Genders and Sexualities in History

Series Editors: **John H. Arnold, Joanna Bourke and Sean Brady**

Palgrave Macmillan's series, Genders and Sexualities in History, aims to accommodate and foster new approaches to historical research in the fields of genders and sexualities. The series promotes world-class scholarship that concentrates upon the interconnected themes of genders, sexualities, religions/religiosity, civil society, class formations, politics and war.

Historical studies of gender and sexuality have often been treated as disconnected fields, while in recent years historical analyses in these two areas have synthesised, creating new departures in historiography. By linking genders and sexualities with questions of religion, civil society, politics and the contexts of war and conflict, this series will reflect recent developments in scholarship, moving away from the previously dominant and narrow histories of science, scientific thought and legal processes. The result brings together scholarship from contemporary, modern, early modern, medieval, classical and non-Western history to provide a diachronic forum for scholarship that incorporates new approaches to genders and sexualities in history.

Life among the Ruins: Cityscape and Sexuality in Cold War Berlin is a groundbreaking study of the destroyed urban landscape of post-Second World War Berlin and the relationships between urban geography and sexuality in the post-war reconstruction and political and ideological division of the city in the Cold War years. In this seminal book, Jennifer Evans provides a meticulously researched, incisive and fascinating analysis of the shattered Berlin cityscape as a primary actor in the historical narrative of the post-war period. Through its focus on urban space and geography, this book challenges the usefulness of political benchmarks in German history (such as 1945, 1949 and 1961) and examines instead the relationship between the fabric and spaces of Berlin and the processes of reconstruction, and the ways in which these were intimately connected to, and shaped, identity, sexuality and gender in the divided city. In spite of a chasm of difference in ideology, the nascent East and West German authorities shared a highly idealised notion of the traditional family unit as the basis of morality. The mass rapes in the immediate aftermath of German surrender, the shattered family units, the ruined spaces in the city fostering casual sexual encounters and the economy of prostitution, the remarkable resurgence in the ruined post-war cityscape of pre-Nazi-era spaces of the sexual avant garde, all fostered concepts among the authorities and Berlin's citizens of a moral geography of deviance that shaped the physical rebuilding of the city and attitudes towards use of public space. *Life among the Ruins* recasts the history of sexuality in Berlin in a radical new light, and repositions our understanding of society and reconstruction in Cold War Berlin. In common with all volumes in the Genders and Sexualities in History series, Jennifer Evans's *Life among the Ruins* presents a multifaceted and meticulously researched scholarly study, and is a sophisticated contribution to our understanding of the past.

Titles include

Cordelia Beattie and Kirsten A. Fenton (*editors*)
INTERSECTIONS OF GENDER, RELIGION AND ETHNICITY IN THE
MIDDLE AGES

Matthew Cook
QUEER DOMESTICITIES
Homosexuality and Home Life in Twentieth-Century London

Jennifer V. Evans
LIFE AMONG THE RUINS
Cityscape and Sexuality in Cold War Berlin

Christopher E. Forth and Elinor Accampo (*editors*)
CONFRONTING MODERNITY IN FIN-DE-SIÈCLE FRANCE
Bodies, Minds and Gender

Dagmar Herzog (*editor*)
BRUTALITY AND DESIRE
War and Sexuality in Europe's Twentieth Century

Jessica Meyer
MEN OF WAR
Masculinity and the First World War in Britain

Jennifer D. Thibodeaux (*editor*)
NEGOTIATING CLERICAL IDENTITIES
Priests, Monks and Masculinity in the Middle Ages

Hester Vaizey
SURVIVING HITLER'S WAR
Family Life in Germany 1939–48

Genders and Sexualities in History Series
Series Standing Order 978–0–230–55185–5 Hardback
978–0–230–55186–2 Paperback
(*outside North America only*)

You can receive future titles in this series as they are published by placing a
standing order. Please contact your bookseller or, in case of difficulty, write to
us at the address below with your name and address, the title of the series and
the ISBN quoted above.

Customer Services Department, Macmillan Distribution Ltd, Houndmills,
Basingstoke, Hampshire RG21 6XS, England

Life among the Ruins

Cityscape and Sexuality in Cold War Berlin

Jennifer V. Evans

First published 2011 by
PALGRAVE MACMILLAN

Palgrave Macmillan in the UK is an imprint of Macmillan Publishers Limited, registered in England, company number 785998, of Houndmills, Basingstoke, Hampshire RG21 6XS.

Palgrave Macmillan in the US is a division of St Martin's Press LLC, 175 Fifth Avenue, New York, NY 10010.

Palgrave Macmillan is the global academic imprint of the above companies and has companies and representatives throughout the world.

Palgrave® and Macmillan® are registered trademarks in the United States, the United Kingdom, Europe and other countries.

ISBN 978–0–230–20201–6

This book is printed on paper suitable for recycling and made from fully managed and sustained forest sources. Logging, pulping and manufacturing processes are expected to conform to the environmental regulations of the country of origin.

A catalogue record for this book is available from the British Library.

Library of Congress Cataloging-in-Publication Data
Evans, Jennifer V., 1970–
   Life among the ruins : cityscape and sexuality in Cold War
   Berlin / Jennifer V. Evans.
     p.   cm.
   Includes bibliographical references and index.
   ISBN 978–0–230–20201–6 (alk. paper)
   1. Berlin (Germany)—History—1945–1990. 2. Berlin (Germany)—Social conditions—20th century. 3. Sex customs—Germany—Berlin—History—20th century. 4. Sexual ethics—Germany—Berlin—History—20th century. 5. Sex role—Germany—Berlin—History—20th century. 6. Prostitution—Germany—Berlin—History—20th century. 7. Civil society—Germany—Berlin—History—20th century. I. Title.
   DD881.E93 2011
   943′.155087—dc22
                                          2011013743

10 9 8 7 6 5 4 3 2 1
20 19 18 17 16 15 14 13 12 11

Printed and bound in the United States of America

To Jason, Gillian, and Gwen

Contents

List of Figures

Map

Following the conclusion of the Potsdam Conference, what was formerly greater Berlin was divided into four sectors, administered jointly by the Allied powers (the United States, Great Britain, France, and the Soviet Union). This map shows the boundaries of the four sectors, which remained formally in place until 1990. After the building of the Berlin Wall in 1961, however, it became increasingly clear that the division was purely one of East–West. Within West Berlin, there were hardly any dividing lines between the sectors administered by the Western Allies. As the map shows, Berlin had unified transportation systems, including railroads and the S-Bahn (suburban railway), which still existed in 1949. It was not until 1961 that this situation began to change radically. (A. Kunz)

Map 1   Berlin (September 1, 1945)
Source: GHI-GHDI/Server IEG-Maps, A. Kunz/J. R. Moeschl

Acknowledgments

I am proud to be in a position to thank all those who have accompanied me on the long journey toward the completion of this book. I first began to think about sexual regulation and rebuilding while at SUNY-Binghamton, and benefited in untold ways from the support of that institution and from Jean Quataert in particular, who continues to provide me with unflagging encouragement. Short-term grants and conference invitations from the German Historical Institute in Washington, DC gave me the opportunity to fine-tune my thoughts at crucial stages in the project's development while offering numerous opportunities to meet with interesting colleagues working on similar and related themes. Richard Wetzell's friendship and support has been another fortuitous outcome of these occasional visits to Washington. The American Historical Association's Bernadotte Schmidt Grant and the Berlin Program for Advanced German and European Studies allowed me to collect vital archive sources in the United States National Archives and Records Administration in College Park Maryland and in Berlin in 2002. My home institution, Carleton University, was generous in granting me leave during the initial year of my appointment to travel to Berlin, and the current Dean of Arts John Osborne has continued this spirit of intellectual support, providing much-appreciated funding to secure the illustrations published in this book. Finally, some of the research for this book was supported by a Standard Grant from the Social Sciences Historical Research Council of Canada.

I am grateful for the permission granted to use some of my research that has appeared elsewhere in other forms. Portions of Chapter 1 appeared in "Life Among the Ruins: Sex, Space, and Subculture in Postwar Berlin," in Sabine Hake and Philip Broadbent (eds.), *Berlin, Divided City, 1945–89* (New York: Berghahn, 2010), pp. 11–22, while portions of Chapter 3 were published in "Bahnhof Boys: Policing Male Prostitution in Post-Nazi Berlin," *Journal of the History of Sexuality* 12.4 (October 2003): 605–636. Thanks too to Art Resource New York on behalf of the Stiftung Preussischer Kulturbesitz, the Berlinische Galerie, the Bundesarchiv Bildstelle, the Landesarchiv Berlin, and Bodo Niemann for providing me permission for the photographs used in the book.

While navigating a path through the sources, I was aided by a fleet of archivists at the Archiv Diakonisches Werk der EKD, the Berlinische Galerie, the Bundesarchiv-Lichterfelde, the Filmarchiv, and the Landesarchiv, where Bianca Welzing-Bräutigam was particularly helpful in providing access to newly accessioned police and court case files. Friends Jens Dobler of the Schwules Museum, Andreas Pretzel, and Ralf Dose of the Magnus Hirschfeld Society shared with me their company and extensive knowledge of the city's underground history. Those in Carleton's Interlibrary Loan Office, especially Christine Taylor, located hard-to-find texts and turned a bit of a blind eye when my preoccupation with getting the manuscript done meant I'd missed yet another due date.

Much-needed moral support has been given for some years now by Heather Gumbert, Atina Grossmann, Dagmar Herzog, Erik Huneke, Angus McLaren, and Annette Timm, while colleagues and graduate students at Carleton kept me focused, calm, well-read, and en pointe. My current complement of German history graduate students have been especially forgiving during my feverish pursuit of deadlines in the final months. Special thanks to Jane Freeland for critical last-minute help with manuscript preparation and Stefan-Ludwig Hoffmann for providing top-flight suggestions for how to shape the manuscript in the first place. Paul Betts, Monica Black, Lisa Heineman, and Bob Moeller have helped me in more ways than I can enumerate. When my exhaustion was most palpable, their friendship, encouragement, and good humor buoyed me. They are exceptional scholars, but, more importantly, they are living examples of the true meaning of collegiality. I can't thank them enough. My friends Sarah Caspi, Cindy Maraj, Suzanne Banks, Ged Sutton-Long, Lil Krstic, and Jennifer Fijalkowska insisted on conviviality and coaxed me out of the den for some much-needed writing breaks while Ian Roy read the entire manuscript and shared a writer's insight about narrative and storytelling. Michael Strang and Ruth Ireland of Palgrave Macmillan have been a pleasure to work with, and I send warm thanks especially to the series editors Sean Brady, John Arnold, and Joanna Bourke for creating such an important and imaginative space for a discussion of genders and sexuality in history. I owe much gratitude to my copyeditor Caroline Richards and indexer Cameron Duder for their careful attention and enduring patience.

While archival and institutional support may have made this book possible in terms of access to documents and time to write, it was my family's emotional support that ensured it all came together during the ups and downs of this past decade. Dayle Allan, Cathy Cameron,

Karen Ray, Duane Evans, Spook Bennett, and Peter and Annalies Neumann taught me to live as much in the present as in the past. Alvarina Mendonca took loving care of my girls in the early years, while Rhonda, France, Kimalji, and Amanda continued to keep watch over them at the Devonshire School Age Programme, reminding me every single day that our accomplishments are intimately tied to the labor of others.

I can only wish that my parents were here to see this book in print. Despite coming from vastly different backgrounds and totally unfamiliar with university life, they were always proud, forever encouraging, and truly supportive. They allowed me the latitude to make my own way, gave me the freedom to explore, and the space to figure things out. Most importantly, they taught me never to ignore the plight of the average person, the socially marginal, and the powerless, for it is often from their stories that we have the most to learn. For someone who writes about intimacy, I find it mildly funny that I struggle to find the words with which to thank my partner Jason Bennett. He's seen and dealt with it all, from the very beginning. I dedicate this book to him, and to my own private feminist revolution, Gillian and Gwen, who perhaps more than anyone else these last years have done the most to alter and shape my own emotional geographies and everyday encounters.

Introduction

> We can distinguish types of cityscape: those, which are formed
> deliberately, and others, which develop unintentionally. The
> former derive from the artistic will that is realized in squares,
> vistas, arrangements of buildings, and effects of perspective,
> which Baedeker generally illuminates with a star. The latter on
> the other hand come into being without having been planned
> in advance.
> Siegfried Kracauer, *Straßen in Berlin und anderswo*, 1924

Walking through the remnants of the German capital in the winter of
1945, British officer Richard Brett-Smith could not help but be amazed
at what he saw. While searching out what remained of the fabled
beer bars, cinemas, and cafés he had read about in preparation for
his eight-month deployment overseas, his eyes became transfixed on
"the shadows of gutted houses and towering, lonely walls" which, he
recalled with some trepidation, looked curiously like "the battlements
of some weird castle." Far from the image of storied Old Europe or even
the demimonde atmosphere of the Kurfürstendamm's libidinous sexuality, Berlin's countenance was "a baleful fairyland: not even the snow
could change that."[1] As was the case for many of the visitors, refugees,
and citizens cast into the cauldron of capitulated Berlin, the city they
found was a far cry from the one ensconced in their dreams, imagination, and memories. In this spectral atmosphere of near total collapse,
Berlin appeared more like a character in an expressionist film, one that
seduced the curious, the weary, and the horrified with glimpses of what
once was, what remained, and what might be gained again. Just as Brett-
Smith continued his afternoon search for some convergence between his

beguiling expectations and his stark experiences, so too did each person encountering the city attempt to reconcile the fairyland they found with the one they hoped to discover.

In March of the following year, this process of discovery and reconciliation between the population and the urban environment assumed a truly cinematic dimension as camera crews and lighting technicians set to work with their cast on the streets of the city. Their efforts culminated at the Admiralspalast in October 1946 with the premiere of Wolfgang Staudte's film *The Murderers Are Among Us*, a melodramatic meditation on militarism, tyranny, and the slaughter of innocents and the first German film to be produced at war's end.[2] While Hildegard Knef and Wilhelm Borchert received top billing for their portrayal of two Germans attempting to rebuild their lives in the shadow of the war, the most interesting character was the city itself. Much more than a passive backdrop to the unfolding plot and storyline, Berlin's sinister streets, grim facades, and bombed-out buildings buoyed the actors from one scene to the next, giving their thoughts solemnity and actions meaning while showcasing their ever-changing mood. A constant reminder of the tragedy of total war, in the film Berlin's shadowy cityscape enabled a reckoning with the past while pointing the way to a new beginning thanks to the redemptive power of love among the ruins. Here, as in the countless diary entries from the "zero hour" – the term given to the period between the cessation of battle and first efforts at rebuilding – the former capital was much more than a stage upon which reconstruction simply happened. It molded experiences, galvanized a sense of shared history, fate, and identity, and created contexts for a range of encounters, from violent interactions and reprisals for past crimes to opportunities for banding together in the face of common challenges. In *The Murderers Are Among Us*, the ruins heralded the redemption and triumph of intimacy and compassion over violence and murder. In the actual streets of the defeated capital, moral reckoning would not come so easily.

At its core, this book is a history of reconstruction sites, physical, cultural, and sexual spaces and places that comprise the collective story of Berlin through the first decades of the Cold War. Fundamentally, it argues that the city is not merely an assemblage of architectural features and administrative functions but a primary actor in the historical narrative of the postwar period, both materially and discursively. It lent shape to people's memories, sights, emotions, and experiences, conditioned their choices and sense of self, and mitigated their day-to-day encounters with fellow citizens, occupation authorities, and representatives of the nascent East and West German state. The book focuses on the problem of aftermath, and the lengths to which people, communities, and governments went in the quest to reclaim and rebuild their city after widespread devastation.[3] It looks at the gendered assumptions at work in the pursuit of normalcy and stabilization, and questions the usefulness of political benchmarks, like 1945, 1949, and possibly even 1961 as markers of change and transition in the social and sexual arena.[4]

Site of Germany's first foray with democracy, home of sexual excess and experimentalism, and birthplace of the Final Solution, Berlin exemplifies the dizzying heights and monstrous lows of the age of industrial capitalism and urban modernity. Bombed into submission in World War II, it emerged out of the rubble a shell of its former self but despite (or perhaps because of this) it would go on to become the iconic center of the Cold War, occupied and divided for well nigh the remainder of the twentieth century. Its fate provides the perfect starting point for an analysis of twentieth-century modernity.[5] Given the city's symbolic importance, it seems natural that the period between capitulation in 1945 and the building of the Berlin Wall in 1961 would merit our attention in seeking to find out what happened to that period of embattled exuberance "before the deluge," as *Newsweek*, *Time*, and *Saturday Evening Post* editor Otto Friedrich eloquently put it in 1972. The book is organized around a single problem: how did postwar attempts to rebuild infrastructure and identity necessitate an engagement with past practices set in motion before 1945? If, as Dorothy Rowe has pointed out in her study of the sexualization of Weimar culture and aesthetics, "Berlin had become a metaphor for a modernity both feared and desired," what became of this Janus-faced legacy, which Eric Weitz has reminded us recently held great promise as well as unparalleled tragedy for central Europe and the world.[6] If we take seriously the category of sexuality as both a marker and agent of modernity, one which reflects the twin goals of emancipation and domination that came out of the Enlightenment project, we can't help but see that post-Hitler Berlin was filled with numerous reconstruction sites where these forces clashed in the quest for a new beginning.[7] Focusing on select places within the city's urban geography where people came together, where they created bonds of intimacy and shared a sense of community, home, and belonging – often, but not always at odds with the state – the book analyzes East and West German attempts to manage and control the city's resurrection amidst the particular anxieties unleashed by conditions in the former Reich capital.

Despite the prominence of the physical destruction in contemporary accounts of capitulated Berlin, the historiography has been slow to take up the issue of the city's broken landscape as a fundamental feature of reconstruction. Whenever the physical environment does surface, it is almost exclusively hinged to analyses of the Cold War division in aesthetics and urban planning, including the similarities and differences in architectural practices on either side of the Iron Curtain.[8] While many important social histories have furthered our understanding of the impact of mass violence, fraternization, displacement, and resettlement on local politics and occupation policy, surprisingly little attention has been paid to the place of the city itself in the discourses and practices of social and political unrest and renewal.[9] This is most curious given the fact that reunification in the final decades of the twentieth century bore witness to a flurry of interventions on the subject. In this literature, the city's structural and imaginary spaces acquired a heightened role in discussions of modernization, urbanity, self-formation, and the politics of memory.[10] Yet, despite attention to the vicissitudes of urban experience, the layering of memories, and the spaces where these came together in collectively remembering (and sometimes forgetting) the city's multiple pasts, with few exceptions this literature has stopped short of analyzing the complex ways in which Berlin's history has been fundamentally shaped not only by clashing aesthetic ideals and shifting political valorizations, but by the dynamics of human sexuality made material in the changing physical environment. How did people live their lives after 1945 and to what extent did doing so mean conjuring up memories of life before capitulation?

To get at this question, this book suggests that efforts to combat nonconformist sexual behavior and practices must be viewed over the *longue durée* as an important, if overlooked, element in the story of twentieth-century sexual modernization. To understand this, we have to tell a different story than moral regulation and social control. To be effective and lasting, the generation of new knowledge about sex relied on mechanisms of enticement as well as coercion, power and pleasure, surveillance and seduction, in an uneven process of fits and starts. This haphazard evolution of new sexual norms created possibilities for subversion alongside ongoing social regulation. But there have been certain moments in history when opposition to accepted norms was easier to marshal and sustain, suggesting the need to historicize the conditions at work influencing changing social morays and the places where they took form and root.

Although Frank Mort has succeeded in historicizing the rise of a permissive society in post-World War II London by drawing on a mix of historical geography, history of sexuality, and changing patterns of leisure and consumption, surprisingly, historians of Berlin have yet to take the spatial turn and assess the city in light of a decade's worth of writing in queer and urban social history.[11] This is especially curious since it was Berlin, and not London, that served as a refuge for sexual dissidents and *anders Denkende* (oppositional thinkers) and was home to sexological definitions of homosexuality and sexual difference. It hardly bears repeating that it was the city on the Spree that served as ground zero for Nazi efforts to harness and control the productive potential of sex, often in extremely nefarious ways.[12] Part of the difficulty, of course, is that one never really analyzes postwar Berlin in isolation; with two competing ideological systems, four sets of Allies, and vestiges of Nazi, Weimar, and imperial German government directives in health, education, and policing, the terrain is muddy indeed. A solution is to draw on its unique and complicated history as an integral part of the story.

Michel Foucault provides a useful guide. Over his career, he outlined a trajectory for understanding sexual modernity as linked to the rise of capitalism and the cultivation of the bourgeois self. As Greg Eghigian's fascinating work on East Germany has shown, it is possible to draw on this methodology to better understand the technologies of self-formation and control in both halves of Germany.[13] In surveying the different forms of intervention at work in East and West Berlin, from the promotion of certain gender norms and sexual practices as central features of productive citizenship to more direct forms of policing out-and-out transgressions, the book charts the shifts and changes in customs, behaviors, and practices that evolved out of capitulation, and attempts to surmise what was at stake in individual and institutional strategies for dealing with collapse and reconstruction. To do so requires a wide range of evidence, from eyewitness accounts of visitors and citizens to more institutional sources that help outline the regulation networks employed by Allied and German police, social service caseworkers, and the denazified judiciary and district courts. In historicizing the cumulative effects of war, defeat, rebuilding, and division on changing social and sexual mores, the book makes cityspace an actor in the analysis to examine how otherwise ubiquitous places like the ruins, the cellar, the train station, the darkened city street, bars and cafés, and the workhouse and remand home became hosts to changing estimations of sexual danger, victimization, endangerment, and also excitement for those who inhabited them. In other words, it uses the divided city as a device to explore how the exigencies of danger and desire, pleasure and panic were mapped out amidst the challenges of the early Cold War before the advent of the so-called sexual revolution of the late 1960s.

The relationship between space, place, sexuality, and history is particularly poignant in a city like Berlin where rebuilding took profound spatial, gender, and sexual dimensions as well, exemplified in the deep concerns German authorities and average citizens continued to voice about the breakdown of traditional mores in the urban setting.

Despite swift attempts to reestablish moral authority and resurrect certain policies and institutions from pre-1945 Berlin, this is not a story of doom and gloom. Although certain regulatory measures to combat the perils of city life were adopted by most postwar occupation governments and city officials in all four sectors, confusion over jurisdiction provided Berliners with more than a few opportunities to subvert the intrusion of the authorities in their day-to-day lives; in some cases, such as juvenile sexual nonconformity, youthful intransigence in listening to rock 'n' roll, consuming American products, or exhibiting more advanced forms of antisocial behavior would remain a sore point for both regimes well into the 1970s.[14] With the regulation of same-sex sexual practices – although men and women were increasingly straitjacketed by the 1950s as the spaces of companionship and community underwent surveillance as part of a more concerted effort to bring back a family-based politics of conformism – many Berliners still managed to tap back into subcultural sensibilities from before the war. While both the Konrad Adenauer and the Walter Ulbricht regimes in the West and East promoted pro-natalism and the family idyll in virtually all areas of social policy, a spatial analysis of sexual encounters provides a means by which to uncover the political agendas of each regime in seeking to concretize heteronormative codes of conduct and comportment as a basis for sexual citizenship and belonging.[15] It also brings into view coping strategies and forms of accommodation and resistance that transcended the benchmark of 1945. Shining a light on moments when authorities worked together to enforce decency despite the increasingly palpable ideological and physical divide, the book provides a glimpse into the unique issues raised by formal division itself as citizens coped with a more or less open border, competing agendas, and divergent understandings of the law and its deployment in everyday life.[16]

Toward a Historical Geography of Postwar Berlin

This book takes as its springboard ideas emanating out of historical geography about the mutually reinforcing ways in which metropolitan life has shaped and been infused by the sexual practices and gender performances undertaken in the city's many spaces. Nowhere is this more palpable than in Cold War Berlin.[17] Among the many tasks facing the occupation forces and the newly established city government alongside rubble abatement, the reestablishment of city services, and the denazification of the population was the more elusive and abstract hope of returning some semblance of normalcy to everyday life. To be lasting, reconstruction would have to take place on a variety of fronts, from structural rebuilding to emotional support for the beleaguered population. And at some point in the process, Germans and their occupiers would have to address the restitution of healthy social mores – an especially difficult task given the mass rape of as many as a quarter to a half of the city's women and girls in the week before the armistice was signed in May 1945. As a compatriot of Brett-Smith remarked in his own memorial account, the situation at war's end was dire indeed since the city's "morals as well as its buildings (lay) in ruins, its families shattered as well as its houses."[18] Here, the physical environment serves as a barometer of moral depravity and dysfunction, measuring the depths to which Germany had sunk in waging (and losing) such a calamitous war. The connection between material conditions and social mores was not lost on other ground-level witnesses to the destruction, however. Even though the draconian Morgenthau Plan had been jettisoned as too harsh and exacting a punishment for Germany, commentators like poet Stephen Spender, Isaac Deutscher, and Manual Gasser reported back to their readers that Berlin had been bombed not just into submission, but back to the Stone Age. In the preindustrial wasteland that remained in the historic center of what poet Gottfried Benn referred to derisively as the "Mongolian border town provisionally still called Berlin," former busy streets and cosmopolitan squares now stood empty and silent. Alongside the remnants of sidewalks grew "nettles as tall as men, and where sleek lines of traffic used to move along, grass is secretly gathered at night for whatever livestock is hidden away at home."[19] What better example of the crisis of civilization and the unmaking of a capital city than the destruction not only of its buildings, roads, and infrastructure, but of one of society's most hallowed institutions: the family, and the gender roles and sexual practices that undergirded it? Behind the surreal facades of decimated tenement blocks, crime was on the ascendance, fraternization challenged Allied authority, and the city still reeled from the after-effects of the Soviet rapes, which left in their wake a host of concerns from public health and abortion provision to how to mobilize this already demoralized population for the enormity of the task at hand: rebuilding structure and society in occupied and divided Berlin.[20]

If not a feature of this most recent literature, the association of materiality with social, sexual, and political reconstruction was very much in evidence in *The Murderers Are Among Us*, where redemption and love between a former political prisoner and returning soldier can only be nurtured in the emotional refuge of an otherwise ramshackle apartment. Not insignificantly, it is the warmth of home and hearth that successfully transforms this broken dwelling into habitable space. In addition to the facilitation of physical rebirth, intimacy and companionship held the potential for re-masculinization, enabling the resurrection of a strong and healthy masculinity out of the shambles of war. To put it somewhat crassly, it is the love of a good woman that guides the main character away from madness, ensuring his rightful place within a postwar orbit as a loving partner, contributing member of society, and future husband.[21] In the film, as in the day-to-day encounters of average Berliners, social interactions were rarely benign. As this book shows, the form and shape of urban encounters was of supreme importance to the scope and pace of reconstruction. If broken houses connoted broken morals, and severed families served as both sign and symptom of societal collapse, then city spaces and the emotions attached to them must be viewed as important sites of intervention in the reconstruction of appropriate gender roles, sexual practices, and political belonging in the early Cold War.

The sexualized nature of life in the city was not lost on Walter Benjamin and Georg Simmel, whose aesthetic and sociological interventions, alongside the more seamy insights of Hans Ostwald and Curt Moreck at the turn of the twentieth century, explored the ways in which city streets, pubs, parks, and squares provided a window into highly fraught social worlds of modernity-in-the-making.[22] Here the *flâneur* ambled about town, directionless but with purpose: to witness and participate in the new forms of leisure, looking, desire, and contemplation, made possible amidst the clamor and noise of the ever-evolving city. In Simmel's work, especially his 1903 essay "The Sociology of Space," he argued that conditions within the modern city played a definitive role in the construction of modern subjectivities as well as providing new forms of social control.[24] As Dorothy Rowe has pointed out in her own spirited discussion of gender and modernity in imperial and Weimar Berlin, "the exclusivity of space, the significance of boundaries and of spatial proximity, movement through space, social organization, solidarity, empty space, and the effects of nightfall and darkness on the psychological fantasies of the individual within the mass" that took shape in Simmel's sociology of the city also percolated into visual representations of the period as a marker of modernity as rapaciously female, conforming to the rise of the New Woman and the anxieties posed by her ascendance in the new spaces of leisure and consumption.[24] The fear of unleashed urban sexuality was the stock in trade of the boulevard press, and guidebooks to the city's hotspots sold in great numbers to the never-ending stream of enthusiasts interested in accessing the underground worlds Curt Moreck marketed as "wicked Berlin."[25] The connection between new spaces of leisure and "debased" forms of sexuality was certainly not missed by contemporary moral purity campaigners, who fought vociferous battles over the regulation of obscenity and the consumption of erotic literature in knock-down, dragged-out battles over appropriate and illegitimate use of urban space, leading to anti-smut legislation to limit youth from accessing dangerous sites of moral corruption, whether the newsstand, kiosk, pub, or cinema.[26] In this way, Benjamin and Simmel, together with the morals police and well-intentioned if misguided legislators of imperial and Weimar Berlin, drew overlapping cartographies of everyday morality and experience, mixing dominant with subaltern assumptions about sexual morality in the urban landscape. This book seeks to uncover what happened to those maps of modernization and desire after 1945.

For contemporary historical geographers who have mapped the comings and goings of everyday life, the city emerges as a place where new forms of community, consumption, identity, and cultural practice are ushered into being and made visible. Echoing Simmel, Frank Mort and Lynda Nead point out in their influential collection of essays from 1999 that city spaces are inherently sexualized and can play both liberating and limiting roles in the "cultural and social formation of metropolitan modernity."[27] While it is true that the city created new opportunities for consumption, sociability, work, and transgression, whether in shopping arcades, factories, universities, or urinals, these same spaces that marked the transition from premodern to modern also held in their very makeup the potential for subversion by acts not originally contemplated within the official plans of use. In response to this challenge, a host of city authorities – chiefly police, court, and social workers – developed their own strategies to deal with transgressors, drawing in the process their own moral geography of deviance and intervention through the regulative differentiation of legitimate from illegitimate use.[28] In surveying trouble spots, identifying behaviors deserving of intervention, and setting out policies for dealing with them, they helped crystallize in public parlance what constituted both normal and at-risk behavior, linking actual spaces of transaction to the markers and traits of transgressors themselves.[29] This battle may have taken place in the police precinct, in the courthouse, in the remand home, and the city streets, but it was invariably inflected with historically specific socio-spatial anxieties, customs, and concerns. By looking at post-1945 Berlin and the different assumptions at work underpinning certain sexual practices as appropriate, desirable, and healthy building blocks for societal recovery and Cold War competition, this book explores what geographer Phil Hubbard has described as the way "dominant moral codes" quite literally map onto urban places with the hope of providing a fixed point from which to "construct boundaries between good and bad subjects."[30] In other words, reconstructing Berlin was as much about physical rebuilding as it was about hammering out new forms of citizenship and morality in a city besieged by competing ideologies. Despite the incredible visibility of Berlin in Cold War rhetoric, ideological refashioning often occurred on the smallest of scales, in otherwise overlooked spaces where attempts to purge Hitler's legacy were designed to cement a foundation for societal renewal. In exploring spaces of sexual encounter through the lens of official attempts to impose law, order, and authority on a destroyed and defeated city, we gain a glimpse into the everyday life of average Germans while unearthing the complex web of regulation, enforcement, memory, and resistance available to them at war's end.

Spatiality, Sociality, Historicity

Given Berlin's prewar status as the locus of excess and experimentalism in art as in life, to say nothing of the political symbolism of its metropolitan aspirations, a socio-spatial analysis promises to shed new light on something geographers such as David Harvey, Henri Lefebvre, and Edward Soja have examined for some time now: the relationship between spatiality, sociality, and historicity.[31] How these three categories interact, what impulses they draw upon, and the relationships, encounters, and identities they engender lends insight into the way in which the struggles, pace, and shape of urban life helped create notions of place, subjectivity, belonging, and experience for average citizens and the governments that claimed to represent them. Alongside the material underpinnings of subjective experience – how the environment shaped not only what transpired but also the meaning it engendered for individuals, the state, and society at large – this relationship between landscape and identity was supremely gendered and sexualized. Historicizing what behavior was tolerated, what actions were idealized, and what practices fell foul of these supposedly universal norms demonstrates that the family compact remained more of an ideal than a reality for many citizens in both halves of the city. Indeed, the supposed transparency of heterosexuality belies the fact that for many people, citizens and state authorities alike, it remained elusive. Although East and West Germany sought a return to traditional gender norms and sexual practices, often the very institutions designed to impart these messages and correct behavior were unable to do so given a host of organizational and economic restraints. In surveying how experiences of encounter, exclusion, control, and resistance functioned in the changing landscape of postwar East and West Berlin, a socio-spatial analysis suggests that city spaces were highly charged sites of interaction in the Cold War arena.

Not only were certain spaces fraught with myriad assumptions about the health and welfare of citizens, but also the challenges people faced and the solutions proposed by city and Allied authorities owed as much to the changing urban environment as to the ideas that circulated about those same places from the period before 1945. The way people gave voice to their day-to-day travails, how they sought food, shelter, leisure, love, and liaisons – sometimes among the same spaces that may have housed more violent memories of war's end, mass death, and the near total breakdown of civility – provides insight into the place of the past in guiding how Berliners understood their current fate, the scale of destruction, and the pace of normalization. In other words, spatiality is not simply about the physical terrain and spaces of interaction. It also evokes a sense of what has transpired before. Here, the third component of Harvey, Lefebvre, Soja-inspired trialectics of space – historicity – was made manifest in the importation of memories of "the time before" alongside the structural inheritance of practices, policies, and more institutionalized environments over the 1945 divide. A socio-spatial analysis must heed how past impressions generated by these same places lent shape and meaning to contemporary experiences and encounters. Asking how certain spaces were designed to function, at least according to past practice, before outlining alternative uses that arose out of the creative intervention of average citizens allows insight into the life worlds of Berliners and their relationship to their own changing environment. Reading official sources against the grain to explore the interaction of voices at work in the city's liminal landscape before the building of the Berlin Wall in 1961, when this complex set of relationships abruptly changed, the book uncovers the way the divided city was territorialized, how its borders were negotiated and contested via a variety of scripts wielded by a broad range of actors.

Allies, visitors, refugees, and returnees, as well as those who had stayed behind cowering in bomb shelters or fighting in the *Volkssturm*, drew on elaborate, and in some cases preexisting mental maps of the city, ones which helped define their own encounters there. Teasing apart the layers of this textual topography unearths the importance of circulated print media, pre- and postwar guidebooks, feuilletons, and crime sections of the newspaper, in addition to the published reminiscences of expat excursions in the Kreuzberg underworld or the more rarified white-collar climes of the Kempinski Hotel or the Hotel Adlon. The ways in which people continued the practice of what historian Peter Fritzsche has called "reading Berlin" through a wide range of city texts provides a cultural currency for how they navigated their course through the postwar city.[32] These prewar Berlin tales were peppered throughout postwar diary accounts and memorial projects, serving as a template for contemporary encounters with what remained of the city. This reliance upon prewar texts extended beyond urban dwellers to members of the occupation forces, many of whom had a rudimentary education in some aspect of the city's notorious past. Even quasi-literate street youth relied on the insights of their peers about where to find quick and easy transactions and which parts of the city might hold more opportunity for independent living. Although there were palpable changes to the built environment as the two Berlins evolved along separate paths, this discursive landscape, like the physical remains of prewar architecture, had a history that continued to resonate through subsequent decades, where it would inform official and popular notions of place and identity. The year 1945 did not herald a radical break from what came before, but 1961 certainly did.

Moral Rebuilding

With the rise in sexual crime at the end of World War II, members of the Allied forces, the hastily reconstituted Berlin police force, jurists, and social workers – as well as everyday citizens – came face to face with a host of concerns regarding the threat of widespread criminality. Variously understood as remnants of Nazi teachings, products of a world turned upside, or the evils of capitalist or communist influence, if there was one source of agreement amidst the cacophony of voices it was the need to prop up faltering social institutions like the family if occupied Germany was going to survive the challenge of rebuilding. Carving out zones of operation to match the physical division of the city, civic and military authorities sought ways to contain licentiousness and promote abstemious behavior. Rising Cold War tensions meant law and order issues acquired new political ambience; indeed, by the late 1940s, no area of local governance could sidestep the growing ideological confrontation. Suddenly, issues of morality and comportment acquired greater urgency as officials sought to rebuild the framework for regulating and rehabilitating offenders and those deemed to be most "at risk." At stake was not just the jurisdictional rebuilding of the city in view of shifting political imperatives but the promotion of certain behaviors, roles, and identities as healthful, appropriate, and in fact normal. In other words, the policing of encounters in the city's ruins represented a moral regulation, perhaps even a moral economy of behavior, ascribing distinctions between "good" and "bad" sexual practices and identities, and forming a foundation for heterosexuality as a supposedly natural condition of successful social and political rebuilding.

The book presents moral rebuilding as linked to the process of policing encounters in the various spaces where men, women, and youths came into contact with one another, and where transactions often ensued of a distinctly (if not always overtly) sexual character. In doing so, it emphasizes three main themes: the role of denazified moral authorities (broadly defined) in setting standards of behavior and comportment, the attempts of average people to negotiate their place within this framework, and the implications of both efforts for Berlin's political reorientation in the early years of the Cold War. Framed around the sites of encounter themselves, it seeks to demonstrate that from the earliest days following capitulation, efforts to promote and regulate behavior represented highly politicized struggles for power between city, state, and Allied authorities, as well as between classes, sexes, and sexualities.

What this book is not is an empirical social history of policing and persecution. Instead, it seeks to cast the net widely to capture how agents of moral control and the people whose lives they affected lent voice to a new history of Berlin, one free of its Nazi imbrications. While it was one thing to tackle Nazi population policy and social engineering, it was quite another to solve the challenges of urban life, especially in a city in a state of collapse. Chapter 1 explores the swift transfiguration of the city's defensive underworld from a place of war preparedness and refuge to a site of danger and desire as its structural integrity was compromised in the bombing campaigns that ravaged the city at the end of the war. That both possibilities were housed in the same structure reflects the productive and destructive potential of the urban environment, especially when impacted by total war. Chapter 2 emerges out of the rubble and out into the street to gauge the emotional connection fostered by life in the city. Streets and boulevards dissected Berlin into quadrants of competing authority as the Allies assembled within the city perimeter. Some, like Unter den Linden, Friedrichstrasse, and Kurfürstendamm conjured up competing memories of the 1920s, and the imperial grandeur (or bombast, depending where one stood) of the last century. Creating a sense of affective connection to city streets, districts, and neighborhoods was of strategic importance to establishing legitimacy of purpose on both sides of the Iron Curtain, and both halves of the city competed to narrate their version of events; this demonstrates the lingering importance of boulevards and streets to questions of order, authority, and identity in the aftermath of the war. Chapter 3 applies this argument to the city's train station portals to explore the liminality of the city's borders despite advancing political tensions. Amidst the anonymity of transit spaces, new coalitions emerged to tackle the problem of street-level sex, especially male prostitution, creating unique partnerships out of otherwise antagonistic forces. Chapter 4 follows the exploits of postwar *flâneurs* as they ambled about the city's streets and alleyways in search of sexual adventure in the bars and cafés of a bygone age. It argues that the internal boundaries between East and West, however porous and permeable in the 1950s, nevertheless played a prominent role in the shift away from traditional contact zones toward new climes. Still, both the physical and sexual topography of the city was not so altered by division that some semblances of its earlier scenes were not in evidence. The question on everyone's mind at the time was "Whither Weimar?" Was it to be found in divided Berlin? Chapter 5 moves away from sites of refuge, transit, exchange, and pleasure toward places of confinement. If city spaces were controlling as well as enabling, then an important part of the postwar urban field were the incarceral spaces designed to treat the perilousness of city life for the legions of youths whose lives were shattered by war. In uncovering the moral imperatives at work in these sites of encounter, a spatial analysis of licentiousness and love, violence and desire, provides a unique lens through which to gauge the push and pull of sexual modernization and societal renewal. In these spaces, the city's subalterns were brought together in unique ways in their attempts to thwart and mitigate regulation. Male and female prostitutes, huddled together in train station waiting rooms and in ruined bomb shelters, sometimes went so far as to proclaim fake marital unions to cast off police suspicion. In this way, although certain sites in the city were identified as places of temptation, danger, and corruption, the people forced to enter them, walk through them, or live their lives in them challenged regulators to refine and defend their methods and tactics of moral reform, sometimes laying claim to the same notion of respectability that regulators sought to defend. In the shifting terrain of Cold War politics, where definitions of deviance were themselves up for grabs, changing motivations for enforcing moral norms meant average Berliners had to seek out new and creative ways to navigate the system, a key theme in this book.

1

The Cellar and the Bunker

"The New Berlin will not rise out of the ruins, but will live under them. Prost!"

A conversation between two German
journalists, November 27, 1943[1]

Returning to his quarters in the Hotel am Zoo in the once classy district of Charlottenburg shortly after the war had ended, an officer in Montgomery's staff looked down from his balcony at the broken landscape. Everywhere Wilfred Byford-Jones cast his gaze, he saw heaps of rubble, "elms and firs blasted and shattered" and streets littered with war wreckage. At the spot where the Kurfürstendamm met the Tauentzienstrasse, where as late as 1944 Berliners breathed in what little frivolity remained in the struggling nightspots of the West End, the "broken ribs" of the Memorial Church spiked ominously out of the grey dirt, a reminder of the end of an era[2] (Figure 1.1). In surveying the rubblescape, he seemed to crib from Siegfried Kracauer's essay on the view of the city through a window ("Aus dem Fenster gesehen"), except that instead of the hustle and bustle of a busy Charlottenburg intersection, Byford-Jones was confronted with what little remained of this once great city. Drawing on a familiar lexicon of martial imagery from Europe's last great war, he described the desperate march of the city's "troglodytes (who) crept [sic] over piles of rubble or burrowed their way into cellars." Despite vastly different circumstances, the view from the balcony, like Kracauer's window vista, continued to frame the contradictions of metropolitan life, only now it did so by drawing the reader's attention to the time that had elapsed between Weimar's decadence and the destruction of the ruins.

Figure 1.1 The ruins of the Kaiser Wilhelm Memorial Church seen from the Tauentzienstrasse, Berlin, 1945. Photographer: Hildegard Dreyer.
Photo credit: Bildarchiv Preussischer Kulturbesitz/Art Resource, NY.

Clearly, area bombing, street fighting, mass rape, and occupation put a violent end to Berlin's metropolitan trappings. In the districts that fell within the central light rail system (*Stadtbahnring*) – those most heavily affected by the two-year bombing campaign – very little remained of Berlin's former glory.[3] Statistics paint a grim picture of the scale of destruction. Over 350 air attacks dropped more than 45,000 tons of explosives on the waiting city, mostly by the Royal Air Force with help in the final years of the war from American bomber pilots. Between 49,000 and 56,000 people met their fate in the incendiary fires unleashed by direct hits, some so devastating that firefighters lost all ability to control the blaze.[4] Almost half of the 1939 population of 4 million had sought refuge in the eastern hinterland, while others sought out family and sent their children to safety in Bavaria.[5] From late 1944 onward, those settled in the eastern territories quickened their pace westward in advance of the steamrolling pace of the Soviet troops, which heralded the end of the war.

Although not completely razed, the city encountered upon their return, especially the central districts of Mitte, Tiergarten, and Kreuzberg, was well nigh unrecognizable. With over 28 square kilometers of its prewar surface area destroyed, generating anywhere between 55 and 100 cubic meters of rubble – one-sixth of all the rubble in Germany proper – Berlin was a debris field. Recently installed US commander of operations in the city Frank Howley remarked famously that it was perhaps "the greatest pile of rubble" that the world had ever seen.[6] Although one might make the same statement about any major German town in 1945, in one sense he was right. Nightly bombing had completely transformed the physical geography of the city, leveling buildings, leaving behind mounds of rebar, concrete, and sand in giant rubble mountains like the *Teufelsberg* (Devil's Mountain) and *Humboldthöhe* (Humboldt Height), which would later be repurposed as a ski hill and an urban hiking trail for the city's sports enthusiasts.[7] Potsdamer Platz, once the symbol of the city's modernity with its automobiles and six-sided traffic light, was catapulted violently back in time, left to resemble a preindustrial steppe inside the city limits instead of a bustling urban roundabout. Left fallow, it would remain undeveloped until unification.[8] A few steps adjacent to the former roundabout, craters and cesspools existed where not long before parkland and canals beckoned *flâneurs* in search of an urban oasis. The Tiergarten's ponds, once laden with fish and lined with sunbathers in Berlin's seasonable summers, were suddenly choked with oil.[9] (Figure 1.2) While statistics vary as to ultimately how many buildings were destroyed, roughly a third of all prewar apartment houses lay in tatters with countless more tenements damaged beyond repair.[10] Ambling about the wreckage visitor and citizen alike could not but wonder what had become of Old Berlin, the city on the Spree, so easily sacrificed by Hitler and Goebbels in the service of mass hysteria and utopian dreams.

Berlin had survived the last days, but its infrastructure, housing, and spirit were broken. After weeks of frayed nerves, spontaneous crying, hushed tones, and realized fears in the dark recesses of underground hideouts, a momentary calm followed the immediate cessation of fighting.[11] Despite the silence, the capitulated city was anything but settled. Streams of refugees continued to make their sad trek into the city, East European slave laborers and recently liberated Jews contemplated their fate, and in some respects, as Atina Grossmann has compellingly observed, some survived the crisis of the early postwar years in better shape than their former oppressors.[12] Demobilized (and

Figure 1.2 Trees in the Tiergarten being cleared due to the urgent need for firewood, 1946. Photographer: Friedrich Seidenstücker (1882–1966). © Copyright BPK.
Photo credit: Bildarchiv Preussischer Kulturbesitz/Art Resource, NY.

often disoriented) teenaged and elderly *Volkssturm*ists, former prisoners of war, and returning soldiers were forced to watch in bewilderment as their sisters, mothers, and wives cavorted willingly or otherwise with occupation soldiers in a sad picture of self-preservation and sacrifice.

Yet, Berlin was more than a simple stage or a show place (*Schauplatz* – as diarist Ruth-Andreas Friedrich would call it) upon which this drama of capitulation unfolded. If Georg Simmel saw the imperial city as creating unique contingencies for the creation of social identities, behaviors, and experiences, constructing boundaries and enforcing borders between the licit and illicit, the extraordinary and the mundane, then the ruined landscape certainly provided a context for the negotiation of new relationships of identity, power, and morality among the burning embers of the embattled Reich capital.[13] Far from passive or neutral backdrops to social and cultural transformation, city spaces, even broken ones, play a constitutive part in shaping social identity and the operation of power. This chapter explores the relationship between morality and authority and the ways in which these were mapped on to the layered landscape of zero-hour Berlin. It suggests that by focusing on Berlin's subterranean world, its bunkers, cellars, and ruins, we see that city space held multiple functions in the final weeks of the war. During the years of aerial bombardments, bunkers provided sanctuary and a sense of community for a war-weary population, with their own clearly delineated sense of rules and order based around the carefully monitored division of the space into civilian and military zones. This sense of refuge and orderliness was short-lived, disrupted in the extreme in the last week of the war by the street fighting and rapes. A product of Nazi war planning designed to buttress the city's defense and engender support for the war, bunkers and cellars became transformed into sites of chaos and disorder, resulting in multiple struggles to reestablish authority over the space. Despite (or perhaps because of) the haphazard attempts to regulate and manage the places where people congregated, where they shared intimate moments, discussed the war, and survived its consequences, the ruins became an important part of a moral geography of danger and desire, giving insight into the way these city spaces could be both obstructive and essential to the moral reconstruction of postwar Berlin.[14] Just as the rubble represents a layering of the past and present, conjuring up memories of the faith in modern engineering amidst recent Nazi war bluster, the reclamation of these postwar subterranean spaces reveals the logic of modernity and its perilous blind spots in an era of total war.

Although it was not the only urban center to experience the devastation of aerial bombing, Berlin's iconic status invested in it a particular resonance, casting this city as a mediator in the negotiation of new relationships, self-projections, and visions of personal and political renewal. Although broken and in tatters, Berlin remained, as poet Stephen Spender noted, "an organism which could survive when its heart has been destroyed."[15] Unlike Wilhelm Hausenstein's 1932 characterization of its spiritual emptiness as a city seemingly "built on nothing"[16] with no sense of tradition or of a past, it was the city's idiosyncratic history, loved and loathed, modern yet provincial, red and brown, home to both progressive and regressive impulses, that loomed large over every chance encounter, conversation, and policy decision in the weeks and months after the war. Those who conquered, administered, visited, and lived in the post-1945 city wrestled with the full weight of Berlin's tortured history at every turn. For some observers, this could be overwhelming. When poet and Berlin enthusiast W. H. Auden returned in the summer of 1945, he anguished over the city's sorry state as though a piece of his own youth was buried under the rubble. Unlike the Weimar-era critique of Berlin as the quintessential parvenu, the "urban monster" at the center of the Mark Brandenburg's sandy plane, for Auden the city never possessed more "soul and gravity."[17]

When visitors like Auden and Byford-Jones, Stephen Spender, and journalist Curt Riess toured Berlin's ruins, they saw a palimpsest of past

desires, both personal and political. There were remnants of the imperial desire for control and power in what remained of the architecture
of Schinkel, the turn-of-the century tenement housing projects, police
precincts, and traffic arteries once designed to better manage the frenetic
growth of the modernizing city. They recalled the search for subversion and escape in the cafés, bars, and restaurants once so popular with
the city's bohemians and literati. And they recognized in the pathos
of destruction the unmistakable remnants of Nazi attempts to combat
the aerial war through the construction of flak towers, bunkers, and
concrete-reinforced defensive facilities. Like an old parchment that has
been written over while still bearing the marks of its previous inscrip-
tions, the ruins conjured up competing pasts, competing emotions,
and diverse stories and experiences. As the architectural historian Alan
Balfour has noted elsewhere, "the projection of so many opposing ideals" virtually ensured that in Berlin "the presence of the past [would]
persistently interfere with the promise of the future."[18]

Although all cities contain spaces designed for particular purposes
that are reappropriated for alternative uses at different moments in
history, Berlin's cellars and bunkers provide unique insight into the
changing plans for and use of space from wartime to peace while highlighting the different ways in which Berliners positioned themselves,
reluctantly as well as purposely, within these grand designs. They also
serve as a vital link between the prewar, wartime, and postwar city, illuminating the changes in how state and society understood notions of
sanctuary and protection. Finally, they raise the thorny issue of moral
imperative and the obligation of the state to safeguard the health and
well-being of its population against whatever ills might befall it. While
the bunker was envisioned as a potent symbol of war preparedness,
as the war continued into its end phase it heralded nothing short of
defeat and desperation, calling into question the very morality of a
regime intent on waging an intractable war at all costs. With the dust
barely settled and the wounds of Russian revenge still fresh, Berliners
sought to take command of the broken spaces that remained, leaving
postwar authorities struggling to wrest control back from those who had
appropriated them for their own purposes.

The Order of Things

Trumpeted as a symbol of the capital's righteous resistance to its enemies, the 1940–2 bunker-building campaign was designed on Hitler's

order to create between 700 and 1000 large- and small-scale concrete facilities with sleeping arrangements for over 160,000 Berliners.[19]
Germans had grown accustomed to air-raid drills in the years before
the war since the Nazis used the image of the air attack to help lay
the groundwork for general war readiness.[20] In addition to the over
40 large vertical bunkers commissioned in 1942, plans were made to
integrate civilians into the city's four large flak towers, to build bunkers
adjacent to major transit arteries and train stations, as well as construct
reinforced neighborhood shelters in both the city center and the outlying districts. Despite extending two floors underground, with elaborate
ventilation systems, meeting rooms, and centers of operation, these concrete structures had been conceived and built before the war, and as
such, according to the writer Karl Friedrich Borée, planners were unable
to anticipate how the campaign for the city might unfold. Aside from
the flak gunnery atop the larger bunkers and the barricaded doors, these
buildings were largely unprotected, acting as large mousetraps for a captive and frightened population.[21] Curiously, the building of the bunkers
was rarely framed in terms of the state's moral obligation to protect its
civilian population. Instead, the bunker building program was imagined
by planners as a purely preservationist attempt to rationalize the war
effort on the home front. Even in the case of increasing vulnerability
of the civilian population to RAF and US air force attacks, the Nazis
construed what was essentially a defensive endeavor as a safeguard for
future success.

Whether Berliners realized at the time that the teams of workers active
on the city's many building sites were largely slave laborers remains
unclear. What is known is that the vast network of neighborhood
bunkers and cellar shelters communicated a sense of refuge from the
hail of bombs just as they served to further align essential social services
to the Nazi cause. Monitored by civilian spies in addition to the under-
cover *Wehrmacht* officers who worked in league with the Propaganda
Ministry and sometimes aided by Hitler Youth volunteers, the bunkers
extended the reach of the state into the nightly rhythms of the citizenry
at a time when they were most vulnerable. In 1940, city dwellers could
still evince some old-fashioned *Berliner Schnauze* (wit) in joking about
the disruption to their nightly sleep patterns, laughing off advice given
to them by city officials to go to bed early and get a few hours' rest
before the evening air raid alarm sounded. As journalist William Shirer
recounted, "when they headed to the cellar, some said 'good morning'
indicating they had been to bed early, as requested; others said 'good
evening' showing they had not managed to get any shut-eye." "A few

arrive and say 'Heil Hitler,'" indicating, Shirer noted sardonically, that "they have always been asleep."[22] By 1945, there was an obvious change in tone as Berliners' propensity for *Schadenfreude* began to acquire a kind of funereal aloofness. Richard Brett-Smith recalled hearing stories about guerrilla graffiti and the tagging of bunkers. In one instance, he noted that the letters L.S.R. were clandestinely painted on the walls of a number of air raid shelters – short form, he learned, for *"Lern Schnell Russisch"* or Learn Russian Quickly.[23] Hiding out in a bunker near the Charlottenburg Bridge on the Havel in the western district of Spandau, teenaged *Volkssturm*ist Helmut Altner recalled how citizen opposition was countered by propaganda designed to underscore the enormity of what was at stake in these final days. He remembered how on Monday April 23, 1945 the "gentle music of the radio (broke) off and a voice announced" a menacing last-ditch appeal by the Reichsminister and Defense Commissar for Berlin. As two children breathed in silent slumber on the sofa nearby, a lieutenant turned up the volume slightly just in time to hear what would happen to "all those traitors who hoist the white flag on their homes and buildings." For those who contemplated abandoning the Reich in its hour of need, the listening public was reminded of the stakes of waging total war: "all the occupants of such buildings, not just the traitors themselves, will be regarded as traitors."[24] Despite the occasional anonymous opposition to the faltering war effort, bunker and cellar space was never benign, neutral, or beyond the reach of the heinous Nazi state.

Rituals of Refuge

Even with the extra intrusion and surveillance, many Berliners preferred to leave the confines of their apartment cellar for the city bunkers. The actress Hildegard Knef, then just a teenager alternating between her grandfather's cottage in Zossen and her mother's apartment in Schöneberg, remembered fleeing the "wobbly cellar in Nr. 6" for the safety of the large bunker at the Bahnhof Zoo, where, bunker pass in hand, she waited together with a huge crowd for the doors to open[25] (Figure 1.3). Outside the concrete havens, there was a carefully constructed set of rules and rituals. Citizens were instructed to listen nightly for the so-called "Kuckuck-Ruf" on the radio notifying them that enemy aircraft were approaching. This alerted them that they could begin to make their way to one of the bunkers with a single pre-packed suitcase in tow. The call to hide was given in a kind of code, with exact locations of impending hits communicated with alternative place names

Figure 1.3   Zoo bunker – women and baby carriages, February/March 1945.
Photo credit: Bildarchiv Preussischer Kulturbesitz/Art Resource, NY.

that the civilian population recognized from rehearsals. Upon hearing that "a formation is nearing Gustav-Gustav (that is Berlin!)" Inga Pollack recalled, "a wild chase ensued, from the house, to the yard, and into the cellar."[26] This system was designed so that they would arrive in an orderly fashion well in advance of the air raid sirens signaling a pending hit. Once the Americans began daytime bombings in 1943, it was even more difficult to sound the alarm in time, leaving people scrambling for their possessions and making their way to the bunker often just before the initial barrage of bombs forced the doors closed "in the last minute."[27] This system was far from flawless. Herr Homa remembered how panic-stricken a waiting crowd was that had assembled outside the Zoo flak bunker when the two heavy doors remained shut while the sirens sounded all around. This delay caused him to spend the duration of the raid on the cold staircase instead of assuming his regular seat (*Stammplatz*).[28] It was not uncommon for the crowd to devolve into an angry and scared mob, or what Ursula von Kardoff likened to a "herd of human animals."[29] On the night of February 24, 1945, over 1000 people, mostly women, were so unnerved by the delay in letting them into the shelter that they opted to take matters into their own hands, shouting and banging violently on the doors of the Hermannplatz bunker in Neukölln. Earning the reproach of authorities, since their actions resisted the logic of rituals and established protocol, one woman retorted that she'd rather "be safe than sorry and it was, after all, lights out."[30] Despite complex rules and regulations, and their heavy-handed enforcement by air raid wardens and street-level neighborhood guards, the destabilizing effect of the air war meant it was impossible to fully domesticate the defense of the city (Figure 1.4).

While the population of entire city blocks huddled around makeshift stoves and lanterns with oil-matted hair to keep the lice at bay, many languished in underground catacombs and sleep chambers, forging distinct subterranean communities each with their own "quirks and regulations" and rituals of coping.[31] Despite the commonality of experience, survival strategies varied significantly from cellar to cellar. Some communities practiced holding cloths over their mouths during an attack, while others, Karl Friedrich Borée found, rehearsed the breathing exercises they had learnt in the prewar air raid drills.[32] Horst Götsch described the nightly trek he made with his family as they scurried to the flak bunker on the leafy Nachtalbenweg in the eastern district of Weissensee. Although each Berliner was allocated a spot in their neighborhood facility, Götsch recalled how even during the heaviest of attacks

Figure 1.4 In a provisional air raid shelter, Berlin, early 1945.
Photo credit: Bildarchiv Preussischer Kulturbesitz/Art Resource, NY.

the doors to his bunker remained open so that "anyone who sought shelter might find it here." Most of the inhabitants came from the Fairytale Land (*Märchenland*) garden community, and they knew to station their bicycles, wagons, and strollers neatly outside the door, even if they had the tendency to disappear occasionally under the cover of darkness.[33] With each night's attack, Berliners retraced these same steps with somnambulant precision.

These coordinated efforts, reenacted with every bombing, evolved into what geographer David Seamon has termed a "place ballet," communicating a sense of common experience, local identity, and dwelling in these extraordinary times.[34] Although the atmosphere underground could be plagued by nervousness and anxiety, it was not atypical for some Berliners to recall with nostalgia the time spent in the company of select neighbors, at least, up until the final weeks of fighting. Manfred Woge described this time as a kind of suspended existence, where children might seize the opportunity to form playgroups with neighborhood buddies and people would forge lasting friendships with the lady across the way. In these "bunker communities," as Gertrud Zscharnt characterized them, Berliners forged a much-needed sense of solidarity to help navigate the deleterious impact of the war on the home front.[35] Johanna Barthel remembers how in the middle of her cellar in Kreuzberg's Görlitzer Strasse there may have been a single cooking stove for "eleven women, two men, and five children including two toddlers," but "in this distress we still were a wonderful community [*Hausgemeinschaft*]."[36] Meanwhile, in Hohenschönhausen, some blocks to the northeast, Hildegard Müller, a 22-year-old teacher, felt the same sense of solidarity that came with sharing such close quarters. Since their fortified cellar was located in a semi-rural section of the city, they even enjoyed freshly harvested chicken and rabbit until the last week of April 1945.[37] Annaliese Herwig could still boast of her "communist collective in the cellar" where three men, six women, a child, a cat, (and two canaries!) had almost all the comforts of home, including sofas, a carpet, and a complete set of table and chairs.[38] Functioning telephone lines kept many of the "cellar people" in contact with other basement dwellers across the city, who snuck upstairs intermittently to fetch water, cook a quick meal, and check in with friends for up-to-the-minute word of the state of the fighting.[39]

Designed as a reassurance of Nazi war preparedness through the regulation of space and emotion, bunkers and neighborhood cellars communicated the message that air war could be rationalized with minimal civilian impact outside of a brief disruption to daily rhythms. Since well

before the war, entire city blocks practiced drills for swiftness in following posted signs and locating available shelters. In the larger bunkers,
soldiers and police led Berliners to their respective underground cabins, taking them from floor to floor in search of available space. Shelter
wardens, usually elderly men or women in uniform, ensured people followed the house rules, including keeping silent and refraining from
smoking, and spray-painted signs (along with the occasional elbow,
groan, or nudge) helped reinforce that message. Some rooms were
reserved for the infirm, some were fitted with electric lighting so people
might read or sew, while other bunkers had a number of small cabins for
sleeping.[40] Civilians could even receive medical care underground and
the Charité Hospital in Mitte's Invalidenstrasse had a particularly well-
apportioned bunker complete with operating facilities and after-care
chambers. Perhaps reflective of the disproportionately high percentage
of women using the facilities, the *Nationalsozialistische Volksfürsorge* or
NSV maintained a birthing unit in the underground bunker in neighboring Chausseestrasse and many of the larger compounds had on-site
midwifery services where infants born behind concrete walls could
apply for their birth certificate on the spot, indicating, in one example,
they were born "in Berlin, in the Flakturm Humboldthain." One woman
remembered that her birth certificate boasted a drawing of the two towers and a handwritten inscription that read: "You made your first cry
under the protection of the tower in Humboldthain, in a difficult but
grand time"[41] (Figure 1.5). If their stated purpose was to replicate life
above ground as accurately as possible, they achieved this in large part,
but once the front approached the city limits, it became increasingly difficult to maintain morale as belief in victory proved as unstable as the
failing structures that buckled under the barrage of bombs.

Sites of Adventure and Encounter

Despite the worsening situation, for Berlin youths like Götsch and Knef,
the bunkers could be sites of excitement and adventure, especially when
looking back through the lens of memory. If it hadn't been for the
quickening pace of bombing campaigns from 1943 onward, for many
Berliners the bunker and cellar experience might have remained a simple extension of their everyday lives. Bringing together people from all
walks of life from neighboring streets or different parts of the city, these
sites functioned as highly charged places of social interaction and intimacy that provided the opportunity for a quick game of charades, a
story or two, or casual flirtation. The Nazis had sought to render the

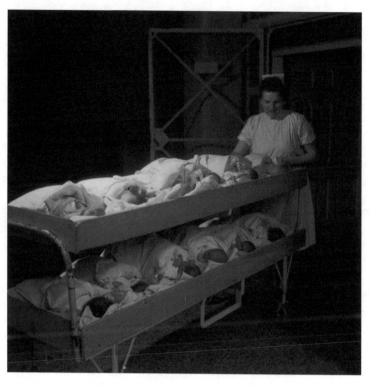

Figure 1.5   A nurse in a bunker taking babies to an elevator, Berlin, 1944–5. Photographer: Hedda Walther.

Photo credit: Bildarchiv Preussischer Kulturbesitz/Art Resource, NY.

state of siege as normal. And they almost succeeded. The constant air attacks, Jacob Kronika recalled, were incorporated into children's playtime as they used shovels and spades to build their own bunkers in the city's sandy plane, challenging themselves to construct the strongest facility.[42] Whereas the reality of war went unquestioned by some, or was at least accommodated in the hopes of simply muddling through, the intrusion of the war into life's daily rituals could be quite disconcerting for others, especially when social mixing challenged sexual sensibilities, personal space, and notions of propriety and intimacy. It is not surprising to learn that weeks on end in the bunker or squirreled away in a cellar shelter, while mind-numbingly boring, might also yield a host of erotic possibilities, breaking down carefully established social, class, age, and racial boundaries as bunker dwellers were forced to sit cheek by jowl on overcrowded benches in the far-flung antechambers of these concrete facilities. Jeanne Mammen, for one, was not quite sure how to interpret the kisses and embraces she witnessed in the smoking room of the U-Bahn bunker she inhabited alongside a work crew of Ukrainian foreign laborers.[43] Ursula von Kardorff claimed it was common to stumble upon amorous couples groping in the darkness of the bunker towers, especially in the ironclad winding staircases that led up to the gunnery turrets. Perhaps their vain search for privacy, and the fact that they were German and not foreign work details, shielded them from the full brunt of the author's scrutiny. For Horst Lange, all of these instances were simple proof of the breakdown of bourgeois values as the air war created conditions challenging "property, morality, and the separation of the individual from the mass." Not just outside, on the front lines, but in the rarified space of the air raid shelter, "frivolity, a lot of alcohol, erotic self-indulgence, ruins and disintegration" were increasingly becoming the order of the day.[44]

Despite the perception of lapsed values in the underground city, social boundaries were still promoted, policed, and reinforced in these subterranean spaces until immanent collapse made this no longer possible. Until they were assigned to the last-ditch defense of the city, the youthful battalions of SS flak gunnery operators atop the Zoo and Humboldthain bunkers used whatever free moments they had in between attacks to pose with the machinery or to relax in the sun, reinforcing in the process a sense of youthful self-confidence and male bonding as core components of the city's air defense (Figure 1.6). But beyond the puerile fetishization of virile bodies and weapons of destruction, which would disappear from view in the final days of fighting, the Zoo bunker's very location cultivated a sense of mystique by drawing a larger than average selection of famous citizens – so-called *prominenti* – who lived along the linden-lined streets off of the Kurfürstendamm.[45] Class boundaries and status were certainly at work in the Adlon Hotel's private bunker, where the hotel's swish occupants took a hidden staircase to the site, where they might linger over a glass of red wine or savor their cognac under the protection of a three-meter concrete wall.[46] Until the bunker and hotel fell into the hands of the invading Soviets, who cleaned out the wine cellar, one could rest here "without the nervous looks and tense sounds."[47] Still, despite the pretense of exclusivity, the frequency of the bombing forced people from all walks of life to penetrate these rarified spaces as they pushed in bunker doors and clamored for protection. Ursula von Kardorff noted that one of her most cherished memories of "the time before" occurred in the Adlon bunker, when she

Figure 1.6 Air raid helpers in their free time on the lower platform. Flak tower III Humboldthain, taken some time in 1944. Photographer unknown.
Photo credit: Landesarchiv Berlin F Rep 290 No. 372806 Bunker Humboldthain.

and a troupe of actors were forced into the space by a daytime raid, only to pass the time with hotel guests and a game of charades. She notes with some glee that "even some personnel from the foreign office" on neighboring Wilhelmstrasse joined in.[48] Social encounters and the breakdown of accepted forms of interaction and moral codes were occasioned by the uniqueness of the space under the cover of war. Despite official attempts to maintain a prewar sense of normalcy, the air war gradually undermined the regime's attempt to fully control the war effort, casting a range of its ideals into doubt with each passing day's call to seek shelter.

Image Versus Reality

Superior engineering and war preparedness was not what the average citizen experienced underground. Indeed, after sprinting to the closest facility, most Berliners languished in what turned out to be less-than-stellar accommodation. They slept on bedding sullied with flies and bedbugs and sat, if lucky, on wooden benches in overcrowded rooms short on oxygen and airflow. By the last week of April 1945, they tried in vain to drown out the hysteria of the city's pending occupation and defeat.[49] While the bunkers succeeded in providing sanctuary to those

Berliners who held the necessary bunker pass (*Bunkerkarte*), in the war's final days total chaos had broken out, which made the highly ritualized trek difficult to organize and control. Most of the bunker wardens had been pressed into the defense of the city only to be replaced by ill-prepared *Volkssturm*ists who took over the flak gunnery, leaving the task of organizing nightly entry in to the bunker to the ad hoc efforts of the civilians.[50] The loss of regular housing meant more and more people searched out long-term shelter in the already overcrowded facilities. All this combined to further erode confidence in the regime as the authorities lost all ability to stifle the swell of gossip that had overwhelmed efforts to clamp down on public opinion. In the tower bunker at Gesundbrunnen, inhabitants were increasingly defeatist by the spring of 1945. An unknown *Wehrmacht* officer tasked with scribbling clandestine situation reports noted that some bunker dwellers openly voiced their desire for Stalin to put an end to the insanity. Boldly, they chimed that chief among his tasks should be the hanging of party members.[51] In the cellars, the mood was not much better. Stuffed from floor to ceiling with a hodgepodge of household items, children resorted to "sleeping on bundles of bedding." Successive bombing attacks gradually took their toll on the structural integrity of the space and feeble attempts to reinforce the cellars with "wooden beams provid[ing] improvised support for the ceiling" may have given the impression of stability but, according to 17-year-old Helmut Altner, was "worthless in the event of an attack."[52]

Like the collapsing ceiling, feverishly reinforced but inevitably unstable, these fortified sanctuaries evolved into a caricature of themselves as these places of civil defense and war bluster heralded the absolute collapse of state authority. As the last remaining men and boys were rounded up for service, these "catacombs of fear" transformed from emblems of engineering and modernity to feminized spaces, inhabited mostly by a mix of women, the elderly, the underage, and the discarded – those whom the anonymous diarist in *A Woman in Berlin* suggests were "unwanted at the front, rejected by the *Volkssturm*."[53] As the bunkers and cellars eroded under the barrage of bombs, with them went the last vestiges of social organization and order as "the Nazi world – ruled by men, glorifying the strong man – [began] to crumble, and with it the myth of the 'Man' "[54] (Figure 1.7). In the confines of the Bahnhof Zoo bunker, Hildegard Knef bided her time sitting on her luggage while children cried all around her. The wailing was pierced only by the efforts of an elderly man "who lost his wife in the last attack" and "kept showing us a photo of her." Amidst the chaos, she

Figure 1.7   Propaganda sign on a bunker in Berlin: "Men between the ages of 16 and 70 belong in use – not in a bunker," 1944–5. Photographer: Hilmar Pabel.
Photo credit: Bildarchiv Preussischer Kulturbesitz/Art Resource, NY.

was unimpressed by the lackluster efforts of what remained of the formerly brazen boy flak soldiers, who, "with tacking on their shoes, slid across the floors like children on a frozen pond."[55]

Although Berliners were accustomed to a degree of flexibility in intermittently moving above and below ground during each passing raid to fetch fresh water, cook a quick meal, or telephone a friend across town for an update, the final battle for the city sent citizens underground for the *longue durée*. As Marta Mierendorf put it, from April 20 onwards she traded "the sweet daylight for cellar darkness" as the nights blurred into day accompanied by sleepless anguish and the steady hail of artillery fire outside.[56] Depending on troop movement and the level of resistance within the various districts of the city, Berliners were corralled underground anywhere from seven to 14 days. In some cases, they remained locked in their cellars even after the Russians arrived, either voluntarily to wait out the pillaging upstairs or as captives for the inevitable raping that frequently followed.[57] According to Annaliese Hewig, the nine days underground passed remarkably quickly between the burial of the first Russians and the blooming of the chestnut trees that overlooked their makeshift graves on the grounds of the Church of the Apostle in Tiergarten.[58] Although she would stay put in her hiding place, on April 22, 1945 the postwar period had already begun for shoemaker Franz Gröpler, himself an air raid warden, who, although initially wavering because of Goebbels's propaganda, ultimately raised the white flag over his cellar sanctuary beneath the rectory of the Protestant church in the Dorfstrasse, where he had hidden together with several women and children from Hohenschönhausen.[59] As the days lengthened into a week or more without the benefit of clean water, functioning ventilation systems, or useable toilets, the ranks of cellar dwellers continued to swell as Nazi supporters took their place alongside the occasional Jewish German *"Uboot"* or "submarine," the slang term given to men like Robert Sachs, who had miraculously managed to elude deportation thanks to the help of his committed social democrat neighbors Kedwig and Otto Schrödter.[60]

As racial, class, and temporal boundaries broke down under the weight of battle, the spatial conditions of the end of the war likewise brought a change in gender performance. While many women and children cowered in the darkness or shrieked in fear, others fought to retain a degree of civility in their embattled subterranean enclaves. In the western district of Spandau, German soldiers like Helmut Altner sought shelter from the brewing storm, only to be confronted again and again by brusque and frightened women who served as gatekeepers to the shelter, challenging the military presence as endangering all those gathered there. Only occasionally did they allow him access inside for a rest. Suffering from shell shock and the trauma of street fighting, overburdened soldiers cowered in the face of these women's emboldened authority over the cellar. One soldier could not even bear to look a bunker nurse in the face after she pleaded with him to leave since "there are women and children down there who have not been out in the air for days." She feared the Russians would kill them all "if they come and find soldiers in this bunker."[61] The bitterest irony, of course, is the fact that nothing could prevent these protective havens from turning into the most ominous of sanctuaries when the ubiquitous calls of *"Frau Komm"* ("woman come") trumpeted that the Russians had arrived.

The Private Is Public

As "bedrooms, living rooms, and reception rooms for the first to enter Berlin," the shelters became host to private degradations carried out in plain sight. In the extreme, the rapes (both the threat and, especially, the realization) confirmed the spatial reorganization of bunker space from a place of protection and community to one of danger and depravity.[62] In anticipation of coming events, women's efforts to control their environment resulted in some members of the cellar communities undertaking the dreadful task of deciding which of their fellow women might best placate Russian desires for the collective good.[63] Others deemphasized their own sexuality, donning men's pants and waistcoats. In the air shelter in Treptow's Beermannstrasse to the east of the city center, Ursula Trappiel resorted to desperate measures by cutting her daughter's face with a straight razor. As she recounted over 20 years later in a West Berlin memory project, her cellar community came to the decision collectively, banding together in the face of impending danger. "Thanks to the blood the Russians left her alone and so we prevented another rape."[64] Subterfuge did not always work. While some women continued to view the bunkers through the lens of security, believing they were safe underground because, to their minds, the raping only occurred on the street or in apartment building stairwells, what they found most often was that no amount of creative intervention could prevent the inevitable once the Russians stepped over the threshold. When the Russians arrived at the Sellerstrasse bunker, the women were separated from the men and held captive in the catacomb cells until May 3.[65] Although some tried to use the darkness of the bunker to their advantage, acting as mentally deficient when the Soviet soldiers shone flashlights in their faces, others resorted to desperate measures, smearing themselves with the excrement that had collected in the corners.[66] Despite the futile attempts to recast the gendered nature of the space, bodily assault was often a ubiquitous feature of the transition from war to peace. Although almost all women were in danger of rape, Russian preferences sometimes dictated that a particular kind of femininity was most sought after. Although there was indiscriminate sexual violence, sometimes the Russians might gravitate toward a specific vision of womanhood in selecting, for example, the robust over the skeletal. While the very old, the very young, and even the infirm did not always escape unscathed, as in the case of Marta Mierendorf's mother, who willingly sacrificed herself so that her daughter would go unharmed, the bespectacled and mannish lesbian in the woman's shelter managed to avoid their attention, as did some heavily pregnant women.[67] Reading the space according to a culturally bound sense of sexual preference and gender norms, in the anonymous diarist's words the Russians were "horribly normal."[68]

In addition to the sexualization of the space through the Soviet conquest and the different notions of femininity brought about by defeat, similarly the rapes engendered a recalibration of men's gender projections and self-understanding. In some cases, men were able to appeal to the Russians as fellow men, as fathers, and possibly even as allies provided they could speak some Russian or, at minimum, Polish. Seventeen-year-old Karin Friedrich recalled how the women in her cellar owed their survival to the pretend paternalism of fellow dweller Leo Borchard, who convinced the Russians in their own language that all those gathered were "Maja Dotschka" (my daughters).[69] For all the examples of bravery and luck, though, most diary accounts suggest the opposite to Friedrich's rendition; despite the language of bravado and hope that seeps through the accounts, most men were poorly equipped to deal with the vengeful Russians. The cellars were unforgiving sites of gender negotiation, where the traditional rules of battle – to say nothing of social organization – were violently recast. Agnes Trost recalled the wanton cruelty of "a batch of Mongols" who searched her cellar one day in late April, separating the few old men from their families. Claiming they had been fired upon from one of the corner houses, they exacted their revenge for the two men killed from their battalion. Despite their innocence, eight men, including her husband, were shot in retaliation.[70] Most depressing of all for Kurt Wafner, a committed leftist who served as a soldier before his release in 1943 forced him into the civil defense as an air raid warden, was the fact that he had to sit helpless while families were subjected to the grossest of indignities in public view. Defeat was far less depressing than the fact that the Russians, whom he admired as the "bearers of the world revolution and of socialism," confirmed rumors of sexual excess as they overtook the city. The vengeful Russians forced Wafner to question his political sympathies and assumptions, and they also took a personal toll on his relationship with his fiancée, who questioned whether he'd be able to protect her from the rapaciousness of the conqueror. For Wafner, who served as a police officer after 1945, this feeling of vulnerability continued into the postwar period, when he was explicitly warned not to intervene in Soviet–German fraternization. Even in cases of rape, he was not to "prevent things from happening." "Most depressing" of all, he noted, was the inability to help endangered women and girls; as he recounted some time later, "we always knew who was master."[71]

The rapes may have highlighted women's sexual vulnerability, but they also played a vital role in staging men's emasculation on both a personal and national level, as German power and privilege unraveled first on the front lines and then amidst the timidity and fear of the city's bomb shelters. As Atina Grossmann and Elizabeth Heineman have shown quite convincingly, for many Berlin women, encounters with the enemy were understood in explicitly racialized terms.[72] Men's experiences in the cellars could equally be infused with propagandistic notions of Russian atavism, demonstrating the parallel importance of race, ethnicity, and masculinity in the spatial negotiation of subjectivity on the home front. While this was very much the "hour of the women," to quote Heineman, male identity was vitally shaped by this sense of powerlessness. Karl Willy Beer, who published his reminiscences in 1946 in *The City Without Death* under the pseudonym Matthias Menzel, recalled knowing evil was afoot upstairs when he heard Russian voices ringing out above his cellar enclave, strange voices that he described as "unnaturally loud, menacing, rumbling, and foreign." Confirming this notion of a regressive, almost animalistic, masculinity, Menzel went on to recall that after the initial visit by a 16-year-old Soviet soldier, his cellar compatriots knew no peace: "young and old came in and left, upright figures and square-jawed wanderers, clear, vital figures and craggy-faced Mongols...we can no longer keep the door closed..."[73] Karl Friedrich Borée was even more circumspect in outlining his encounter with the Soviet forces. This was no simple battle, but an out-and-out attack on European values: "our quiet place was taken over by an exhausted horde of creatures that appeared to us between human and animal, eerie, inapproachable, untamable, and unpredictable."[74] If these reminiscences are to be believed, in casting the Russian onslaught as a clash as much of masculinities as of culture, male memoirists continued to understand German comportment as respectable, proper, and civil. Capitulation may have violently broken apart German mastery over the tropes of masculine power and authority, but in the crawl spaces of underground sanctuaries all across the city, the rapes served as a kind of *coup de grâce*, the ultimate indignity.

Transfiguration

Although the bunkers were envisioned by Hitler and Speer as buttressing the war effort by providing shelter to Germany's citizens (largely, it must not be forgotten, so they might continue to work for the Reich), as places of refuge, containment, and ritual, their design and function was as an essential element in the militarization of daily life while providing opportunity for further state control. Yet this is only half of the story. The breakdown of military authority together with the destruction of the capital ensured that these spaces rarely lived up to their grand design. With each night's bombardment taking a toll on structure and spirit, the facilities that corralled Berliners together provided ample opportunity for the questioning of authority, whether the righteousness of the Reich or male privilege. When faced with certain defeat and the inevitable encounter with the enemy, these spaces could no longer serve as a protection against a gruesome end.

Once the guns stilled and the armistice was signed in the district of Karlshorst to the southeast of the city center, the fledgling civilian government, with the backing of the Allies, sought new uses for Berlin's underground. Many bunkers were leveled, albeit with considerable difficulty, while others were put to use as jails, hospitals, makeshift schools, and venereal disease stations. Indeed, the *Kurier* newspaper, published in the western sectors, lauded the ingenious recasting of these "last bastions of security" which had been "built at tremendous cost." Once symbols of aggression and warmongering, these buildings were suddenly converted "into places of peaceful industry." The district of Wedding's revenue office (*Finanzamt*) rented out the floors of the once-mighty Humboldthain bunkers near the Gesundbrunnen train station to a paper supply company, while another floor stored empty kegs from a local brewery. During the Berlin Blockade, these bunkers were stockpiled with extra foodstuffs, demonstrating the continued importance of these facilities to the city's civil defense, which, given the quick emergence of the Cold War, remained a central function of most remaining bunkers until 1989. The Zoo Bunker was called upon "to heal the wounds of war" as an extension of the Robert Koch Hospital[75] while the famed Adlon bunker became a well-known restaurant for occupation troops.[76] Some bunkers formed temporary shelter for refugees while others housed German POWs soon to be marched off to the Soviet Union. In one of the most curious postwar uses, the 20-meter-high facade of the Humboldthain flak bunker was repurposed into a mountaineering wall for the city's climbing enthusiasts, for whom a trip to the Alps "remained a wistful dream" given the austerity of the day.[77] These spaces of death, rape, and retribution were resurrected swiftly to help lessen the impact of privation on postwar living conditions. By November 1946, the Allies hoped to spring many of the larger bunkers so as to affirm Germany's commitment to peace and pave the way for new urban planning initiatives. Not surprisingly, this move was met with skepticism from some Berliners, many of whom took pride in finding alternative uses for these former military spaces.[78]

Attempts to reconfigure the city's topography, motivated by public safety, democratization, and morale, began to reflect new Cold War priorities once Marshall Plan money started trickling into city coffers.

Plans were set in motion in the districts in the French, British, and American occupation sectors to transform the city into "a window to the West."[79] The Ministry of Greenspace and Landscaping (*Hauptamt für Grünflächen und Gartenbau*) set about the task of "greening" the approximately 15–20 million cubic meters of rubble through elaborate city park projects, especially in the northwest of the city, which had been hit especially hard due to the placement of heavy industry. For planners like soon-to-be famed architect Hans Scharoun and the director of the city's landscaping ministry Günther Rieck, the scale of the destruction offered a tremendous opportunity to finally correct the mistakes of the unbridled growth of the nineteenth century. Aside from the obvious desire to eradicate the blight of war-related buildings, the springing of the bunkers fit nicely into designs for more rational urban planning. Here was an opportunity, as outlined in a 1950 memo from the Wedding district burgomaster's office, to reconnect to a kindler, gentler preindustrial part of the neighborhood's history. Instead of shouldering the burden of forever being known as Red Wedding for the street clashes between Nazi and communist youths in the early 1930s, civic authorities cast their glance back to the 1869 consecration of the Humboldthain hill and surrounding park named in honor of humanist Alexander von Humboldt.[80] An extra incentive to remodel the park into a premier site of recreation and repose was the fact that the view from the hill gazed directly over the inter-German border, where one could easily spot the fruits of a planned economy in the building projects of socialist urban design, especially the mass housing project in the district of Marzahn. This spectral chest beating was cemented in stone in 1961 – the year the Wall was built – with the well-timed unveiling of a monument atop flak tower G in the name of a hopeful reunification of the two halves of the city (*Mahnmal zur Wiedervereinigung der Stadthälften*). Ideas for the park were anything but benign. Beautification drew meaning and inspiration out of the layered events of recent history.

Once it became clear that the concrete bunker could not be totally removed from the landscape given its proximity to the railway bed below, city planners and politicians sought to incorporate it more fully into their leisure and recreation designs. On both sides of the boundary, the transformation of city spaces into places of recreation and consumption helped communicate the effectiveness of each economic system in not just meeting but exceeding the needs of the population. Paralleling the increasing importance of consumerism and the domestic economy in the stabilization of the East and West German economies, bunkers were dynamited and former rubblescapes were cleared to make room for playgrounds, parks, and recreation facilities.[81] In Wedding, plans were hatched to build a cable car to take citizens to the top of one of the two hills in the Volkspark Humboldthain, where a couple might enjoy a drink or a meal in the comfort of a proposed brew house while their children played in one of the adjacent playgrounds. To cement the transfiguration of the space, a competition in 1952 was held to rename the three hills that the city constructed out of the detritus of the bombing. Organizers were inundated with over 950 suggestions, from the banal ("The View of the North") to the strange ("Big Bosoms"). Ultimately, the hill acquired the suitably sober moniker Humboldt Heights (*Humboldthöhe*) in honor of one of the city's most esteemed citizens. Despite efforts to cleanse these sites of the Nazi stain, places like the Humboldthain bunker hindered even the best-laid plans. Like the stubbornness of the seven-story Wedding bunker that refused to yield to detonation, these spaces could not easily be reconfigured to suit postwar needs. If these concrete structures remained impervious to human intervention, it was even more difficult to eradicate the memories they housed, to say nothing of the divergent ways in which people reconfigured the spaces for their own purposes.

Housing Delinquency

While city architects took to their drawing tables to design plans for Berlin's future, MPs, police, and public health and welfare workers combed through the rubble day and night to provide a sense of order and rule of law. The bombed-out bunkers and air raid shelters were no longer simply symbols of Nazi war bluster and a militaristic past; in the popular imagination, they were a tangible sign of the immorality of victor's justice and the depths to which Germany had sunk in defeat. After capitulation, they acquired an additional meaning as important sites of communal identity, this time for the legions of children and young people left orphaned, homeless, or in the care of psychologically damaged parents. More than just a physical shelter for Berlin's towering number of street youth, the bunkers provided emotional relief from the quotidian challenges of life after Hitler with black marketeers, rent boys, and fallen women camping out together in subterranean cliques and gangs.

Just as the rapes solidified in public consciousness the danger and immorality of these underground spaces as sites of racial mixing, emasculation, and bodily assault, in the postwar period the bunkers and ruins posed unique challenges to German sensibilities and the politics of rebuilding. If city planners and civic authorities sought to connect these spaces with a pre-Nazi past through rubble abatement and innovative design, police and welfare authorities were unknowing participants in a similar struggle over the city's moral geography. Whereas urban planning initiatives promoted recreation and "greening" to turn rubble mountains into ski hills and bunkers into climbing walls, street-level policing and custodial intervention for at-risk populations were important initiatives in promoting a vision of respectability and sexual normalcy via the transformation of urban space. But just as city planners struggled with the ineradicable nature of these solid structures, police and welfare authorities met considerable resistance in their attempts to neutralize the deleterious effects of the past on the present population. Juvenile delinquents, teenaged cliques, loose girls, and boy prostitutes brought into view the shame of defeat, while simultaneously conjuring up the image of a generation lost to Nazi influence, postwar privation, and the trauma of rape. Alongside clean-up operations, attempts to tackle the comings and goings in bunker squats, cellar hovels, and rubble mounds brought into plain view the war's enduring valence.

The night in November 1946 when Officer Behr of the women's police detachment was called to the Schlesischer train station to investigate reports that a clique of undesirables had barricaded itself in an abandoned bunker nearby provides a case in point. What she found there flew in the face of German mores on a number of fronts. Six youths – two girls and four boys – ranging in age from 11 to 15 had been living in the bunker for the better part of a year.[82] Until that night, they had managed to sidestep convention by creating a world unto themselves, without adults, caregivers, rations, or responsibility. Living rough, they had sidestepped Allied denazification strategies and shirked enrollment in school, two important sites of ideological reorientation for the Americans and Russians respectively.[83] If this behavior continued, they would be unable to take part in the rebuilding of Berlin, whether clearing of rubble or working in industry. Most pressing was the fact that they lived beyond the boundaries of the family or the state, creating their own nascent community, stealing to survive, prostituting themselves if necessary, and confirming in the minds of police and welfare authorities that Berlin's ruins served as a "hotbed of asocial elements"[84] (Figure 1.8).

Living in underground clusters of 10 to 15 individuals, street youth created a world with their own distinctive hierarchies, ranks, and rules. As Silvia Koerner recalled for a memorial project conducted by the German Historical Museum in 2000, "after everything we children and adults went through, it was no wonder we built cliques... they held us

Figure 1.8   Thieves' den in the underground, Berlin, March 1949. Photographer: Walter Heilig.
Photo credit: Bundesarchiv Berlin, Image 183-S83920. Photographer: Walter Heilig.

together, helped us create community, and gave us a sense of security."[85] Although forged out of necessity when parents could no longer provide for their children, these cliques also provided their members a sense of adventure and romanticism, if tempered by the recent experience of war. The underground crevices still served to ignite the imagination, as they had during the bombing campaigns. Koerner recalled the fantasy world of the underground, where abandoned cellars and bunkers held untold secrets as well as opportunity for a war-ravaged population. One served as a cache for her gang's stolen grocery loot, while another, in General-Pape-Strasse, was stocked with letters, which they took turn reading with great anticipation. They gleefully tore out the stamps and took them to a neighborhood collector, distracting him while members of the gang stole his most valuable lot. They even had the gall to approach the collector a few days later to sell him his own stamps. "We didn't care why he didn't recognize his own collection. We were just happy to get the money."[86]

While gangs like Koerner's viewed the rubble as sites of mischief, not all youths viewed them with the innocence of childhood. For many, these spaces still housed memories of the taking of Berlin, which was understandable considering estimates that as many as 1 million women and girls may have been assaulted by advancing troops.[87] This fact was certainly not lost on street youth who returned to the city's subterranean nooks and crannies in search of shelter and community. As one chain-smoking, teenaged "gangster's moll" remarked to journalist Curt Riess in the underground hideaway she shared with fellow teenagers, "you know, we haven't forgotten what the Russians did when they came in."[88] In case the full meaning was lost on the journalist, a boy reminded Riess of the space's dark history, "for Christ's sake, where do you think you are? This is Berlin." What may have seemed like a carefree existence without parental control had more in keeping with Rossellini's image of the rapacious ruins in *Germania Anno Zero* that spelled death for its young hero. As Curt Riess reminded his readership, for the legions of youths raised "in a world of slogans, of resounding phrases, of wild curses and promises" (and many of them were former members of the *Volkssturm*, the Hitler Youth, and League of German Girls), this hunger "for life, for love, even for vice" came at a cost, with prostitution and stealing the only ways to earn the semblance of a living.[89] The war continued to intervene in the natural rebellion of teenage life – only in divided Berlin the cost could be high indeed.

While public streets, bars, and clubs attracted the scrutiny of MPs and health authorities on the look-out for girls "on the make," the rubble provided shelter for youths in search of community. The city's semi-destroyed train stations were a natural draw for Berlin's bombed-out teens. Bustling with activity at a time when entire city blocks remained idle and deserted, train stations still served as vibrant, if ramshackle, nodes of activity. An engineering marvel given the Mark Brandenburg's sandy plane, the construction of these stations formed part of the modernist project to aid with the flow of human traffic, streamlining how people moved from domestic to commercial space. In addition to lending shape to traffic and travel, these stations were urban stages not unlike the street or boulevard, where the flow of people forced the creation of a new language to better organize, standardize, and regulate which actions, styles of clothing, postures, gaits, or facial expressions would be countenanced as suitable to that particular space.[90] While transit police and beat cops might try to dictate the pace of circulation and proper behavior, these spaces did not always lend themselves to control and management.[91] The sheer number of the dislocated compounded the problem; even staff in train station restaurants could not help but notice the throngs of soiled youths loitering around the waiting rooms, accosting would-be passengers with knowing glances and sideways looks, and heading out among the rubble in search of a private site of exchange.[92]

Police were well versed in how to spot male prostitutes thanks to the inherited strategies of surveillance and on-site interrogation they had acquired from their Nazi-era colleagues, to say nothing of the fact that some police and judicial authorities continued in their positions after 1945.[93] Focusing on suspects in station waiting rooms, watching how they (using their terminology) "gadded about" ("*umhertrieb*"), with whom they shared glances, if they winked and motioned hither, beat cops tagged their perpetrators-in-the-making and surreptitiously followed them as they ambled out onto the street. When beat cops followed Enrico P. and Gunter M. into a bunker ruin along the Reichstagsufer from their meeting place at the Friedrichstrasse train station, however, it did not matter that they had yet to have sex. Enrico declared at the scene that he "leaned towards homosexuality" and the boy had been observed leaving the station with another man earlier in the night.[94]

Although police tried hard to find physical evidence of transgression to substantiate charges, this was not a prerequisite for questioning or even arrest. Where it did matter was in sentencing. While men and boys served time and paid heavy fines for sex in the rubble, sometimes judges evoked the shadowy character of the ruins themselves as spaces that at least fell outside of the public eye.[95] Given the haphazard application of the law against homosexuality, it is not difficult to understand why rent boys and their johns believed there was shelter if not protection in the cavernous underground of the city's bombed-out bunkers.

If forced into a detention facility to await further investigation by child protection services, in the eastern sector boys could be sent to the Dircksenstrasse police station's youth wing, itself a ruin, chronically overcrowded, and fitted with beds and bedding from a neighboring bunker. In the west, they were channeled into a detention facility that had been built into the Fichtebunker in Kreuzberg – one of three gasometer bunkers in the city, measuring 26 meters in diameter and

12 meters in height. Constructed as part of the Nazi program to create three giant bunkers to house up to 6000 people, its basement had been converted during the bombing campaigns so that police could house inmates without fear that they might flee. "Liberated" by the Soviets on April 27, its official postwar function was to provide temporary shelter for displaced persons. But it also jailed delinquents like "Freddy," who had spent time in the Fichtebunker youth jail for "stealing anything that wasn't nailed down to buy cigarettes and chocolate" and even "socializing with known homosexuals."[96]

While the Fichtebunker or the Dircksenstrasse facilities might provide temporary holding for the so-called *"Besprisornies of Berlin"*[97] (a term that emerged out of the Russian Revolution for the street children of Moscow and Petrograd), many youth advocates believed long-term rehabilitation was most achievable outside of the city's corrupting spaces in one of the neighboring workhouses resurrected in 1946 as a means to neutralize the rise in youth criminality. Despite attempts by the divided city administration to reclaim the ruins, positioning them to serve productive purposes as prisons and detention centers, they could not yet fully rehabilitate the fallen, as the image of sending boys to rural homes suggests. In a sense, only a limited order could be imposed on these physical spaces through policing and the law. The desires of the ruins could not be redeemed within the ruins themselves. As we will see in Chapter 5, only hard labor outside of the city offered true reformation and a connection to healthful and productive manhood.

In other words, although Berlin's underground was built as a testimony to a "rationalizing" state, the physical transformation of the bombing campaigns and the experience of occupation transformed these same sites into spaces of irrationality and confusion. At the moment of capitulation, the Nazi state lost all hope of ever rationalizing the space, organizing the behaviors it inspired, the emotions it engendered, and the memories it housed. In the postwar period, attempts to regulate the comings and goings in the ruins likewise proved challenging, as Berlin youth chose their subcultural identification over official attempts at channeling moral renewal. In thinking about the place of gender in these spaces of conflict and desire, here too we see evidence of a shift in orientation. While the underground "caves," as the anonymous Woman of Berlin calls them, were feminized sites of violent desire and places of emasculation for German men, they remained highly charged places of sexual exchange. No longer simply heteronormative, however, these spaces played host to shifting notions of femininity, masculinity, and an evolving youth and homosexual subculture in the postwar orbit.

Inextricably linked to the recent terror of war's end, Berlin's underground was host to predation, crisis, death and decay. Within the muck and the mire there could be frivolity and mischief, but the shadow of war was felt by many of the women and girls who experienced the violence of capitulation at first hand. As spaces of disorder, they emerged as much more than a passive backdrop to postwar rebuilding. Certainly, they represented the breakdown of traditional authority. But they also helped shape the dynamics of a wide range of human sexualities and experiences, reflecting a host of concerns about the way in which sex, gender, and immorality were represented, perceived, and remembered at war's end. In some instances, those memories gained expression through official channels, in diaries and memorial projects. In other cases, ruined bunkers and cellars foregrounded experiences that remained truly subterranean, buried in archived police ledgers and dusty court dockets. This "onion skin" effect shows quite clearly that geographer Doreen Massey's claims for contemporary Berlin also hold true for the immediate postwar period: that the city's story is a product of "intersections of multiple narratives."[98] Hidden in plain sight, fragmented, decaying, pointing to a lost, invisible world, yet heralding something still to be articulated, Berlin's underground was much more than a "fossilized region where life no longer existed." In the face of death and decay, Berlin's "troglodytes," as Byford-Jones called them, used these spaces to map out a range of desires, connecting the ruin's shadows with those of the prewar city. In other words, the city's underground was not only a space of violence and disorder; it was also a site of subversion, nonconformity, and visibility for a host of subcultures, proving that the rupture of war's end was also accompanied by continuities as well. Byford-Jones conceded as much when, after scrutinizing the city below, he turned from his apartment window and "went down amid its ruins" since there was much "to learn from its secrets."[99]

2
The Street

> The song of the city: light and serious, cocky and melancholy,
> beguiling and alienating all at the same time.
>
> Georg Holmsten, *Berliner Miniaturen.*
> *Großstadt Melodie*, 1946

Sitting in the number 46 tram sometime in 1960 and passing through the intersection of Invalidenstrasse and Chausseestrasse just to the north of Unter den Linden, Monika Maron, the daughter of a prominent GDR (German Democratic Republic) minister and soon-to-be celebrated writer was momentarily overcome by swells of emotion for her native city. "Looking through the back window...at the hot asphalt on this ugly, war-damaged junction" she felt a rush "of disquiet and delight in equal measure." Searching for words to describe her conflicted state, she realized "the only appropriate word is love." Reminiscing about the event 40 years later, Maron remembered that all she wanted was "to lie down flat...with my arms out wide and embrace the street, the city."[1] Amidst the otherwise bleak descriptions of homely East Berlin neighborhoods (and the lingering image of a prostrate woman kissing the earth), two things jump off the page: the use of the affective register in describing her sense of belonging and the image of the still-broken streetscape in triggering such an intense emotional response. Not only is it curious that an otherwise banal act of traveling on a tram could bring on a host of associations, but the contemporary reader is certainly somewhat surprised at the suggestion that the dreary eastern portion of the city might actually inspire a profoundly pleasant memory from one of its citizens.[2]

Perhaps such a strong reaction is not so out of the ordinary after all. If geographer Nigel Thrift is to be believed, city life has always had the ability to instantiate "rolling maelstroms" of emotion whether through moments of intense activity like a brisk walk through a bustling crowd or even more mundane, repetitive tasks like the grind of the daily commute.[3] Certainly, Berlin was no stranger to emotional turmoil. A mix of disquiet and excitement lined virtually every page of the nineteenth-century chronicles of the city's budding modernity. Its unyielding vitality pulsed through the veins, unleashing anything from enervating to dizzying effects.[4] When "the shock of the new ceased to be shocking," as film theorist Patrice Petro has put it, life in the capital could also become tremendously boring, banalized, and routine, leading to a pronounced state of ennui.[5] In Berlin, at certain times the boredom of routinization gave way to raw passion, as general strikes, street fighting, and the climate of revolution and reaction brought about pure bloodlust, which some authors, like Klaus Theweleit, have notoriously linked to the eventual rise and appeal of the right.[6] Josef Goebbels had recognized the productive power of emotions in the 1920s when he claimed, "Berlin needs its sensations like a fish needs water... the city lives off them." Harnessing the human passions was essential to the success of the movement. "All political propaganda will miss its target if it does not recognize this."[7] Despite economic misery and protracted hardship, for a lucky few Weimar Berlin still managed to impart a "sense of freedom and exhilaration."[8] But as we all know, the use and abuse of public sentiment ultimately won out, a fact not lost on Walter Benjamin and Siegfried Kracauer, both of whom devoted considerable ink to the cinematic manipulation of space and emotion in garnering Nazi hegemony.[9] In staging the fascination and fears of the spectator and participant in Nazi torchlight processions, and showcasing the jubilance of the crowd during the 1936 Olympics, Berlin's city spaces were chockablock with affect and emotionality in the years leading up to World War II. Securing some measure of control over these spaces, and the emotions they engendered, was a central element of Nazi strategy.

Although it was based on observations of Moscow and not Berlin, Walter Benjamin provides an alternative way of viewing the emotionality of the street in his analysis of the role of bar, café, and street life on the course of early twentieth-century bourgeois identity formation. Well known for his city texts, most notably his description of his own childhood in Berlin and the Paris *Arcades* project, Benjamin's exegetical reading of the Soviet capital provides an interesting discussion of competing socialist and bourgeois modernities based on a spatial analysis of how people move through urban space. In his lesser-known work *Moscow Diary*, written after a two-month visit in 1926 while he was in pursuit of an elusive romantic relationship, he suggests the rhythm of the street served as an important gauge of the city's changing moral and political landscape. He was particularly struck by the movement of the Muscovite crowd. All over the Soviet capital, people seemed to march together in syncopated proximity with little regard for personal space. To his mind, this proved that the Soviets had successfully sub-limated their sense of the personal to the will of the collective.[10] He then went on to suggest that this economized claim to public space was itself a commentary on Soviet subjectivity and the purported with-ering away of privacy under communism. Instead of functioning as a place of alienation, as much of the writing on metropolitan modernity seems to emphasize, in Moscow city streets surfaced as the source and site of consciousness building and community, where individuals ham-mered out a new social compact. Whereas his earlier work on Paris and Berlin envisioned the city as a privatizing force, one that created a sense of bourgeois identity in contradistinction to the dangers of the street, under communism it had the opposite effect as a site of radical de-privatization in the spirit of the collective.[11] Although he did not live to see how fascism would transform his native Berlin, it is worth ask-ing what comes of his vision of the spatiality of selfhood within these different notions of modernity. This is especially interesting in such a hotly contested place as Cold War Berlin, where borders and boundaries between two competing ideological systems were porous until 1961, when crossing from one sector to the next meant simply turning the cor-ner, riding the S-Bahn from one side of the city to the other, or traversing the street.

As we will see in this chapter, urban space played an indelible part not just in the negotiation of memory and the regulation of bodies, but also in the solicitation of support for various ideological plat-forms and regimes. The Nazis may have been iron-fisted and extreme in their approach, but it would be foolhardy to suggest that attempts to control the emotional register of the city were excised completely after capitulation. This chapter looks at the changing valuation of Berlin's city streets from symbols of rationalization, cosmopolitanism, and modernity before the war to a highly fraught staging ground in the negotiation of authority between the occupation forces and average Germans. It then moves away from ground-level street altercations to the visual depictions of street life itself to analyze the role and place of photographic propaganda in legitimizing division. It explores a series of photo books that emerged on the scene during the Berlin Crises of the late 1950s and argues for the ongoing importance of the visual imaginary and emotional register in molding support for reconstruction efforts in both halves of the city. What at first glance appear as glossy images of street scenes and café culture were in actuality sophisticated appeals to secure the hearts and minds of the population. The exertion of control over the street, whether in regulating behavior or in sentimental depictions of a day in the life, was an essential component of the Cold War battle for Berlin.

Streetscapes of Modernity

Whether the storied Unter den Linden, where well-attired couples strolled serenely under the triumphal arch of the Brandenburg Gate, that gigantic portal standing 65 feet high on whose precipice stands the Goddess of Victory in her chariot, or the stony sobriety of the nearby Wilhelmstrasse, home of the Foreign Office, the Reich Chancellery, and Germany's beleaguered bureaucrats, or even the artful Kurfürstendamm in the city's West End, which Kaiser Wilhelm II had tried to domesticate through the building of the Memorial Church in 1905, city streets, boulevards, and intersections have dominated the landscape of modern Berlin. Although narrow cobblestone streets, claustrophobic tenement rows, and a hodgepodge of medieval alleyways remained a testament to its bizarre pattern of growth, the metropolitan narrative has generally hinged on a few major streets. To move off the boulevard would require a radical rethinking of metropolitan modernity. In actual fact, historic Berlin is a textbook study of anachronism and contradiction. Despite its status as an icon of urbanity, bourgeois sobriety, industrial might, and imperial bombast, the largest European metropolis between Paris and Moscow presented visitors with a curious mix of urban and rural life, with over 800 farms and 200 waterways within the city limits. Before World War II, more than half of its topography was still made up of parks, forests, and gardens, offering accessible respite from the challenges of city life via a short walk or a ride by bicycle, omnibus, or suburban train (S-Bahn).[12] Although much of this greenery burned in the bombings or was used as firewood, in no time at all its craters and rubble gave way to the inevitable cycle of life (Figure 2.1). British documentary filmmaker and one of the founders of the Mass Observation Organization at the University of Sussex, Humphrey Jennings, was stunned to find "hedges and trees and weeping willows growing finely in between the ruins and up and down what were once streets."[13] Just as the city housed the country, amidst mass death there was also life.[14]

Berlin's streets and avenues were more than urban stages of lives once lived, or simple symbols of unbridled growth, commodity fetishism,

Figure 2.1 Berliners swimming in water hole in front of Zoo Bunker, 1945.
Photographer: Otto Hoffmann.
Photo credit: Bundesarchiv Berlin, Image 146-1982-028-14.

street fighting, and interrupted modernity. They showcased and made
possible a host of new experiences, contacts, and feelings that tell us
much about the city's history. But just as the remnants of the pre-1945
Berlin still dotted the landscape, pushing through the new growth of
weeds and grass, these encounters owed much to the continued presence of these multiple and conflicting pasts. The inheritance of many
of Berlin's prewar structures of feeling – what Benjamin and Simmel
referred to as the range of emotions between outright boredom, extreme
overstimulation, and fascist manipulation – provides a useful methodology for historicizing how Berliners gave voice to their struggles in
the postwar city.[15] If the modern thoroughfare "made the city walka-
ble," as historian Joachim Schlör has argued, bringing hitherto unseen
parts of the city into plain view and providing new opportunities for
self-exploration, then the craters, rubble, and bombed-out streets of
capitulated Berlin certainly provided new terrain for self-discovery and
introspection.[16] It must be said, however, that these physical, topo-
graphical, and personal spaces of subjectivity did not necessarily mean
there was a uniformity of perception or experience. If anything, the jum-
ble of life on the street unearthed a complex set of sensations as varied
as the range of possible encounters. In this way, the bombed-out street

remained a potent symbol of the contradictory conditions of memory and modernity.[17]

Just as there were conflicting ideas about life in post-1945 Berlin, so too must we not rest on a reductive view of what came before. As might be expected, there were competing estimations of the changes brought about by the worsening political situation, the Nazi seizure of power, and the eventual mobilization of the home front for another total war. Our casual romanticization of the demimonde atmosphere of imperial and Weimar Berlin would benefit from further nuance. The humanized coupling of abject poverty in satirist Heinrich Zille's etchings receded by the early 1930s, when the romance of the underworld gave way to a more pessimistic, even ambivalent, tone. As Curt Moreck described in his *Guide to Depraved Berlin*, it was as if the temperature itself had cooled, leaving the climate in this former hot spot changed by degrees. Friedrichstrasse was no longer the measure of licentiousness; suddenly, it failed to impress. It was as if "the melancholy of the transitory has percolated everywhere."[18] Now revelers followed the trail of money to the bright lights of the city's New West, to the neon-lit restos and nightspots along the Kurfürstendamm and Tauentzienstrasse. Whether numb from the sensory overload of the penny amusement industry, which Joseph Roth claimed was a European-wide conspiracy against the introspection of the night walker, or simply blinded by the buzz of city lights, by the early 1930s people increasingly retreated indoors, leaving the pleasures of the street for the comfort and sanctuary of known haunts and hangs.[19] This uniformity had replaced decadence far before Hitler emerged on stage. Cheap and banal amusements had supplanted the variety of experiences formerly countenanced on metropolitan streets, as everyone sought to cash in on the craze. What mass culture had begun, the Nazis had ended as they embraced the street with particular verve, clearing away the homeless, pursuing an aggressive platform against criminality, and furthering the use of street lights to rationalize the night in the service of their law and order agenda.[20] Far from completely philistine, however, they actually allowed nightlife to continue, as long as it could be subjected to party control. Hitler Youth trolled about urinals as stool pigeons (*Lockvögel*), preying on unsuspecting men interested in temptations of the flesh. Using similar tactics a few short years later, *Wehrmacht* and Propaganda Ministry agents huddled together in bunkers, bars, and cafés, listening for anti-Hitler jokes and tirades against the regime.[21] Defying the pleas of moralists and social purity campaigners, Hitler's crew upheld the utility of these highly monitored gathering spots in maintaining power at home and promoting a law and order public image abroad.[22] Night marches notwithstanding, during the initial years of Nazi rule they managed to carry off this conquest of the street relatively unnoticed. Indeed, one had to look closely for evidence of intervention. Martha Dodd, the daughter of the US ambassador to Germany and future Soviet spy, initially saw few differences between Berlin and any bucolic American town. In her memoir of the time she spent in the company of her family in a palatial house on the Tiergartenstrasse, a short walk from the American Embassy, she felt, in fact, that the Hitler state had been much maligned in the press. She took it as her mission "to proclaim the warmth and friendliness of the people," drawing on the example of "the serenity of the streets."[23] Given her highly stage-managed tours of the city, she could not be completely faulted for succumbing to the official image promoted in Nazi propaganda. Even that *enfant terrible* of British letters Christopher Isherwood noted in *Goodbye to Berlin* that one had to look deeply to see evidence of the changes afoot. In many respects, "things seemed very much as usual, superficially."[24] While Isherwood saw the writing on the Wall and fled Berlin in 1934 – a good thing too given his taste for rough young boys – the scales would only fall from Dodd's eyes after she witnessed the tranquility of the streets replaced with sheer emptiness in the wake of the notorious Röhm Putsch.[25]

As we know now, all was certainly not what it seemed in Hitler's Germany, and in the lead up to war it was hard not to notice the changing climate as all eyes turned to what was happening in Berlin. The 1920s had drawn a sizeable number of visitors, tourists, and students to the city in search of its much-ballyhooed hedonism. After the so-called "seizure of power," the question on everyone's mind was how this new political animal would institute and realize its much-touted social revolution. With as much if not more vigor than the literary outpouring that followed the end of World War I, writers, diplomats, tourists, and artists poured in to the city, unleashing in their wake a torrent of dispatches, essays, and memoirs detailing their impressions of life in the Nazified capital. As might be expected, what surfaced was not one but multiple, coexisting Berlins: one was almost always rendered in perpetual twilight, static, and ambivalent, while another still teemed with tension. To many intellectuals and well-heeled observers, it was one thing to question the legitimacy of the Nazi Party and quite another to see clearly the fate of things to come. To make sense of what they saw, writers often gravitated to a particular set of bodily and spatialized metaphors to help lend color and contour to their tales of Berlin's precipitous decline. One such example came at the hand of prosaic American writer Thomas Wolfe, whose love for Germany eventually gave way to a pronounced sense of alienation after the promulgation of the Nuremburg Laws in 1935. In his novella *I Have a Thing to Tell You*, serialized in *The New Republic* in 1937 and re-released in an edited collection in 1961, Wolfe's narrator could almost smell the changes in the air when "in the center of the street..., the fine trees had...lost their summer freshness." As his train rolled out of the Zoo Station bound for exile in Paris, his once treasured city grew ever smaller in the distance. All that remained was "a world hived of four million lives, of hope and fear and hatred, anguish and despair, of love of cruelty and devotion, that was called Berlin."[26] Presaging Maron's narrative frame of gazing at the city while in transit, Wolfe similarly uses the affective register to sketch out his thoughts about the city's decline. Also like Maron, whose reminiscences were penned after the GDR's collapse, Wolfe's sense of nostalgia was communicated with sentimentality in linking taste and smell to the longing for a now defunct past. American reporter Howard Kingsbury Smith similarly used olfactory sensation to make known his displeasure at the changing political situation. In his dispatches from the Nazi capital in wartime, one could literally smell the mix of resignation and overwork on the bodies of Berliners.[27] For Smith, to know the city one had to simply walk its streets; to know its people required something more intimate: a descent into the belly of the beast, as it were, by which he meant into the city's vast subway system, where he watched Berliners scurrying off to work. Just as his observations signified a retreat into the body, which would normally suggest a commentary on private life or the private sphere, his focus on the bowels of the city was used as a device with which to gauge the depths to which Germany had sunk morally as well as politically. In other words, it was through the intensely private metaphors of taste, smell, and intuition that Smith attempted to chart the instrumentalization of private life in the service of the Reich. Bodily experience and body knowledge, attention to gesture, behavior, and the rhythms of everyday life was anything but apolitical but formed an integral part of the way in which people attempted to make sense of their world. It is through the author's use of metaphors of affect and embodiment in the confined spaces of the city's underground that one begins to sense for oneself the extent of the regime's intervention in the life course of its citizens. In Smith's account, the process of decivilization had already begun long before Allied bombs rained down on the city.

This indictment of the Nazis as ushering in a period of deep-seated cultural decay did not just animate the writing of Wolfe and Howard, but impacted a range of writers who remained in the city – in some cases, until well after the outbreak of war. The writer Karen Blixen, who toured the city in the days before her native Denmark was overrun, was particularly opprobrious in her reproach of the city's management, noting that the Nazi allocation of resources for war preparedness came at a huge cost. She bristled at the sight of the barren city streets, barely cleared of dark and dirty snow, indicating that the city's priorities clearly were focused elsewhere. The neglected environment paralleled the sentiment of its dispirited population, politically neutered and culturally inert. Hers is a somber Berlin, where the citizens ambled about draped in gray togs and last year's fashions, humorless, demoralized, and detached. Although she fails to see actual street urchins (*Lumpen*), the war-addled population displayed little to no elegance. Unlike her view of Weimar Berlin, where the streets were alive with perpetual spectacle, without responsible cultural stewardship "the city was as uniform as hopelessness was universal."[28] Matthias Menzel's account of the Kurfürstendamm was similarly oppressive, where between seven and eight o'clock at night there may have been great evidence of citizen energy, only it took the form of a grey mass of passersby quickly shuffling about their business before the nightly blackout. Indeed, the once "colourful, noisy, light and life-filled street had grown still" in anticipation of the pending hail of bombs.[29] If streetscapes functioned as barometers of social experience and political practice, as sites not just countenancing but conveying cultural caché, providing some measure of military preparedness, and political legitimacy, their description by foreign observers suggests that once the pomp and circumstance of night marches and parades gave way to total war, Nazi Berlin was a drab and colorless place indeed.

Whereas most observers saw the street scenes as emblems of demoralization, some of the regime's most ardent critics were surprised at the perseverance of Berliners who clung desperately to vestigial memories of the 1920s. Theo Findahl, a Norwegian newspaper reporter in the capital during the final years of the war, was shocked to see Berliners promenading along the Kurfürstendamm despite the presence of fresh ruins from the numerous bombing raids. There is an anthropomorphic element to his telling when he describes the street's own emotional investment in resurrecting its "reputation as a promenade and erotic hunting ground." The bombs might shake the earth beneath their feet, the fires churning clouds of smoke into the sky, but the next morning, "Eva does her hair, looks in the mirror, applies some colour to her lips and cheeks and sets out in search of her Adam."[30] With all the demands of total war, in outlawing dance bars, variety shows, and wine and liquor bars, the cinemas, cafés and streets were the last arenas of elegance. Whatever flirtations continued to exist along the Kurfürstendamm were not signs of the survival of the human spirit, however, but emblematic of the triumph of the banal over the carnivalesque. The New Woman of the 1920s, "whether in bed, on the streets or at the beach" had been a hallmark of the heights of urban modernity.[31] In war-torn Berlin, her fleeting attempt at self-adornment was but a harbinger of the coming apocalypse. The feigned elegance of Berlin's women, so obviously artificial and contrived, was, Menzel tell us, the inevitable offshoot of a morally bankrupt regime. For him, the street underscores the economy of scarcity via a gendered and sexual parable.[32] Not only is the regime unable to make good on the provision of advertised consumer items such as cosmetics, making this image of coquetry utterly unsustainable in real time, but the demands on the home front, to say nothing of the bombing campaign, had well nigh stifled the last vestiges of intimacy and desire once omnipresent along the city's promenades and high streets.[33] If "war and the danger of death (are said to) spur on the erotic," this was certainly no longer sustainable in Berlin. With the closure of other meeting places, what little desire remained on display was relegated to the Kurfürstendamm, and even there, it was only noticeable for a few hours each day in the afternoon and early evening.[34]

While the prewar metropolis came to life amidst the throes of modernity, the 1930s saw its city streets transformed from spaces of frivolity, flirtation, and conviviality to the syncopated whimsy of a morally bankrupt regime. The war-torn city bore little resemblance to the mix of Prussian militarism and eroticism Kracauer noted in so many of his essays.[35] Where once Berliners strolled about in leisured harmony, shielding their eyes from the glare of flickering lights while stopping to linger in front of shop windows, darkness now descended on the city, literally and figuratively. Through metaphors of light and shadow, Berliners lost all semblance of individuation, and were rendered instead a dark mass of deluded citizens. In this way, foreign observers mapped the city's boulevards and streets with alternating frequencies of emotional detachment and intensity, contrasting their memory of the 1920s with their growing sense of unease and disenchantment during the war. The material conditions of life in the city made a very real impact on the senses, and shaped how these observers understood Nazi Berlin. The link they forged between social space and moral authority emerged through acts of walking, observing, smelling, and tasting the atmosphere of the city, evoking a kind of phenomenological linking of life's rhythms to the changing pulse of the city. Aside from an intensely emotional experience, this was also an extremely gendered and sexual-ized practice of social observation. If the war represented pure barbarity to its critics, with the power to unmake a civilization, nowhere was this more palpable than in the arena of intimacy and the erotic. Street life had been transformed from a hub of energy and erotic exchange to an instrumentalized, empty, dead space, where honor in valor and sacrifice no longer reigned supreme. Turning to an analysis of the zero hour, the question becomes, to what extent did these metaphors con-tinue to shape the way in which Berliners understood and experienced war's end?

At the Crossroads

If Berlin's streets once pulsed with life as urban stages upon which cit-izens acquired the tools of self-presentation by learning how to read and reproduce cosmopolitan affectation, persistent air raid sirens, lights out, shortages, and the brutality of capitulation snuffed out any hope of Berlin resurrecting its former status as one of Europe's most exciting metropolises. Well before the end of the fighting, observers believed the rise of the Nazis heralded civilization's unmaking – understandably so, given the view of the city that awaited them upon their arrival. Cul-tural historian and critic Wolfgang Schivelbusch was the first to point out the reliance upon such narratives of apocalypse at the zero hour.[36] For anyone living through Berlin's capitulation at the end of April 1945, city streets acquired additional meaning as sites of danger, of last-ditch defense, of first encounters with the enemy, and death on a mass scale. Although the street had once functioned as part of the negotiation of identity and spectacle, this did not completely cease in 1945. As the political situation evolved from dictatorship to four-party rule, Berliners cut a path through the destroyed streetscape with renewed vigor. In pro-viding a window into social relations at war's end, their reminiscences help us understand how Berliners imagined themselves in relation to the changing terrain. But, more importantly, they tell us that the prac-tice of establishing control over the city was simultaneously an exercise in reasserting authority over the use and meaning of city space. In this sense, cleaning up the rubble may have been the immediate goal, but reestablishing symbolic mastery over the streetscape was a core com-ponent of social and political normalization. It would take a variety of strategies to convince Germans that they could feel safe again in the streets of Berlin. Alongside attempts by both East and West Berlin gov-ernments to rebuild their halves of the urban environment with symbols of their benevolent rule, whether in the form of housing reconstruction or the building of recreation facilities, the greatest challenge lay in expunging citizen fears and anxieties over what had become of their cherished city.

As Soviet soldiers from the 1st Belorussian Front, led by Marshal Georgy Zhukov, started the steady shelling of the city on April 20, 1945, ultimately dropping more tonnage than that dropped by Bomber Command and its US allies combined, the city would defend itself for a little over 10 days before the last battalions of *Wehrmacht*, *Waffen-SS*, Hitler Youth, and *Volkssturm*ists resigned to their fate and surrendered.[37] During those fateful days, civilians were paralyzed with horror and retreated from above ground to whatever sanctuary could be provided in underground cellars and air raid bunkers. For those who bore witness to the hopeless defense of the city, the streets formed an important physical and psychological barrier between the occupying forces and the soon-to-be vanquished civilian population. In the space of days, it was transformed from city space to an urban wasteland, one littered with the bodies of those who had tried in vain to reach a new hiding place, retreat to their units, or retrieve cherished belongings from their home. (Figure 2.2) Hitler Youth and *Volkssturm* battalions familiar with the city now searched the streetscape for clues to the enemy's position. As the teenaged Helmut Altner recalled on April 26, 1945, they literally learned how to read the street as a text for signs of recent changes. They especially scanned the sightline to see if doors to apartments were kept open since this was a clue to Soviet presence inside the building.[38] As we saw in Chapter 1, encounters with Russians in cellars and apartments were anything but peaceful. On the streets, courtyards, and alleyways, they were almost always deadly.

During the siege of the city between clouds of dust and debris, even the *Volkssturm*ists became disoriented amidst the quickened pace of fighting and constant flow of adrenaline. In this quick-paced environment, soldiers struggled to identify the shattered features of the streets that went "past like a film strip, building after building, ruin after ruin."[39] Despite this strain on the senses, including the collapsing of time and the blurring of night into day, street fighting brought about an eerie sense of violation, fear, and ever-present danger, as the boundary between the military and civilian worlds was continually breeched through sniper attack, errant bullets, and life in the crossfire. People died where they lived and it was not uncommon for a soldier or civilian to come upon a body a few short blocks from a home address, as desperate Berliners took advantage of occasional lags in fighting to return to

Figure 2.2   Soviet Soldiers and a fallen German after the battle for the center of Berlin, April/May 1945.
Photo credit: Bildarchiv Preussischer Kulturbesitz/Art Resource, NY.

their dwelling, gather a few provisions, or telephone friends in an outlying district for a quick update on troop advancement. The same was true for combatants, given the fact that the Nazis' impressment scheme meant many *Volkssturm*ists were boys and seniors from the local *Kiez* or neighborhood, ill equipped to deal with battle; with overwhelming frequency, they too fell close to home.[40] Of course, adults and soldiers weren't the only ones to perish on city streets, and the killing of hundreds of thousands of men, women, and children quickly overburdened municipal officials.[41] Indeed, the presence of bodies in the streets in the spring of 1945 was so ubiquitous that no postwar account fails to make mention of it.[42] Red Army reliance on mass graves to stave off a pending public health threat and the inability of German authorities to provide pious, individualized burial in the short term forced Berliners to take matters into their own hands and carry out emergency burials anywhere they could – in gardens, along pathways and sidewalks. Crosses and makeshift grave markers soon dotted the landscape of the city.[43] At the same time that the presence of bodies signified the chaos of the transition from dictatorship to capitulation, reinforcing the sense of Germany's unmaking, for some the scene could also convey an air of macabre serenity, signifying the extent to which Berliners had become accustomed to the sight and smell of death in the streets. Altner describes the image he witnessed while in the eye of the storm:

> on the street are lying a lot of dead who look as if they had been suddenly mown down. Torn bodies, burnt corpses, women, civilians, and bits of baggage are strewn around. A policeman in his pale green uniform lies in the gutter his face a smashed-in mess. Dead children look as if they are asleep, their wounds hardly discernable. Women, girls, and men. Between and over them lie the remains of the cables and wiring from the street lighting. A solitary soldier's boot shows a bloody stump in the leg. A dead man leans against a dark doorway as if he has simply fallen asleep.

This passage is universally significant for its detached description of total war. But it is also city-specific, as the author evokes the image of street light cables and electrification – symbols of Berlin's inelegant brush with modernity at the turn of the century, reminding the reader yet again that what the Baedeker tourist guide once termed "the greatest modern city in Europe" now stood at a crossroads the proportions of which had never been seen before.

The battle for Berlin may have been fought on city streets, but its memory was constructed in the realm of the senses. In their recollections of these city spaces, witnesses drew a sensual map to communicate feelings of fear, nostalgia, demoralization, and security. In this telling, streets emerged as much more than simple lines on a map. They were highly charged emotional spaces of transition between what had come before and what lay ahead, between life and death, and between collapse and reconstruction. More importantly, these were places where citizens and occupation authorities intermingled often in unique and interesting ways. For Albert Speer, the craters in his carefully manicured streets brought home the fact that this was not simply the end of any war, but the end of war as previously known. Searching for words to describe his emotions as he surveyed the ruins of the city from the air en route to his prison, he recalled that the "whine and burst of mortars and 'Katyushas,' the moan of rocket guns, the sharp defiant note of rifles, or the abrupt drilling noise of a Spandau from heaps of wreckage" continued to ring in his ears.[44] Indeed, metaphors of hearing were often employed by Berliners, who, in resorting to the blackness of the underground, strained to hear the sounds overhead for "the hurrying footsteps of the advancing Russians."[45] After hearing rumors of Soviet rapes from German refugees who had made the trek westward, the sound of alien voices overhead followed by the smell of alcohol on the breath formed some of women's first encounters with the occupiers. Although the sound of boots meant the Soviets had made it as far as the streets, many women believed public space offered salvation from the horrors to come. Walli Sohrade could almost hear her heart pound in her chest as she sprinted like a schoolgirl out of the cellar, past her attacker and the two soldiers he had asked to stand sentry at the door, to her compound. She had heard officers would offer protection if only she made it to the street.[46] Though she was lucky, many others were not. In capitulation Berlin, the streets offered no sanctuary.

Although they were responsible for mass rapes, kidnappings, and the continued brutalization of civilians well into the occupation, the Soviets were the first to claim they brought order to chaos in the streets of Berlin. On the one hand, this claim was true insofar as they were indeed the first of the occupation powers to administer the city until the three – and later four – power Allied Kommandatura could be established in the middle of the summer of 1945. On the other hand, this statement is imbued with obvious ideological invective, and was part of the rhetorical battle for legitimacy in this contentious space. Putting politics into practice, before he succumbed to a motorcycle accident later that year, the first Soviet Military Commander of the city Georgy Bersarin quickly resolved to call back into life key city institutions like the police, judiciary, and social services "in the interest of a quick reconstitution of normal life for the people of Berlin."[47] That sense of normalcy would remain elusive, however, especially in light of that summer's persistent rat problem, the lack of running water, and the pressing need for DDT to disinfect school children and refugees entering the city through the major train stations.[48] Peace may have reached Berlin, but as far as Richard Brett-Smith was concerned it would take some time to return the city to its past course. Not known for mincing words, he illustrated his point with an image from one of his many walking tours of the city. "You could walk for miles in the middle of the city, starting, say, from the Brandenburger Tor or from Belle Alliance-Platz, and see nothing but destruction, with the sour smell of death and corruption rising from the Spree, which was hardly more than an open sewer."[49]

The entry of the Americans, French, and British did little to alleviate the stress facing the city. Curt Riess noted that summer that "the streets were still an unimaginable chaos."[50] In a trip in June 1945 to his command in Schöneberg, John J. Maginnis traveled a full two and a half hours from Babelsberg before reaching the city center, where "except for the main thoroughfares, the streets were filled with rubble and in many cases not discernible at all. It had been hot for the past several days, and the stench from the dead among the ruins further proclaimed the awful condition." Conditions were dire indeed. As one of his press bulletins outlined,

> when Allied Military Government went into effect on 12 July 1945 Berliners had almost exhausted their food supplies... Dysentery was killing 65 out of every 100 babies born in the city. Typhoid and diphtheria were making huge inroads due to the weakened condition of the population. Sewers dumped directly into the city's waterways. There was no postal service in Berlin. A handful of street-cars jerked spasmodically through the streets as the battered power plants tried in vain to keep up with minimum demands for power.[51]

It isn't difficult to understand Maginnis's questioning of the entire occupation effort; from what he saw during that two-hour drive, he "was forced to wonder... whether this ruined city was really worth bothering with."[52]

What for Maginnis and the US military government represented a pressing challenge to successful governance for city planners and architects was initially greeted as an opportunity to refashion the city's outdated and ailing infrastructure on a street-by-street basis. Concentrated as it was on the central districts, the bombing had decimated much of the nineteenth-century architecture and urban planning, blowing open wide holes in the topography. Leftist historian and journalist Isaac Deutscher, writing dispatches for *The Economist*, echoed the apocalyptic overtones of other observers when in September 1945 he noted that the city streets in the center of town looked like a desert, with the once wide Kurfürstendamm barely discernable amidst the destruction.[53] Interestingly, national rebuilding initiatives had already been in development before the end of the fighting as urbanists were called upon to make plans for a postwar greening initiative to turn crowded tenement blocks and narrow streets into gardens, parks, and green spaces. The political importance of these initiatives cannot be overstated, since working-class districts like Prenzlauer Berg, Friedrichshain, and Wedding had long been recognized as a blight not just on the city's landscape, but as deleterious to societal welfare given their link to generations of political opponents and petty criminals.[54] Many city planners, like Hans

Scharoun, first appointed by the Allies to the city building council and named director of the *Abteilung Bau- und Wohnungswesen des Magistrats* (Department of Building and Municipal Housing), were optimistic that "mechanical loosening" during the war provided fertile new ground upon which to build a more modern, rational city.[55] Berlin may not have been completely razed, but it certainly provided a suitable canvas upon which to imagine a new relationship between the built environment, the circulation of capital, and societal renewal, as Scharoun himself noted in his Berlin Plans speech (*Berlin Plant – Erster Bericht*) presented in September 1946 in the ruins of the old Hohenzollern City Palace – before he too caught whiff of the changing political winds in the Kommandatura, and relocated to the western portion of the city.[56]

For the city's amateur gardeners and academic botanists, the rubble-strewn city streets were anything but deserted spaces devoid of life. To this day, Berliners are reminded of the giant vegetable gardens in the felled fields of the Tiergarten central park, which sustained the hungry population in the immediate postwar years. All manner of *Kraut* was grown wherever it could be nurtured – along sidewalks, on cobblestone streets, even under the canopy of a balcony in a bombed-out apartment house (Figure 2.3). Alongside the home garden, new species of flora flourished among the ruins. In evidence-gathering expeditions, botanists meandered down paths and walkways, along the Havel and Spree, in between buildings, discovering new forms of vegetation brought into being by the conditions of total collapse. In forging their path through the ruderal landscape, they were quick to turn their sampling expeditions into formalized knowledge via articles in academic journals and dissertations. Despite worsening political relations between the two cities after the formation of two German states in 1949, botanists on both sides of the boundary found ways to continue collaborating, and, even after the building of the Wall in 1961, they continued an informal correspondence by mail, reinforcing the transcendental power of rubble and renewal in the scientific imaginaries of the two Germanys.[57] The new canopy of green that spontaneously burst forth over the city streets did not just unite Berliners in the pursuit of knowledge; it also did the unimaginable, according to botanist Cornel Schmidt. In a clever reference to Johannes Becher's anthem in praise of the newly christened German Democratic Republic "*Auferstanden aus Ruinen*" ("Rising from the Rubble"), Schmidt remarked in a 1950 journal article that nature had "pushed itself forwards into the city and has thereby achieved what several city councils have failed to achieve: rubble heaps have disappeared, at least to the eye."[58] But the city's

Figure 2.3 A former living room is made into a balcony, where laundry can dry, Berlin, 1946. Photographer: Hildegard Dreyer.
Photo credit: Stiftung Preussischer Kulturbesitz.

vegetation growth had achieved something more than simply masking reality. As Jens Lachmund has argued, the ebb and flow of nature brought about quiet but significant changes to the postwar environment, opening up new avenues of debate and exchange along with changing vistas, despite a worsening political situation.[59] At the same time that tensions brewed between the Allied powers, this veil of green defied the political boundary-making exercises of the early Cold War. As we will see in the next section, the greening of the natural environment may have covered over remnants of the end of the war in a floral blanket, but it could not completely expunge the ongoing presence of the past in the burgeoning rift between the eastern and western portions of the city. How authorities and citizens on both sides of the inter-German border struggled over boundary enforcement initiatives goes far in underscoring the place of the emotional register in reconstruction efforts after the war.

Despite the ceaseless pace of nature's reclamation of the city, by 1948 nothing could cover over the growing tensions within the Allied Kommandatura and city government. By the end of that year, as Paul Steege has argued in *Black Market, Cold War*, for all intents and purposes the city was split firmly in two. There were two mayors, two police forces, two currencies and two independent bureaucracies.[60] This administrative realignment had been percolating for some time, and archival documents give ample evidence of the burgeoning ideological split well before the Berlin Blockade reinforced the borders between the Soviet and American, French, and British sectors. The declaration of two separate Germanys in 1949 did have a real impact in terms of how police and social services approached the problem of street-level crime. Years of collaboration between sectors suddenly required rethinking. For many Germans across the city, both the old and new police structure had little bearing on how they perceived the street and threats to their own personal security. Whether in Weissensee or Wedding, for the city's women especially, the street remained a dangerous place that fell outside the bounds of respectability and control. How East and West Berlin authorities tackled the problem of street-level violence, including the policing of prostitution, and fraternization between German youth and members of the American and Soviet occupation troops, goes a long way in illuminating the difficult road that lay ahead for Allied and German authorities. General Bersarin's intentions for an imminent stabilization notwithstanding, Berlin's city streets promised anything but personal security after the war. For occupation authorities and average Germans desperate to bring a dose of normalcy back to daily life, access to and conduct in public space only served to highlight lingering social, political, and economic tensions. Moreover, the lack of personal security meant the occupiers had failed to make good on one of their most basic of guarantees, a return to law and order. This broke down in highly gendered ways, and confirmed the function of the street as a highly charged emotional conduit in the negotiation of postwar notions of respectability, community, and self-understanding in the aftermath of the war.

Pathologizing the Street

As Henri Lefebvre showed in *The Production of Space*, how people conduct themselves in public space, where they shop, how they dress, move through, and navigate the street, which establishments they opt to frequent and what behaviors they display there serves as a litmus test of broader social, economic, and political value systems. Similarly, what actions arouse attention and the form intervention takes forges a sense of the limits of toleration, of just what society is willing and able to countenance at a given historical moment.[61] As Benjamin noted, how people occupy space individually, clandestinely or in groups, under the cover of darkness or in the light of day, and how they negotiate their claim to visibility and right to privacy speaks volumes about the assumptions circulating within wider society.[62] Nowhere is the boundary between comportment, subjectivity, and social tolerance clearer than in contraventions of popular morality, for it is here, at the train station, in the GI bar, and especially on the street, that notions of respectability and identity were made visible, contested, and reinforced.

Given the dearth of living space, the requisitioning of housing by the Allies, and the taxing living conditions under which most Germans lived, a serious lack of privacy marked day-to-day life in both halves of the city until the housing boom in the late 1950s.[63] Dorothea von Schwanenflügel Lawson recalled being outraged at the American requisition of over 2000 apartments in the southwestern district of Zehlendorf, a sentiment that even made its way into a 1976 memorial campaign years later in *Der Morgenpost* designed to commemorate Berliners and their postwar struggle.[64] In that campaign, Erna Saenger won fifth prize for her humorous rendition of the housing requisition. Of course, it had taken decades for her to finally be able to spin her yarn about the abrupt confiscation of her family home.[65] Despite her tale of triumph over adversity, for the most part shared living had such a deleterious impact on family relations that it was a constant theme in the early Rubble Films (*Trümmerfilme*), the melodramas and romantic comedies that dominated screen and celluloid in the first four years after the war. These films often offered trenchant social commentary on the struggle for love, desire, and family under the difficult material conditions of the early postwar years.[66] Far from the tempered optimism of *The Murderers Are Among Us* one year earlier, as the title suggests the amorous couple in Hans Deppe's 1947 film *No Room for Love* (*Kein Platz für Liebe*) ultimately fail in their quest to find a quiet place to explore their feelings for one another. For them, there could be "no place for love" amidst the deadened tree trunks of the felled Tiergarten park in central Berlin, where they, like so many couples before them, strolled the once secluded pathways in search of a sliver of privacy in the big city. In 1947, privacy was in short supply regardless of the sector in which one lived.

Despite different administrative structures for tackling the housing shortage, there was surprising similarity in the way in which East and

West Berlin authorities pathologized and policed public space in the immediate years after the war. At the same time that the Blockade made explicit the ideological differences at work in either half of the city, both Berlins countenanced a similar concern over the immorality of the street, especially given the rise in venereal disease transmission.[67] Just as policy dealing with VD and prostitution bore certain similarities, so too did the patterns of daily life on both sides of the divide. Although where one lived after 1961 would contribute to the rise of differing interpretations of family structure, kinship, and social mores, until the building of the Wall, life on both sides of the boundary was more similar than different.[68] Even differences of personal taste and public decorum bore little distinction. Unlike the stultifying cleanliness Benjamin portrayed upon his return from Moscow, a symptom of modernity run amok, Berlin city streets bore few remnants of consumer complacency and fascist spectacle. Still, in their infinite brokenness, with ruins scattered about into the late 1950s, both halves of the city continued to make visible a host of new anxieties over how to structure societal transformation.

Although tentative at first, because of fears of sexual reprisal, Berliners eventually surfaced from their cellar hideaways, reclaimed their bombed and broken apartments, and took stock of the damage. While adults coped with the stress of survival, the city's children took to the streets in search of escape, merriment, and levity to broker some semblance of a childhood among the ruins. While some roamed aimlessly in search of lost parents and kin, others found shelter and solidarity amidst the rubble. A fixation of photographers like Friedrich Seidenstücker and Herbert Tobias, whose images injected a degree of beauty into the dark and somber portrait of capitulation, the sight of children in the streets of Berlin was anything but exceptional. Allies, police, average citizens, and foreign observers were heavily drawn to the plight of youth as both a tangible feature of the calamity of war's end, and a metaphorical symbol of Germany's infantilization through destruction and occupation. Like the weeds that quickly overtook the graves of hastily buried soldiers and citizens, children grew wild in this terrain, running about the streets, collecting soldier uniforms and paraphernalia (much to their parents' chagrin, since they could be shot for this), hiding "in upturned tanks," and scurrying about the rubble. Fun took many forms, from playing blockade with mini planes to blowing up elongated "balloons" pilfered from the machines inside train station pissoirs.[69] Although there was some sympathy for their plight initially, before too long children – and to a far greater extent adolescents – came under greater public scrutiny as emblems of a derailed generation.[70] The experiences of 1945 were so stark that even sociologists like Helmut Schelsky saw in them the roots of a skeptical generation of unruly, oppositional, emotionally detached youth.[71] As they played hopscotch, initiated a game of tag, or lingered and loitered under the S-Bahn arches, the actions and behavior of children and teens garnered the attention of a host of Berliners, who saw in them evidence of war-related moral decline and social decay. While the celebrated photographer Friedrich Seidenstücker saw in them an image of the city's rebirth, juxtaposing their vitality with the destruction all around, most Berliners were less charitable (Figure 2.4). Although the Soviets had conquered the fighting in the streets, these spaces would require additional monitoring and control to ensure Berlin was set upon a course for reconstruction.

One of the greatest problems facing the city was the swelling numbers of children and young people prostituting themselves for food and shelter. While child prostitution had long been a feature of the imperial and Weimar streetscape, it had been relegated to clearly definable city blocks where one might venture in search of a broad palate of offerings.[72] Sexual liaisons, treating, and the selling of sex after the war fueled a renewed sense of desperation and malaise, particularly because it was so visible and widespread. While women donned their kerchiefs and

Figure 2.4 Young people meet at the destroyed memorial to Frederick the Great in the Tiergarten, Berlin, 1946. Photographer: Friedrich Seidenstücker.
Photo credit: Stiftung Preussischer Kulturbesitz.

took to clearing the rubble mounds in exchange for the coveted worker ration card, "their youngsters ran wild in the streets," at least, according to Judy Barden, a reporter with the *New York Sun* whose special feature "Candy Bar Romance" outlined the impact of the war on women's lives.[73] The streets of divided Berlin showcased to the world the moral transgressions of German youth, and as such forced a renewed debate over the deleterious impact of urban space on fragile social mores. Some contemporaries sought to counter this image of despair with jaunty photographs and colorful vignettes, perhaps tapping into the same desire for escapism that Eric Rentschler notes drove audiences away from the rubble films[74] (Figure 2.5). While Georg Homsten attempted to lighten the mood with his 1946 "song of the big city" (*Großstadtmelodie*), his effort to shore up a sense of levity serves as a window into the general malaise that had swept the city. For many Berliners, the image of jaunty girls on the city's main thoroughfares conjured up a host of images, not all of them innocent.[75] Amidst Holmsten's own narrative, the author employs the occasional saccharine description of the "sweet girl from the Kurfürstendamm" who is "somewhat thinner, lighter in weight and morality" than before. Rest assured, he tells his reader, "she has held up nicely," a fixture along the famous boulevard where she could easily

Figure 2.5   The twins Hilde and Helga Fischer in a beer garden in Berlin, 1948. Photographer: Friedrich Seidenstücker (1882–1966) © Copyright BPK
Photo credit: Bildarchiv Preussischer Kulturbesitz/Art Resource, NY.

be spotted walking with "carefully calibrated, swaying gait," returning men's glances with a sharpness so deliberate it could only be construed as lewd. In the pictoral and narrative space of postwar accounts of the city, encounters with popular morality were inevitable.[76]

While the bombing had decimated many of the city's more traditional red light districts, the ruined city attracted people from all walks of life in search of work, companionship, and play in the city's hastily recalibrated spaces. The Kurfürstendamm retained some of its allure in part due to its prewar importance as the center of the New West. More important was its location at the intersection of the British and American sectors and near Zoo Station, the underground and regional train terminus that connected Charlottenburg to the eastern districts of Kreuzberg and Friedrichshain via the 10-kilometer U1 line, the precursor to the more famous U2 and one of the oldest in the city's U-Bahn network. But there was a price to be paid for such easy access to public space, especially for women, who paid dearly for their newfound visibility in popular parlance and daily encounters with the military and civilian authorities.

Scrutiny came in many guises, and not just from the Allies. In fact, the image of fallen youths and women was omnipresent in how Berliners remembered the crisis years, galvanizing people's fears about the social cost of transition. Beyond the general perception that women's identities were forever altered by separation from husbands, war rationing, and the widespread rapes, the American servicemen's magazine *Stars and Stripes* claimed there were upwards of 250,000 full- and part-time prostitutes ambling about the city spreading social disorder and disease at a rate far higher than official estimates, many under the age of 18.[77] The increased visibility of compromised moral values was remarked upon again and again by returning soldiers, eager to survey the changes to the neighborhood they had left behind for the front. Almost as soon as he got home Heinz Friese headed out to the fledgling market stands near the Bülowstrasse train station to take stock of the changes to his old haunt. Passing by the black market, he was shocked at being propositioned by a young girl loitering near the entrance to the station. She claimed she needed money, and would provide sexual services on the cheap if he followed her into the nearby ruins. Offended to learn she was just 14 years old, he recalled later that this deeply disturbed him at the time. "What better image of a lost war?"[78] While certainly the selling of sex was not new, especially in the streets surrounding the art nouveau Bülowstrasse train platform, what was unique was Friese's condemnation of the girl's offer as a symptom of defeat.

Friese was not alone in linking the sex trade to the social problems facing the defeated city. When economic stabilization after the currency reform of 1948 failed to curtail the practice completely, prostitution slowly acquired additional meaning as part of the ideological struggle to differentiate the two systems of governance. Increasingly, youths that solicited for sex in the streets of East Berlin were seen by health and welfare authorities as neglecting their duties as citizens. Despite claims to have "cleaned up the streets" as part of the transition to socialism, one East Berlin Ministry of Health and Social Welfare report from 1950 noted that the Worker's and Farmer's State was still taxed by the ongoing presence of youths on the stroll, leading one man to wonder, having been propositioned by an aggressive adolescent, if he really was in the "democratic sector of the city." Although it was commonly known that the state condoned prostitution during the yearly Leipzig Fair, another man initiated a letter-writing campaign as a result of the embarrassment he experienced at the hand of a streetwalker while shepherding guests from Moscow around East Berlin.[79] As the head physician of the Central Office of Venereal Disease Control noted in a letter from 1954 to the local burgomaster, the insouciance of the youth was no longer simply a product of defeat but a veritable threat to reconstruction generally. In exalted tones, Dr. Gross underscored the importance of sexual sobriety to nation building: "If we wish to build a technical state, we need the strength of the youth for work; we don't need it for sexual games."[80]

Just as the bombs had opened up new spaces for play, mischief, and exploration for children and youth, they also democratized deviance by bringing the stroll out of the inner city and into the suburbs. In paintings by Hans Baluschek we see that Berlin's outlying districts were already colonized in the 1920s by the *Vorstadtdirne* or suburban prostitute.[81] After the war, the problem gained an even higher profile considering the growing number of people involved in the trade, the fact (as we shall see in Chapter 4) that it involved a good number of boys as well as girls, and was no longer simply a problem for German authorities but for the Allies as well, whose barracks and bases were often located in the far reaches of the city. The war had also decoupled prostitution from its original moorings as a problem of industrialization and forged new links to social dislocation based on war, division, and occupation. Social scientific accounts of Germany's largest cities confirmed the overwhelming sense of powerlessness circulating amidst the war-torn population. Empirical sociologist Hilde Thurnwald collected story upon story of youths from broken homes for whom a "sexual lack of restraint" was the result of years of *erschütternde Daseinsbedingungen* – the life-altering existential experiences associated with the hunger years after war's end.[82] Sex education literature went so far as to claim that the lingering trauma of war actually made a physiological impact on the earlier onset of puberty, making youths sexually mature, and by extension, sexually curious at a much younger age – although, granted, they had borrowed much of this insight from the work of anthropologists in the wake of World War I.[83] There was something new about this generation of pleasure-hungry youth, thirsting for adventure amidst the graying ashes of the broken cityscape. They no longer strolled solely along the Friedrichstrasse or in established sexual zones but might be more easily seen on the streets of the southwestern district of Steglitz or hanging about the waiting room of the Wannsee train station, challenging social service workers and police to find appropriate methods to deal with this new social category. Even more difficult, given the democratization of deviance, was differentiating between "loose girls" and upstanding citizens.[84] Authorities used Paragraph 361 of the pre-1945 criminal code to police lewd conduct in the streets surrounding schools, parks, and houses with children, while a 1947 memorandum from the Allied Kommandatura authorized the use of raids and spot checks to clamp down on rampant disease transmission. But these new tactics failed to curtail the problem completely. As one Ministry of Health and Social Welfare memo noted in the eastern portion of the city, increased enforcement only "pushed the problem off of the main streets and out of the public eye."[85] And there were many places where one could hide from the police in postwar Berlin. Unsurprisingly, these structural problems of enforcement failed to curtail a rise in crime and disease transmission. Added to the mix were the streams of refugees from the formerly occupied eastern territories and, after division in 1949, from the outlying districts of the GDR. Taken together with the lack of adequate housing, it is easy to see why it was so difficult to find a working solution to the promiscuity of the youth.

On a purely material level, the infrastructure simply was not there to fully safeguard morals and ensure public safety. Although the Soviet-backed *Berliner Zeitung* lauded the safety of the streets thanks to the "banishment of darkness" in June 1945, in actuality it took until December 1945 to restore proper street lighting, according to the illustrated evening paper the *Nacht Express*, and even then it was emergency lighting that was installed over the threshold of tenement houses at the expense of the fledgling city government.[86] Such avuncular pronouncements, complete with illustrated images of happy and thankful citizens,

were designed to mask the dire material conditions under which citizens continued to live. Shrouded in darkness, which in that part of
Germany could come as early as four o'clock in the afternoon in winter
months, was it any wonder that crime statistics were off the chart? Given
the lack of available housing and shelter space, women and girls were
increasingly forced to the street with few available alternatives. In one
report from the Zehlendorf district health authority from September
1946, despite every effort to educate school girls in the upper classes
about the "disastrous aftereffects of non-marital sex," the dire material
and economic conditions meant that "in the last weeks the number of
infected youths has increased and the running around of these youths
has either been encouraged or simply condoned by parents."[87] Health
service workers across the sectors especially lamented the spatial constraints they faced with barely enough space to house those rounded
up in the nightly raids. Although they offered their muscle and services in policing known strolls, the Allies left the actual administering
of health policy to the Germans.[88] To meet the challenge of the rising
disease and crime rate, the Berlin police service on Dircksenstrasse heralded the return of the newly reconstituted criminal department, which
included special uniformed commissions to tackle "sex crimes, prostitution, and other abnormalities." City marriage counseling services, which
as Annette Timm has shown had a long history dating back to Weimar,
were likewise brought on board and given the responsibility of advis-
ing clients of available treatment.[89] Although each of these initiatives
was designed to allay citizen fears about the early occupation, reading
between the lines it becomes abundantly clear that neither the fledgling
police service, nor the assurances of the Allies could reinstill a sense of
security in the postwar city.

Joyless Streets

For many Berlin women, fear remained a constant companion during those early weeks and months after capitulation. The Soviet sector
German Women's Collective (*Deutsche Frauenbund* or DFD) lamented
the difficulties they faced coaxing women out of their houses to attend
evening films and panel discussions. This, they argued, severely hampered their efforts at politicizing women in support of the cause.
Indeed, the rapes may have cost the SED (*Sozialistische Einheitspartei
Deutschlands*) more support among women than any other policy undertaken by the occupiers.[90] Interestingly, these fears could also serve their
own purposes, as when the DFD sought to pin responsibility for the

lack of interest of Schöneberg women on the aggressive behavior of American forces policing their district. "As soon as it gets dark," according to one report, "women don't allow themselves to be viewed on the street" for fear of unwanted attention.[91] During the tense atmosphere of the summer of 1948, Soviet representatives of the soon-to-be-defunct Allied Kommandatura questioned their depiction in city statistics for VD transmission, rape, and prostitution, citing deliberate "cooking of the books" to make them look solely responsible for women's woes. In a letter of complaint by Soviet-sector police chief Markgraf in June 1948, he accuses the Americans of not playing fair in failing to submit their statistics on disease transmission, despite the fact that the French and British had. What at base should have been concern for women's safety in the streets was quickly elevated to Cold War rhetoric over which occupation power provided best for the population of Berlin.[92]

Barring these propagandistic flourishes, it is not an overstatement to say that access to the city's public and private spaces was severely mediated by gender and the fear of sexual violence. Simply put, women were not safe in their homes, and they certainly knew no security in the street, whether from the lascivious glances of occupation troops or the prying eyes of nosy neighbors known for perching at apartment windows and observing the comings and goings of the neighborhood.[93] Like the newspaper-thin coverings used as windows, the separation between public and private space was equally fragile since women could be – and frequently were – attacked in their bedrooms while they slept. Cases soon flooded into the murder squad, whose situation reports outlined the rising number of widows, teenagers, and single women murdered in their beds. In July 1945 alone, according to reports to the chief of police, there were over 123 murders and 598 "crimes of morality" (*Sittlichkeitsdelikte*) committed in the city, a term that included any offense of a sexual nature up to and including rape.[94] Countless cases were logged ranging from assault to *Lustmord* in all four quadrants of the city. And the aggressors weren't all Soviet. Edith T. was raped in Berlin-Schmargendorf after refusing to share her rations; Ingeborg S. was enticed into a car without a license plate near the Weidendammer Bridge, only to be driven through Tempelhof to the outskirts of the city and gang raped by three former Polish forced laborers ostensibly exacting some form of revenge for their treatment during the war. Using his service wagon as transport, mailman Johann S. pretended he was a transport police officer and threatened to take 15-year-old Edith S. to a youth home if she did not accompany him in his truck, where he ultimately violated her. If killed, itself a frequent occurrence, women were left where they lay; some were even placed in sadistic positions, kneeling, clothes partially removed or strewn about, and in one horrific case from the largely rural northwest district of Reinickendorf, with a 1.45 meter iron bar protruding for all the world to see.[95] If the Weimar fixation with sexual crime served as a commentary on war trauma and modernity, urban pathologies, and women's changing place in society, then the prevalence, form, and location of these crimes against women suggest both the randomness of extreme violence in postwar Berlin and the blurring together of boundaries in total war, as personal privacy and bodily integrity gave way to whim and capriciousness on a grand scale.[96] If women had lobbied for equal access to public space, they were sharply reminded that access came at a cost.

Even as the months passed, the specter of sexual danger remained at the forefront of women's minds. It continued to define how they organized their day, how they moved through city streets, where they shopped, how long they stood in line, whether they braved going out alone or in groups, and where they chose to socialize, live, and relax after a difficult day. It was not uncommon for women to be accosted as they bicycled to work, went grocery shopping, or returned from visiting friends and relatives. While women and girls have always shouldered the burden of self-protection, learning street smarts in order to navigate the urban environment, nothing could prepare citizens for the dangers of the postwar city.[97] And still, as the days became shorter, they continued to attempt to exert control over their situation, going to the local police detachment or Allied representative and making sure to lodge a complaint if they survived an assault. While the women of imperial Berlin may have drawn guidance from the 1913 *What A Woman Must Know About Berlin* to help shape their enjoyment of all the city offered, the amusements on offer in the postwar city carried with them considerable risk to body and soul.[98]

The boundaries between public and private were not the only ones transgressed and blurred in divided Berlin. Assaults occurred across age, race, and gender barriers, on city streets, in apartments, and along isolated country roads as women roamed beyond the city limits in search of food. The increased number of crimes against Berlin women could not solely have been committed at the hands of foreign troops, and indeed police records and court martial documents suggest former forced laborers from the east, returning Germans, and American servicemen were not above committing sexual assault. Although it has yet to be proven statistically, since these records are piecemeal and scattered between social welfare organizations, the police service, and four separate military authorities, extant sources do suggest that women reported incidents of violent sexual encounters with Soviet soldiers at a higher rate, although these charges begin to taper off in the late 1940s. As might be expected, the conditions of scarcity in the early "hunger years" exacerbated existing social cavities, exposing young girls to exploitation at the hands of family members or intimates. Thirteen-year-old Katharine W.'s case was forwarded to the Kreuzberg youth service bureau once police learned that her mother had encouraged her to secure liaisons with Soviet soldiers if the opportunity arose while searching for food along the dusty roads around the perimeter of the city.[99] In fact, charges of *Kuppelei* or procurement are equally high among the *Sittlichkeitsdelikte* represented in police ledgers. In other words, although there were certainly degrees of difference between pro-curement and sexual assault, Soviet soldiers were not the only ones responsible for a culture of abuse, fear, and intimidation.

Less well known are the crimes committed by American service-men. Indeed GI delinquency, whether petty theft or more vexing cases of domestic-style violence, emanated out of the southwest districts of Zehlendorf, Wilmersdorf, Steglitz, and Friedenau in concentric circles around the large army bases on Finckelsteinallee and Kronprinzallee (later renamed Clayallee in honor of the American general who helped guide the city through the Blockade as military governor of the US Occu-pation Zone).[100] We do know that Berlin's precarious physical and social condition at war's end contributed to a higher crime rate than other regions under American occupation.[101] In fact, for a five-month period in 1946, Berlin actually ranked first on three occasions with the high-est arrest rate, compared to 16 Criminal Investigation Division (CID) detachments in Germany.[102] This finding is particularly salient consider-ing that other CID detachments were responsible for arrests over a larger geographic area. Additionally, the figures reported from Berlin reflect arrests made solely in the American sector of the city, and excludes the British, French, and Soviet sectors which account for nearly two-thirds of Greater Berlin and its population. While American Military Police, on the whole, found Germans somewhat passive and less prone to general acts of criminality, prostitution posed an entirely different set of chal-lenges, and radically reoriented the way public space was represented, gendered, and policed. The US military relied on military justice to deal with abusive encounters between soldiers and civilians as a symbol of its commitment to good governance, yet many citizens saw the influx of occupation troops as playing the determining role in the further loos-ening of women's social and sexual mores, claiming soldiers were the reason why women were more licentious than they had ever been. Civic officials in the southwest neighborhoods of Steglitz and Lichterfelde found that the problem of female prostitution warranted the repeated arrest of girls suspected of spreading disease. Of course, not all girls chatting on street corners were "on the make," as one Steglitz raid made all too clear when the police forced two girls returning from a Christmas shopping trip to undergo painful gynecological examinations despite their repeated claims of innocence.[103] In this example, simply congregating on a busy street was enough to unleash the vice squad, suggesting the time-honored link between public space and public women.

Indeed, public safety was a priority, and offenses committed were monitored at the highest levels by officials at the Office of the Military Government of the United States (OMGUS), first in Frankfurt and then in Berlin.[104] German crimes against US installations were not the only preoccupation of OMGUS statisticians, however. In his report for the Historical Division of the United States Army, Oliver Frederiksen commented in 1953 that in the early stages of the occupation, the German population "caused no difficulties in regard to the maintenance of law and order." Relying on commonly held stereotypes prevalent at the time, Frederiksen observed that "the traditional German respect for authority, resignation to loss of the war, and even relief at the overthrow of the Nazi regime" explained why the Americans found so little disorder in the months following the war. Interestingly, the most dangerous threat he found to public order in the initial year of occupation was not a result of subversive German organizations or activity, but was due largely to "juvenile delinquency, black marketing, depredations by displaced persons, and assaults by American soldiers."[105] If German behavior was not a problem, American actions certainly were. And if American crime was on the radar, it was even more of a problem in divided Berlin.

During this early phase of the American presence in Berlin, smaller streets surrounding the army bases became highly sexualized sites of contact between prostitutes and GIs, with girls hanging about at the entrances to the gates, winking at the sentries and disturbing the suburban quality of the neighborhood. The tree-lined streets that survived the bombing, complete with dense hedgerows, numerous parks, and the paths near the Teltow Canal, provided cover for all manner of sex acts between servicemen and youths. The furtive assaults on young children, hidden away in police ledgers, suggest that no area of the city was immune from soldier intransigence. Male prostitutes claimed they were initiated into the scene after having been molested by servicemen, and in one case, a child as young as 4 developed venereal disease after a similar encounter. In most of these instances, which never made it to court, the GIs remained faceless, known only via the impassioned recriminations of an angry parent or the claims of a fallen boy.[106] If the side streets and bushes provided cover for individual attacks, soldiers likewise benefited from traveling in packs, so much so that even broad boulevards could sometimes shelter anonymous assaults. Such was the case in March 1946 along the 3.7-kilometer stretch of the Kaiserstrasse (later renamed Bundesallee in celebration of German federalism), which linked the art nouveau apartment houses of smart Friedenau to the bustling Tauentzienstrasse. Despite the presence of an American Military Police detachment nearby, neither the daylight nor the watchful eyes of passersby could prevent the gang rape of a heavily pregnant woman on her way home from work.[107]

If assaults took place with reckless abandon during daylight hours, nightfall posed distinct challenges and further impinged on women's mobility. Late on the night of July 23, 1946, Ursula V., accompanied by her mother, two sisters, and infant niece, were accosted by three American soldiers who had offered the family a ride to their home in Wilmersdorf. Making moves on her sister as soon as they mounted the truck, one of the privates of the 16th Constabulary threatened to set Ursula down in the Soviet sector, toying mercilessly with popular fears of the dangers young women faced in Russian hands and suggesting the extent to which rumors of Soviet aggression had penetrated popular knowledge. Ursula's predicament was similar to her sister's. She was first fondled, then groped, and ultimately forced to remain behind once her mother and sisters dismounted the truck. The Americans drove off as Ursula wept, testifying later that she was "afraid of what might come next."[108] As the truck sped away, she heard the discharge of a gun in the front cab, which got the attention of a nearby US MP (Military Police) Special Investigation detachment that had been patrolling the area conducting ad hoc venereal disease checks. While the servicemen claimed the girl was a longtime sweetheart, Ursula stole the opportunity to explain to one of the officers that she was being held against her will.[109] Interestingly, although the victim's predicament was thoroughly documented, the sexual assault was not the focus of the materials recorded in the private's court martial. Rather, it was the discharged pistol, and the threat to public order, that garnered the interest and attention of the military court. Indeed, the trial documents underscore that the army's primary concern was with the unlawful use of a weapon outside of military jurisdiction. Although the prosecution did assert that "it [was] a battery for a man to fondle, against her will, a woman not his wife," in the end the soldier was found guilty for besmirching the reputation of the US military effort and forced to relinquish $50 pay over a period of five months.[110] The psychological damage and attempted assault fell outside the boundary of military jurisprudence and official concern. This example, one of many gathered in the courts martial files of OMGUS suggest that for Berlin women, regardless of which sector they inhabited, the stationing of servicemen impacted the way they conducted their lives, how they organized their day-to-day comings and goings, and infused the spaces they accessed and traversed with the air of sexual excitement and adventure when it came to fraternization and dating, but also with the ever-present potential for sexual violence as well.

When it came to attempts to deal with concrete issues of disease containment and the policing of morals, the increasing visibility of solicitation around army bases forced occupation authorities to participate more directly in rounding up women suspected of "frequent exchanges of sexual intercourse" (*häufig wechselnde Geschlechtsverkehr or HwG*) – the official term used to connote the behavior of promiscuous women with multiple intimate partners. Dr. Eugene E. Schwarz of the Public Health Office of the Office of Military Government Berlin Sector (OMGBS) said as much in a letter to the Burgermeister of Berlin from July 9, 1947, in which he argued that military installations served as hot spots for prostitution. Most egregious of all was the fact that "nightly a great number of girls are soliciting and accosting soldiers."[111] Given the preeminent position of venereal disease (VD) abatement, Berlin women always had to fear being carted off on an MP or police wagon simply for loitering on the street, lounging in a bar, or taking in a film at the cinema, thanks to the youth protection legislation and venereal disease measures carried over from before the war. Countless newspaper articles from outraged women reinforced the randomness of forcible VD testing. One letter to *Der Abend* from August 4, 1947, details both the desperation of authorities in seeking an end to disease and also the idiocy of sexualizing certain gathering spaces. In a mass raid of "harmless Berliners" in the *New World* ballroom, 650 women were rounded up and taken to the nearby Britz Hospital in the western working-class district of Neukölln. After hours of waiting without enough seating, of those forced to undergo pelvic examinations, a mere four cases of disease were found.[112] Upon being asked for clarification by the American authorities, the local police inspection in Neukölln corrected the newspaper's findings, and argued that the 34 confirmed cases demonstrated that "the actions carried out, from a health and police standpoint, were entirely justified."[113] Raids must have appeared as pernicious since stories about wanton soldier and police aggression quickly became the stuff of ideological posturing. The Soviet-backed *Tägliche Rundschau* newspaper ran a story lauding its district officials in the East for not raiding the *Neues Brett'll Schall und Rauch* bar on the Friedrichstrasse despite the overwhelming presence of single women.[114] While this example has the aura of opprobrium and level-headedness, it is also reminiscent of the laissez-faire attitude of the Soviet administration when it came to their role in spreading disease through the mass rapes their soldiers perpetrated on a large scale at the end of the war.

Although skyrocketing disease transmission rates was a public health nightmare that could not be ignored, the process of actually differentiating between upstanding and fallen women was often quite muddied. At the same time that the simple act of *being* in the street was often enough to arouse suspicion, how one moved, what one wore, whether one paced, lingered, or acted out one's intentions played a distinct role in how police and social services measured the level of endangerment and depravity. Films like the 1948 *Street Encounters* (*Strassenbekanntschaft*) and the DEFA newsreel *Berlin Under Construction* (*Berlin im Aufbau*) make this point quite clearly in focusing in on the shoes women wore in public; those rubble women deeply ensconced in rebuilding Berlin would never be found wearing high heels – at least, not by day when they toiled for rations in the city's numerous construction sites. The association of manner of dress with lapsed morals was a convenient if not wholly accurate of measuring deviance. As with the VD raids, the police reserved the right to bring in anyone that raised suspicion. In a letter from the chief of police before the division of the force, officers were given free rein when it came to the problem of wayward youth. "When their behaviour on the street, in open spaces, and publicly accessible places arouses suspicion that they lead an amoral lifestyle," they could be forwarded first to the juvenile police unit in the Dircksenstrasse facility near Alexanderplatz, from where they would be transferred on to the Youth Service Bureau (*Hauptpflegeamt*) for interrogation and further processing.[115] These actions belie the fact that, in actuality, the law was quite clear on what counted as lascivious behavior and which spaces requiring extra monitoring. Until it could be amended and altered in both East and West German jurisprudence in the early 1950s, police and welfare workers drew guidance from standards already hammered out in 1943 in the Youth Protection Law together with its corollary, the Police Provision for the Protection of Youth from that same year.[116] Although both have their origins in Weimar legislation and were designed as curative measures for youth transgressions, the Nazi version emphasized wide-sweeping regulation over reeducation and was even more precise about how to deal with the perils of public space.[117] Police were to ensure youths were not "on open streets and squares after dark if under the age of 18, do not gain access to bars under the age of 16, and cannot attend cinematic performances after 9pm at night." According to this Nazi legislation, youths should not drink or smoke before the age of 18, and if found in a wrestling establishment, a bar, cabaret, or revue unaccompanied by an adult, the owner of the establishment was likewise open to enforcement.[118] The moral panic surrounding the danger to youth was so great that neither jurisdictional boundaries nor temporal or ideological ones mattered more than bread-and-butter issues of regulation and control. As we will see in Chapter 5, where divisions in method and actions do begin to harden is away from the street and in the city's homes and correctional institutions, where behavior was not simply observed and monitored but restructured along the axis of (re)productive citizenship.

Although the street represented enough of an allure for women of all backgrounds that officials could never be entirely sure who was innocent and who was guilty, and urban streetscapes retained the link to pre-1945 discourses of vice and immorality, policing comportment in the postwar city retained a distinctly spatial component. In a 50-volume series of *Big City Documents* (*Großstadt Dokumente*) published between 1905 and 1908 under the editorial eye of left-leaning social critic Hans Ostwald, the city's underground sex scenes were mapped according to the dictates of imperial sensibilities, both dominant and subaltern. These fascinating texts provided the first major glimpse into the form and function of Paragraph 361 of the Penal Code and the way it dealt with suspicious behavior near schools, homes, and public spaces. Like the protective youth legislation, which had its origins in the 1920s, the treatment of prostitution in both halves of postwar Berlin harkened back to imperial and Weimar measures, a time when certain forms of prostitution were allowed if regulated by a special section of the morals police (*Sittenpolizei*). Prostitutes were given an eight-page booklet detailing the terms of semi-legality, which outlined the limits to mobility placed on them if they sought to ply their trade. To safeguard public morals in the city's best neighborhoods, working women were not allowed to access the central districts of the city nor enter its major parks and gardens. They could not walk near churches, royal or public buildings, or military barracks. Touring theater groups, circuses, exhibitions, museums, and the major transportation nexuses were likewise out of bounds. Aside from outlining what counted as off limits, the guide also stipulated what behavior would be countenanced as legal on the street, in establishments, even within the confines of their own homes. They could not smoke in bars or meet men's glances; they were banned from singing or otherwise drawing attention to themselves; and they certainly could not offer their services in public, or communicate their wishes through manner of dress. These restrictions of space and access even spilled over into the realm of interpersonal relationships. Regulated women were discouraged from forging relationships with children, for example, and were forbidden from cohabitating with former clients. As if these restrictions to personhood and privacy were not already strict, they were also required to allow police access to their homes on the whim of an officer and often at a moment's notice. Indeed, according to these instructions, one is left wondering what possible benefit regulation might have held for women involved in the trade.[119] What these strictures do suggest, however, aside from the obvious disempowerment of working women, is the collapsing of boundaries between physical and moral categories, and how space-centered the licensing of prostitution had become during the city's modernization. On the one hand, it appears as though it was the spaces of transaction and exchange that most required monitoring, while on the other, in the case of cohabitation, women themselves emerged as the sole source of danger and disorder. Divided Berlin may no longer have been the pulsing metropolis (*Großstadt*) it once was, but the level of intrusion into everyday lives suggests that important remnants of this legacy of regulation and control lingered over the benchmark of 1945 and could be easily felt into the postwar period when police, social services, and case workers stepped out into the streets of the destroyed city to survey, measure, and contain the damage.

The *Großstadt Dokumente* provide a uniquely precise description of the street-by-street selling of sex and urban subcultures, serving as a kind of map for the layperson to Berlin's erogenous zones. They outline all that the night offered, including where amusements might be found, and began the process of affixing an identity to the teeming masses of otherwise faceless streetwalkers, brothel workers, and male and female hustlers. They even drew on contemporary sexological maxims in order to provide color and nuance to the phenomenon of street sex. Although post-World War II foreign observers sought to rekindle this ethnographic tradition through their own travelogues and guidebooks, their accounts often fell short on detail and analysis. Social observation on this scale was relegated instead to the annals of crime reportage, social service caseworker file records, and church memos, where new maps of endangerment were crafted with the hope of carefully planned intervention. Making visible the thoughts, behaviors, and actions of those underworld characters typically shrouded in the twilight of the demimonde, these accounts played a vital role in maintaining the focus on the street as the source and emblem of social disorder. While the Allies sought to monitor movement across the sectors, police, church, and state welfare caseworkers enforced boundaries of decorum in monitoring the streets and alleyways of the former capital. In doing so, they developed new mental maps of the city that borrowed from these past templates while adapting them to the pressing needs of the emerging Cold War. And while they were technically policing sex, in actuality officials were complicit in the construction of a sense of community, one based on the exclusion of sex workers whose presence in the streets of Berlin undermined the hope for moral rebuilding.

Spaces of Subversion

Although statistics suggested a reduction in youth crime, emotions ran high in the 1950s regarding juvenile sexual promiscuity. While girls felt the brunt of street-level enforcement through raids and spot checks, young men came under scrutiny for hanging about in gangs and failing to live up to the dictates of responsible citizenship. In border zones, especially those that cut through existing working-class districts like Wedding/Mitte and Kreuzberg/Friedrichshain, and in the major commercial centers and leisure spaces of East and West Berlin, authorities saw in these supposed layabouts challenges not just to stabilization, but to the successful functioning of the state, since they were accused of perpetual unemployment and shirking their responsibilities to the goal of economic recovery. A series of *Halbstarke* (teenager) riots in 1956, in both East and West Berlin, captured public attention, and together with a German-wide critique of American popular culture and social science fascination with deviance in general, a new terminology was coined for understanding antisocial youth. Whether in battling clandestine jazz clubs, or more overt forms of oppositional behavior, youth welfare organizations and police believed they faced an uphill struggle in controlling the *rowdys*.[120] West Berlin police redoubled efforts in monitoring public gatherings, patrolling open spaces like the penny carnivals (*Rummel*) that set up shop in undeveloped stretches of land between bombed-out tenement buildings. Large-scale operations like the famed Circus Busch returned to the city in 1952, heralding a return to prewar spectacle of amusement parks, fairs, and animal performances, while other events moved into the storied Luna Park grounds near the Halensee at the end of the Kurfürstendamm.[121] Smaller, more humble varieties like the shooting galleries and beer tents of Anton Beuermann's "Kreuzberger Volksfest" struggled to secure licensing to run their operations despite their hope of instilling some levity and luster to the grey march of quotidian life.[122] While parents and neighborhood groups objected to the constant noise and dubious morality of those who worked there, suggesting as one article in *Der Tag* did in June 1955 that "it was too much for our nerves, which through war and postwar have not gotten any better yet," the West Berlin police force was more concerned with youths like 17-year-old Erhard S., who learned from his peers at the *Rummel* about the potential for earning income as a rent boy at the Zoo Station.[123] Closer inspection of Erhard's Plötzensee youth jail case file records adds another dimension to the reaction of the authorities, since his Soviet sector residency meant that in addition to his "girlish demeanour" he was also a border crosser (*Grenzgänger*), one of the legions of youths who crisscrossed the boundary in search of employment, entertainment, or companionship in the western sectors. At the same time that the GDR had moved away from charging homosexuals as aggressively as in years past, the problem was so great that the West Berlin Senator for Youth and Sport broached the idea, in a 1955 memo, of adding the Bahnhof Zoo and Stuttgarter Platz to the sites outlawed by the Law for the Protection of Youth.[124] The fact that over 53 rent boys with eastern addresses had made their way through the system, and were at risk of reoffending since they could not be housed in an appropriate correctional facility, contributed to the sense of powerlessness youth protection workers felt in tackling the transient population of at-risk teens. The porous nature of the border, and lack of material support for these youths (since they failed to count as refugees under current legislation) only exacerbated the feeling of helplessness.[125]

For the Protestant welfare organization *Innere Mission*, the influence of occupation soldiers together with the search for material goods and entertainments severely hampered moral development.[126] One report even went so far as to insinuate that delinquency and the threat to the family was part of a well-organized conspiracy of homosexuals themselves, who took to the streets to spread their "propaganda" and seek out prey.[127] Across the border in East Berlin, similar fears percolated about the offices of the Ministry of People's Enlightenment (*Abteilung Volksbildung*) concerning the throngs of youth gathered around train station platforms, whose capability for rowdiness and petty thievery meant they were shirking their responsibility to the socialist state.[128] As one gray-haired East German judge proclaimed, in sentencing three boys accused of fondling a girl's breasts outside a state-run restaurant in 1961, "why don't you utilize all the free facilities for sports and recreation that are available for our citizens instead of hanging around on the streets?" "In our part of Germany," she continued, "we must try to guarantee the security of the individual... you have to take responsibility for our republic and for your own lives."[129]

This image of lawlessness and the social causes of juvenile delinquency surfaced not only in ministerial accounts, court transcripts, or welfare memos, but also found its way onto celluloid, where filmmakers struggled for artistic license to realistically portray the social problems plaguing life in the GDR. The East German production company DEFA commissioned a series of introspective "Berlin Films," some from Kurt Mätzig and others from director/writer duo Gerhard Klein and Wolfgang Kohlhaase, to explore the impact of postwar listlessness and division on the younger generation. These films, Mätzig's *Roman einer Jungen Ehe* (Story of a Young Marriage) (1952), and Klein and Kohlhaase's *Berliner Romanze* (A Berlin Romance) (1956) and *Berlin – Ecke Schönhauser* (Berlin – Schönhauser Corner) (1957) provide an intimate portrayal of the lives, choices, and decisions of working-class Berlin youth struggling to find a place in an unstable and changing world.[130] In these films, and a number of films in West Germany that likewise used Cold War Berlin as a backdrop, borders and boundaries emerged as important tropes with which to explore contemporary barriers to intimacy, love, and personal fulfillment at work and in the home. Often set around star-crossed lovers, one with roots in the East while the other lived in the West, the DEFA films positioned socialism as the salve for postwar malaise, generational strife, and the quest for the good life. The divided city was often enlisted as a character in the plot as the protagonists navigated the schizophrenic city streets in search of answers to the mind's troubles. To ground this political messaging, they often incorporated actual events, political scandals, or high-profile crimes to lend gravitas and credibility to the storytelling arc. In *Roman einer Jungen Ehe* (1952), as an example, this took the form of the actual scandals surrounding famed Nazi director Veit Harlan, whose reemergence in the West Berlin theater district in the 1950s had actually caused a quasi riot. Using this device in a film about an actor couple torn between the prospect of career success in the West and artistic integrity in the East, Mätzig offers a commentary on the widespread sense of emotional and erotic displacement that plagued postwar society.[131] The chasm that divides Agnes from her western beau may be exacerbated by the distance between their worldviews, but it is concretized spatially through a moral geography of emotion and collective action literally carved into the cityscape. Leaving behind the theater scene in Charlottenburg after the fictionalized Harlan affair, she finds a spiritual center in the collective building project of the Stalinallee, once one of Berlin's "worst destroyed streets."[132] In the film's spectacular final scene, she is called upon to use her extraordinary oratory skills to provide a dramatic reading of a poem by the real-life writer's union luminary and central committee member Kurt Barthel (known by the penname KuBa). With full dramatic flair, and the blurring of fiction and reality, she concludes the film with her rendition of this ode to comrade Stalin, in whose name the street has been built:

> Peace came to the city on this street; the city was dust, we were dust and broken glass and dead tired. But tell me, how should one die; Stalin himself had taken us by the hand and told us to raise our heads with pride. And after we cleaned away rubble and made plans, conceived of the little parks and the blocks of houses, we were victors and the city began to live. The path on which the friends came led straight to Stalin. Never should fires be reflected in the windows, the empty, new windows. Tell me, how should one thank Stalin, we gave this street his name.[133]

With beatific pride in father Stalin and faith in belonging, Agnes finds strength of purpose in sublimating her subjective desires to the fantasy of socialism. In this tale of two streets, the decadent, bourgeois Kurfürstendamm and the wholesome Stalinallee, industry trumps romantic love, and communal effort offers psychic wholeness, peace, courage, and harmony in transcending the erotic ideal for something much more concrete, a mythologized fantasy of completeness of person – a far cry from the cut-throat world of industrial capitalism that reigned across the border. In the alternative modernity of East Berlin, to bring back Benjamin for a moment, Agnes finds individual wholeness in the collective. Over the border, amidst the quickened pace of life of the West End theater scene, Agnes succumbs to a nervous breakdown. Socialist humanism, at least in this idealized form, really did hold the keys to health and happiness. The fact that this search for affective harmony was untenable under the material conditions that reigned in the 1950s, conditions which had the opposite effect on the actual workers on the Stalinallee site, who flocked to the streets in revolution in June of 1953 protesting unrealistic work norms, the day's events did little to detract from official narratives of belonging in East Berlin.[134]

A few years later, in *Berliner Romanze*, East and West collide once again along the Kurfürstendamm where the main characters this time are young adults who exchange glances and conversation one sunny afternoon after a chance meeting in the street. She, an aspiring model from East Berlin, is wooed by what she believes is a handsome (and monied) West Berlin suitor. Buoyed by the prospect of furthering her career with his willing material support, she enrolls in a fancy modeling school only to learn that he has exaggerated his income in the quest for her affection. Fleeing the arrangement, she eventually relents and invites him to live with her and her mother in their cramped East Berlin apartment. Despite all that is lacking in terms of worldly possessions and glamour, ultimately it is the simple life in the eastern portion of the city that nurtures the couple as he finds a market for his mechanic's skills in the socialist state, something that had eluded him in the West. The pursuit of love and personal fulfillment, or at least the realization of a unitary self, far from the fractured realm of dueling worldviews and border crossing, could only be found in the socialist east.

In the West, Berlin likewise featured prominently in several melodramas, but surfaced more frequently in madcap romantic comedies. Veit Harlan's 1957 feature film *Anders Als Du und Ich* (Different Than You and Me) takes the viewer inside the villas of the tony Grünewald, where modern music (to say nothing of Greco-Roman wrestling) tempted the likes of the young and impressionable Klaus, who quickly finds himself under the spell of the sartorial – and most certainly homosexual – Dr. Boris Winkler. From the director of the controversial Nazi-era film *Jüd Suß* came this morality tale revolving around a teenager's exploration of his sexuality and the lengths his parents would go to "set him straight." In this film, borders and boundaries take on added meaning as social, racial, and even temporal divisions are questioned and ultimately reinforced by the plot development. At one point the camera follows an Afro-German motorcycle youth from the Zoo Station through the streets of West Berlin en route to the clandestine party space, reinforcing the transgressive composition of this milieu by conjuring up Nazi-inspired images of the link between African Americans, drug use, motorcycles, and jazz music.[135] Beyond the whiff of Nazi-era propaganda, the lingering impact of Nazi-era jurisprudence was felt in the continued illegality of homosexuality that gives the film its narrative thrust. Adding to the mix the director's checkered past suggests there remained a significant structural inheritance from Nazi Berlin. Despite Harlan's efforts to enlist the help of prominent sexologist Hans Giese, and the obvious tipping of the hat to Magnus Hirschfeld's 1919 film *Anders als die Anderen* (Different Than the Others), the film reinforces the notion of the high social cost of abnormal sexuality. Interestingly the film was released in theaters at the pinnacle of postwar gay persecution as same-sex desiring men were forced to deal with the fact that there were in actuality more arrests than there had been in Hitler's Reich.[136] If Dr. Winkler's Grünewald basement was not safe from the prying eyes of the state, the street was certainly no place for gay sociability, whether on screen or in the everyday.

While *Anders als Du und Ich* revolved around the antics of an overzealous mother in safeguarding her son's sexuality, Billy Wilder's *One, Two, Three* (1961) took the comic register even further in this romantic comedy about a Coca Cola factory executive tasked with keeping an eye on his boss's young and vacuous daughter, who is seduced by the charms of her hygienically challenged "rebel without a cause" boyfriend from communist East Berlin. Shot in the months leading up to the building of the Wall, this film takes shots at all sides, poking fun at communists and capitalists alike. A veritable tour de force for James Cagney, it turns on an image of Berlin as the quintessential Cold War city, while also drawing on its storied Weimar and Nazi past. It is a debased city, inhabited by black-clad Soviet henchmen and former Nazis – no match for the naivety and innocence of an expat southern belle. In turn, the audience is introduced to Cagney's dour wife and curvaceously conniving mistress, as well as a cross-dressing former SS assistant, and the innocent if humorless boyfriend played by ur-Berliner and teenage heart-throb Horst Buchholz, fresh from the set of the not-yet-released *The Magnificent Seven*. With circuitous plot twists, the film could be read as casting aspersion on the overtly didactic tenor of the Berlin films. Unlike the DEFA films, in *One, Two, Three* love may turn the world upside down, but instead of reinforcing boundaries it succeeds in transcending them. Based on the play by Hungarian playwright Ferenc Molnar, himself a victim of the Nazis, who fled for the United States in 1940, Billy Wilder's Berlin holds little in the way of gravitas, opting instead for a tone of irreverence ill-suited to the time in which it was released, quite possibly the major reason it failed to achieve box office success or recognition at the Oscars. It was hard to find levity in August 1961 once the comic liminality of division turned a porous boundary into a cement border virtually overnight.

The Optics of Division

With the high participation of young adults in the 1953 workers' uprising, the incessant allure of American popular culture, and the seemingly
endless threats of blockade from the Soviet Union, it was only logical that the visual realm would emerge as an important venue in
the struggle over the hearts, minds, and actions of those who lived
at the epicenter of East/West confrontation. Indeed, the photographic
and filmic portrayal of life in the streets of divided Berlin coincided
with a series of attacks on Berlin's unresolved status as a frontier city.
In this chapter's final section, it is worth exploring more fully the ways
in which both regimes sought to construct a sense of normalcy and
"everydayness" out of the disruption of division through geographies of
emotion and the visual register, especially in the final five years before
the building of the Wall. Whereas the street played host to violence
and fears of sexual reprisal, in film love had been instrumentalized
in the service of the mid-century civilizing mission, whether as madcap comedy or political satire. In mid-1950s vernacular photography,
on the other hand, public space was reclaimed in all its infinite ordinariness. Although the inner boundary was extremely visible "in the
heart of the city," at least according to journalist Jörn Dorner whose
dispatches captured the mood before the Wall changed everything,
Berliners appeared to have struck a balance in their daily lives.[137] Division may have spawned new city centers and alternative art, erotic, and
entertainment scenes, but if these photos were to be believed – and of
course that was the intention of their creators – citizens on both sides
of the German/German boundary had come to terms with the city's
exceptionalism.

By the late 1950s, the physical transformation of East and West
Berlin may not have been quite complete, but if city officials were
to be believed great strides had been made in removing the scars of
war. Despite grand pronouncements heralding the promise of repose
and consumption along the Stalinallee and Kurfürstendamm, city planners were not always successful in fully covering up the blemishes.
Indeed, visitors and citizens alike were not appreciative of moments of
solemnity like the decision to keep the "gutted and blackened shell"
of the Memorial Church in the midst of West Berlin's "gayest, and
most modern shopping and entertainment district."[138] Beset and bedev-
iled by rampant commercialism along the Kurfürstendamm, William
Conlan claimed reconstruction had changed its character "from a Berlin
'Broadway' to a 'Fifth Avenue,'" dwarfing its restaurants and cafés in

favor of "lavishly decorated and exclusive shops."[139] Similarly critical of the pace of change in the East, Jörn Dorner evoked the spirit of Weimar social critic Alfred Döblin when he claimed that even the streets leading from Friedrichstrasse to Alexanderplatz fell prey to the ill-planned efforts of city magistrates whose efforts to cement an alternative shopping district in brick and stone threatened to erase "the last mementos of Hans Biberkopf's milieu."[140] Efforts to revitalize these areas were a conscientious attempt at reorienting Berliners around an alternative city center. Whether the imitative splendor of the Stalinallee, the exercise in officialdom along Unter den Linden, or the glitz and glamour of the Kurfürstendamm, these streets played an indelible role in the self-fashioning and struggle for legitimacy in East and West Berlin. Indeed, the scope and symbolism was not lost on contemporaries. Like the highly fraught symbol of the Memorial Church, which *Die Welt* columnist Anna Teut called "more curious than convincing," street spaces more generally were intimately bound up with struggle to find normalcy in the abnormal, to render common and quotidian that which to most people remained glaringly anomalous, unusual, and strange.[141] Despite official efforts to realize new mental and physical maps of these counterbalancing city centers, they still operated within a fractured cityscape. As a consequence, these projects struggled to gain resonance within the multiplicity of meanings conjured up by the city's ruinous spaces. Like the Memorial Church which symbolized at once the lost city center and new downtown, these spaces formed an important part of a much-hoped-for normalization not simply of relations across the political divide, but of life in its midst. And it was this projection of contentedness, of social harmony, of community, fulfillment, belonging, and love that motivated state-sponsored photographers on both sides of the internal divide to develop an optics of normality in this otherwise chaotic place.

In addition to serving as portals and gateways to a lost era, city streets were perhaps most notorious in the divided city for the way in which they bounded off neighborhoods, sectors, and nations. In his introduction to *This Is Germany*, Arthur Settel remarked that the story of Germany itself at least from "the war until 1950 was written on the West side of a city where a single street was the border between democracy and totalitarianism."[142] In 1955, Austrian writer Franz Kain used the porous nature of the boundary space as a setting for his contribution to a long line of Berlin stories. In *Romeo und Julia an der Bernauer Strasse* (Romeo and Julia on Bernauer Street) published with the East German Aufbau publishing house, Kain located his story of love on the border between working-class Wedding in the West and Mitte in the East. Of course, he could not have known at the time of writing how prophetic his words were when he wrote: "Bernauer Strasse became a wall, which divided families."[143] It was here that the border cut just in front of a row of tenement apartments with the street and sidewalk below marking the western edge of the city. After the elderly Ida Sieckmann plunged to her death on August 22, 1961 – the first casualty of the Wall – apartment windows along the street were bricked in to prevent other escape attempts and the bad press they had obviously engendered. Long before these harrowing stories became part of the public memory of the building of the Wall, however, the interstitiality of these street spaces represented a tactical problem for contemporary politicians, and, as the 1950s unfolded, the East German leadership itself was painfully aware of the drain on resources posed by the so-called *Grenzgänger* or border-crossers, those citizens who lived in the East and worked in the West, many of whom fled the GDR in ever-increasing numbers for greater financial security and a sense of permanence in the FRG (Federal Republic of Germany). Moving between worlds was so normal by the mid-1950s that even the West Berlin public transport company, the BVG (*Berliner Verkehrsvertrieb*), introduced a return ticket for East Berliners in GDR currency.[144] Things came to a head in November 1958 when Nikita Khruschev issued his famous Berlin ultimatum to the Western powers, calling for the withdrawal of Allied presence in the western portion of the city as a precursor to a future reunification, ostensibly on Soviet terms.[145] Three years of diplomatic wrangling failed to produce a solution to subsequent standoffs, culminating in what many believe was the order to build the Berlin Wall.

Although most of the literature on the Berlin Crises of 1958–61 have focused exclusively on international relations and the Cold War confrontation broadly defined, Patrick Major suggests that a more bread-and-butter approach may be beneficial in understanding the smoldering storm. In his erudite analysis, 1958 remains a key moment in time, but the city of Berlin plays a more active role in its own undoing a few years later. Chief among the issues shaping GDR policy on border crossing was the fact that Berlin's metropolitan makeup was simply incapable of preventing flight to the West. Visa restrictions had been put in place limiting the number of people who could legally depart for the FRG. As long as many side streets intersected with the west-bound suburban or underground train lines, however, Berlin would remain the preferred place of departure for those disgruntled citizens seeking to flee socialism. Added to the mix were a number of hard-nosed policies aimed at universities and medical elites which served as "push factors" for an already angst-ridden population. Given these conditions, Major argues, it could no longer be shocking that one in six citizens were opting to flee the country. Beyond these antagonisms lurked the discrepancy in wages and buying power between those with addresses in the East and those living in the West, which the 1958 end of postwar rationing failed to rectify completely. Baked goods sold out by noon with little in the way of restocking, and butchers often sold the last sausage well before the final shopper in the queue reached the counter. By the time the astronaut Yuri Gregarin reached the stars in 1961, disgruntled Berliners could be heard joking aloud that he'd likely find more dairy in the Milky Way than in the stores back in the bloc.[146]

Considering the general sense of malaise – to say nothing of the changing tenor of diplomatic wrangling – it is not surprising that these tense final years of liminal division would witness the publication of no fewer than three books of photography documenting everyday life in this exceptional city. In these visual portraits, some which would garner their chroniclers immeasurable hardship and artistic isolation, we see evidence of yet another Berlin, one in which the everyday struggles of average people were solicited in support of the larger ideological struggle to concretize and close the boundary. The extent to which this new visual register helped articulate an embodied sense of division between East and West is open to debate, but what is clear is the way the streetscape functioned in these photographs as a new stage upon which to showcase the passionate politics of the Cold War city.

It comes as no surprise that Berlin would capture the artistic imagination of photographers after the total destruction of World War II. Just as writers and poets flocked to the broken Reich capital, so too did German, expat, and foreign photographers focus their eyes on the city on the Spree. In addition to the likes of Henry Ries or Friedrich Seidenstücker, already established names from before the war, young men, some of them former soldiers like the American Will McBride and Herbert Tobias, came to the city to hone their skills with shots of damaged streets and broken people. In photojournalistic snapshots and carefully crafted *mise en scènes*, these photographers further mapped the city streets along an axis of emotionality and reverence, humanizing the plight of the people while poking jabs at the city and federal authorities overseeing reconstruction. Chief among their fixations, in addition to documenting the plight of children, was the question of parallelism and mirror effect. Frequently, their photos served as meditations on the theme of dualism, of the coexistence of life and death, and the search for the simple life in the eye of a burgeoning storm. As ethnographies of everyday life, these image makers did not simply circulate their photos as supplemental documents of the Berlin Crisis; they played an active, constitutive role in formalizing the visual representation of the city divided. That these photographers seized on street scenes and images of youth is especially telling since it was in leisure spots, like the Wannsee Beach in the furthest reaches of West Berlin, or amidst the hustle and bustle of a curbside market, the bus stop, and traffic circulation that the landscape of war and destruction was reconfigured to suit a new master, that of competing ideological systems desperate to win over the hearts of its citizenry. But alongside the ideological struggle another force animated the actions of the artists: the quest to negotiate aesthetic integrity amidst the instrumentalizing force of current history.

"Does Berlin have a soul?" asked Lynn Millar in the introduction to the book she edited with Will McBride. In *Berlin und die Berliner: Von Amerikerikanern Gesehen* (Berlin and the Berliners as Viewed by Americans), with over 80 photos of "neighbourliness," comradeship, love, and the ordinary, Millar and McBride used their dual-language publication as an explicit testament to an American way of seeing that sought out a "sense of balance between the ruins of yesterday and the boundaries of today." Their Berlin was one where division had become a way of life. "Hypnotised by the sound of the air hammers and the sight of the concrete and glass walls shooting up over night," like the moderns who squinted at the neon signs sprouting up around the Kurfürstendamm at the turn of the century, McBride described how exhilarating it was to "feel the pulse of the rebuilding of the city."[147] Despite his best effort not "to harp on the subject," McBride could not help but notice the differences that animated daily life in both halves of the city. Schooled in the style of Henri Cartier-Bresson's photojournalism, which stressed that authenticity lay in capturing "the everyday moment," Millar and McBride rendered commentary on the political situation in the city through quiet depictions of daily life. Images of children looking askance during a May Day parade in the East were twinned in the book's layout with the mesmerized expressions of window shoppers anticipating Christmas. On another set of pages, the orderly precision of a traffic police officer with his stash of holiday gifts is paired with the image of a busy interchange along the "massive, cold, and empty" Stalinallee. Most striking are the mildly erotic images of youth culture, whether turtle-necked blondes in an artist's studio or a flirtatious couple embroiled in conversation in a smoky jazz cellar. The only image of unbridled *eros* and pure emotion is staged completely out of doors, as the camera lingers over the form of a couple literally twisted in embrace and almost hidden by the long grass and reeds of the Pfaueninsel, an island in the Havel river to the west of the city in the American-controlled district of Zehlendorf. In this photo, it is as though love, or at least bodily lust, cannot be tamed by grid patterns, city streets, and the worsening political crisis slowly enveloping the city in the latter half of the 1950s. At the same time that the beaches along the Wannsee are featured as sites of release and repose, the lack of a similar image from the pools, parks, and green spaces of Berlin's eastern half is itself telling. In a city with two zoos, two major parks, two promenades, two rival circuses, and two competing universities, the misplaced mirror effect underscores through its absence the notion that youthful desire, self-realization, and sexual fulfillment may only truly flourish under the watchful eyes of the American protectors (Figure 2.6). Curious is the fact that these photos seem intent on reclaiming sites that continued to garner unwelcome attention at the hands of police, social welfare, and health authorities. This contradiction is resolved if we look at these photos as harking back to images of a pre-1933 Berlin sociability, in which case Millar and McBride's photos suggest that the West is the true heir to this historical legacy – before, at least, Hitler, the war, and division unhinged it from its course.

Whether through oblique referencing or more deliberate framing, the grafting together of positive emotions with particular city spaces leaves an indelible imprint on the viewer, linking life-affirming messages of love, happiness, and mutuality to a life lived on the western side of the boundary. The correlation between city space and emotion was anything but ambivalent or peripheral to the larger machinations of power and authority over the divided city. Instead, these visual templates and cues worked by associating a particular emotional response to the places where they transpired, whether spaces of leisure and recreation or entertainment and the mundane, day-to-day life, or the lustiness and loveliness of erotic attraction, wherever they may be found. In essence, photojournalism, and photos of divided Berlin especially, created an emotional geography of the Cold War city that was a supremely important means of communicating the supposed naturalness of a way of life safeguarded and protected on *this* side of the boundary. Well before the building of a bricks-and-mortar wall between two opposing ideological systems, the simple association of happiness with one side of the city linked memory, self-actualization, comfort, and desire to a particular political system.

Figure 2.6 Young people eating popcorn at the Wannsee, 1959. Photographer: Will McBride.
Photo credit: Bildarchiv Preussischer Kulturbesitz/Art Resource, NY.

Nowhere was this message more doggedly pursued than in two books published at the height of the Berlin Crisis, when premier Khrushchev threatened once again to block trade and travel in and out of the city lest American troops withdraw from West Berlin. Edith Rimkus and Horst Beseler's *Verliebt in Berlin* (In Love with Berlin) was published by the New Life Publishing House in the GDR in 1958. It was followed by the 1959 West German publication *Berlin: Bilder aus einer großen Stadt* (Berlin: Pictures From a Big City) by Hans Scholz and a well-known *Stern* photo-journalist from Cologne known mostly by his last name, Chargesheimer (a contraction of his given name Karl Heinz Hargesheimer). Both books traded on this very same linkage between city space and emotional optics during this especially tumultuous period in the city's divided history. Like Millar and McBride's, these books purported to be simple photo essays of daily life. Replete with images of circus acts and the now ubiquitous scenes of children playing in the ruins, each was a carefully crafted primer on the contradictions of life in Berlin, again turning on the dualistic rendering of emotional geographies and the inter-German divide.

In the tradition of DEFA's star-crossed lover films, Rimkus and Beseler's account, which called itself "a diary in pictures and words," took the form of a fictitious epistolary correspondence between a suitor and his lover. Recognizing that "symbols are themselves pale and empty," Wolfgang paints a picture of the city for his beloved Sabine in words and images so as to communicate to her his desire that she too might adore the city, and him by extension.[148] Although Sabine initially fails to see things beyond simple black and white – like the images between the covers – by the book's end she is persuaded. In a statement resembling marriage vows, she professes she'll continue to love Berlin "in the fog and damp" and in the heat of summer.[149] Although their visual love affair unfolds with the help of countless anonymous Berliners, who, smiling and posed, appear to have willingly agreed to participate in the drama, the city is itself the biggest personage in the morality play, looming largest in the portrayal. Beseler knew the city well, as a former technician with the Soviet occupation authorities, and had developed a sense of its flair and pulse as a regular reporter for *Neues Deutschland*. Riding the success of this book, he would go on to be one of the GDR's most celebrated writers of children's literature, while Edith Rimkus would serve as his muse, collaborator, and life partner. Happily for the GDR cultural authorities, the love affair at the heart of this book extended into the lives of its authors in a curious twist of art imitating life.

As in the Millar and McBride text, this Berlin story revolves around distinct emotional geographies, only in this telling, the West is set up as the site of callousness and capitalism run amok, while the East houses an earnestness, frankness, and honesty found in the faces and movements of those whose images grace the pages. Upon finishing the love story, there is no doubt that East Berlin will serve as the future home of Wolfgang and Sabine (as with Horst and Edith, before they relocated to the countryside in the 1960s). In an unwritten postscript, one may assume not only that Sabine falls for Wolfgang, but that the reader will likewise succumb to the book's rhetorical and visual persuasion, like the crowd of demonstrators at the graves of Karl Liebknecht and Rosa Luxemburg that Sabine admires in the story's final lines, who could not help but be caught up in the desire "to live freely, work, and be happy" in the East.[150]

Rimkus and Beseler's fate was very different from that of Arno Fischer, a far more recognized and talented East German photographer, whose eight prints from his own Berlin series were selected for publication in the 1958 issue of *US Camera Annual*, a leading journal in the field which included work by celebrated photojournalist Robert Frank. The warm reception he received abroad was doubly surprising since his photography was denigrated at home in East Berlin. At a gallery in the eastern district of Weissensee, he was derided for not realistically reflecting the lives of Berliners according to the abiding cultural policy of the day. Unlike Rimkus and Beseler, Fischer was appalled at the emotional bankruptcy and sense of alienation in East Berlin, and did not shy away from letting this seep into his photography. To be fair, he reserved a good bit of visual criticism for both halves of the city, but since this ambiguity fell foul of current cultural trends and failed to paint the distinctiveness of the East in stark tones and sharp lines, his work was unable to find a publisher in the GDR despite the fact that he secured financial support through a benefactor and an ally in the publishing business. The story goes that one day before the building of the Wall in August 1961, the final mock-up of the series was ready to go to press. Only the most neutral of Fischer's East Berlin photos remained in the book, and the textual accompaniment to the West Berlin ones was rewritten according to the preference of the day. Under the title *Situation Berlin*, it first surfaced in the fall 1961 book fair in Leipzig, where its press heralded its arrival with elaborate banners and signage. As art historian Ulrich Dornröse tells it, when the Minister of the Exterior surveyed the offerings on display as part of an orchestrated state inspection, members of his coterie responded with great displeasure to the suggestion that Berlin's status was in any way out of the ordinary. Upon hearing one handler exclaim "Comrades, comrades, Berlin is no longer a situation," he was heard to remark "Oh yes, take that away!" Although Fischer would go on to acclaim as a professor of photography in Leipzig, he turned his back forever on the city of Berlin, and the story went down in public memory as the book that was never published, until it was resurrected after the fall of the Wall by the Berlinische Galerie. Unlike Rimkus and Beseler, who were beatified for their emotional geography of the two Berlins, Fischer's treatment at the hands of the state underscores the consequences of artistic malfeasance. His passionate portrayal of privation, want, and loneliness created a firm and lasting boundary, not between East and West as was hoped, but between integrity and duplicity.[151]

Even West German visual depictions of Berlin's status were less pointed than Fischer's, highlighting once again the depths of his aesthetic independence. Drawing on virtually the same form, structure, and content as Millar/McBride and Rimkus/Beseler, a West German take on the situation in Berlin emerged onto the scene in 1959, only a few short months after Khrushchev's ultimatum in November 1958. In this cauldron of swirling propaganda, amidst fears of another possible blockade, Chargesheimer the photographer and Scholz the writer sought to paint the "open, plaintive, and unadorned face of the city ... this indestructible city, the German capital." Of course, even this statement is highly charged, considering the implication that Berlin was the rightful heir of German unity. Although the face painted in these photos was certainly more relaxed and moderate than those claiming to represent an "American view" or a story of love and adoration, in the book's front sleeve the tried and true juxtaposition between East and West was once again in evidence: "after the Second World War curbstones became border zones, barbed wire divided children from parents, and metropolitan Berlin became two cities: one mute and grey and the other blooming and blossoming under the tutelage of the irrepressible Ernst Reuter" – the first Lord Mayor of West Berlin.[152] Chargesheimer, who according to one biographer possessed "the uncanny ability ... to capture events, landscapes and buildings as well as the life and emptiness of cities with precise verisimilitude," would release over 20 photo books over his vast career, with the bulk of them published in the turbulent years between 1957 and 1961.[153] His images of vibrant street scenes and lively beach crowds resonated with similar motifs found in the many Berlin stories published in the mid-1950s, which depicted the city as a green, natural, oasis – an island – in a sea of red.[154] Best known to postwar audiences for his work on Cologne, Chargesheimer's Berlin is a clear blending of genres, from the more theatricalized staging of middle-class portrait photography to the point-and-click blurriness of photojournalism's captured moments. Indeed, most of the subjects in this book are caught off-guard, either looking askance out of the frame or hazarding a cautious look at the photographer. Snapshots of citizens going about their daily affairs, traveling by train or tram, are juxtaposed against more recognizable emblems of the reconstructing city, whether shots of those gathered in observation of the construction site surrounding the Memorial Church or queued in a line awaiting vegetable delivery outside an East Berlin grocery store. Sidestepping the temptation to cast Easterners as masses of automatons on the work site or marching in unison at a demonstration while Westerners linger over coffee, conversation, and cigarettes in one of the many quaint cafés along the Kurfürstendamm, nevertheless he included occasional images of well-filled streets and happy consumers and juxtaposed them against the sober idleness of a near-abandoned stretch of an East Berlin U-Bahn line. Although it is clear from the gloss and texture of the page that this is a West German publication, the demarcation line between East and West is less well policed visually than in the book by Rimkus and Beseler. In fact, only an insert in the back pages allows readers to decipher precisely which images were taken where. Despite the opening missive about the true meaning of division that linked quality of life with life in the West, these images of parades, cafés, street culture, and transit are less pointed than the cover sleeve suggests. In actuality, without the aid of the penultimate site directory, the reader might never truly guess the location of many of these shots. Unlike Rimkus and Beseler's more partisan account, Scholz and Chargesheimer's view of the divided city might be read as a call for moderation.[155] Additionally, what we see here are images of a moment in time when normalization (i.e., separation) was indeed the norm. This is a city seemingly at ease if not at peace with division, where hard-and-fast differences between neighborhoods and sectors were increasingly less discernable, blurring into the backdrop amidst images of bathing beauties, old couples sipping their schnapps, and children in traditional dress – still playing in the ruins. This is borne out in the emotional tenor underscoring many of Chargesheimer's photos, as many are equally imbued with a sense of quotidian ordinariness, peppered with occasional spectacle and youthful frivolity. Even if, as Scholz puts it in his accompanying text on the city's storied history, "Berlin is once again in danger," he follows up with a perfunctory "as in many times in the past," implying that tension and conflict does a Berliner make.[156]

While photojournalistic accounts continued the tradition of earlier city stories and revisited sites associated with the pre-1945 city's lively beach and bar culture, what was new and distinctive was the way in which they assigned daily life a particular emotional currency, which was then instrumentalized in the service of nation building during the worsening political conditions of the late 1950s. These visual city texts, although presented in the spirit of naturalness, underscored the important place of street scenes, public spaces, and everyday intimacies in the Cold War confrontation.

Although housing strategy, rubble clearance, missing persons searches, and the rebuilding of essential services were implicitly designed to meet the basic needs of the postwar population, the political potential of these initiatives in harnessing popular sentiment cannot be overlooked. Did Berliners feel safe traversing city streets? Would city authorities be able to offset privation and make life bearable in a city under siege? Precisely these concerns animated policy and procedure during the Berlin Blockade, when abstract contingency plans had the enviable result of creating a sizeable shift in support for the American occupying powers.[157] Sexual assaults and sexualized violence more generally by the occupation troops had the reverse effect, undermining legitimacy of purpose and damaging faith in the benevolence of the forces. While Berliners retained a healthy dose of skepticism for the Soviets, given their role in the violence of capitulation, the Americans were similarly at risk of losing the emotional support of the population if crimes against civilians went unpunished. The opprobrium leveled at the Americans could upset the delicate balance of occupation rule. In this way, courts martial were important places where American democracy came under scrutiny, as Germans sought due process. Failure to intercede adequately on behalf of victims jeopardized social and political relations. Although they had initially "come as a conqueror," they could not risk appearing as one.[158] If order could not be established in the streets under American control in southwest Berlin, what hope did the United States have for setting an example for the rest of the country?

While the courtroom served as a site where emotions ran high in the ideological battle for Berlin, coffee table books published at the height of the pre-Wall Cold War likewise reflected the rising tensions over the city's unresolved fate. Photojournalists hoped to tap into popular sentiment and showcase the good life that was to be had on their side of the internal boundary. People continued to map out the city according to their own wants and needs, living in more affordable accommodation in the East while working in the West, or traveling across the city boundary for leisure, a film, or an after-dinner drink in an across-town bar. However, by the late 1950s, in visual culture at least the boundary between East and West was becoming even more fixed. At the same time that the flurry of international news stories and photo essays heralded a return to something resembling world-class status, the reliance upon street scenes and daily life was not simply an easy, breezy way of capturing the essence of big city life. Each photo spread's intended purpose was to promote identification on an emotional level with each system of government by tapping into past visual metaphors of modernity, escape, and leisure.

Given Berlin's special status, the stakes were high indeed. In historicizing the desires, anxieties, and frustrations of Berliners living through these tumultuous times, we see that urban encounters and the diverse passions they engendered – the fear, loathing, love, lust, anger, contempt, and ambivalence – were not just responses to life in a constrained environment. They were moral arrays around which citizens organized their thoughts about past, current, and competing regimes. Emotive reactions to the use and manipulation of city space serve as a barometer of how Berliners understood and made sense of their place in the early Cold War. In revisiting the symbol and place of the street as a crucible of belonging, this chapter has suggested that a more phenomenological appreciation of the spatialities of feeling, whether real or discursive, are of central importance not just in accessing the culture, texture, and feel of life in the divided city, but in understanding the subtle ways in which power circulated at both the subjective level and the international scale. The association of the street with modernity, fascism, order, danger, eroticism, and leisure reemerges with particular strength in the 1950s. Although it takes on different hues on both sides of the inter-German boundary, it nevertheless indicates the political importance of emotionality and affect in Cold War Berlin.[159]

3
The Train Station

> The S-Bahn is one of our intimacies. It is ours, the puzzling over
> the peculiar old shades of paint going round the trains, the dark
> carmine, the ox-blood red, the stolid yellow on top. We rec-
> ognize the sound without thinking, the rattling passage, the
> respiring brakes and approach at night, the singing accelera-
> tion. The green neon signs on the bridges and stations, the
> white S: Stadbahn: it belongs to us, we know where we are.
> Uwe Johnson, "Postscript on the S-Bahn," 1961 (1970)[1]

"Always in a good mood, always a boost." That was how Gustav
Spielberg characterized Frau Kupke, a metropolitan train station attendant with the Berlin Transportation Authority (BVG). Among the feuil-
letonists, physicians, technicians, district majors, and rubble women he
approached for perspectives on the fall of Berlin, Frau Kupke's story
stood out. No one had managed to capture the collective trauma of
capitulation as vividly as she had, and in so few words. Faithfully attend-
ing her post in the Mehringdamm underground station in Kreuzberg,
every 2½ minutes she warned the city's frustrated and overburdened
travelers to mind the doors as the trains hurtled in and out of the station. Steeped in steely optimism despite the drudgery of the day, Kupke
made certain she held tightly to the schedule, all the while thankful not
to be "stuck at some dead train station, where the trains come every 20
minutes." She needed "this tempo, this bustle" after her lengthy illness,
brought on by what she termed rather euphemistically as the "excitement of the last days of the war." Her embrace of the orderly chaos was
remarkable given the scope of her personal struggles. Less than a year
ago, united with her husband and two small children, she felt certain
she could endure the transition from war to peace. This all changed

shortly before armistice on May 8, 1945, when within the space of two days she lost her parents in a bombing raid and her young family in a grenade attack on their tenement house while she was out searching for provisions to help survive the final assault.[2]

Released from a 10-month sojourn in hospital for a nervous break-down, she faced an upward battle to regain her bearings. Having spotted the BVG poster advertising a job search, possibly at one of the city's work exchange kiosks that jostled for preeminence amidst the swarm of notices for lost loved ones, she hoped her situation might improve. And it did. The din of the daily commute provided a welcome respite and the mix of people coursing through the station ensured a daily dose of levity, distraction, even humor. Indeed, the platform and tunnel system, not long ago home to street-fighting insurgents and fleeing civilians, had been transformed into an oasis of rhythmic precision amidst the noise and racket of reconstruction. Still, despite the occasional flirtation, the sideways glances of elderly black marketeers, and the quickened gait of tardy theater goers, Frau Kupke's thoughts never could fully transcend her plight. "Perhaps I'll marry again," she said wistfully, "so as not to be so alone with the troubles of the everyday." But before she totally succumbed to her grief, which was never far from the surface, the trusty southbound train brought a much-needed reprieve, hurtling into the station loaded with its human cargo.

Although for most Berliners it likely conjured up Nazi-era images of the cheerful BVG attendant, a frequent feature of 1940s photospreads of League of German Girls performing their war service, for Frau Kupke, the train station provided a sense of comfort, regularity, and order – a hopeful return to normality both technologically and existentially. But for the legions of refugees entering the city, to say nothing of the throngs of Berliners clambering aboard trains to beg for food from sympathetic farmers, it acquired an entirely different meaning as a symbol of the howling privation of war's end. Police and social service workers had more pressing concerns. For them, the train station served as a portal of crime and delinquency, a place that brought client and trade together and guided naive new arrivals into the waiting hands of eager recruiters. Amidst the tension of the early Cold War, there was another layer still, that of the place of the train network itself within a swiftly dividing cityscape, where transit lines played a not insignificant role in carving up the city terrain between East and West. For all these reasons, train stations were supremely important to how Berliners navigated and understood the impulses at work in the reconstructing city. Beginning with an exploration of the cultural heritage of the train station as embodying the contradictions of urban modernity, including their function as part of Nazi genocide, this chapter charts the changing function of these spaces after 1945 as they evolved from sites of transit to places of combat and sexual transgression. Viewing them as sites of mobility, encounter, and exchange, it argues that the culture of the train station may have broken down conventional boundaries such as those between city and suburb, upper and lower class, but it also created a context for greater intervention in policing boundaries of respectability, decorum, and identity, especially in treating the problem of sexual transactions negotiated there. In the final section, it looks at the way in which train station sex galvanized a sense of common purpose by building allies and coalitions out of otherwise antagonistic elements. It argues that efforts to regulate these liminal spaces of transit and exchange may have been time-honored traditions of big-city life, but in Cold War Berlin they represented in microcosm many of the challenges, conflicts, and struggles over the form and shape of reconstruction itself, the result of which could herald profound alienation for those caught out of step with the new face of change. Still, just as the moral remapping of urban spaces like the train station hardened, in police procedure and social welfare policy, into a vision of the endangered boy prostitute, it also had the spin-off effect of positioning the hustler at the center of definitions of a more legitimate homosexuality, understood in contradistinction to the effeminacy and debasement of filthy station boys. While many men still bore the brunt of Nazi-era anti-sodomy legislation, the demonization of train station youths and cruising played a significant part in the negotiation of homophile respectability.

Heterotopias

As Wolfgang Schivelbusch and Todd Presner have shown, the train station was a crucible of modern cosmopolitan consciousness and identity formation.[3] Representing the faith in and fear of mobility and change, simultaneously embodying the "emancipatory hopes and the destructive nightmares of an epoch," it serves as an important site for any investigation into shifting moral sensibilities after the war.[4] A liminal space, characterized by alternating moments of movement and stasis, it enabled a degree of sociability, bringing people together in unique and interesting ways that challenged existing social divisions and replaced them with a host of new possibilities.[5] It was in the train station, after all, that people were thrown together regardless of age, sex, race, or status, where for fleeting moments all of society coexisted in a single space before being cast out to class-specific waiting areas and wagon cars or to destinations of work, leisure, or consumption. In the late nineteenth century, train stations marked the distinctiveness of city life by reinforcing the separation between the urban and the provincial, between old money and the nouveau riche. They reinforced the differences between the leisured and working classes, who could barely, if ever, afford the trappings of luxurious travel. Transit was also highly sexualized, creating new spaces of encounter for men and women, who traveled through city and country unsupervised, beyond the constraints of family convention. They were brought together in carriages, in waiting rooms, and in the neighboring establishments that took root in the city's new leisure spaces and café culture. As it merged with the metropolitan transit system linking the newly amalgamated districts to the center, train travel and the stations at the end of the underground and suburban train lines became important nodes of mobility, anonymity, and encounter between high and low as men and women of various backgrounds made use of this mode of transportation to sample the city's charms.

Train stations, in addition to being symbols of modernity, were also resplendent with multiple, coexisting meanings. As heterotopic sites in the Foucauldian sense, they disrupted conventions of order, bringing into being a range of identities, experiences, and meanings for those who occupied the space, however fleetingly. Heterotopic sites are common and familiar, and yet in their infinite ordinariness they also manage to expose the uncanny and the strange – the conditions, lives, and experiences that fail to live up to the dominant meaning of the space in question.[6] The train station's main function, of course, was economic: to shuttle labor and capital to markets and places of exchange. But they were also markers of technological innovation and imperial power. In the past century they helped forge German unity, connecting Berliners to centers of business, culture, and history. They were metonyms for modernization with cathedral-like train stations heralding Germany's engineering prowess as a newcomer to the world stage.[7] The balustrades and columns, sweeping staircases, and great halls may have communicated a sense of grandeur but the brash belief in progress and cosmopolitanism masked larger fears and anxieties as citizens were forced to accommodate considerable changes in perception through the mechanization of everyday life. Whether hurtling through vast swaths of countryside en route to the capital, or commuting from newly amalgamated suburbs to the cultural and industrial pockets of the inner city, in poorly sprung carriages, on bumpy track, soiled by soot and smoke,

Berliners unwittingly became participants in the technological reordering of traditional ways of life. Trains forged a distinct separation between the metropole and the countryside, creating new forms of interaction between city folk and rural dwellers and redrawing the boundaries between working and "respectable" classes. Suddenly men and women might ride together in a train car, unsupervised, jostled about in ways that historian Peter Bailey has shown in the English context excited the imagination as well as breaking down inihibitions.[8] Aside from instituting "railway erotics," these interactions and experiences forged a new cultural lexicon through the negotiation of common knowledge of what it meant to live in the capital, which increasingly included an awareness of how to navigate the urban maze of streets, cafés, and squares amidst the distraction of consumer culture and the sometimes welcome, other times unwanted glances of anonymous strangers. As Simmel noted in an now-forgotten chapter from 1910 titled "the Adventure," metropolitan life heralded great potential for new understandings of power and adventure but modernity also brought its share of alienation and dislocation for those slow to adjust to the dizzying pace of change.[9]

As sociologists Gayle Letherby and Gillian Reynolds have noted, train stations have always served as "sites of conflict and negotiation," engendering a range of culturally and historically specific social interactions.[10] Variances of interpretation might be extremely individual, depending on the circumstances of a particular person, but they also reflected dominant and marginal social attitudes as well as the political values that shaped the contours of self-reflection. In the story of Fritz Haarman, the real-life Hannover mass murderer portrayed by Peter Lorre in Fritz Lang's *M*, who ambled about the train station in search of teenage boys, the concourse epitomized the sense of atomization and malaise of post-World War I Germany. The claustrophobic atmosphere of Weimar Berlin was similarly cast in relief by a character in satirist Erich Kästner's 1931 novel *Fabian: The Story of a Moralist* who sought refuge and escape from the stifling metropolis via the famed Anhalter station. Conversely, Pamela Swett has shown in her discussion of train stations in pre-World War II Berlin that these same sites of desperation might also represent places of possibility for women plagued by outmoded notions of propriety, as in Irmgard Keun's novel *Gilgi*, released the same year as *Fabian*.[11] Train station spaces, like any other historical sources, therefore require historicization to best understand the link between the cultural imaginary, lived experience, and the changing physical environment which gave it form and structure.

During the Hitler years these sites played a distinct role in the domestic and foreign policy agendas of the regime. Seeking to tame the legions of *flâneurs* and window gazers to better control leisure time and the pace of circulation, Hitler's notorious architect Albert Speer crafted a vision of the city center that imbued urban planning with measured and controlled theatricality. In his vision of the Street of Magnificence (*Prachtstrasse*), more commonly referred to as the North–South axis, columns of soldiers would embark upon their three-mile pilgrimage to the soon-to-be-constructed Great Arch via two central train terminals in order to pay tribute to the idylls of Germania.[12] Speer, together with Director Leibbrand of the Reich Traffic Ministry, saw in these designs the possibility of a large-scale reorganization of the city's train network to reflect the idealism and mastery of the Hitler state. But, while the design for the major train station at the southern end of the Prachtstrasse epitomized Nazi largesse, it simultaneously drew on modern notions of space and circulation. As Speer himself described the plans to build a four-level structure, dwarfing New York's Grand Central Station, "the idea was that as soon as they ... stepped out of the station they would be overwhelmed, or rather stunned, by the urban scene and thus the power of the Reich." Perhaps more impressive were the plans for the station plaza, a full "thirty-three hundred feet long, and a thousand feet wide," which was to be furnished with "captured weapons, after the fashion of the Avenue of Rams, which leads from Karnak to Luxor." While Hitler drew explicit inspiration from the ancients, the final details of this structure owed much to Baron Hausmann's Paris design, since Speer conceived these plans after his visit to France in the fall of 1941.[13] Forged from concrete, steel, and marble for all the world to see, "the avenue between the two central railroad stations was meant to spell out in architecture the political, military, and economic power of Germany."[14] In the very center, under the triumphal arch of the Great Hall would reside the most powerful man in Europe – at least, according to the design.

For the city's subjugated populations – forced laborers, dissenting Germans, and Jews – these same sites of Nazi heraldry, rationality, and urban planning had a much more direct impact as places of horror and deportation. But although the transit lines embodied the megalomania of the Nazi regime, these spaces could not always be wholly subordinated to the racial imperatives of the Hitler state. In one notable instance, the sophisticated network and its clockwork regularity actually saved the lives of at least two Jewish Germans in hiding. Ellen Lewinsky and her mother Charlotte spotted a former childhood friend and notorious "Jew-catcher" at a restaurant adjacent to the Friedrichstrasse station.

Before they were discovered, they jumped on one of the waiting trams before transferring to a bus and then subway en route to a safe house where they reported to friends about their near miss.[15] This story could have ended badly for the women, suggesting that the transportation grid, something simultaneously orderly and chaotic, held within its design the potential for great tragedy as well as triumph.

Just as the rail lines served a new purpose under Hitler's racial policies, occasionally subverted by serendipity and happenstance, these places of transit acquired additional import for the civilian population during the air war and block-by-block defense of the city that ushered in the conflict's final days. To meet the challenge of sheltering the city's women, children, aged, and infirm, Berlin's underground train stations took on new symbolic and material importance as its tunnels, platforms, and stairwells became transformed from 1920s emblems of commercialization and mobility to places of entrenchment and sanctuary, as the "world turned upside down." Under the barrage of the katyusha rockets that heralded the arrival of the Russians, they underwent further alteration as host to sexual violence on a mass scale.

Spaces of Civility and Militarism

The city's unique place as a civilian front line meant the spatial meanings of these sites and the memories they engendered bled into future constellations in profoundly racialized, sexed, and gendered ways. For feuilleton editor Ursula von Kardorff, writing about the final year of the war in her diary, they showcased essential differences between Berliners and the vast pool of foreign laborers working on a range of public and military works projects in the city. According to her diary account, foreign laborers dominated the scene at the Friedrichstrasse train station in 1944. Claiming that their mere presence decivilized the space, she described how the bombing campaigns forced Berliners begrudgingly to share the underground dwellings with the impressed workforce. Likening the scene to a crowded square in mythic Shanghai, those "tattered, quaint figures in quilted jackets" were actually quite easy to spot given "the high cheekbones of the Slavs." Between the gangs of Eastern European workers, there even "circulated light blond Danes and Norwegians, coquettish French girls, Poles with looks of hatred, and frozen Italians – a mix of nationalities never before witnessed in a German city."[16] Although many foreign workers entered into forbidden liaisons with Germans, their presence in Berlin's air raid shelters was not always embraced by the crowds cowering there.[17] Jeanne

Mammen's vitriol was palpable in January 1943, when she was forced to find alternative shelter since the train stations were too overcrowded. At the Potsdamer Brücke, she found some space, but even the smoking room was "so damn full, I thought I was actually somewhere in Russia; [everywhere there were] leather caps, lambswool jackets, and Asiatic shoes with bent back tongues."[18] Although the workers were housed in workers' tenements and makeshift labor camps adjacent to factories, separated by fencing from the city's civilian population, Kardorff and Mammen's accounts suggest the transit network provided numerous occasions for intermingling beyond the worksite. Ostensibly, foreign workers were so visible along Berlin's train corridors that she labeled them a kind of "Trojan horse," undermining morale from within. In the bars and restaurants adjacent to the train station, the "girls moved from table to table" together with "long-haired boys with neck scarves," possibly armed with weapons and trading in illegal radios.[19] According to local lore, many of them were secretly in league with the advancing Russian troops, who gave them hints on how to steal weapons and hide them in the cellar underneath the train station, where they might then be used in the final confrontation with home front SS detachments.[20] If their presence in train stations, bunkers, and bars was not disconcerting enough, the unwelcome glances and sexual assertiveness of drunken and loud French POWs on the north–south Oranienburg to Wannsee line confirmed that social control mechanisms, policing, and fear-mongering had little impact as the war erupted all around.[21]

For those teenaged *Volkssturm*ists forcibly enlisted to defend the homeland in its final days, even the familiar sight of the city's train nexuses acquired an otherworldly hue, transformed amidst the smoke and shrapnel into a battlefield that extended well into the underground rail network. Pockmarked with bullet holes, the station platforms lost all luster of their art deco or marble-studded glory; even simple light switches were stripped away by ration-weary Berliners. The maze of train tunnels linking the city's underground stations formed a substantial part of its final defense, and the ragtag defense forces were slow to relinquish control over these subterranean spaces, especially given the fact that they enabled reliable if slow transit to various strategic positions within the urban front. As one might imagine, fighting underground posed unique challenges. East Germany's most celebrated feuilletonist Heinz Knobloch recalled years later a conversation he had had with a former SS general, whose passage from the city center to the northern district of Pankow via the Friedrichstrasse station was hampered not by opposing Soviet forces but by Berlin transit workers with an emboldened sense of self-importance. Despite the ready threat of his machine gun and the authority of his *Leibstandard* uniform, General Mohnke continued to encounter opposition when the transit workers refused to grant his company passage through the tunnels. Ultimately, his entourage was forced back above ground, where they were left no choice but to follow the overground rail lines on foot, a more difficult path since it necessitated traversing the Spree River and tramping through the ruins before finding shelter in a nearby brewery. Seeking some levity, Knobloch remarked that for the transit workers "the Hitlers come and go, but the U-Bahn must go on" – an offhanded reference to a popular Soviet sloganeering campaign at the end of the war. Looking back on the incident, the general still respected the moxie of the workers and their attempt to maintain civilian control over this increasingly militarized space. As a soldier, he was "accustomed to think in terms of orders and obedience." Indeed, the workers' sense of duty, a trope Knobloch used to appeal to a postwar GDR audience, had "compelled [his men] to obey."[22] While the subterranean space yielded material for a subtle morality play, above ground was far less forgiving, a point Knobloch made quite clearly when he shifted the focus away from quaint nostalgia to details of another confrontation those same fateful days, the result of which saw the bodies of two fleeing soldiers strung up from the arches of the very same railway station.[23]

While East Berlin authorities felt the need later to instrumentalize the sacrifice of young lives at the Friedrichstrasse train station via a memorial plaque, the militarization of Berlin's underground needed no such marker. For generations, seared into public memory was the notorious SS flooding of the north–south line near Potsdamer Platz in which hundreds of women, children, elderly, and infirm perished minutes away from Hitler's bunker. Fearing a Soviet assault on the city's core via the U- and S-Bahn tunnels, at 7.55 a.m. on May 2, 1945 the order was given to blow up the protective bulkheads that barred the waters of the Landwehrkanal from entering the underground system – causing water to stream into the tunnels. Water from the canal flowed as many as two stations northward toward Oranienburger Strasse and the Stettiner Bahnhof. Alongside the soldiers furrowed underground, hundreds of civilians crouched on the subway platforms and in abandoned train carriages as these spaces served as ersatz bomb shelters when neighborhood facilities were either full or inaccessible. Placing full faith in the imperial infrastructure and the city's defensive air strategy, those who sought refuge could not have anticipated that militarization would bring death and not deliverance at their own government's hand. While filming scenes for the newsreel *The Eyewitness* (*Die Augenzeuge*), Kurt Maetzig, director of the DEFA films *Marriage in the Shadows* (1947) and *The Story of a Young Couple* (1952), recalled in a postwar interview how his footage was unfit for public consumption given the graphic horror he and his crew encountered in the catacombs.[24] Despite the efforts of all four occupation authorities to drain the water in a timely manner (since this was as much a public relations issue as a public hygiene concern), a diver, Willi Besener, biliously described how bloated remains of mattresses, pillows, benches, and, of course, human forms lingered in the waterlogged "underbelly of Berlin a full six months after capitulation."[25]

The permeability of the boundary between civilian and militarized space that belied the neat separation of the battlefield from the home front may have marked the public memory of total war, but it failed to take hold in the visual imaginary of the Soviet-backed film industry. Although Maetzig could not stomach the actual footage of the Landwehrkanal slaughter, Wolfgang Staudte's 1949 film *Rotation*, filmed for DEFA six years before the director's falling out with the regime and subsequent move to West Germany, reinforced the idea of spatial separation, serving less as a full-on public reckoning with the Nazi past than as a momentary engagement with issues of personal responsibility and mass death in the Allied air campaigns against the city of Berlin. Staudte's film is a discussion of complicity and suffering, with a focus on the exploits of a single German family from the period before Hitler's ascendance to the regime's final days. Although he had access to Maetzig's film footage of the underwater carnage, he too opted to restage the breaching of the Landwehrkanal in the actual tunnels beneath Potsdamer Platz, as well as on a sound stage on the grounds of the famous Babelsberg studio in neighboring Soviet-occupied Brandenburg. Although the images are infused with the sense of beauty in destruction – a common thread in the visual representation of the end of the war, from photography to rubble films – the mood is certainly one of confinement, claustrophobia, and pending doom.[26] Even with its avowedly anti-fascist message – the director was a staunch critic of jingoism in any form – it manages to employ a compassionate lens through which to view the scale of German blindness, carefully balancing victimization with culpability. If spaces acquire meaning through their use, as feuilletonist Heinz Knobloch believed, then the drownings under the Landwehrkanal – both the staging of the tragedy and the horrors of the actual event – served to underscore the sense of hubris that was Germany's hallmark of modernity. Whatever may have remained of the trenchant belief in salvation through technological innovation, the honorable fight, or the separation of spaces and spheres, no amount of architectural knowhow and engineering could shield Berliners from the horrifying blowback of total war.

After the Deluge

Once lauded by Siegfried Kracauer for the way in which their cafés, vitrines, vending machines, and newspaper stands pulsed with life, these hubs of modern cosmopolitan consciousness were literal and figurative shells of their former selves at war's end.[27] April 1945 still saw 18-year-old Annaliese Holzhausen-Rohr shopping for sausage in the S-Bahn arch stores of the Bellevue train station despite the best efforts of artillery barrages to drown out Franz Lehar's ironic operetta "Aren't you happy luck," which was playing on the shopkeeper's gramophone, but by the first week of May, the market squares adjacent to the city's train stations stood eerily silent and Berliners only emerged from their hovels to dart about the streets in search of provisions.[28] Decimated by aerial attacks and a last-ditch tank battle, Alexanderplatz, which urban planner Martin Wagner had once envisioned as the "crossroads for a whole transportation network," lay smoldering in tatters.[29] Swedish-Finnish writer, journalist, film critic, and later politician Jörn Donner noted in the late 1950s that some stations never retained their old form, like the Nordbahnhof station, "where the earlier long-distance train traffic [was] now only a memory in the midst of rusty rails, unused warehouses, and ruins."[30] Unlike the years following World War I, when attention turned away from revolution toward the quick resuscitation of Berlin's world-class status, post-1945 rebuilding was thwarted by total collapse and the breathtakingly quick onset of fratricidal infighting among the Allied occupiers.

The cessation of fighting brought with it a host of material, structural, and environmental concerns not least of which was the gargantuan task of cleaning up the mountains of debris. Makeshift anti-tank barricades littered the streets, while corpses, both human and animal, hampered traffic circulation and endangered public health. Water mains "were ruptured in at least three thousand different places" and the city sewer system "slopped over into the canals and lakes, still not cleared of bodies."[31] In his first trip through the city in June 1945, American envoy John J. Maginnis noted that with the exception of the main thoroughfares, "the streets were filled with rubble and in many cases not discernible at all."[32] Although the US Army Engineers pumped out the underground to the extent that "one half of its 625 miles of track in the American zone was operating in limited service by Christmas," streetcars, trams, and buses were slow to resume service since they had been more severely damaged or bombed.[33] According to Landrum Bolling of the Overseas News Agency, S-Bahn cars were in short supply since many of them had been carted back to the Soviet Union, where they could be seen running on the Moscow metro system, a symbol of the rapacious appetite of the Russians, who were suspected of pilfering anything from pots and pans to the fine art collection of the famed museum island.[34] In the city's central districts, few bridges were left intact, inhibiting movement except for bicycles and foot traffic. Whereas Berliners once mapped out their city by the time it took to travel by rail, bus, or streetcar from one destination to the next, now they ambled about the smoke-laden landscape willy-nilly, sometimes for hours if they dared venture out of doors at all. With little recourse to the comfort and ease of rail travel, people employed whatever mode of transportation was on hand, ranging from "horse-carts, hand-carts in their thousands, expensive and shoddy cars, mostly commandeered, smart and not so smart military vehicles, bicycles, trolleys, wagons, and lorries, many of which looked rickety enough to be museum-pieces."[35] Plagued with distorted vision – so-called "cellar eyes" from days on end spent underground – they crept as best they could through the craters and debris that rendered the city unnavigable. Indeed, walking was often the most reliable form of transportation.[36] Besides the rocky terrain and dearth of reliable transport, there were additional dangers. Diarist Margret Boveri learned from friends not to trek along the east–west corso since the Russians continued to pilfer bicycles, or, worse, drag women off into the ruins where rapes continued to mark the everyday experience of many Berliners well into 1947. Beyond the threat to personal security, Boveri's options for getting around the city in May 1945 were few since it would take weeks before sporadic bus and streetcar travel was functioning again.[37] By September, much of the network may have been up and running again, but it did not necessarily alleviate the daily struggle. In Lichterfelde in the city's south end, Marta Mierendorff was jubilant at the sight of running water and electrification, yet she reserved sober judgment for train travel since it forced one to encounter other people's unending tragedy. Unlike the days before the capitulation, where travel through the city took on an air of insouciance and adventure, in defeated Berlin "every step through the ruins hammers chaos, violence, desperation into the head." For Mierendorff, using public transport was "an experience out of Dante's Inferno."[38]

Despite the image of sin and suffering conjured up in Mierendorff's metaphor, it was during the Blockade that the sight of train cars packed with scrounging day-trippers in search of a farmer's goodwill provided observers the opportunity to articulate a sense of German victimization. As the first major showdown between the superpowers, it aided in transforming the image of civilians from Nazi supporters to victims of circumstance. The vastness of the broken landscape carved out new spaces for rendering visible the disparity of people's experience. While the Blockade reinforced a new sense of boundaries to the relationship between the formerly united Allied powers, economic hardship coupled with ruin also cast new light on individual experience. Amidst the grayness of the city, where Richard Brett-Smith could not remember seeing a single Berliner with a ruddy complexion in 1945 and 1946, slowly there emerged hues of contrast, as citizens began to acquire definition and form as victims first of Soviet callousness and then of circumstance more broadly.[39] This willingness to dispense with outright condemnation for supporting – or at least acquiescing to – the Nazis found its way into the memoirs of servicemen and foreign observers. Train travel and the train station itself played an important role in bringing about this transformation of opinion. It served as a physical site of suffering showcasing the cumulative effect of hampered mobility, privation, disorder, and decay. A gathering house for the city's abject, a backdrop to the anonymous masses in search of a toe hold on security, and imbued with multiple levels of meaning and memory, it both reflected social malaise and refracted the gaze away from culpability in the war. In other words, the comings and goings of citizens through the city's train terminuses, along its lines, and in the bombed-out buildings in their vicinity played a vital part in recasting German victimization and complicity in the war.

Slow to come around to this idea in the early months after capitulation, the chief correspondent for London's *Daily Herald*, Denis Martin, was surprised by his own change of heart. Sharing Mierendorff's sense of anger at the Germans for having supported Hitler in the first place and bringing upon themselves and others such widespread misery, by 1949 he still could not shake the image of the legions of refugees, that "veritable army of despair," which huddled for days amidst "their bundles of dirty clothes and bedding" in the waiting halls of the Lehrter Bahnhof, "camped out on the platforms and on the waste ground facing the station."[40] The sheer number of faceless masses of women, elderly, and children humanized his view of the millions who had marched westward from the occupied territories in the East. While empathetic to their collective plight, his compassion was augmented by the macro-level politics of the early Cold War, which colored the way he saw them, not as beneficiaries of Nazi resettlement policies and the former occupiers of Polish and Ukrainian lands, but as victims of circumstance and the conditions of defeat.

While the sight of the refugees made an impact on individuals stationed or sojourning in Berlin, photographs and film images of their poverty helped communicate this new tone to a wider audience, embedding in public memory the presentation of select Germans as worthy of compassion. It is not surprising that Berlin railway stations were frequently a common point of focus in this visual reimagining. To the untrained eye, these sites might appear as simple backdrops to the staging of sacrifice and ruin. But they also formed an inextirpable part of a longstanding cultural imaginary that lent certain photographs historical currency and resonance. In this vein, it is not insignificant that Wolfgang Staudte selected the Stettiner Bahnhof as a location shot for his 1946 film *The Murderers Are Among Us*. In this world turned upside down, where brooding shadowplays of the ruins serve as constant reminders of the city's spiritual bankruptcy, at a particularly poignant part of the opening sequence Staudte has ingénue Hildegard Knef's character amble out of the Stettin train station upon her return from a concentration camp. Purportedly built upon ground that once housed a gallows, up until World War II the Stettin station was one of the most well-known long-distance stations (*Fernbahnöfe*) in Berlin. From its location near Chausseestrasse to the north of the city's central district, Berliners boarded trains en route to the Baltic coast, the playground of the city's bourgeoisie, and later home to a large Strength Through Joy (*Kraft durch Freude*) vacation facility.[41] The curved entrance arches beckoned visitors with thoughts of the journey that awaited them. It was this spirit of wanderlust that saw husbands flock to the station on Friday afternoons to catch the cumbersomely named "straw widow express" (*Strohwitweexpress*) to the island of Usedom to meet up with their wives and children on a hot summer weekend.[42] In his childhood reminiscences of Berlin, Walter Benjamin likened the sandy plane upon which the station was built to the beaches of the northern resort towns, illustrating the role of the station in the city's cultural geography as a conduit of adventure and escape from the crowded industrial metropolis.[43]

The war may have altered the majesty of the northern hub both as a physical structure and as a symbol, but it failed to completely bury its meaning under the rubble. However, the Stettiner Bahnhof would not remain a feature of the postwar network for long. The writing was on the wall already in 1945 when the *Wehrmacht* sprang the Karniner Bridge, severing the direct route to the Baltic. A few years later, the station's name would require changing when the GDR recognized the Oder–Neisse Line as its eastern boundary in 1950 because Stettin, now Szczecin, became part of Poland. Although it was deemed superfluous to the city's rail nexus and decommissioned in 1952, standing idle for the remainder of the GDR's history, the station's rhetorical and visual power continued to have resonance for a postwar Berlin audience. Photos like those by Erich Zühlsdorf in the late 1950s continued to tap into the spirit of escapism and leisure, except that they added the requisite messaging from the Soviet-backed regime regarding the collective efforts of the population in clearing a path through the rubble to build an outdoor swimming pool so that the little ones "without danger could splash around in the cool water" (Figure 3.1). Not only does this 1959 photograph's caption suggest the lingering importance of the ruined landscape a full 14 years after the cessation of fighting, but it employs this image as a trope of political reorientation and rebuilding. In the shadow of the station's arches, leisure and summer sun might still be had. Most striking of all is the near complete absence of fathers in the

Figure 3.1 Summer fun in the big city, 1959. Photographer: Erich Zühlsdorf.
Photo credit: Bundesarchiv Berlin, Image 183-66636-0001.

picture, a testament either to the continuity of traditional family values in the Worker's and Farmer's State or the lingering stain of social imbalance brought about by total war.

Shot during the airlift in August 1948, the train station photographs of *New York Times* photojournalist and German Jewish expat Henry Ries similarly employ the multi-hued memories of the train station to reinforce the humanizing impact of images on public opinion. Gone was the rawness of Mierendorff and Boveri's diary accounts of the depths to which the Germans had sunk in defeat. In a series of images taken in and around the Anhalter Bahnhof in the American sector, Ries wished to capture the "hungry, the miserable, and confused" without passing judgment. Anhalter, that magisterial train station, which Heinz Knobloch once joked acquired its name from the many trains that stopped there (a pun on the word "halt" in German – "weil viele Züge dort anhalten"), once saw "more than 800 specially trained stone workers... employed to craft the extravagant ornamentation covering the entire structure, ranging from terra-cotta relief figures and sculpted arabesques to detailed friezes, ornate columns, and flowering capitals."[44] In the decrepit state in which Ries found it, precious little of this prewar splendor remained. Inside its bombed-out skeleton lurked pure human squalor. Whether released prisoners from Russia, expellees from Silesia, black market operators, grandmothers with wicker baskets, or children, the deep lines on his subjects' faces communicated the "tragedy of the war and the catastrophe of the Hitler dictatorship." Himself a victim of Nazi tyranny, Ries was struck by the pervasiveness of the poverty he witnessed around the station. He was not alone. Montgomery's aide Lieutenant Colonel Wilfred Byford-Jones described the station refugees in atavistic terms. To him, those huddled together on the platform, the "old men, unshaven, red-eyed, looked like drug addicts, who neither felt, nor heard, nor saw."[45] Ries preferred to shoot the more marginal figures such as elderly women and the infirm. In these times of "privation, of hunger, homelessness of widows, and cripples," he wrote, "who was I to expect discussion of responsibility?" Indeed, as Dagmar Barnouw has shown, Ries viewed his craft as a kind of silent witnessing whose purpose was to initiate discussion by documenting the range of emotions on display.[46] His only role was to "remain silent and let my camera hold the memories captive."[47] Of course, Ries was no passive onlooker, and his carefully wrested images were anything but neutral. In actual fact, they reflect a curious fascination with life course and sexuality. In the overwhelming number of photos of huddled masses, more than a few document wrinkled grandmothers, a shy child hidden among her mother's belongings, and, in one particularly poignant photo, a coy blonde woman seductively poses for Ries as tendrils of smoke circle around her well-managed curls. Juxtaposed with the images of wrinkled, elderly women shying away from the camera or reluctantly captured on film, Ries crafts a narrative of capitulation as emasculating and feminized, linking the broken remnants of engineering mastery to civilization's decline in the form of the women, elderly men, and children camped out along train station platforms. Humanizing the Germans as victims of circumstance, he does so through highly gendered means.[48]

Like the remnants of ticket stubs and cigarette butts that littered the station grounds, these people were Berlin's discarded. But they were much more than that. Ries's subjects occupied a precarious position both in and out of time, as products of the difficult conditions of capitulation and – like Anhalter's giant clock which remained fixed at precisely three minutes past twelve – as emblems of the supposed universality of suffering brought about by the war. But, of course, suffering was anything but equal, let alone quantifiable, and the same space that conjured up images of precipitous decline held emotional import of a different sort for those who remembered it as one of the city's so-called "farewell stations" (*Abschiedsbahnhöfe*), where frightened Jewish parents bade farewell to children fortunate enough to leave before the mass deportations. Here, silent witnessing was an impossible task given the spectral presence of the dead amidst the ruins' persistent screams.

In addition to photos and films, trains and train travel also garnered the attention of songwriters and cabarettists like Erika Brüning, famous for her 1950 hit "Berlin boys are alright" (*Berliner Jungens, die sind richtig*). In the song's lyrics, she likewise employed spatialized metaphors of seeing and hearing to draw attention to privation and want:

> The trains are always packed to bursting,
> Only the pushiest get a seat,
> And once you're sitting squashed up in there
> You fall asleep from the stuffy heat.
>
> All the windows badly boarded,
> Wind whistles in through all the gaps
> And in one or other corner
> A hungry child whines and yaps.[49]

Complete with blown-out windows and unregulated heating, Brüning's image of the carriage draws its sense of gravitas from the murmurs of a hungry child, audible amidst the overcrowding and anonymity of the train car. It is a quintessentially metropolitan story of vying for space within the push-and-pull of quotidian life. Where mobility once connoted cosmopolitanism and adventure in an age of technology, as we saw in Ries's photography it could also strip passengers of all the accoutrements of civility. One need only think of the images of overcrowded trains bound for the countryside with Berliners hanging onto the roofs for their chance at trading clocks and ornaments for foodstuffs from willing farmers in neighboring towns. This scene also points to the fundamental inability of postwar Germans to conceptualize and concede victim status to the Jews, those most directly impacted by the technological precision of mechanized mobility.[50] Although it remains difficult for a contemporary audience to disassociate the image of the train car from the history of mass deportation, it is interesting to consider that an image so pregnant with meaning did not appear to conjure up such associations, either because the experience of the Jews was not yet fully known or, more likely, had failed to garner a place in the dominant moral economy of German deprivation and suffering.[51]

Despite competing claims to victimhood, nothing connoted innocence more than the image of a childhood lived among the ruins. Indeed, the city swarmed with lost children. Byford-Jones hypothesized that Berlin's population of wastrels, many of them air-raid orphans and refugees, totaled somewhere in the realm of 53,000. At the station, "every train that came brought its quota of pinched, pale-faced babies, and old elf-like children whom no one owned."[52] Juxtaposing their wild nature with the former opulence of the train station surroundings, the unclaimed children resorted to living "in holes in the ground beneath the ruins," or, as we saw in Chapter 1, in the bombed-out remains of the city's bunkers.[53] Given their sheer numbers, it is not surprising they made their way into the cultural topography of the city. A favorite of photographers Friedrich Seidenstücker and soon-to-be *enfant terrible* of the West German art scene Herbert Tobias, the image of children playing in the broken landscape became a leitmotif of the postwar condition, connoting innocence lost and hopefully regained. Not all depictions of life amidst the chaos was as bleak as those in Roberto Rossellini's neo-realist 1948 film *Germania Anno Zero*, where the young protagonist hurls himself from the window of a destroyed apartment block after being tempted into depravity by the charms of a pedophilic Nazi sympathizer.[54] Shots like Ries's were certainly more commonplace, often positioned in the feuilletons sections of the city's newspapers for a mass audience. Friedrich Luft, celebrated theater critic and contributor to

RIAS (Radio in the American Sector) and the *Tagesspiegel* (Daily Mirror) newspaper, preferred the short story medium to paint his picture of a seven-year-old boy waiting for his mother in a busy U-Bahn station. In this quirky 1947 tale of redemption and moral rebuilding set amidst the traffic of the concourse where commuters are "in such a hurry, so serious, so active, so important, so willing to aid in reconstruction, with quickness of breath as they rush to the trains," our attention is drawn to a single boy standing idle and erect as he waits for his mother to return from the ticket counter. Nothing about the scene is remarkable, except, perhaps, that the boy has his finger lodged indiscreetly up his nose. Bucking convention, the boy stands there, mouth agape, and bored, "his two open, brown, clear child's eyes" replete with "the innocence of childhood and sweetness, two little windows into life, open to the world." In a humorous twist (as if the image of a child rooting around his nose was not funny enough), Luft describes his attempt to engage the boy, reminding him that picking one's nose was not exactly desirable in public, only to be told in no uncertain terms and in a thick Berlinish brogue, "Piss off, sir, it is my nose after all!"[55] While this story ends with the author's description of the innocent encounter, Luft toys with the reader's sensibilities by hesitating to impart the man's true intentions, going so far as to suggest that he might have had even more duplicitous interest in the youth since, we are told, it was quite odd that he was traveling without the requisite day bag or briefcase. What turns out to be a quaint little ditty about big city humor might actually have played itself out quite differently considering the sexualized terrain of the train station and the shifting meanings of postwar urban space.

Staging Sexuality

As a staging ground for emotional reunions, a gathering place for dirt-encrusted refugees, and a site of dangerous encounters between leering occupation soldiers and hungry Berliners en route out of the city, what remained of the city's modern railway network played host to the daily drama of lapsed social boundaries and compromised moral values. Home to slumped refugees and hurried passengers, train station platforms were a study in contradiction, while neighboring side streets and alleyways beckoned black marketeers, "loose women," and girls who relied on quick transactions under cover of the crowd to lure customers away from the eyes of the police. City dwellers knew implicitly to hold tightly to their children's hands when traversing train station concourses, given their motley crew of characters. In Hanover, the lasciviousness of the train station space entered into the vernacular, with the red light district acquiring the moniker "Platform 6" (*Bahnsteig 6*).[56] As we have seen, these places had a long history of embodying wider societal fears and anxieties as a sign of the Janus face of modernity. Ralph Herrington has suggested that "the railway station provided a concentration of many of the aspects of modern life which were widely believed to be injurious to health: anxiety, pressure, worry, noise, bustle, crowds, constant movement."[57] Within its brick facade the contradictions of city life flourished. Traditional hierarchies were made plain while other barriers were transgressed, allowing class, race, and gender anxieties to bubble to the surface amidst inescapable interaction and social mixing. Despite the presence of transit police, the promise of regulation, and the regimentation of the schedule, the incessant movement and bumping together of bodies brought back the specter of the mob as the veneer of security and sociability was tested amidst the hustle and bustle of the concourse, in what Herrington terms the "traumatic encounter between technological modernity and the human constitution."[58] This feeling of anxiety was even more pronounced in the aftermath of the war, when social boundaries were further challenged by the legacy of carpet-bombing, mass rape, and widespread privation. Even the stabilization of the economy in 1948 failed to quell the anxiety, and the city's train stations retained a degree of fascination, fear, and loathing as police, welfare authorities, and the newly resurrected ecumenical Travelers' Aid Societies (*Bahnhofsmission*) redoubled their efforts to protect weary travelers from the sinister forces that shared this transit space.[59]

These new spaces opened up by the ruins, together with the sheer number of refugees, invested the train station with new purpose and meaning. Not only did the scale of destruction have the effect of forcing sympathy for the German population and forgetting Jewish trauma, but it also provided important cover for the city's clandestine sex trade. Although historically associated with working-class districts, prostitution remained a feature of the city's transit network and transcended East and West much like the *Deutsche Reichsbahn*-controlled S-Bahn, which continued to transect the internal border throughout the Blockade and up until 1984, when a treaty turned over responsibility for its operation on West Berlin territory to the BVG transport authority[60] (Figure 3.2). The gradual stabilization of the economy had failed to fully eradicate the trade in flesh, and although the black market would subside after the currency reform, prostitution could be found in every sector of occupation, in central districts as well as more suburban stops along the far-flung reaches of the network. In other words, despite

Figure 3.2   Warning sign for S-Bahn riders, Berlin, 1953. Photographer: Friedrich Seidenstücker.
Photo credit: Bildarchiv Preussischer Kulturbesitz/Art Resource, NY.

varying efforts to combat the more structural reasons why people fell into the trade, prostitution remained a hallmark of city life in post-1945 Berlin. For some – visitors, largely – it preserved a hint of the famed debauchery of Berlin's gloriously perverse past, as in Scottish journalist Ewan Butler's rather cheeky comment in 1955 that in the concourse of the Zoo Station in the refurbished West End, "travelers can satisfy any need at almost any hour."[61] For others, meanwhile, it served no greater purpose than to rub salt in the wounds of an already struggling urban population. Among the many reasons why it irked city and Allied officials was the participation of under-aged youths, both girls and boys. This was made even more prescient in the 1950s when East and West Germany targeted youth in a series of high-profile moral purity campaigns. But already after formal division of the city (and of Germany proper) in the fall of 1949, street walking gave a human face to the continued disparity of income between those citizens with addresses in the East and those who settled in the West, and it was a constant reminder to German authorities of the debasement brought about by war, amplified by division, and the lingering impact of defeat.[62]

If prostitution along the city's transportation corridors belied the permeability of internal boundaries, it also called into question the boundaries of respectability and decorum, especially surrounding important social taboos like intergenerational sex and sex between men. But boundary making and the reinforcement of certain social norms also held important spatial–temporal moorings. In the ideological battle to denazify the criminal code, jump start the economy, and democratize (or socialize key) institutions, loosened sexual mores threatened to uncloak a range of unsavory episodes in the city's recent past, like the Soviet mass rapes or even occasional American transgressions, which, when made public, might hamper the enlistment of citizens into the larger political struggle. But the laws themselves, policing procedures, and guiding criminological theories of debasement posed an even more wide-reaching problem insofar as they exposed the extent to which both postwar states continued to rely on pre-1945 methods of sexual regulation. The policing of street-level sex, in other words, forced an unwilling population to further engage the specter of the Nazi past, whether in the form of NS laws against homosexuality that remained on the books, or, more sinisterly, in the words and actions of police and social workers who hoped to stamp out the trade. While the ruins afforded the opportunity of cover, new building projects failed to dislodge these associations, now firmly implanted, between transportation nodes and sexual encounters, bartering, and exchange.

As the former hub of a racially defined empire, unceremoniously occupied, divided, and administered by foreign powers, Berlin's transit networks provide a perfect opportunity to revisit the link between the city's shifting physical and sexual boundaries. Once illustrative of Germany's famed order and murderous efficiency (although it was in Mussolini's Italy that the trains purportedly ran on time), during the Cold War the train station served as a gateway to freedom in the West and an access point for cheap goods and services from the East. In the 1920s, it exposed the raw and attenuated existence of those who were caught in the ebbs and flows of rapid modernization, with the beggars, vagrants, whores, and street youth congregating in the train station waiting rooms seeming to enact a scene from a Weimar-era Alfred Döblin novel. While a certain degree of debauchery went hand in hand with the development of this metropolitan space, in the years following capitulation social disorder of this magnitude increasingly reflected the moral depravity brought about by defeat.[63] In time, the sexually delinquent youth who gathered under the train station's arches began to generate fears about national renewal. The police regarded them as delinquent homosexuals-in-the-making, reformers and betrayed clients as blackmailing turncoats, and criminologists as passive asocials.[64]

Perhaps more than ever before, the train station and its denizens came to symbolize a Germany at a crossroads, still reeling from the recent Nazi past and torn between an emerging Soviet-style dictatorship and a consumerist Christian democracy. Rent boys crossed over the internal sector boundaries for evening liaisons, tempting fate and risking possible incarceration under the slow-to-be-reformed Nazi-era anti-sodomy legislation, revealing in the process some of the tensions associated with Berlin's homosexual subculture as it evolved, after years of Nazi persecution, amidst Cold War debates over policing, social welfare, and criminality.[65] From the records generated by these agencies, we can map the topography of transgressive sexuality in postwar Berlin, exposing to the light of day the contours of an urban subculture that survived Nazi assaults on homosexuals.[66] Indeed, despite the concerted efforts of the Gestapo and criminal police to destroy Berlin's reputation as an Eldorado for same-sex desiring men and women, the train station remained an important site of non-normative sexual expression in the years after the war, a situation that prompted renewed efforts to regulate it.[67] At the same time that unlikely allegiances were forged in and around the city's train stations to combat the threat of homosexuality, haphazard efforts to control transit space afforded boys and men the prospect of mediating their own experience of regulation, providing them with much-needed avenues of resistance and lending insight into the uniqueness of Cold War Berlin.

Catacomb Lives

Like their predecessors in the Wilhelmian and Weimar periods, in the years following World War II boy prostitutes led catacomb lives.[68] In the bombed-out bunkers that dotted the city's landscape, in pay-by-the-hour hotels, rented rooms (*Absteigequartiere*), and pungent pissoirs, they turned tricks to help support their liminal existence. Their lives were less ordinary than most, marked by loss, poverty, violence, and crime in such extremes that the state appeared unable to understand, much less solve, their problems. Who were these train station youths? Were they hardened criminals, moral misfits, or mere unfortunates who merited social welfare and state intervention? To the denazified social workers and newly recruited police officers walking the beat in capitulated Berlin, train station boys, whether operating alone or in cliques, presented a host of paradoxes, to be sure.[69] Often in contact with social services, whether escaping from a remand home or spending time in youth jail, initially they were viewed in conflicting ways, as both victims of and contributors to postwar instability. This view would change, however, and by the late 1950s their presence in and around the city's train stations would be viewed by police on both sides of the boundary as a potentially destabilizing force hazarding the development of healthful social mores. More disheartening still was the fact that even among progressive advocates for legal reform of the anti-sodomy paragraph they received little help and no sympathy. Contravening much fought-for homophile respectability at a time when persecution was at its postwar height, rent boys bore the stench of the street and as such were an unwelcome reminder of the furtive glances and uncontrollable passions of the cruising scene. In the years before Stonewall, train station sex could not form a part of respectable urban gay identity.[70]

Of course, concern about male prostitution was not solely a postwar phenomenon; it had an elaborate history that predated Hitler and the Nazis. The lineage of Paragraph 175 of the German Penal Code, which penalized consensual liaisons among adult men, can be traced back to Paragraph 143 of the Prussian Penal Code, which criminalized all forms of bestiality.[71] Upon the creation of German statehood, this paragraph was adopted by the newly united Germany in Bismarck's 1871 legal statute (*Reichsstrafgesetzbuch* or RGSt). In the 1920s, policing practices and new rules of evidence ensured that fewer charges of sodomy were laid when compared to the Weimar fixation with male aggressive, lewd, and violent behavior more generally.[72] Nevertheless, same-sex desiring men were anything but free from the fear of police intervention.[73] This sense of powerlessness only increased after the National Socialists gained power in 1933, when efforts to enforce Paragraph 175 were intensified, especially after the "night of the long knives" on June 30, 1934.[74] What began as an assault against Ernst Röhm's authority within the Nazi Party and an indictment of his previously tolerated sexual proclivities signaled a decisive shift in attitude toward the issue of homosexuality.[75] In vitriolic campaigns against all "deviants," which at times linked Jews, communists, and homosexuals together as one mutually reinforcing group, the Nazis sought to foster public support for their vision of "healthy social mores" (*gesundes Volksempfinden*).[76] By 1935, as Edward Dickinson has argued most persuasively, the Nazis had succeeded in undoing many of the gains of Weimar legislation that safeguarded individual sexual freedoms in order to weave the nation's moral fabric into a pattern more suitably aligned with the party's emerging social and racial policies.[77] Since homosexuality represented a challenge to the racial regeneration of the nation, the state had to ensure that transgressors were suitably punished. Through the use of Article 6 of the Law for the

Amendment of the Criminal Code, Paragraph 175 was altered to reflect this changing political ambiance. In the Federal Court decision of June 28, 1935, it was officially rewritten to expand the notion of malfeasance to include any behavior that represented the "shameless" use of another man's body for the purpose of sexual excitement. Gone was a previous stipulation requiring material evidence of an "intercourse-like act"; the Nazi version allowed prosecutors to rely upon rumor and innuendo and prohibited mutual masturbation, sexual touching, kissing, and even letter writing.[78] The boundary between guilt and innocence had become porous indeed.

While widening the range of homosexual acts subject to prosecution, the new version of Paragraph 175 also sharpened the focus on same-sex prostitution by splitting the original imperial paragraph in two. Paragraph 175 continued to govern sex between consenting adult men, while Paragraph 175a subsections 1 through 4 criminalized forced intercourse, the use of one's position of authority as a teacher or youth services worker to solicit sex with someone in care, sex with minors (boys under 21), as well as the buying and selling of sex.[79] Although offering oneself for the purpose of sexual arousal was illegal under the old code, the penalties for transgressions under the Nazi paragraph were amplified considerably. As many as 100,000 charges were laid according to Paragraph 175, with 10,000–15,000 men perishing in cannon fodder regiments, in prisons, jails, mental institutions, and concentration camps.[80]

Following the collapse of the Third Reich, the Allies began the daunting task of dismantling key Nazi institutions, including the police and judiciary. To eliminate many of the laws deemed reflective of Nazi authoritarianism, the Allied military government issued Army Order Number One.[81] Curiously, Paragraph 175 was not among the scores of laws revoked.[82] Despite numerous Allied Control Commission statements and the explicitness of article 3 of the military government's order outlawing the future application of laws smacking of National Socialist dogma, German courts, especially those in the western zones of occupation, continued to prosecute homosexuals according to the 1935 law.[83] Although a number of state courts in the Soviet-occupied eastern zone argued that the Nazi version of 175 and 175a should be annulled as tainted legislation, others, primarily in the West, opted to observe the unaltered Nazi-era code.[84]

In many ways, postwar decisions about which version of the law should be upheld broke down along the East/West axis. In the Soviet Occupation Zone, which in 1949 became the German Democratic

Republic (GDR), the Supreme Court of Berlin decided on February 21, 1950 that the 1935 variant of Paragraph 175 – which expanded the definition of what constituted a homosexual transgression – was an "instrument of power for the Nazi state to prepare for war."[85] Thus, in the emerging GDR, charges that consenting adult men had transgressed Paragraph 175 again required physical proof, which was not the case in the western zone. In West Berlin and the Federal Republic of Germany, the 1935 variant of Paragraph 175 was retained for several more years. However, in considering the second part of the code governing homosexuality – the section that criminalized bought sex and sex with minors (Paragraph 175a) – the Supreme Court of Berlin upheld the Nazi variant since it promoted "sexual integrity and thus the healthy development of the youth." As Günter Grau has argued elsewhere, when it came to safeguarding the sexual mores of young males, the East and West upheld similar images of respectability and moral endangerment.[86] While the collapse of the Reich set in motion changes in the process of identifying homosexual transgressions, Nazi-era attitudes about the protection of youth continued to influence the regulation of male prostitution in both Germanys.[87]

Policing a Divided City

If the legislation governing same-sex sexuality was confusing, so too was the prospect of policing a divided cityscape like Berlin, where travel between sectors was relatively unencumbered until the building of the Wall. Here, male prostitution flourished. A problem affecting larger urban centers generally, according to Klaus Ulrich Klemens in his 1967 analysis of extant criminal case files, West Berlin's insecure geographical and political status, not to mention the pull of its diverging economic system, made it a particularly alluring site for johns interested in a quick pick-up.[88] The stationing of Allied troops in the vicinity also added a sense of allure, with liaisons often occurring in the bushes near the train stations placed closest to military bases.[89] Although sector boundaries posed challenges to the enforcement of legal norms, border checks did not hamper same-sex desiring men from finding available trade. In fact, the vagaries of legal statutes, together with the mishmash administration of the city's central and suburban train stations, may have actually facilitated contacts.

Added to this was the fact that in the initial postwar years at least, the homosocial mapping of the city's male sex trade resisted the rigidity of ideological borders. It was also not unusual for police in the Soviet sector to ensnare West Berliners buying sex there. Conversely, boys traveled over the sector boundaries frequently in the 1950s to service the needs of gentlemen in the Western half of the city. As late as 1955, the Reinickendorf welfare agency in northwest Berlin noted that it had over 50 boys listed in their register with eastern addresses, many of whom wound their way through the court system and into one of West Berlin's youth jails and remand facilities.[90] Despite the increasingly hostile climate among the Allies in civic affairs, to say nothing of the separation of the police force and mayoral office along strict ideological lines, some degree of cooperation existed between the eastern and western police. One night in May 1948, for instance, a police task force conducting a raid at Zoo Station in the heart of the British sector asked Horst D., an 18-year-old resident of the western district of Neukölln, why he was frequenting this "known hangout for homosexuals and rent boys." Since Horst had "neither identification nor money on him," he was sent to the local police station for questioning, whereupon it was discovered that he was wanted on charges of assault and robbery at two eastern sector precincts.[91] With little fanfare or opposition, he was promptly sent eastward for processing. While the police might cooperate in the name of public morals, the general population tended to be less emboldened to act, however, especially if crossing the internal boundary was required for testimony. By 1950, one year after the establishment of not just two separate city governments but two independent states, the political climate had changed so much that two West Berlin witnesses in a case against Hans L. refused to cross into East Germany to attend the young man's hearing. Although it might seem like an act of defiance, and perhaps it was, the fact that one of the men was responsible for initiating the charges suggests either that he was pressed into making his claim by the police – which would not be surprising considering this was a tactic inherited from earlier regimes – or that he had tangible misgivings about the possibility of leaving East Berlin territory once he crossed into it.[92] While Berliners crossed the boundary daily for work and pleasure, the permeability of the border was not something one took for granted in dealings with the regulatory apparatus.

Although people in the gay scene continued to imagine the city as a geographic whole, as a series of strolls, scenes, bars, parks, and meeting places where same-sex contact was possible, encounters with the courts made the political divide more palpable, as Horst's example makes clear. It was here too that the divergent applications of Paragraph 175 in East and West Berlin jurisprudence were concretized in sentences, social policy, and welfare initiatives to promote what authorities believed were more healthful sexual practices. The situation befalling Otto N. provides an interesting example of the mental mapping of the gay scene and the ways in which men and youths confronted the limits to mobility and sexual expression through the process of regulation. The tale of his escapades one evening in 1951 begins in the file of a West Berlin Youth Bureau (*Jugendamt*) caseworker. One night Otto picked up a young man at the pissoir near the Friedrichstrasse train station, a known node within the East Berlin cruising scene. He recognized the boy was a prostitute by the way he had carried himself in the station, making particular reference to how he sauntered, and the forthright way in which he returned his glance. Approaching the young man, he carefully negotiated the terms of exchange and made the necessary arrangements for sex, taking a moment to guarantee the boy's age of majority. Settling on a price of five East German marks, they struck a deal quickly and, we are told, fulfilled its terms. Later that same night, when their paths crossed a second time at a local movie house – another place of concern to the vice squad as a site of intemperance for gay and straight Berlin youth – the pair took advantage of the chance encounter and arranged another rendezvous. Leaving the eastern sector this time, they drove to the West Berlin district of Neukölln in search of a particular underground bar. At some point in the evening, they befriended another man, and all three made plans to reunite later that morning once Otto's wife had left for work. Although he avoided his spouse's suspicions initially, in time (although we are not privy as to how), Otto fell into the dragnet of the West Berlin police force and had his case heard in front of the Tiergarten district court (*Amtsgericht*) in the famed Moabit courthouse.[93]

With prior convictions in both the Nazi and postwar years, Otto was in a legal bind.[94] In a gambit to secure a lighter sentence, he implored the court to understand that he had been under the impression that in the eastern sector, where the pick-up occurred, their action (mutual masturbation) was no longer a crime since the rules of evidence were different in East Germany. Demonstrating an amazing amount of legal knowledge, what Otto did not realize at the time was that although the rules of evidence differed in the GDR, the actual arrest took place in the West. Of greater significance was that the boy he cruised was still considered a minor according to West German law. What began as an innocent pick-up at the Friedrichstrasse train station resulted in another six-month prison sentence.

Although an aura of order surrounds this faded file, whose yellowed statements are neatly preserved in Berlin's city archive, confusion is its hallmark. Among the many insights it provides into the postwar scene, chief among them is the tenacity of same-sex desiring men in taking on the befuddled regulatory apparatus. This included the care with which men sought out contacts at the train station and the knowledge many displayed of the legal system and its statutes on age of majority legislation. More telling is the way it underscores that political division had not yet imprinted itself on citizens, who still conceived of the city according to their own compasses. Just as it was common to travel across sector boundaries for a film or a night out at a local bar, so too might men crisscross the sector borders for liaisons and sexual encounters. In this instance too, the intra-German border came to matter most when Otto attempted to transgress social boundaries in the name of pleasure, access, and desire, moving away from the relative anonymity of transit space to a bar, his apartment, and a park. There, the vice squad and youth bureau caseworkers could intervene more directly in policing the boundaries not just of public and private space, but of age, class, and gender as well. Despite the worsening relations between the two Germanys, where one might imagine greater unanimity of policy and procedure, in actual practice police, welfare, and court authorities held considerable power over when and where jurisdictional lines of demarcation might be enforced, suggesting flexibility as well as rigidity in the spatial enforcement of social and sexual mores. Where there was no debate was in reading train station spaces as uniquely gendered sites of barter, encounter, transgression, and exchange.

Gendering Deviance

If legislating and policing behavior was a complicated matter in postwar Berlin, the gendering of deviance further hampered enforcement. Within the reorganization of the police department after 1945, as in the pre-Nazi legislation governing sexual crimes, male and female prostitution were understood as distinctly different infractions requiring different forms of regulation.[95] We see this in the administrative units assembled to deal with the train station trade. From its headquarters on Dircksenstrasse, only steps away from the Alexanderplatz U- and S-Bahn station, police chief Paul Markgraf swiftly reassembled the vice squad to investigate crimes against morality (*Sittlichkeitsdelikte*).[96] Task force MII/4 of the criminal police, staffed with two detectives and a rotating number of lower-ranking officers, as well as occasional policewomen (*Weibliche Kripo* or *WKP*), was charged with investigating cases involving seduction, rape, molestation, incest, and same-sex prostitution. Theft, sabotage, youth crime, and female prostitution were left to other units, reflecting the different juridical importance placed on these crimes.[97] Although female prostitution compromised the standards of healthful morality, it was linked to health (venereal disease transmission) and poverty and not to aggressive male sexual desire, providing a degree of cover for male prostitutes and the johns soliciting their services.

The invisibility of male prostitution is reflected in the historiography, where little exists on the plight of train station boys despite great interest in recent years about the impact of the war on women's sexual vulnerability. Part of this oversight is owed to the sources, part to the way in which the field of women's and gender studies has developed, and part to the emphasis within the gay and lesbian movement of the 1970s and 1980s to foreground the history of activism and organization over the eroticization of the street.[98] The diarists whose eyewitness accounts helped define this chaotic period as the "hour of the woman" were conscious of the gender imbalance. After all, those raped en masse following the Russian entry into Berlin were women; the faces that Allied authorities saw waiting in line for rations were typically female; and the survivors who worked to clear Berlin's debris-congested streets were "rubble women" (*Trümmerfrauen*).[99] And in all four corners of Berlin, it was women who assumed sole responsibility for those under their care. Although male prostitution had a long history in the red light district of the prewar Friedrichstadt, and cottaging was commonplace in train station urinals long before the war, little information has surfaced regarding the plight of young men outside of the narratives of returning soldiers.[100]

Perhaps owing to the overwhelming number of women selling themselves for food at war's end, the separate legal statutes for male and female prostitution, the widespread public health crisis posed by women and venereal disease (VD), and the lack of a contemporary discourse for speaking about male sexual vulnerability, the invisibility of rent boys nevertheless belies the fact that they often stood cheek by jowl with women in the city's solicitation zones. In effect, the feminization of street and train station space sheltered their activity, rendering them invisible. In a national conference on postwar criminality in 1959, a well-respected West Berlin police officer went so far as to make the audacious claim that there were few to no hustlers working city streets in the early aftermath of the war.[101] Despite the misgivings of some authorities, hustlers were very much on the radar of police and welfare workers, only often their visibility was linked to gendered notions of deviance and divergent understandings of masculinity. And while they had not shared the experience of mass rape, there may have been other points of convergence in the sexual histories of young women and men. As an example, some boys claimed they fell into the trade after being initiated into "abnormal sex" by members of the occupation forces.[102] And hustlers, like female prostitutes, were thought to be attracted to the "easy life," languishing about, smoking cigarettes, and spending what little money they had on cheap amusements. Still, they presented a different set of challenges to police. Did they choose this life out of necessity or was this a reflection of ingrained desire and orientation?[103] Did they merit society's protection or its punishment? In developing a viable policy for the surveillance and arrest of those boys suspected of willfully "polluting themselves," the Berlin police navigated a path lined with contradictions.[104] Despite the confusion surrounding boys' particular predicament, the enforcement of moral norms often began and ended at the train station.

Since it was commonly accepted that venereal disease originated with women, rent boys were spared the humiliation of night raids, where the mere presence of women congregating at the station could be grounds for forced VD testing. Of course, not all girls emerging from the underground or chatting on street corners were "on the make," as a raid near the Rathaus Steglitz metro made all too clear when the police forced four 15- and 16-year-old girls to undergo a mandatory pelvic exam. One of them, it was later confirmed, was in fact a virgin (*Unbescholten*) as she had claimed, while another was a survivor of Soviet rape.[105] These measures may have provoked outrage, but as one police officer was quoted as saying, in the divided city "it is impossible to differentiate between good and bad girls" since even those from good homes have "discovered their bodies as a means by which to live an easy life.[106] While simply being female was grounds for intervention, hustlers typically had to be caught in flagrante delicto or, at the very least, acting in an aggressively "rent boy-like fashion" (*nach Strichjungenart*). This differential portrayal of debasement was predicated on a variety of factors, chief of which was the American command's influence over the West Berlin police force in regulating amoral troop activity by aiding in the crackdown on female prostitution. But it also betrays the extent to which train station space itself was imagined, at least by police, as a uniquely heteronormative place of contact and exchange. Hustlers may have dotted the landscape, but unlike girls, station boys had to go out of their way to arouse suspicion, remaining hidden in plain sight. The mere presence of women laying claim to public space, unaccompanied or in groups, after dark and even during daylight hours, almost always garnered the immediate response of the police. In postwar Berlin, public space was broken, dangerous, disorderly, and unruly, and frequently gendered female. The mapping of the space as heterosexual by police provided boys and their customers welcome cover while causing undue harm and stress to Berlin women seeking to go about their daily business. In this symbolic ordering of the space, the attempt to remove a disorderly sexual presence from the scene caused police to inadvertently privilege the public boy over the public woman. But as we will soon see, this was not about the essential differences between men and women, but spoke more to the mutually reinforcing structure of space and sexuality, and the important role of gender in definitions of deviance. Although station boys benefited from their social status, some male prostitutes – especially those who appeared by virtue of their gait, gesture, and appearance as effeminate – were themselves rendered more public than other boys. Sharing a gender coding with women and girls, effeminate boys engaged in the sex trade were a risk to postwar social mores. More significant still, as we will explore in Chapter 4, they posed challenges to homophile activists hoping to secure the repeal of Nazi-era anti-sodomy laws still in force in West Berlin.

A 1946 report of one spot check conducted at the bunker neighboring the Schlesischer station in Berlin's eastern sector provides a case in point. In her log entry, Officer Behr of the WKP noted that the women's detachment had found six youths blocking the entrance to the facility. All were sent to the precinct for processing, but the brothers Georg and Gerhard B. and a friend described only as S. were set free after a short interview. Rolf R., not quite 15 years old, was transferred to the youth welfare station at Dircksenstrasse since he was homeless, underage, and without either a ration card or identification. The two girls in the group, likewise without identification and in the exact same situation, were sent to police detachment MII/3 where they were held on suspicion of prostitution. One of the pair was even forced to undergo a gynecological exam, known to be invasive, embarrassing, and often quite painful.[107]

Officer Behr's log entry outlines the process in place to deal with wayward youth. Those found without appropriate identification were automatically sent to youth services if they appeared underage and seemed "endangered." Girls would more likely than not be forced to submit to VD testing since in the eyes of police they were regarded as already compromised. The boys could just have easily been guilty of amoral proclivities since the culture of the train station was renowned for producing such behavior.[108] That they were not investigated further illustrates both the differential understanding of risk associated with the boys' situation and the existence of a gendered double standard. The incongruity of enforcement strategies in this example reflects deeply entrenched societal notions of what was at stake in allowing "asocial" behavior to continue unchecked. While girls were forced to submit to humiliating pelvic examinations in the name of protecting public health, boys, likewise imperiled by conditions, were simply sent to crisis centers to help them cope with the harshness of their social situation, which police believed had forced them to the train station in the first place.

Although the police report never explicitly acknowledged the possibility, Rolf R.'s profile fitted that of the many hustlers who plied their trade either on the train station platform or in its surrounding bunkers and ruins: he was underage, homeless, and without identification and any means of financial support. Doubtless many boys preferred the company of peers over their depressing home lives, although the "freedom" offered by life on the street was hardly carefree. Many youths were unable to obtain residence permits or ration cards, especially if their origins lay elsewhere in the old Reich. Had he not yet turned to prostitution, he might have done soon. Without the support of families, train station sex was often one of the only ways to earn a semblance of a living and word of this possibility spread swiftly through the city's informal network of itinerant and homeless youths, who flocked in steady streams to the stations to try their luck.[109]

As the ranks of "asocial" boys began to swell, and officials noticed they were doing more than taking temporary shelter in train station waiting rooms, transit police appealed to the uniformed officers to intervene more directly. As they did with female prostitutes, they began the process of scrutinizing deviant behavior according to an evolving image of what constituted "normal" masculine identity, which the existence of boy prostitutes actively belied. No longer invisible, hustlers were considered to be dangerous because their presumed effeminacy undermined "productive citizenship" by jeopardizing their own involvement as future contributors to the state. As we will see in Chapter 5, they would be rounded up and sent to youth facilities where they were schooled in a trade, taught how to find work, and sent back into the world with a healthful respect for productive labor so as to better contribute to rebuilding the state.

While police and public health authorities were overwhelmingly concerned with the plight of fallen girls, train station boys failed to garner the same notoriety. Yet that did not mean they were ignored completely. To control male prostitution in divided Berlin, police redoubled their efforts by focusing primarily on Zoo Station, which would emerge after

1961 as both the central transportation nexus for West Berlin and home of its high-profile drug-dealing network.[110] One of the two main train stations near the Kurfürstendamm, this area had gained notoriety in the Weimar era in what Austrian novelist Stefan Zweig referred to in his memoir *The World From Yesterday* as "the Babylon of the world," where "powdered and rouged young men sauntered...and every high school boy wanted to earn some money."[111] Zoo Station was also a major station stop for the city's main U- and S-Bahn lines as well as the hub for all trains connecting West Berlin to West Germany proper. Significantly positioned close to the nexus of the British and American occupation sectors and within walking distance of no fewer than three cinema houses, it was the gateway to entertainment and adventure for an eclectic and mixed crowd of Berliners, expats, and occupation soldiers trading on the cachet of the now not-so-new West End. Given the GDR's control over the S-Bahn network and de facto jurisdiction over Zoo Station – since it was the East German *Deutsche Reichsbahn* concern that serviced all long-distance travel in and out of the city – Allied and West Berlin authorities were effectively prohibited from policing these spaces. But this did not preclude West Berlin police forces from working together with East Berlin authorities to deal with the problem of station sex.

In the eastern sector, where prostitution was seen as a holdover of capitalism, police patrolled three stations where the trade was most visible, corresponding in large part to the prewar red light districts. Alexanderplatz and Friedrichstrasse were well positioned within the pre-Hitler cultural imaginary, while Ostkreuz in the district of Friedrichshain was the main hub of the East Berlin suburban train network and hence a site of frenetic activity that lent itself well to cruising.[112] In combating the trade, officers were surprisingly well schooled in what to look for. Despite the replacement of Nazi officers with new recruits, the divided police force was well versed in the signs of solicitation and knowledge of where to look for illegal activity, like the nineteenth-century urinals adjacent to most stations. In pairs, they would walk first through the station concourse and out amidst the neighboring streets and alleyways, all the while watching for signs of suspicious behavior, which they viewed in explicitly gendered terms. Although most studies of street hustlers suggest they came overwhelmingly from the working class, and as such bore the markers of their social identity, the rent boys that stood out to Berlin authorities were those that they claimed "gadded about" with an elaborate gait, including effeminate gestures and a lingering gaze.[113] Settling on a set of suspects, they would follow them into the neighboring parks or bombed-out apartment blocks where the sexual act typically took place. In their activity logs, they boasted in ritualistic detail how they crouched down and settled in before identifying themselves to the suspects. Using techniques of surveillance honed and perfected during the Nazi period, they strained to gain the best perspective, often turning "on [their] flashlight in order to get a better look."[114]

While women garnered most attention for their defiant claim to public status and space, police understood boys' endangerment through images of passivity and lapsed masculinity. But concentrating their attention on signs of effeminacy could cut both ways. It focused attention on a certain caliber of youth while shielding those who failed to exhibit signs of "advanced rent boy like behaviour." There was the fact, too, that not all boys on the make displayed effeminate masculinities. In this early part of the postwar scene, as Clayton Whisnant has documented, there was a wide array of gender performances, with up-market bar boys presenting themselves in a more feminine manner, including the use of make-up, hair gel, and aggressively feminine gesturing.[115] If not all rent boys were obviously effeminate, why did police and social workers pigeonhole them in this way? On one level, if spaces of transit were understood in strictly heteronormative terms, it is not surprising that boy prostitutes might be positioned on par with station girls in this way since they too were increasingly visible parts of this nexus of barter and exchange that serviced male sexual desire. But there is a material side to the story as well. Social service workers and vice squad police were motivated to intervene out of fear that station boys had been emasculated not by the scene but by the war, whose impact was felt in the development of a deviant sexual appetite. Put simply, what might appear to be a simple act of quiescence or experimentalism could be quickly transformed into outright desire for the sinful pleasures of gay sex. In their reports, social workers pointed to a variety of warning signs related to the breakdown of the nuclear family, one of the hallmarks of societal decline in the aftermath of the war. The lack of fatherly presence or the smothering attention of a doting mother was a recipe for disaster. One mother accused of coddling her son argued euphemistically in her defense that she had developed a particularly strong bond with her son given that "together they had lived through the difficult experience of the Russian invasion." Further hinting at the shared experience of trauma and possibly rape, the boy's father went on record to comment that since that time he had failed to enjoy conjugal relations with his wife, and that this, together with a worsening relationship generally, made it especially difficult to parent their troubled child. Seeking explanations for their son's transgressions, both the boy's parents and the various caseworkers working his file made a link between the emasculating impact of mass violence and the development of healthy adolescent sex drives.[116] East German enodcrinologist Günter Dörner would win a German Medal of Honor for his life's work, which included arguments about the trauma of the bombing campaign, which he believed brought about such a significant hormonal impact in utero that women gave birth to a preponderance of effeminate and homosexual youths in the postwar years.[117] As a cauldron of gender negotiation and trade, the train station was an important locus for discussion of the lingering impact of past transgressions on postwar lives. More importantly, it positioned gender as a uniquely important category of socio-spatial notions of deviance.

In this highly fraught social field, it increasingly took very little to set the wheels of regulation in motion. Since train stations were targeted as sexual hotspots, any boys "acting in a rent boy type way" were monitored from the moment they entered the field of vision: as they traversed the concourse, stood at the entrances, bummed cigarettes, and offered their services for change. Officers were careful to make note of their activities since this "was the main meeting space for homosexually inclined people."[118] In other words, the train station, par definition, was a space of movement and fluctuation; when the normative pace of circulation was challenged by a boy helping older men with their luggage, leaning up against a wall chain smoking, or carrying on an extended conversation with an occupation soldier, this behavior was read as a sign of endangerment and imminent vice, disrupting the tepid equilibrium of heteronormative transit space.

Although hustlers might be picked off for lingering and lounging about, they could also be quite mobile, traveling at a moment's notice from the station across the city to a café, nightspot, or apartment at a john's request. Since they were already close to the transportation network, they could easily hop on a train and travel a few station stops away to complete a transaction beyond the prying eyes of police. This mobility might even serve more sinister purposes, allowing them to rob a client or abscond with his valuables. Carl A.'s pick-up hinted at the prospect of further intimacy but failed to return with the vegetables he went to fetch for dinner.[119] The reliability of the train station for quick and easy sex did not always translate into worry-free transactions of a love unbound.

Policing Trade

While efforts to contain female prostitution and the spread of venereal disease involved joint efforts by the police and the state health office, with occasional help from the Allied power most affected, male prostitution remained the domain of the local police, who received support from youth services. As the first contact that rent boys and johns had with the legal system, the police possessed broad discretion in determining what situations warranted further investigation. Moreover, in recounting the unfolding of events, the police also played an active role in constructing what counted as criminal conduct.

For officers in the field, determining what constituted a criminal offense was a highly subjective act – made more so by the ambiguities of Paragraph 175a. Depending upon the nature of the transgression, who was involved, and how much the officers had in fact witnessed, boy prostitutes and johns could expect anything from having an on-the-spot interview to being arrested and taken to the station house for clarification and processing. In most scenarios, police would force youths to come to the precinct simply for exhibiting advanced signs of "rent boy-like" behavior; but they would release johns on their own recognizance despite overwhelming evidence (in one case the presence of semen and a disheveled appearance). Thus train station boys could expect different treatment than so-called "established" homosexuals, who were sometimes sympathetically viewed as "afflicted" by their sexual persuasion.

Despite its appearance of uniformity, the surveillance process could be implemented quite flexibly. When Gerhard Z. entered a bombed-out building on Georgenstrasse with 17-year-old Karl-Heinz S. after a rendezvous at the Friedrichstrasse train station, he was unaware that two officers on foot patrol had followed them. On that night in early June 1948, Gerhard and Karl-Heinz aroused suspicion since the complex they sought was, according to police, "often used by homosexuals and call-boys for unnatural sex."[120] But officers S. and W. missed catching the suspects in the act, having startled the two before they could begin mutually masturbating. After checking both men's papers, the police admitted in their report that they had little evidence to go on. Despite the lack of physical proof, Gerhard Z. opted to accompany the officers to the station "to explain his actions" since he was married and wanted to ensure that his case would be handled with the utmost discretion. It is doubtful Gerhard was ever sentenced since the "intention" of having sex with a hustler was not technically a crime under Paragraph 175a, at least as it was interpreted in the East. However, the hustler might have been detained because offering himself for the "purpose of abuse" was grounds for intervention.

In a similar case involving an encounter between an off-duty East Berlin homicide detective and a known prostitute, the evidence was sufficient enough to cast doubt on the officer's innocence but not adequate to sustain a charge. Having struck up a conversation with 14-year-old Fred V. in the street near the Friedrichstrasse station, Werner W. invited him to a nearby bar for schnapps, beer, and a bite to eat. Using the same defense as Kurt R. across the border in the district of Wilmersdorf, who argued he was virtually forced into a sexual liaison after missing his train home, the Friedrichstrasse hustler claimed that once they had finished drinking, the trains had stopped running, causing both to search for a hotel room to sleep off the imbibed spirits.[121] On the way, they ran into the back courtyard of a ruined building in order to urinate. It was at this time, in the safety of the ruins, Fred claimed, that Werner touched his penis before placing it in his mouth. The boy purportedly pushed him aside, ran onto the street, and yelled for the attention of two officers on foot patrol who swooped in to make an arrest.

At the police station, the police interviewed both Werner W. and Fred V. in an attempt to sort out their stories. The boy's particulars were already in the card index of known prostitutes, another carryover of imperial policing practices, and no doubt he had most likely offered himself in exchange for food and shelter. But how guilty was Werner W.? A seasoned officer, who had been a member of the force since 1946, Werner W. underscored his "normal" orientation ("ich bin normal veranlagt") by repeatedly mentioning his pregnant fiancée. Unlike in the Nazi period, where the circumstances would justify a charge, the arresting officers felt the need for physical evidence to corroborate the boy's claim and returned to the scene the next day after rounding up a chemist to conduct an examination of the rubble for traces of semen. Sadly for their case, rain the night before had washed away any trace of evidence. Regardless of the fact that their encounter seemed to fit the pattern of most interactions between rent boy and john, not to mention the damning nature of the boy's statement, without physical proof Werner's guilt remained unproven.[122] While Werner W. was ultimately released, the 14-year-old was sentenced to no less than two years in a youth home, with the possibility of being sent away for an indefinite amount of time if he remained hostile to "re-education."[123] Paradoxically, a law originally envisioned as protecting an innocent youth from the advances of a corrupt adult targeted the youth for more extreme discipline. In Fred V.'s case, seduction was not a factor since he was a hustler.

Obviously, it was not the function of the police to judge which suspect should receive what sentence. But the police had to know who and what represented the greater threat to public and private order so as not to squander valuable time in court. Although their actions might vary according to the situation, they were generally swift to combat perceived transgressors. When Werner P. and Karl-Heinz H. entered a destroyed building along the river Spree so that Karl-Heinz could earn his bus fare home, police intervened and questioned both suspects, claiming that they had acted suspiciously near the Friedrichstrasse station. Sixteen-year-old Karl-Heinz answered every question asked of him, including how he and Werner had searched for a quiet spot in order to masturbate uninterrupted. Werner P. was implicated by the youth's confession, and as a result his counterclaims were dismissed out of hand. Interestingly, it was the youth, Karl-Heinz, who was taken to the station for questioning; after making a note of his particulars, the police saw fit to release Werner on site.[124]

As two of the cases above illustrate, johns who followed their pick-ups from the train station to the anonymity of the ruins were often treated differently than the boy prostitute whose favors they had solicited. Did such discrimination connote a different estimation of guilt and transgression? Was the treatment of johns more lenient than that of boy prostitutes? In the police reports, this is often not clear. To be sure, it was a relief to a john not to have to proceed to the precinct to clarify his story on the night of the incident in question. And he could still expect to have his address registered by the police, which ensured that his story would be investigated further and that he might receive a summons to contest the charge in court at a later date. Yet, as these cases demonstrate, both the train station space and the sites of transaction were differentially enforced according to gender in terms of the different ways in which female and male prostitutes were treated, but also across the categories of age, status, and class.

In all these cases, we see the enhanced role police played in teasing out the "truth" in otherwise complicated investigations. They relentlessly pursued suspects before any crime had been committed, created files on known hustlers, and handled situations differently based upon suspects' status. Although both East and West Germany upheld the Nazi variant of Paragraph 175a in order to protect vulnerable young men from the perils of seduction, these cases suggest that by the late 1940s, the vision of victimization embodied in the law rarely shaped the actions of the police. Instead, the police intervened willy-nilly in the city's semi-public spaces to control wayward youth. Without visual or physical evidence of intercourse-like behavior, johns might be able to negotiate their temporary release, but rent boys rarely had such an opportunity. Although the

boundaries between East and West might be porous in terms of policing the male sex trade, once rent boy transgressions moved away from
the street and station house and into the halls of justice, the borders in
question were no longer physical or jurisdictional but temporal as well
as ideological, and they hinged on notions of good citizenship.

New Alliances, Strange Bedfellows

Well into the 1950s, jurists, sociologists, psychologists, and biologists
devoted endless hours investigating the malaise of the postwar generation and its propensity for crime. In their efforts to understand
homosexuality and purchased sex, postwar legal reformers in both
Germanys inevitably drew upon pre-Nazi discourses. While a longstanding argument over endogenous and exogenous factors continued to
animate the postwar discussion of male sexual deviance, proponents
on both sides often marked members of the urban underclass like train
station youth as criminogenically predisposed to asociality. But male
prostitution posed particular risks to society as well. Their criminality
might be passed on to future generations if left unchecked, their actions
jeopardized sexological arguments for decriminalizing Paragraph 175 by
sullying the image of the respectable homosexual, and their presence
raised fears that exposure to same-sex activity threatened the development of "healthful" orientation. Rarely, if ever, was the rent boys'
involvement in the sex trade understood as a protean search for community or intimacy among same-sex desiring men. Fractured and transitory
like the space it occupied, cruising and train station sex was an unlikely
source of positive identity formation for homophile organizations eager
to acquire respectability and rights. What at first represented the evils
of privation and postwar chaos proved through its staying power to be
a larger problem of urban life more generally, a force so potent that
neither German state could solve it solely through regulation.

   If police and courts struggled to deal with the problem of male
homosexuality, station pick-ups occupied an even more dubious position among homophile groups, members of which were under great
pressure not to confirm stereotypes of the preying homosexual child
molester propagated most recently by the Nazi regime.[125] Unlike *enfant
terrible* photographer Herbert Tobias, who took erotically charged photographs of train station boys in the sanctuary of his Grünewald
apartment after pick-ups in western sector locales, in official publications and friendship magazines homophile groups took great pains to
distance themselves from station lads in the quest to establish a basis

Figure 3.3   Photograph of young boy by Herbert Tobias, untitled, 1950s Berlin.
Photo credit: © Estate of Herbert Tobias/SODRAC (2011).

for acceptance away from the stench of the street (Figure 3.3). In fact, most of the imagery in the Swiss homophile journal *Der Kreis* (The Circle) revolved around the fascination with working men and youths; in these magazines nowhere was the jouissance of Tobias's transgressive erotic imaginary to be found.[126] This carefully crafted closetedness and appeal to respectability, deemed self-loathing by the protean gay rights movement, was a necessary position if they were to lobby the West German government for decriminalization. It is not coincidental that one of the most scathing indictments of male prostitution came from Botho Laserstein, an outspoken jurist, critic of the Adenauer regime, and defense attorney in Paragraph 175 cases.[127] In his quasi-documentary account of a typical street boy in postwar Dusseldorf, Laserstein emphasized the immorality of male prostitution. Out of a pastiche of former clients' experiences he reconstructed a cultural milieu within which innocent homosexual men were taken advantage of by cheeky young boys on the make (*auf dem Strich*). In this sordid underworld, instead of confirmed homosexuals corrupting heretofore innocent youth, gangs of station boys plotted blackmail. Interestingly, by representing Karl D.'s entry into the male sex trade at the hands of an uncle's unwelcome advances, Laserstein inadvertently reinforced the seduction motif, bringing him in league with conservative opponents who willfully used this fear to stymie efforts to decriminalize homosexuality.[128] Like many progressives before him, most notably the anchor of the pre-Hitler anti-sodomy campaign, Magnus Hirschfeld, Laserstein claimed it was greed, not sexual orientation, that induced the fall of Karl and other hustlers, whose depravity made them the "worst kind of criminal there is."[129] As long as consensual sex among men was criminalized, Laserstein argued, the train station would continue to yield new clients, thereby putting honest, law-abiding men unnecessarily in harm's way.[130]

By pathologizing rent boys in his quest to see the abolishment of Paragraph 175, Laserstein revealed their precarious and sometimes contradictory position within the West German legal reform movement. While themselves the product of the continued criminalization of an otherwise harmless activity, they in turn made criminals out of otherwise upstanding citizens, and for this behavior they deserved little sympathy.[131] From both progressives advancing the protection of homosexuals and conservatives advocating the protection of society at large, station boys received little sympathy and much contempt. As in the period before Hitler, talk of their victimization was minimal.[132]

As they dealt with the growing pace of homosexual infractions in the 1950s, East and West Berlin officials seized upon different parts of the prewar argument, drawing from diverging discourses to substantiate the city's regulation of intergenerational sex. In the steady procession of cases that passed through the district courts on both sides of the boundary, defendants and prosecutors, judges and witnesses, party officials and welfare officers armed with the most recent definitions of abnormality and deviance picked up where the police had left off in redefining the contours of aberrant masculinity and train station cruising.[133]

Because a hustler's confession (*Geständnis*) was central to the process of laying charges and establishing a john's guilt, it is understandable that in court a john would elect to debate the veracity of his accuser's claim.[134] Given the growing popular and professional belief in the male prostitute's moral depravity, the criminal climate within which he circulated, and his relatively low social position, many johns defended themselves by attempting to discredit their accusers in open court and by arguing that mitigating circumstances needed to be taken into account. In making their defense, they made crafty use of legal maneuvers already embedded in the system.[135]

The case against Horst K., a writer, who picked up a hustler at the above-ground Savignyplatz train station in posh Charlottenburg, a stone's throw from the Kurfürstendamm, illustrates this system of negotiation. After they returned to Horst's apartment for sex, the boy promptly demanded a 50 DM payment, threatening to destroy his host's apartment, give him a good thrashing, and report him to police if his demands were not met. When he received only a portion of payment, the hustler went straight to the police and placed a charge against Horst K. At the precinct, despite his own obvious victimization, Horst confessed to his "crime."[136] Nevertheless, seeking retribution, he decided to contest the charge and forced the process to proceed to court.

In December 1956, without counsel or evidence to support his story, Horst K. appeared in court to outline his situation. Surprisingly the presiding judge took his plight into consideration. Horst's compliance with the police, confession of guilt, lack of a previous criminal record, and upstanding social position all contributed to the judge's sentence of a fine of 100 DM instead of the proposed 10-day prison sentence. The judge recognized that, although an illicit transaction had in fact occurred, the partner was obviously a rent boy and the deed did not offend public sensibilities since it took place in private.[137] Still, sex with a minor, whether out of doors or in the privacy of one's own home, remained a matter of the state, belying the supposed sanctity of the right to privacy in matters of same-sex desire.

In their pleas for leniency, rarely did defendants claim outright innocence or recant earlier confessions; they sensed that admitting some responsibility was the most likely way to secure favor with the presiding judge. In reconstructing their stories to present mitigating circumstances, defendants chose among several different options. Some bravely proclaimed that they were gay and had never had sex with a woman; others employed the "drunk defense" to account for their momentary straying from the straight and narrow; some relied upon marital status as evidence that theirs was a one-time homosexual dalliance; others drew attention to their military experience to explain their actions. If defendants could forge a link between their sexual transgression and their war experiences, the court was even more inclined to grant extenuating circumstances. Although sex reformers and jurists pointed to the homoerotism of all-male environments like the army, prison, and youth-care facilities, defendants rarely acknowledged this aspect of their experience as fostering an interest in same-sex relationships. Instead, they professed that injuries and illnesses sustained in combat or imprisonment made them unable to forge "healthy" relationships with women, sending them to the train station for comfort and release.

When Gerhard P., a 48-year-old laborer, was accused of having sex 15 to 18 times with an underage partner, he offered his wartime experiences in mitigation. It was less the sexual perversions Gerhard "got used to" as a Soviet captive and more the chronic lung condition he developed upon his release that made physical contact with women impossible. Gerhard was accorded some lenience by the court due, in large part, to the belief that upwards of 15–20 percent of returning soldiers with extensive physical and psychological injuries were prone to homosexuality.[138] When his case was heard in the West Berlin criminal court (*Strafkammer*) in 1951, Paul W. offered a similar defense. After engaging in erotic conversation with 16-year-old Gerd W., Paul was accused of initiating an extended session of mutual masturbation. Since the boy accepted money for the transaction (he was after all in social services and met the profile of a rent boy), the court recognized that he too was an active participant and not simply a victim of seduction. To help understand the defendant's behavior, the court solicited a physician's assessment of Paul W.'s personality. The physician, Dr. Weimann, concluded that the laborer was an intelligent man, fully in control of his faculties. Despite an excessively close relationship with his mother, he had little contact with other women, due largely to injuries sustained during the war. Disgusted by the ugliness of his war wounds, the defendant had developed a kind of "cripple neurosis" (*Kruppelneurose*), which no woman could manage to understand. Based largely on this diagnosis, Paul W. was given the relatively light fine of 50 DM or 10 days in jail.[139]

In connecting their current crimes to their wartime experiences, both Gerhard P. and Paul W. were able to draw sympathy to themselves by evoking their war trauma.[140] They did so by relying on a particular image of masculinity as linked to responsible citizenship, honor in service, and personal sacrifice, thereby deflecting any thoughts of the boy's victimization. In these cases, the dangers of intergenerational homosexual sex were downplayed as the defendant's homosexual behavior was medicalized. The courts accepted implicitly some of the same arguments advanced by prominent sexologists of the day, who likewise advocated the repeal of Paragraph 175 by arguing that homosexuality should be treated by physicians and not the police.

As these West Berlin court cases demonstrate, the men accused of picking up train station youth could mitigate the consequences of their acts by drawing on a vision of masculinity that reflected the implicit heteronormativity of the day. Those charged with "hustler-like behavior," on the other hand, rarely escaped some form of incarceration. In cases involving underage youth, social workers made field notes about the cleanliness of a boy's home, his mother's employment status, the parents' emotional stability and, shockingly, even the regularity of conjugal relations. It could not be any clearer that social service investigations still assumed that delinquency was linked to conditions within the overburdened working-class household. These reports might have helped build a case for mitigating circumstances in the event that a youth came from a troubled home, but more often than not they served to confirm commonly held beliefs concerning the true source of depravity. This is certainly what occurred in the case against Peter S., whose advanced endangerment earned him a six-month sentence in a youth facility.[141]

For the boys arrested and tried in East Berlin's court across the boundary in the downtown district of Mitte, mitigating circumstances were even more of a rarity. Instead, the boys were the focus of a multilevel governmental investigation that employed a mixture of welfare and penal strategies geared toward the active promotion of socially useful behavior. Male prostitutes, like other delinquent youth deemed reluctant to contribute to the economic restructuring of the fledgling GDR state, were monitored by various agencies within the purview of the Ministry of People's Education (*Volksbildung*), whose mandate included monitoring children's aid and youth services in addition to promoting socialist principles in cultural affairs. Adolescents charged with crimes in youth court served their sentences in a variety of facilities, but it was another institutional space – the juvenile workhouse – that was considered to have the greatest potential to rehabilitate waywardness by promoting socialist morality through hard work.[142]

Claiming to encourage corrective education and communitarian values, these facilities combined social welfare and penal strategies to inculcate socialist values among the nation's youngest citizens. Not simply a throwback to Weimar-era rehabilitative policy, youth penal policy inherited significant Nazi-era measures as well.[143] Male prostitutes charged with plying their wares at the Friedrichstrasse train station, for example, were charged with transgressions under the general Criminal Code, as well as under the 1943 Nazi-amended Young Offender's Act (*Reichsjugendgesetz*). Eastern sector judges, interested in curbing aberrant sexual behavior among the urban underclass, had no problem employing the Nazi act to sentence the hustlers they deemed most depraved to unlimited sentences (*unbestimmte Dauer*) in one of the regions' youth work facilities.[144] Fred V., mentioned earlier, who had "fallen into homosexual circles at Zoo Station" before being arrested after his liaison with a member of the homicide police in East Berlin, was given a sentence of "no less than nine months and no more than two years," which he served at the workhouse in Neustrelitz in the surrounding province of Brandenburg and at a remand home in Berlin. His case bears a resemblance to a Nazi-era case against the hustler Alfred B., who in 1941 was likewise sentenced to an unlimited spate in a youth facility for rent boy activity around Alexanderplatz.[145] In both cases, the educative measures of the Young Offenders Act were lauded by the presiding judge as affording the youths the opportunity to avail themselves of rehabilitative measures, while still fulfilling the state's mandate to punish the offenses committed. Considering both boys came from troubled families, the redemptive role of hard work in modifying sexual behavior assured state officials of the imperatives at hand. The fact that this often took the form of agricultural labor meant that it might serve as an antidote to the perilous urbanity of reconstruction Berlin and its impact on boyhood sexuality. As with the internal boundaries in the divided city, temporal boundaries were not always as rigid as one might expect, and on the issue of fears over boyhood sexuality, there were considerable continuities in youth policy and policing.

Adopting Nazi-era penal measures and casting them in the language of prewar welfare reform, one thing the East German regulators did do was tread softly around any attendant biological assumptions. Although they certainly inherited these traditions, early GDR policy makers and practitioners emphasized social environment, class struggle, and material inequality as the most significant contributing factors to moral debasement and criminality. Biological explanations of homosexuality, such as those advocated by East German sexologist Dr. Rudolf Klimmer, while circulating in the West, made little impact on legal definitions of deviance in the GDR. Meanwhile, in a nation intent on rebuilding it is understandable that the East German emphasis was placed squarely on the redemptive role of hard work, especially in cases of sexual delinquency. Indeed, it many ways the GDR was much more aggressive than the West. So distrustful was the East Berlin court of biological explanatory models, however, that only after multiple suicide attempts and the intervention of two physicians was one trial judge persuaded to release an afflicted youth from his unlimited sentence.[146] While both East and West Berlin youth services may be seen as inheriting a similar strand of pre-1945 criminology – especially a Lombrosian-inspired analysis of prostitution as passive asociality – in resurrecting unlimited sentences under the guise of humanist social reform, as we will see again in Chapter 5, jurists in East Germany ensured that the state would play a more authoritarian role in resocializing wayward youth.

Despite East Germany's attempts to reform the Criminal Code in the early 1950s, the workers' uprising of 1953 caused the government to abandon its commitment to legal reform. After 1953, the Socialist Unity Party (SED) initiated a series of pro-natalist policies designed to spark early marriages and child rearing to help control the population decline and counteract the effect of the mass exodus of GDR citizens. Viewing homosexuality as a remnant of bourgeois society, the party opted to maintain the Nazi variant of Paragraph 175a, which criminalized same-sex sexuality in the name of the "healthful mores of the working people." West Germany's jettisoning of the Nazi version of Paragraph 175 likewise had little effect on the status of Paragraph 175a. Public debate on male promiscuity remained extremely contentious throughout the 1950s, and a steady stream of infractions made their way through West Berlin's judicial system. Despite increased sensitivity among some progressive jurists about the plight of street boys, a number of high-profile murders in Frankfurt and Berlin, where male prostitutes had actually killed their johns, ignited widespread condemnation of this criminal lifestyle.[147]

Whether a preemptive strike against the possible corruptibility of youth or a natural off-shoot of problematic legislation, the juridical engagement with train station prostitution demonstrates a parallel discourse of state intervention in both Berlins which focused on molding, shaping, and protecting respectable masculine behavior from perceived dangers lurking on the fringes.[148] Despite conflicting beliefs about the impact of so-called "unnatural desire" (*widernaturliche Unzucht*) on otherwise "healthful" and heterosexual maturation, rent boys, more so than their johns, posed a direct challenge to the reconstruction of a respectable German masculinity in the East as well as the West. While contemporary jurists might continue to employ the concept of guardianship to justify their treatment of them, in the mind of the postwar German public, station boys had become predators, not prey.

Among progressive-minded jurists and prominent sexologists, train station boys posed a direct challenge to arguments for decriminalization. While cruising remained a common feature of the scene, a source of excitement, adventure, and desire that literally knew no boundaries in divided Berlin, it remained a thorn in the side of reformers whose case for the extension of full citizenship rights had to be made within a climate of moral conservatism and inherited Nazi-era jurisprudence. With such little wiggle room, it is easy to understand why hustlers were continually vilified as undermining much-desired social gains. Given their closeness to the gutter, the urinal, and the transient atmosphere of the train station where many liaisons were negotiated, rent boys were themselves spatially marginalized within the gay scene. In this way, hustlers assumed many of the characteristics of the spaces they occupied: rootless, untrustworthy, disordered, and dangerous. At the same time, their presence in and around the city's train stations helped give meaning to these sites as liminal, transgressive, and corrupting, necessitating greater intervention on the part of the state to streamline errant masculinity. As we will see in Chapter 5, if the family could not be resurrected to safeguard the morals of East and West German youth, incarceral institutions would be required to buttress the work of home.

4
Bars, Cafés, Clubs

> The best thing... was the wonderful light which flickered over the boulevard. In the twenties there was much less bad and cheap lighting. There were candelabras on the Kurfürstendamm. The tree tops filtered the light and glimmering reflections of the advertisements gave the boulevard an intimate feel, which made every woman's face come alive. The streets did not thunder, they played music, a love song to the women of Berlin. In the twenties, Berlin was a gallant city.
>
> Franz Hessel, *Spazierien in Berlin*, 1929

> Should Berlin one day become a city again, in which we can and do live well, would it be opulent as in my dream, or would it be tolerable, peaceful, and upstanding? The main thing is... maybe... possibly... possibly really soon... that would be nice.
>
> Georg Holmsten, *Berliner Miniaturen:*
> *Großstadtmelodie Melodie*, 1946

In the 1920s, the pull of the Kurfürstendamm was unmistakable. Berliners reveled in the pageantry of the former corduroy road while émigrés and tourists, as many as 300,000 by 1923, flocked en masse to its concentration of trendy cafes, bookstores, dinner theaters, and *Schnellrestaurants* (quick cafeterias).[1] Before the currency stabilization undercut the rouble, forcing many of the well-heeled expats to head for Paris, so many Russian aristocrats, artists, and exiles buzzed around the neighborhood haunts "like flies to a lantern" that some critics, like Soviet pamphleteer Viktor Schlovsky, claimed it felt more like "Charlottengrad" than Charlottenburg.[2] Berlin's fashionable new suburb certainly was addictive. As the writer Christian Bouchholz put it, once one had a taste of its main street, "one feels changed…and cannot do without it."[3] The view from the street during the turbulent years of Germany's first republic was one of exuberance, youthful ambition, and opportunity – provided one had the financial means to partake in the frivolity. The Ku-Damm's smart stores, trendy cafés, and pulsing nightspots galvanized a decades-long shift away from the old money of staid Friedrichstadt toward the flashiness of the New West, the name given to the former towns and cities to the west of the Zoo Station that were amalgamated with the greater city of Berlin in 1920. The city's nouveaux riches were quick to purchase swanky pieds-à-terres in the streets that butted up against the famed boulevard. Their influence was profound, and the street lent its name to a whole new phraseology for describing the modern tastes, opportunities, and sensations on offer there (*Kurfürstendammgeschmack, Kurfürstendammgelegenheit, Kurfürstendammsensation*).[4] Twenty-five years later, the street continued to evoke memories of this storied past, only this generation of Russian visitors came as conquerors and not as artists in exile. Despite the sound of jazz emanating out of its underground bars, Ursula von Kardorff commented in her diary in September 20, 1945 that the Kurfürstendamm was nothing more than a mere backdrop to misery and destruction.[5] Lieutenant Colonel Byford-Jones was even more morose when he described the streets surrounding the once grand Hotel am Zoo. Instead of Weimar's glitz and glamour, all he found in the summer of 1945 was the omnipresent "smell of dampness, of charred remains, of thousands of putrefying bodies."[6]

Although the rubble would be cleared, the zoo reopened, the streets rendered passable, and order more or less restored, well into the 1950s a pall still hung over this central district that had been most affected by the street fighting and bombing. Indeed, the twilight years between war's end and the building of the Wall saw Berliners traverse city spaces still bearing marks of the recent fighting. More important than the physical renderings of the city were the mental maps of these bygone years, as citizen and visitor alike clung to images of the notorious 1920s, which they interpreted in various and sometimes contradictory ways. Often the city was cast as a wellspring of dynamism, a symbol of unending modernity, fluidity, and flux. Other times, it was a rogue space of revolution, inequality, and immorality. The bombing altered the physical topography of the city, making it possible "to see from Charlottenburg to Steglitz across the still flatter ruins of Wilmersdorf and Schöneberg."[7] As people scribbled chalk signs of life on building facades or chatted in line at neighborhood water fountains, the city they commiserated about was mired in contradictions, with some streets completely destroyed while others escaped harm entirely. Well before that fateful day in August 1961, when East Berlin's most famous transvestite Charlotte von Mahlsdorf claimed "everything changed," postwar Berlin continued to spark fascination and awe among the legions of citizens, visitors, and observers who struggled to find their place in the former capital.

As mid-twentieth-century *flâneurs*, crisscrossing their way through checkpoints and train stations, these authors of a new set of Berlin stories moved through space and time in the hopes of uncovering the contours of the once vibrant metropolis, leaving behind lively reportage about where decadence reigned and where it might still be found. These dispatches took various forms, from the quiet condemnation of an expat's personal reckoning to romantic *mise en scènes* of Europe's literati and breezy sketches of story-hungry journalists. These commentators continued the prewar tradition of urban spectatorship in document-ing the life and activities of Berlin's burghers, creating a picture of the unique features of a postwar landscape pockmarked with bullet-holes well into the 1950s[8] (Figure 4.1). Together with police logs, criminol-ogist accounts, and diary entries, they helped map what remained of this vibrant *Weltstadt* among the ruined buildings, bunker squats, movie

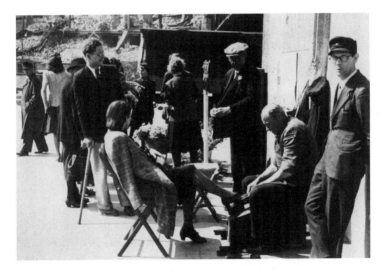

Figure 4.1 Postwar spring at the Zoo Station, Berlin. *Flâneurs* get their shoes polished.
Photo credit: Bildarchiv Preussischer Kulturbesitz/Art Resource, NY.

houses, and bombed-out cellar bars of the destroyed city. Although they looked to the past for evidence of what survived destruction, their meanderings were more than an archeology of waste and destruction. As Michel de Certeau suggests, practices of everyday life like the time spent walking through a city's streets and alleyways are not mere physical acts of getting from here to there but should be seen instead as important acts in the construction of a place's meaning.[9] In their meanderings and reflections, these *flâneurs* helped lay a foundation for new understandings of life under occupation and division. This came about through their constant negotiation of Berlin's past with it's unseemly present.

These forms of observation and spectatorship functioned in three ways, and form the basis of this chapter's organization and argument. Most importantly, they charted the terrain of divided Berlin via an archeology of vice and transgression, as these writers drew points of comparison between the fractious yet exuberant 1920s and the purportedly banal 1940s and 1950s. Second, when combined with police and welfare authority visions of Berlin's trouble spots, these accounts mapped out the moral and material state of Berlin's hackneyed reconstruction. And third, by tracing the comings and goings of the city's subalterns, these authors helped breathe new life into the rubble by casting its broken spaces as repositories of danger, certainly, but also of desire, creating new terms of reference for the "sexual coding of the city."[10] Far from passive backdrops, these new spaces of contact, leisure, entertainment, and frivolity actively elicited new social memories that owed much to the changed but still familiar landscape of the tarnished metropolis. To put it simply, the new Berlin emerged out of the confrontation with past Berlins. In other words, as this chapter will show, for the legions of witnesses, visitors, and raconteurs, the physical city and the memories and experiences it engendered played a constitutive role not simply in the reconstruction of Berlin's gloriously transgressive past, but in the very conceptualization of its future as well.

Myths of Berlin

If Georg Simmel saw the imperial city as creating the contingencies that sculpted modern social identities, behaviors, and experiences, then post-1945 Berlin certainly provided a context for new relationships of identity, power, and morality among the burning embers of the former capital.[11] While Hamburg, Dresden, and parts of the Ruhr and Rhineland suffered terribly under Allied bombing attacks, the scale of

destruction in Berlin together with its symbolic importance as the former Reich capital imbued it with considerable pathos and meaning.
As we saw in Chapter 1, nightly bombing had well nigh completely
transformed the physical geography of the city.[12] In to the 1950s, criminologists continued to sound the alarm that the physical destruction
might create generations of crime, angst, and turmoil. As criminologist
Egon Weingartner put it in his 1951 doctoral dissertation, Germany was
not simply a "rubble heap in a material sense but...had reached an
exceptional low point in a moral sense as well."[13]

This was not the first time Berlin had rehearsed this dance. Christened
by defeat, revolution, and economic uncertainty in the years following
1918, the new republic and its precarious capital played host to a litany
of artists, filmmakers, and progressive and populist politicians drawn
to the city precisely because of its carnival of contradictions. They created this image of the brooding modern metropolis in the pages of the
mainstream and yellow press, while similar city texts surfaced in the
biting social criticism of writers like Siegfried Kracauer, taking visual
form in the avant-garde paintings and photomontage of artists like
Georg Grosz and Otto Dix, John Heartfield and Hannah Höch.[14] The
local government recognized the spectacular potential of the modern
city for attracting tourists. As one official guide proudly proclaimed, the
dynamism, artistry, and cultural diversity of the metropolis was something everyone should behold at least once in their lifetime.[15] Taking
to the streets in an unofficial homage to Walter Benjamin, perhaps the
most famous of the city's *flâneurs*, Kracauer described the contradictions
at the very heart of Berlin. In submissions to the *Frankfurter Zeitung*,
he told his readers that only by disentangling the "phantasmagorical
from the implied" could one truly hope to understand the meaning of
the shifting, bizarre city.[16] Amidst the ruins of the former *Weltstadt*, the
challenge of disentanglement was quite easily met, for, as one observer
recalled, the ruins served as a constant reminder that "one was in the
very presence of history."[17]

In the most war-ravaged sections, defeat in May 1945 laid bare the
otherworldliness of the city, but most Berliners concentrated on their
daily struggles for survival. In their accounts of the days, months,
and years following capitulation, those correspondents, photographers,
artists, and cultural elites with time and resources meditated on the tarnished remnants of Weimar luminosity, drawing explicitly on the literary imaginary that preceded the zero hour. Some, like Byford-Jones and
Hans Habe, had direct connection to the British and American occupation government either as officers, cultural attachés, or correspondents

in various US-backed newspapers. Regardless whether it was a first-time encounter or whether they had cut their journalistic teeth in the prewar trade, their ethnographic observation and self-reflexivity relied on the constant negotiation of past and present.[18] Their stories engaged not-yet-forgotten city texts of Weimar Berlin and viewed them through the crucible of death and destruction.[19] This exchange between the observer and the rubble was a mediated discussion between the writer and the historical or discursive Berlin, its distinctiveness owing much to the con-tingencies of the contemporary terrain. Theirs was not simply an effort to craft a new narrative for a new audience. In traipsing through city streets in search of underground bars and cafés, they lent shape to the very nature of divided Berlin's new social realities.

Resetting the Clock: The Zero Hour

Nostalgia for Berlin's Weimar heritage began well before war's end as a fleet of international writers reported on the war's impact on Nazi Berlin. Long before W. G. Sebald would claim that the air war became a repressed feature of postwar public memory, numerous wartime racon-teurs, from Samuel Beckett to Jacob Kronika and Marie Vassiltchikov, reflected in remarkable detail on their experiences in the eye of the storm. With each night's bombing, they described the assault on the city's infrastructure despite continual attempts by the city government to retain control over the rhythms of everyday life. American correspon-dent Howard K. Smith, second only to Edward R. Murrow in reputation, reflected on the absurdity of trying to proceed as if unaffected. In some instances, city officials went so far as to try and insulate the popu-lation by literally shrouding evidence of the rubble. Charlottenburg's Lietzensee was so filled with detritus that it was covered over with green netting so as to serve as a temporary roadway and hopefully distract Berliners from its real function as an emblem of the city's unmaking.[20]

Alongside the horrible truths contained in their observations, cor-respondent reports could also yield a spirit of hope. In the autumn of 1944 Norwegian journalist Theo Findahl suggested as much when he observed that despite the presence of "fresh ruins that dotted the background of life and traffic in the metropole," the Kurfürstendamm fought hard to hold on to its prewar status as the city's premier "prom-enade district and erotic hunting grounds"[21] until nightly bombing and dwindling provisions forced the last of the thriving nightspots to close their doors to the public.[22] For the steady stream of refugees flee-ing Stalin's katyusha rockets (*Stalinorgel*), the image of Weimar Berlin loomed especially large, rising "before their eyes as someone had seen it, or described it, years before, with its neon signs, its fine streets, shops, cafes, apartment-houses, its traffic, its hotels. Berlin was their Mecca."[23] Of course, the embattled city they found at the end of their forced pilgrimage bore little resemblance to the one in their mind's eye.

With the luxury of shelter and steady meals, international observers romanticized the ruins, beholding them with wide-eyed wonder at the same time that they pondered the crisis of civilization brought about by German support of Hitler. Isaac Deutscher's dispatches for *The Economist* adopted an upbeat tone, noting that Berlin's star might have faded but had not completely disappeared since the debris field still yielded glimpses of its former glory. Similarly, in his 1946 *European Witness* Deutscher's friend, poet, and fellow countryman Stephen Spender managed to find beauty in the destruction, marveling at the "ghostly impressions" the war had unearthed as he found himself going to the ruins "with the same sense of wonder, the same straining of the imagination, as one goes to the Coliseum at Rome." For Spender, Berlin had "the remoteness of all final disasters which make a dramatic and ghostly impression whilst at the same time withdrawing their secrets and leaving everything to the imagination."[24] While the foreign literati were seized with nostalgia, expatriates felt conflicting emotions when they returned to the city of their birth. One such expat, German-Jewish US Army Air Corps photographer Henry Ries, ambled through the ruins in the weeks and months after capitulation "with two pairs of eyes." Viewing the rubble with the eyes of an American, since he had made it out of Berlin in 1938, he beheld the broken streets and alleyways with quiet detachment in recognition of the horror the Germans brought on themselves. "As soon as [he] turned around," however, "[his] Berliner's eyes saw only destroyed people in front of and behind the curtains of a German tragedy. Only there were no curtains, just the remains of the thousand-year Reich." In a passage redolent with heartfelt introspection, he pondered whether his most intimate memories were interminably altered by the enormity of destruction in capitulated Berlin.[25]

The ruins served as markers of the decline of civilization, and indeed, as Atina Grossmann has deftly pointed out, there was no end to the metaphors of antiquity in contemporary accounts.[26] For the legions of women raped in the final days of the war, this was not just the decline of civilization but the end of civility as previously known, as the Orient took its bloody revenge over the Occident. Just as Freud remarked upon reading Wilhelm Jensen's novel *Gravida* set in the city of Pompeii, although a symbol of death, stasis, and misery, ruins also "stirred a feeling that death was beginning to talk."[27] And talk loudly they did. For actor, director, leftist agitator, and concentration camp survivor Wolfgang Langhoff, destruction was the norm and integrity, both spiritual and architectural, was clearly the exception.[28] Nevertheless, the crepuscular nature of the ruins provided the necessary cover for a variety of encounters as the city's destroyed apartment blocks, abandoned buildings, bunkers, and train stations reemerged as highly charged sites of negotiation, memory, barter, eroticism, conflict, desire, and exchange.[29] As zero-hour eyewitness and future University of Southern California professor Marta Mierendorff recorded in her June 25, 1945 diary entry, the twilight nature of the destruction played no small part in ensuring that "cabarets, varieties, dance bars and cinemas were the first to come back online." Capitulation and mass rape may have brought the war home to Berliners, but as Ernst Troeltsch had noted in the aftermath of World War I, somehow the city's youth managed to find escape and abandon in the landscape of defeat, even if it appeared to some to be "a *danse macabre* between death and horror."[30] As one woman recalled years later, as part of a memorial campaign sponsored by the West Berlin Senator for Work and Social Affairs (*Senator für Arbeit und Soziales*), for her teenaged daughter, who came home every night abuzz with the excitement of underground dance clubs, these same ruins that represented the end of a way of life, for her "opened up a whole new world"[31] (Figure 4.2).

Just as the images of burned-out buildings and the odor of rot and burial testified to the unmaking of the city's modernity, in rendering the invisible visible and turning sites of violence into places of escape, the ruins also forced Berliners to confront (and not repress) the contradictions of war's end. Civilian infrastructures like running water, tramlines, and communication networks were restored relatively quickly when compared to the crisis of emotion, the rise of licentiousness, and the breakdown of the traditional family. The capitulated city was already a tremendously gendered place, marked by shifting zones of sexual activity and mixing. Throughout the first four years of occupation, fluctuating numbers of occupation troops, displaced persons in transit camps, and returning Berliners who had either fled the bombings, served at the front, or had been prevented from an earlier return coursed through what was left of the city's major train stations. For observers like Curt Riess, a refugee from Nazi Germany and an American war correspondent, the city remained dreary and bleak, as morally bankrupt as the regime most recently in power. One need not look far for evidence of lapsed moral values. Army barracks, like the American base

Figure 4.2 People can go dancing again. The delayed spring festival is celebrated at Fuerstenhof Casino in Koepenicker Strasse, Berlin, Summer 1945. Photographer: Willi Saeger.
Photo credit: Bildarchiv Preussischer Kulturbesitz/Art Resource, NY.

on Finckensteinallee in the city's southwest, and the bars, cinemas, and cafés where soldiers congregated during their free time were patronized by a steady stream of loose women, who paced outside the sentry post or waited near movie houses for pick-ups until city authorities organized nightly raids to deal with the problem.[32] From virtually the moment of capitulation, each sector's health authority received numerous requests for abortion, testifying to the Russian propensity for lawlessness that for a time transcended sector borders and boundaries. US Judge Advocate General files suggest that Americans were also quite capable of using the city's hidden pathways and bombed-out apartments for their own gain.[33] Despite occasional excess which has done little to tarnish the public memory of the American occupation, Curt Riess thought the men of the 82nd Airborne were "distinctly handsome, decent, attractive fellows…a pleasure to look at, not only in comparison with the Russians but in comparison with the German men also.[34] The virility of the American soldiers stood in stark contrast to the emasculated German men who slowly lumbered back to the city from the front or from sojourns in Soviet prisoner-of-war camps.[35] According to one doctor, the rise in divorce was hardly surprising given the fact that in the "dreary environment of the ruins eroticism could scarcely flourish."[36]

Of course, "the women of Berlin" fared little better. Stefan Zweig was particularly enamored with the alluring self-confidence of the 1920s New Woman, especially the assured way in which she laid claim to public space, places of work, and leisure. Drawing out the link further between modernity and womanhood, Weimar *flâneurs* infused the city with seductive allure, viewing Berlin's modernization as both an enabling and an emasculating force.[37] Within a generation, both the embodied city and the confident New Woman were tempered by the violence of war's end. Like the destroyed Berlin, women "were themselves ruins, compared to what they had once been. Like the houses in which they spent their lives, they no longer tried to impress, or even to please; just as the whole city no longer made any attempt to please, or even to be interesting."[38] In Riess's telling, capitulation had desexualized women and emasculated the few remaining men, who, understandably, could scarcely be expected to play the Lothario on a calorie-weakened diet. What for Riess represented a world turned upside down, where class, status, rank, and background momentarily ceased to matter, could be understood quite differently by other observers. Ursula von Kardorff noted the vivacious beauty of girls on the Kurfürstendamm in her September 20, 1945 diary entry. They jauntily walked about with hair comb and purse amongst English, French, and American soldiers.[39] Twenty-two-year-old captain of the 11th Hussars Richard Brett-Smith was more cynical about the designs of German women. In *Berlin '45: Grey City*, he was without empathy when he sniped that "comparably few women could not be bought at a price or would refuse at all costs to surrender their bodies."[40] Compared to Brett-Smith's brazen critique, Riess's seems almost forgiving, or at least tempered with the wisdom of someone who had witnessed the great upheavals of the first half of the twentieth century playing themselves out a second time.

Terra Incognita

Regardless of how one might evaluate the plight of the Germans, whether as victims of their own passions or misled into submission, the relative normalization of daily life by the mid-1950s did little to erase the specter of destruction. As Scottish correspondent Ewan Butler described in his 1955 book *City Divided*, "behind the front of normality" there often "lurked an uneasiness and a fear, a sense of dark things moving in a half-world."[41] For *New York Times* foreign correspondent

Drew Middleton, any sense of tragedy was eclipsed by the charmless carnality of the postwar city, a "combination of garrison town, wide-open mining camp, [and] espionage center sprawled across acre after acre of dark and frozen desolation. The soldiers of four nations brawled in the streets. Shots sounded in the night. Dives cater[ed] to raw sex, and for those so inclined, every perversion flourished."[42] Correspondents and returnees continued to employ contradictory imaginings of the city in their search for remnants of the Weimar past. For the pre-war intellectual elite, cultural fare was at best transitional fluff, hardly worthy of Berlin's former *Weltstadt* status. "Culturally and politically," as author Elizabeth Langgässer noted in her reminiscences, Berlin was a wasteland that relied on "a dance of ghosts from 1928...[to] propel 'intellectual life' onward."[43] Although critical of claims of German victimization, correspondents similarly conjured up selective and often competing images of the city's past as they set about the task of cementing their own cultural authority as tellers of this new round of Berlin stories. Clearly, these postwar *flâneurs* had read their Hessel, Benjamin, Kracauer, Roth, and Simmel. But they seemed to have also studied the writings of Curt Moreck, whose notorious *Führer durch das "lasterhafte" Berlin* (Guide to Depraved Berlin) served as an armchair guide to Berlin's underground pleasure spots. Instructing his readers to "dive into the turbulent whirlpool" to experience its dizzying labyrinth of streets, dead ends, and roundabouts, Moreck implored those strolling through the city to draw on the wisdom and experience of others to help navigate a course between the city's official and unofficial offerings. Visitors, understood as male, were instructed to romance the city by learning the proper way of "coax[ing] it into showing its Janus-face" since "the depths are the more amusing side of life." After all, if Moreck was to be believed, true "intensity is to be experienced only at the vital sites of life, where polar opposites touch, where contradictions become one, where humanity is blended together like a piquant ragout."[44] For these latter-day *flâneurs*, cultural emissaries, and tourists, the remnants of Weimar's seductive past might even still be attainable in the broken landscape of the divided city.

Seeking to make good on this instruction, Brett-Smith hit the streets on a quest to locate the sexual permissiveness of Weimar Berlin, only to come up empty handed. It did not take long for him to lament that the quest for "vice on the scale that had been known before was rather pointless." Dogged in his pursuit of the erotic, he felt certain that "the same sort of thing went down (on a smaller scale) though it was hard to pin down."[45] Swiss journalist Manuel Gasser had better luck, having learned from a shifty black marketeer that "one can have anything in Berlin, you just have to know the right people."[46] Unable to get anywhere with the nightclub touts who clustered around the newspaper kiosks of the S-Bahn train stations in pursuit of randy businessmen and curious occupation troops, Brett-Smith was forced to rely on an established prewar tapestry of diversion, visiting the postwar incarnations of the better-known Weimar-era night clubs, some of which had quickly resurfaced along the Kurfürstendamm, around Breidscheidplatz, and in the vicinity of Tauentzienstrasse near Wittenbergplatz in the shadow of the ruins of the department store Kaufhaus des Westens (or Ka-De-We).[47] Despite his frustration at all that had been lost, in describing his nightly excursions he painted a lively picture of the residues that remained of Moreck's depraved capital.

It was clear to most visitors that the late 1940s were not the early 1920s, and Brett-Smith lamented that in surveying the landscape "the eye picked out only the *Rio Rita* and the *Femina*." There was still "the *Eldorado*, where the clients came dressed as girls," but this had given way to "the post-war *Tabasco*, and that in time became the *Cockatoo*." Unfortunately, "the *Silhouette*, which used to be attended by a mixture of pansies and Lesbians [sic], the *Geisha* and the *Monocle*, both specializing in the latter, *Steinmaers*, where the dancing partners ogled their customers in bathing-dresses, and the beery, knee-slapping *Haus Vaterland* – all were gone." More upscale dance bars had survived, like the *Roxy*, *Bobby's*, *Chez Ronny*, and the *Rio Rita*, although "the drinks were expensive and the girls cheap." In the *Royal Club*, on the Kurfürstendamm itself, big shots from the black market, foreign correspondents, and American and British officers intermingled with a mixed clientele. There, "for a change, the girls…were beautifully dressed and really lovely." Still, it seemed that 12 years of Hitler's rule, bombing, defeat, and division had forever altered the terrain of the truly transgressive. In the "mushroom glut of cabarets and *Lokale*" in the New West, one feature was ubiquitous: the satirical cabarets were often "introduced by a passé showgirl who addressed her victorious patrons in three and sometimes four different languages, making unsubtle and facile digs at Hitler and the Nazis while (for a time) Stalin looked on phlegmatically from a prominent position on the Wall."[48] Even the most famous of the gay and lesbian bars, the Eldorado, one of the first nightclubs to be targeted by the Nazis upon coming to power, failed to titillate and impress. Ewan Butler's sardonic description of Berlin's nightclub scene made its banality palpable. When a nightclub singer attempted to conjure up an image of gender nonconformity by breaking into a few bars of one of hit-maker

Heino Gaze's more raunchy songs, "I Am a Woman who Can't Say No" ("ich bin eine Frau, die nicht nein sagen kann"), "none of the people sitting round seem to care very much whether the happily married father, who calls himself Dolores, says "yes" or "no."[49] Like Henry Ries's disappointment at not being able to return to the Berlin of his youth, for many the landscape of the past was forever altered by the war's enduring presence.

The Porousness of Boundaries?

At the same time that the temporal boundaries of 1933 and 1945 were routinely blurred in the quest for an archeology of desire, the physical boundaries dividing the city into four occupied quadrants were equally porous. Still, the century's second postwar period would be nothing like the preceding one, understandably, given that post-Nazi Berlin was a far cry from the embattled republic capital. Chief among the differences, of course, was the presence of four occupation forces that ensured a further degree of complication in the negotiation of everyday experience.[50] Sector borders were doggedly policed, but for all the pretense of governance and control, ultimately they were of little importance up until the building of the Wall, as a host of Berliners crisscrossed their way across the inner boundary for work by day and pleasure by night. While they might serve as points of friction and random violence, as Henry Ries noted upon witnessing American MPs shoot wantonly after a renegade jeep made a run for the sector boundary, in some instances, they might even have contributed to the sense of novelty of a particular neighborhood.[51] Potsdamer Platz, that beacon of modernity with its multi-sided traffic light, department stores, and frenetic pace – a locus of activity in the years before the currency stabilization with black marketeering and the occasional boundary disruption – was still little more than a "grassy steppe in the center of the city."[52] In an area that would one day soon rub up against the Berlin Wall, renowned bandleader Heinz Hupperts claimed he particularly enjoyed playing gigs in the *Kaisersaal* of the Hotel Esplanade adjacent to the Platz, given its proximity to the Russian-controlled section of Berlin. Ninety percent destroyed in the final year of the war, the Esplanade stood as the sole venue jutting out of the rubblescape near the Tiergarten's southern tip, only a yard or two away from the Russian sector; in the 1950s Hupperts was quoted as saying with some bemusement that "at 4 o'clock in the morning" when the band packed up for the night "by God, you can hear the Volga rippling!"[53]

Although few areas of the city rivaled the near-total decimation of the core, rebuilding was anything but an overnight affair and by 1949 most of West Berlin still had yet to resurrect its high streets. With Unter den Linden under Soviet jurisdiction, Jörn Donner underscored the pressing need "to create a substitute in the cultured pearl, the Kurfürstendamm."[54] Berliners poured their lust for life into recasting the boulevard as it once had been. Pulling back "the curtain of ruins to expose their bombed out windows," in the fall of 1945 Ursula von Kardorff recalled hearing "hot jazz" flowing out of ramshackle bars "in which there were only hot drinks and no food."[55] By 1946, writer Georg Homsten could barely contain his enthusiasm at finding that the boulevard "lives, lives on, lives again. Without the shimmer and alcohol, without oysters and limousines. Despite ruins and ration cards. The Kurfürstendamm is alive, living out its ambiguous, trivial, seductive and irrepressibly Berlin life!"[56] Marked by a heady mix of high and low, from swanky boutiques to bars and cafés of varying renown, certainly the scene had more in keeping with Hamburg's *Reeperbahn* than the Champs Elysées, at least according to the venerable *Süddeutsche Zeitung* newspaper, whose reportage caused such a stir that shopkeepers took to the street to count the actual number of jewelry shops, beggars, and neon signs on the strip.[57] Even the prewar cabaret scene once clustered around the Friedrichstrasse train station relocated to the neighborhood as relations between East and West steadily deteriorated after 1948.[58]

As it had in the 1920s, the Kurfürstendamm continued to polarize opinion. Viewed as a symbol of mass consumption, modernity, Americanization, Jewishness, and bourgeois vapidity, the nightlife of the New West came to epitomize the ebb and flow of Weimar politics as a tussle between pro-capitalist, leftist, and provincialist voices. Rising economic insecurity after 1929 meant that it underwent even more scrutiny, evolving from the symbol of modernity to what Siegfried Kracauer decried as "a street without memory," eclipsed by crass commercialism and fleeting desires.[59] The tension between the city's democratic potential and its anti-cosmopolitanism played out anew among the observers who combed the post-1945 city for traces of this spectacular, if fractious, past. Not even the Berlin Wall could detract from the street's luster for William Conlan, who described it in 1963 as "never more cosmopolitan, more glamorous, or more hectic than ... today."[60] Jörn Donner was less magnanimous in his choice of words when he reported that it was an "international, worldly street, with gaudy window displays." Like Kracauer before him, he expressed disdain for the subservience of culture to commodity fetishism. Most alarming of all was the sheer banality of the street's nightspots that "imitate[d] imitations, which in turn have imitated something."[61] While signs of a "hidden life" might be found in some of the British and American sector nightclubs and bars, with their hastily reconstructed pneumatic tubes and telephones for flirting on the fly, they seemed more like museums to past glory or catch basins for the litany of provincials, tourists, soldiers, and businessmen traveling through the city. Even the prostitutes that worked among the *Hausballet* of the Remde performed "in hideously prim nakedness, while the star of the show croons one of the over-worked songs of Capri" and "the blondest of the girls sways slowly towards the audience, pale flesh jiggling in time to the music" only to be applauded by "fathers, with their wives and daughters."[62] This search for authenticity, for some vestige of Weimar exuberance, was palpable in both the expectations of patrons and their hosts' pathetic staging of elaborate water shows, revivified dance acts, and choice of *chansons*. Although Richard Brett-Smith faced what he thought was a "well run conspiracy against inquisitive outsiders" in his hunt for the city's "real vice-haunts,"[63] by the late 1950s Jörn Donner somehow managed to fake his way into the street's first "key bar" (*Schlüßelbar*) whereupon, looking about, he admired the red lighting, the blonde bar girls, and amply flowing whiskey that one dancer admitted was more helpful in keeping the showgirls awake than quenching one's thirst. Still, the sight of a German businessman in his fifties "licking and kissing" a girl's hand "further and further up to the armpit" confirmed rather than contradicted Donner's reading of Christopher Isherwood in *Good-bye to Berlin*, who had similarly recognized the Kurfürstendamm was nothing more than "a sparkling nucleus of light, like a sham diamond, in the shabby twilight of the town"[64] (Figure 4.3).

Despite its lackluster offerings and unoriginal fare, some sites, like the multifaceted Femina Palace on Nuremburger Strasse just to the south of the Kaiser Wilhelm Memorial Church, retained vital elements of the post-1945 scene. Stretching 150 meters of an entire city block, the 1928–32 building, designed by architects Robert Bielenberg and Julius Moser in the quiet utility of the New Sobriety style (*Neue Sachlichkeit*), reflected the progressive sentiment of the period, foregoing the ornamentalism of Unter den Linden for a modern functionality of design approach. The Femina dancehall grew to be one of the most spectacular supper clubs of late Weimar Berlin. In its heyday, it boasted over 2000 seats, had two large bars and a smaller one in the vestibule, in addition to three orchestras, a hydraulic dance floor, tabletop telephones and tubular message service to connect the various different bars with

Figure 4.3 Patrons and a musician at the local "Gypsy Bar" on the Kurfürstendamm, West Berlin, 1955. Photographers: Armin and Lisolette Orgel-Köhne.
Photo credit: Bildarchiv Preussischer Kulturbesitz/Art Resource, NY.

their patrons. Of all its features, it was the glass ceiling that was the most spectacular, as patrons were invited to experience the "comfort of sitting under the open skies, to chat, dance, all combined here in beautiful, practical style within the convivial luxury of Femina."[65] Known especially for its record release parties and a lively house orchestra, the Femina's patrons willingly shelled out over a Mark for the opportunity to enter the facility, and the cheapest bottle of wine required an additional five – sums easily out of reach to the majority of the population. Beyond the cost of imbibing, class markers were also reinforced by the selection of alcohol on offer in the various social settings within the site. While beer flowed on tap, it was only available in the vestibule bar where, for the most part, men congregated amongst themselves before joining their parties. Most guests refrained from imbibing in this working-class elixir anyway, viewing it as more suitable to the midday meal than to an evening of conviviality.[66] More enticing than the wine list, of course, was the prospect of flirtation via tabletop telephones and pneumatic tubes, a nightclub craze that had swept the Residenz Casino in Friedrichshain before it was imported to the West End. From the comfort of one's table, as the *Berliner Herold* reported in 1931 – the height of the fad – "the tabletop telephones buzzed, and the acquaintance with the blonde, raven-haired or redheaded, monocle-wearing beauty was made, one was no longer alone, and had twice as much fun"[67] (Figures 4.4 and 4.5).

Despite the Nazi ban on swing music, and the destroyed ballroom, the Femina remained operational and in use throughout the war in one form or another, and was quickly called back into action as soon as the guns had stilled. Reflecting on experiences in the summer of 1945, when the Russians relinquished total control over the city to the jointly mandated Allied Control Commission, John J. Maginnis remembered that

Figure 4.4 Table telephones and dancing at Berlin's "Residenz-Casino," ca. 1925. Colored postcard.
Photo credit: Bildarchiv Preussischer Kulturbesitz/Art Resource, NY.

Figure 4.5 Woman on the telephone at the Resi Ballhouse, Berlin, 1955. Photographers: Armin and Lisolette Orgel-Köhne.
Photo credit: Bildarchiv Preussischer Kulturbesitz/Art Resource, NY.

the famous bar functioned as the unofficial officer's club of the Soviet occupation force. One hot evening in July, a high-ranking Soviet officer actually telephoned over to ensure the prompt removal of partying patrons in advance of an impending meeting. Coming within sight of the bar, Maginnis was shocked to witness a flood of people congregating in the street, angry at having been forcefully removed only minutes before. With more serving girls than guests, the Femina hosted one of the many notorious drinking banquets put on by the Soviets which, upon closer inspection, turned out to be a "kind of farewell party for the Russians who had occupied Schöneberg for two months."[68]

To Richard Brett-Smith, the Femina certainly put on a good cabaret, but their "nauseating bonhomie," "wretched food," and "watered-down red wine" reflected all too poignantly the material realities of a stretched economy.[69] The Tabasco, previously known as the Robby-Bar, on nearby Augsburgerstrasse, managed to retain its edge despite the aura of austerity, and successfully conjured up the abandon of the 1920s with boxing nights and members-only gatherings. Brett-Smith barely contained his enthusiasm for this Schöneberg nightspot that "was still the playground of the pederasts and...Lesbians...of the latter," he assured, "there were many in Berlin." In the bar's current incarnation, "it was genuinely impossible to tell who was a man or a boy and who was a girl. It was apparent that men danced with men and women with women, and sometimes, oddly enough in that atmosphere, men with women; but it was anybody's guess who was who."[70] Perhaps Brett-Smith's *Grey City* was more colorful than he realized. Cabarets remained highly charged venues of social commentary and sexual stratification even if their utility was not always appreciated at the time. Besmirched by the right as decidedly Jewish and homosocial spaces yet allowed to continue in various incarnations throughout the war, cabarets were among the first establishments to embrace the spirit of reconstruction when, as early as June 1, 1945, Brigitta Mira's *chanson* "Berlin is back" ("*Berlin kommt wieder*") in Willi Schaefer's Cabaret of Comics club on the Kurfürstendamm was taken up by the beleaguered population as a kind of unofficial mantra of survival.[71] Already in November 1945, the *Tagesspiegel* conjured up the spirit of Friedrich Hollaender in reporting on the "tingle tangle" programs of the resurrected cabarets, a blatant reference to the cabaretists he had managed before fleeing the Nazis for the United States.[72] But the article was equally wary of the form abject critique might take in the new order. "Can smut ever replace charm? Or an old collection of jokes, spirit? Cabaret is closing in on public nuisance."[73] While satirists like Kurt Tucholsky, Erich Kästner, and Walter Mehring had crafted biting prose to be delivered in smoke-tinged *chansons* and Bertolt Brecht, Kurt Weill, and Hanns Eisler infused the irony of cabaret into their lyrics and song, many observers clearly believed the genre was divested of its original edge and effect. Despite the forced migration of many of Germany's writers, directors, dramaturges, and chanteuses, cabarets staged in underground cellar bars like the one depicted in Billy Wilder's 1948 film *A Foreign Affair* attempted to resurrect the spirit of Weimar vignettes. Often, the reality had little in common with the glamour of Marlene Dietrich or the trenchant wit of Hollaender. Certainly, the inflation-riddled economic disparity of the 1920s and the specter of brown-shirted fascism played a particularly important role in shaping the genre. But although the context was different, the tumultuous conditions of capitulation that Hollaender satirized via Dietrich's four-language rendition of "the Ruins of Berlin" (in which, interestingly, the German verse harkens back to "earlier days" while the English looks wistfully toward a brighter future) ensured that the politics of quotidian life continued to inspire occasional instances of critique and emotion. Sometimes, foreign observers seemed not to understand the self-mockery and introspection of cabaret, especially when the hardships of capitulation became tropes in the staged narrative of renewal. It was clear that *New York Sun* correspondent Judy Barden was taken aback by the way in which Berlin's women employed the cabaret stage as a vehicle to narrate their anguish and victimization. Remembering one evening's fare in a smoky underground room in a bar in Soviet-controlled Berlin, she recalled the "plaintive and bitter song" conjured forth by the young performer, whose face was caked with "rubble dust," her hair streaked, and body clad in a soiled jumpsuit in deference to the much-mythologized rubble woman so popular in the Soviet press.[74] The songstress directed her barbs at the failings of the German man, admonishing him to "stop acting like busted heroes. Help us build something new." After all, she prodded, "we housewives went through more than you. You had your drink and your *Blitzmädels*, your officers' clubs and your medals. We had the American Air Force by day and the Royal Air Force by night, a cold air-raid shelter in which to live and very little to eat." Curiously absent, but not surprising given the politics of occupation, was reference to the Soviet rapes.[75] Although they weren't mentioned explicitly in the lyrics, "when the singer finished" Barden claimed a hush fell over the crowd before a crescendo of "almost hysterical high-pitched applause from the women in the audience." Clearly, "the cabaret turn had scored a hit with her own sex." On many levels, Barden thought, the singer "had given the men something to think about."[76]

"Berlin Is Back"

Cabarets continued to give voice to the city's fractious history even if they were robbed of physical integrity and financial stability. Although portions of it were heavily damaged, the Femina housed a slew of new and fledgling establishments in its expansive chambers and anterooms. In 1948, the postwar jazz legend and promoter Helmuth Brandt established Die Badewanne (The Bathtub) on site, at first a rogue artist and student pub that in no time at all grew into one of the city's premier jazz bars, drawing a mixed crowd of teenaged Berliners, members of the local art scene, and African American servicemen. Although there was a palpable lag in the house band's musical repertoire given the Nazi suppression of jazz, this was soon overcome, and over the course of its existence such legends as Count Basie, Ella Fitzgerald, and Duke

Ellington took to the venue's small stage. Despite jazz's contemporary recognition as a legitimate genre of music, the frequent dance competitions and frenetic moves angered some Germans. Given fears about the ambiguous styles that some contemporaries believed emasculated young men through an emphasis on aesthetics and fashion, and the obvious blurring of racial boundaries, Die Badewanne was almost destined to rub up against West German notions of respectability, perhaps explaining its popularity among young people in search of diversion from the gloominess of everyday life.[77] When not playing host to jazz concerts, *Die Badewanne* also hosted the earliest incarnation of Die Stachelschweine (The Porcupine) cabaret, one of postwar Berlin's most successful attempts at searing social commentary.[78] Drawing a wide audience, the company eventually outgrew their venue. After vagabonding about for a time in cellar hovels like Der Burgfrieden before it too was closed by building authorities out of fear of collapse, in 1965 it finally settled into its final home in local celebrity and industrialist Karl-Heinz Pepper's replacement for the Romanisches Café, the Europa Center.[79]

Its surrounding area, the streets around Breitscheidplatz that fell under the shadow of the ruins of the Memorial Church, had witnessed better days. Referred to by the local papers as the "blemish on Berlin's calling card" (*"der Schandfleck auf Berlins Visitenkarte"*), the square that once coursed with creative energy as writers as varied as Billy Wilder, Vladimir Nabokov, Ilya Ehrenburg, and Gerhard Hauptmann moved about in search of the next great debate, fell into disrepair as a macabre mix of blue movie theaters, shish kebab stands, street prophets, wrestling venues, and "circus people shoveling cow manure" took up shop amidst the rats that still scurried in and around the spaces opened up by the bombing.[80] It is not insignificant that plans for the 21-story showpiece of capitalist ingenuity, the Europa Center, borrowed overtly from American models of marketing (it was crowned, after all, with a giant illuminated Mercedes symbol), least of which was the ingenious way Pepper assembled the 70 million Marks necessary to get the design off the ground. The plans for a multipurpose pleasure palace complete with ice-skating rink, movie theaters, glass vitrines, and the all-too-important mix of business and boutiques confirmed Pepper's vision of the space as the city's answer to the Rockefeller Center, which, when viewed in light of the building of the Berlin Wall and Nazi resistance fighter and major Willy Brandt's enthusiastic support for the project, may be read as the unselfconscious attempt to firmly fix West Berlin along the axis of democratic capitalism and civility. The Europa Center, Breitscheidplatz, and the manicured amusements of Kurfürstendamm nightclubs may have drawn implicitly on the legacy of Weimar, but by the 1950s they were redeployed in the service of Cold War polarization and nation building. It was not irrrelevant that West German industry minister and Berliner Victor-Emmanuel Preusker commissioned the use of the cabaret catchphrase "Berlin is back" to inaugurate an exhibition on the "once and future capital's" transformation over the past 10 years, the hallmark of which was its industrial productivity and economic recovery.[81] Whereas the ruins once bore witness to the lingering stain of war amidst carnivalesque street scenes at the confluence of the Kurfürstendamm, Tauentzienstrasse, Nuremberg, and Budapester Strasse, huge architectural projects like the Europa Center coopted the already once-refracted spirit of Weimar in the promotion of an ethic of competition and prosperity.

If the ballhouses, cafés, and cabarets in the western neighborhoods of Charlottenburg and Schöneberg self-consciously dusted off their Weimar credentials, forgetting to emphasize that they had remained in service during the war, bars in the Soviet-controlled sector of the city faced far greater challenges. Using a 1928 guidebook to navigate the eastern half of the city, similar in kind to what Brett-Smith employed in the west, Jörn Donner sought out the remnants of the eastern vice center vividly depicted in Heinrich Zille's turn-of-the-century charcoal etchings of the poor and downtrodden. Beginning at the corner of Leipziger Strasse before circling around to the Friedrichstrasse train station, he cut to the quick: "it would be an exaggeration to say that there are traces of the cabarets and night clubs, the homosexual pubs, and the traditional beer halls."[82] No longer as "powdered and painted," perhaps, as on the 1920s canvases of Otto Dix and Georg Grosz, following the upheaval of World War II "female beauty" was still discernible amidst the gray-scaled stucco of East Berlin's tenement houses. Lounging in pairs among East Berlin's bohemian elite in the Presse-café of the Admiralspalast, a former bathhouse dating back to the imperial period, replete with indoor ice rink, opera house, and entertainment center known in GDR hagiography as the site of the famous handshake between Otto Grotewohl and Wilhelm Pieck upon unifying the SPD and KPD in 1947, Donner bemoaned the fact that these women remained out of reach even with fists full of western currency. As one popular German song put it, "one can't buy that with money."[83] Even the streets and alleyways of the former paradise of vice (*Sittenparadies*), the area surrounding the ruined House of Technology (*Haus der Technik*) was devoid of activity, a far cry from the sordid imaginings of Grosz whose paintings of these "whore-infested streets" cast an indelible mark in Donner's memory of the numerous "ladies of pleasure" who once stood in the doorways "like sentinels dangling their handbags, the sign of their guild."[84] Smaller, unassuming East Berlin hovels retained the broken atmosphere of capitulation, like the Hajo cabaret and dance restaurant, housed in nothing short of a "scantily-repaired ruin."[85] East and West Berliners mixed freely until the wee hours of the morning in these dug-out cellar bars until the worsening political situation made access to nightspots itself troublesome. The cheap liquor of the Kleine Melodie bar was out of reach for most Berliners without a permit stating that one's residence was in the eastern portion of the city, and the informal visits of the People's Police ensured compliance. "Eroticism certainly flowered here, both the cheap and expensive," but, as Donner noted somewhat crudely, in paraphrasing the bartender, what "Berlin bitch would have any desire to sell herself for Ostmarks?"[86] University students, a few spies, and even Karl-Eduard von Schnitzler, the future East German television personality, propaganda mouthpiece, and host of *Der Schwarze Kanal* (The Black Channel), turned their backs on these East German dens preferring instead to cross over the sector boundaries to Nollendorfplatz when the Hajo bar relocated westward to take up residence in the theater complex where epic theater dramaturge Erwin Piscator had formerly staged his masterpieces of Weimar social criticism. Donner lamented the bar's upward mobility, since he had found more than a single night's pleasure at the old location dancing with modest and impressionable eastern local girls and forgetting briefly "that peculiar odor of death" which to him "belonged to both the idea and the city of Berlin."[87] Indeed, in many observer accounts, the dim lighting, the unimaginative fare, the spartan surroundings, and tiny dance floors simply reinforced the view that East Berlin lagged behind West Berlin. Across from the Stettiner train station (renamed Nordbahnhof in 1950), the Hotel Neva's restaurant turned out its lights by 1 a.m., and despite rumors that Ulbricht made a habit of stopping by nightspots in the eastern sector, it too "will be as dark and secret as all the houses which lie about it already are."[88]

Toward a New Cultural Imaginary

While the bars and pubs in the central Berlin districts of Mitte and Schöneberg, near the Friedrichstrasse train station, and along the Kurfürstendamm struggled to rekindle Weimar's lost glory, the foreign observers' sampling of Berlin after dark points to the lingering impact of political, cultural, and material devastation that continued to make itself felt well into the 1950s. Despite the entrepreneurial efforts of various nightclub owners to tap into the cachet of Weimar, unbound revelry was not to be found in the hastily resurrected nightspots, dance bars, and cabarets of the divided city. If police reports were a reliable indication, the remains of a truly transgressive subculture were not to be found in the prewar sexual imaginary but in the twilight spaces that came onto the scene along the quickly consolidating border between East and West that became home to one of the city's varied and diverse gay scenes.

In September 1949, Werner Becker wrote an article in the Swiss homophile magazine *The Circle* (Der Kreis) telling of the burgeoning nightclub scene in Berlin where "already in the early days after war's end the first bars and restaurants opened their doors." Sure enough, another set of venues competed for space with the chic and sophisticated supper clubs of the New West and the pokey backyard bars of the red light district surrounding the Friedrichstrasse train station. Although many would be forced to change location due to prying eyes and public opinion, Becker was pleased to report signs of survival, given the 23 men's clubs and 15 ladies' clubs in operation. Some, like the Zauberflöte in the Kommandantenstrasse, had attracted an established following in the 1920s through its lesbian nights in which, according to Ruth Margarete Roellig, "a wave of light flowed over the mostly young, thin, women's forms, that harmoniously swayed in blithesomeness from mirror dance to waltz ... "[89] Regarded by many as a tad pretentious and bourgeois with a heady love of schmaltzy music and rigorous entry requirements gendering access along a butch–femme axis, various women's clubs, like the Monbijou and Violetta, hosted their dances there until the Nazis closed it in March 1933, which did little to stifle spirits and only forced a change of venue.[90] In virtually the same space 21 years later, on May 17, 1949, the Zauberflöte continued the tradition of irreverence by holding a tongue-in-cheek birthday party "in celebration" of the seventeenth day of the fifth month, a not-so-veiled reference to the notorious anti-sodomy article in the German Penal Code, Paragraph 175, which still outlawed sexual relations between men.[91]

While some of these dancehalls were steeped in history and built on tradition, others were decidedly more low key, like the Artistenklause on the Lausitzer Platz in Kreuzberg, housed in a series of simple, spartan gathering rooms tucked neatly into residential tenement blocks. Here, despite the austere surroundings, patrons were promised a range of "colorful programs" regardless of the fact that few of these establishments held official ordinance or proper licensing, given the fears of site inspection and the continued illegality of gay sociability. In the case of the Artistenklause, the owner experienced the full force of the law's injustice when her husband's wartime homosexuality surfaced to light. In a meeting on November 27, 1951, members of the police licensing committee, which included representatives from the West Berlin youth bureau, select members of the hospitality industry, and, of course, the Allies, determined that in addition to the prior convictions of her husband, the Artistenklause must close shop since it was obviously a meeting place for "known homosexuals." As the police stated in their report, "nothing about the place inspired confidence" that it would ever be anything but a hook-up bar.[92] Despite an elaborate plan to divorce her husband and secure a temporary license, few of the commission members actually believed she would refrain from holding "dance parties for gays and allow entry to youths." Despite these concerns, curiously, the bar was allowed to eke out an existence. Taken over by Mamita, West Berlin's famous transvestite dance promoter who would soon fall victim to an untimely death in an automobile accident, mini-galas continued to be billed for Mondays, Saturdays, and Sundays, and advertisements graced the back pages of the city's newspapers and friendship magazines until anti-smut laws forced them from print.[93]

In order to avoid the scrutiny of the vice squad, whose raids only increased in frequency over the course of the 1950s, many bars and dance clubs like the Artistenklause returned to the elaborately themed parties so prevalent in the 1920s and early 1930s to cloak revelers in the security of masquerade. In the various ballhouses on the Kommandantenstrasse and Alte Jakobstrasse in Kreuzberg, cross-dressing remained a feature of friendship circles, balls, and ladies' clubs well after Hitler came to power. Since lesbianism was not outlawed by Paragraph 175, women's clubs were somewhat shielded from direct intervention, although many, like the parties organized by members of the Comical Nine (*Lustige Neun*), remained on the Gestapo's radar as late as 1940.[94] Observation reports noted that men in drag also attended these masquerade balls, but, given the gender confusion, they were often taken as mannish women. On the parquet dance floors of Friedrichshain's Residenz-Rooms (*Residenz-Säle*) and the neighboring Concordia Hall (*Concordia-Säle*), the ambiguous sexual performances blurred categories and sometimes succeeded in shielding participants from prying police eyes. The legal system in both halves of the city remained quite rigid; homosexuality was an offence punishable by jail, and homosocial spaces engendered continual monitoring via the albeit haphazard scrutiny of law enforcement. Yet more was required than simply transgressing known danger zones in order for charges of public nuisance or same-sex sexuality to be laid. In the twilight topography of bombed-out Berlin, somewhere on the border between decorum and debauchery some semblance of sanctuary might still be found.

Cross-dressing has had an elaborate history on the stage, enabling actors to destabilize sexual binaries and comment on the rigidity of social boundaries.[95] Beyond its explicitly performative function, as in theater and stage plays, cross-dressing in the everyday also served as a device that enjoyed particular resonance in Weimar Berlin, whether as part of the so-called "voluptuous panic" of street-level prostitution or as an erotic drive and claim to identity.[96] Whether amidst peers in the Eldorado or in the antechambers of private cigar clubs, cross-dressing among Berlin's sexual subalterns created moments of dissonance that disrupted easy categorization, exposing to light the explicitly constructed nature of sexual and gender roles and subjectivities, creating what Marjorie Garber has termed a "category crisis" by pointing to the liminality of bounded and corporeal imaginings.[97] In some cases, it was suggestive of sexual play and frivolity, but it might also have a more declarative function, as in Claire Waldoff's 1929 adoption of a more masculine register in her version of the rough-and-tumble song "Hannelore," whom "nobody can tell is a girl or a boy."[98] Not only did the song embody cross-identification of voice, but it also transcended public and private space, with Hannelore's walking through the street in all her ambiguity and Waldoff performing the story in the comfort of a cabaret. Although it invokes the image of experimentalism and play, in German sexology cross-dressing operated more plainly as a claim to subjectivity, an intermediary notch on Magnus Hirschfeld's sliding gender scale. Interestingly, queer spaces of sexual nonconformity, which relied on the pronounced ambiguity between the respectable and the profane, between gay and straight worlds, between the corporal and the demonstrative, formed a vital part of the sensationalist guides to Berlin, which provided bourgeois readers a tantalizing if safe point of access into the scene. As Curt Moreck described in his alternative guide to Berlin's pre-Nazi night life, "the young women, who weren't women, but so confidently moved about in their long ball gowns, danced together or with other young men. Only their hands gave them away, which were a bit too course, together with their naked arms, which lacked any sign of feminine smoothness"[99] (Figure 4.6).

Whereas the respectability of marriage could not deflect scrutiny away from the stain of previous convictions for homosexuality, sometimes the more raucous and ornate the party, the better the chance of evading the police gaze. Kisses on the cheek, over-the-top posturing, and camp shielded revelers from suspicion while providing cover for expressions

Figure 4.6 In the transvestite bar Eldorado on Motzstrasse, Berlin. At left, the only woman in the group, 1926.
Photo credit: Bildarchiv Preussischer Kulturbesitz/Art Resource, NY.

of desire and feeling. Underscoring the ways in which interior and exterior spaces might differentially shelter oppositional behavior, except in situations where a confidant turned tail as an informant, four men "in extremely flamboyant clothes, short women's skirts, panties, but without stockings" were taken to the police station by Acting Inspector Hans Pingel, who had been called to the scene not to raid the bar but to investigate a charge of "unnatural desire" in a neighboring housing block.[100] Although they had just left the ball, their behavior and dress was only deemed offensive when they emerged from the confines of the twilight spaces of the ballhouse.[101]

The end of National Socialism failed to completely alter the standards of evidence and proof required to sustain a charge of homosexuality in West Germany. As in the Nazi period, under the applied statute in force in West Berlin, touching, groping, and kissing were grounds for a visit to the police station. Although East Germany relaxed the standard of proof for homosexual transgressions, returning to the Weimar-era statute that required proof of intercourse in order to mount a charge, it nevertheless remained essential for police to strike a balance between the open expression of frivolity and outward displays of affection. But camp remained an important feature of homosociability after 1945. Flamboyance could similarly cloak revelers in the relative safety of artistic expression. Raids were still conducted on suspicious nightspots, but parties organized under the rubric of artistic installations could minimize attention. For the young artist and recently decommissioned *Wehrmacht* soldier Eberhardt Brucks, whose provocative sketches of amorous men adorned the pages of *The Circle*, the parties put on by the newly minted Fine Arts Guild of Berlin (*Berufsverband Bildender Künstler Berlins* or BBK) in the ballhouses surrounding Zoo Station were opportunities for self-expression as an artist and contact with other like-minded men. Here the boundary between bohemia and the gay scene was exceptionally fluid. The Bright Lanterns (*Bunte Laterne*) Mardi Gras festivals, co-sponsored by the Association of Handicrafts, gave local artists the opportunity to design entire installations in separate chambers within the vast ballhouses. These fests were well attended, above all by the city's gay and lesbian patrons, who, perhaps drawing from prewar experiences and memories of the glory days, "made a great stir" with their creative costuming and disguises.[102]

Such a mix of high and low, of bohemia and the everyday, was also palpable in the north end of the city, in the working-class district of Wedding, where from 1949 lesbian actor and sculptor Toni Höyenborg ran Café Münschhausen, which drew a steady business as the preferred gathering place for journalists, writers, and artists in pursuit of the "light and airy frivolity" that Brucks claimed marked the gallery-like openings, Christmas parties, and Mardi Gras festivities.[103] While many of these parties were open affairs, advertised brazenly in newspapers and in the announcement pages of the various friendship magazines that circulated openly in the early 1950s, before the 1953 Law for the Protection of Youth (which was really a revivified version of the Nazi Anti-Smut Law) outlawed all gay and lesbian periodicals, informal communication networks ensured information was passed to those in the know.[104]

Despite the engagement of Berlin's police, youth, and licensing services, and the exacting influence of the censor, dance halls reemerged among the city's ruins. Although the gallantry of the ballhouse festival captivates the imagination, it was the smaller, more ramshackle venue that provided comfort and companionship for the less well connected; and in fact, in time, it was spaces like these that galvanized the burgeoning scene. Nook-and-cranny bars hidden among the ruins, like the Berliner Kind'l-Diele, later called the Schnurrbartdiele – and then F13 for its Friesenstrasse 13 address – were simple wood barracks on a piece of abandoned property near the Tempelhof airfield.[105] Like many of the watering holes catering to a predominantly gay male clientele, the F13 came under the scrutiny of the police-directed licensing committee whose primary purpose was to enforce building codes and public morals. Faced with the threat of closure, the F13's owner opted to take his case to court, only to receive a verdict in his favor. In his address to court, the judge evoked sexologist Magnus Hirschfeld's notion of constitutional homosexuality and questioned whether the committee's energy might not be better served in "not prohibiting every men's dance" but by treating "this impossible to eradicate vice" by protecting "normal oriented people" from stumbling into one of these establishments unawares.[106] After the court decision, the bar continued to operate more or less without difficulty, and the new proprietors, Hermann and his partner Werner, held dances complete with a three-piece band. Gottfried Steckers recalled in his memoirs how he frequented the bar after fleeing as a refugee from the East, fending off elder suitors who, bowing courteously, politely asked "May I have this dance?" The older crowd of suited, mustached men danced under the watchful eye of the "boss lady," who took her position at the entrance and decided with a quick "he comes in" who was (and was not) allowed access.[107]

Although Christopher Isherwood's edgy Kit Kat Club and the notorious Eldorado hold court in the Anglo-American imagination as the premier icons of the gay and transvestite scene, if notoriety and rumor are markers of cult status, another bar is arguably more deserving of the moniker. Ellis Bier-Bar in Kreuzberg, housed across from the arches of the Görlitzer train station, was lifted to iconic status after it was portrayed in activist filmmaker Rosa von Praunheim's 1970 film *It's Not the Homosexual Who is Perverse, but the Situation in Which He Lives*. Although purported to be a meeting place for such notoriously gay (if politically polarized) luminaries as Klaus Mann and Ernst Röhm in the 1920s, it only emerged onto the scene as a gay bar in 1946, when Elli Hartung resurrected the bomb-damaged space her mother had rented since 1912. Despite her own highly dubious political status – she was personal friends with the NS Women's League chairwoman Getrud Scholtz-Klink, and herself a NS party member from 1939, causing delayed denazification by the Allies – Elli built her bar into a central meeting space for the West Berlin gay scene, drawing a cross-border clientele until the building of the Berlin Wall. Finally awarded an operating license in 1948, Elli undertook the daunting task of clearing the facility of rubble since the house had been adversely affected by the bombing. Beer was hauled by wagon from the neighboring Schultheiss brewery while patrons chatted by candlelight because of the short supply of electricity. Prone to embellishment and a big personality, in an interview with a Berlin radio station Elli took pride in having fitted the entrance with a door pilfered from the SS guardhouse in the Behrenstrasse and a chandelier from Goebbels's propaganda ministry. The fact that the bar was only outfitted with a single toilet for its patrons, forcing women to trek upstairs to use a neighbor's facilities, garnered the attention of the Kreuzberg police who conducted the first of many visits on October 20, 1951.[108]

Despite constant troubles with the police, and a nasty dispute with her landlady that resulted in a letter-writing campaign against the establishment, Elli continued to operate the bar and, in 1952, after she had added the requisite number of toilets, was granted permission to hold dances. Instead of stemming the tide of surveillance, however, the raids continued and even increased in number. The bar surfaced in contemporary criminological literature, when Detective Superintendent Schramm reported on the establishment at a meeting in April 1959 of the Federal Criminal Authority, which had convened to discuss the ongoing problem of sexual morality and sex crimes. In a raid conducted on November 10, 1957, over 100 people were questioned, of whom 33 were forced to give further testimony in the neighboring police precinct; 14 were eventually charged, although the specific charges were not discussed in any detail. As justification, Schramm added that given the general atmosphere of bars like Elli's, "anyone who entered such an establishment had to reckon with police action." The motivation was clear: police claimed it was well within their authority to gain access to gay bars in order to investigate possible infractions against Paragraph 175 and 175a, which governed male prostitution. Using a variety of laws on the books, ranging from police procedural articles, health and welfare ordinances, and juvenile law, criminal police conducted raids to regulate the spread of venereal disease, protect the youth, and also protect public order.

While Schramm was well known within the West Berlin criminal police as overseeing the city's fight against homosexuality, in the 1960s this position was taken over by Dr. Karl Kaiser, affectionately referred to by regulars of the beer bar as "the empress," a pun on his name in German. To protect itself from the raids, Elli's, like many of the underground clubs along the Kurfürstendamm, installed a doorbell to regulate entry and, more importantly, provide enough time for patrons to "straighten themselves out" in advance of a pending raid. One bar owner at La Boheme actually went so far as to offer the police a key to the establishment to mediate the need for raids – but the police promptly turned this down, claiming it took away the element of surprise. Elli didn't need to take such a stance since she had a mole within the police service; as luck would have it, Kaiser's own son was gay, and a patron at the bar. With advance warning of a raid, Elli notified preferred guests to vacate to the backyard in the nick of time, sacrificing in the process some of her other guests. As the writer Peter Jürgen Fabich remembered, the police often gravitated toward the more effeminate "Tunten" (sissies), throwing them into the wagons, while he escaped out back. By 1965, Elli took a more proactive role, warning her guests not to dance too closely, to refrain from kissing on the mouth, and avoid the "grabbing of the sex area" just in case. She even had a sign installed to enforce the house rules.[109]

As police practice shows, despite the ongoing presence of Paragraph 175 in the West German legal code, in the years leading up to the decriminalization of homosexuality in 1969, it was not a crime to *be* gay, nor to operate a gay bar. It was unlawful to cruise and flaunt one's masculinity, whether effeminate, tough, leather, or transsexual. Other bars managed to escape the kind of scrutiny reserved for Elli's, even though they hosted masquerade dances, balls, and mixed crowds. Elli's was different, and, together with a few other similarly mixed venues, police used a range of laws to claim access to bars such as hers in order to safeguard public morals, protect the youth, and limit the spread of vice.

Elli's Bierbar was without doubt one of the most colorful attractions in postwar Kreuzberg. Elli herself was nothing short of remarkable; she made a tidy living from the bar, drove fancy cars, owned property, and lived out her days as hostess to an increasingly eclectic crowd, which over the course of 40 years included actors like Hildegard Knef, writers like Günter Grass and painters like Fritz Muehlenhaupt, and even musicians like Udo Lindenberg. Before the Wall went up, nightly gays and lesbians from the neighboring districts made their way across the sector boundary, including Charlotte von Mahlsdorf (born Lothar Berfelde), proud wearer of traditional German *tracht*, which on one occasion caused Elli personally to lift her up onto the bar and yell for all to hear, "you are my own ornamental doll."[110] Although, as von Mahlsdorf wrote in 1961, "overnight, it was all over," Elli's continued to draw a mixed crowd from the West Berlin scene until it changed hands in the late 1980s once Elli was forced into a nursing home. In the early 1990s, it was no longer salvageable, as the building required much more money and attention than the landlord was able to invest.

Elli's is one of many examples of the burgeoning and competing homosexual subcultures that came back into view after the war and despite police regulation and morality enforcement in the 1950s and 1960s. One of many lesbian-owned and -operated establishments, it projected an air of tolerance among the community itself: hustlers, transvestites, sissy boys, "half-naked young men, in fancy evening dresses or in enchanting almost transparent flimsy garments," and mannish women sought sanctuary from prying eyes and judgmental hearts. A throwback to the 1900s in terms of decor, complete with a framed picture of Berlin as it once had been, "within this topsy turvy turmoil, there was one stable rock: the host [Elli], wearing a striking motorcycle outfit."[111] Harking back to what Richard McCormick has characterized as the quintessential mark of 1920s sexuality – that sexual practices had not yet gelled into hard-and-fast identities – then certainly the Bierbar continued this tradition of sexual fluidity: the mixing of high and low, and the intersections of same and opposite sex-desiring worlds.[112] Although establishments such as Elli's were shuttered when the Nazis came to power, Hitler's regime was less concerned with innate desire than with those who externalized it. In other words, for the Nazis too, it was not a crime to be gay but to act on one's desires. This did not stop men from wanting to be in the company of other men, and, once fighting ceased, we see the staying power of queer sociability in the way in which same-sex desiring men and women sought out love, lust, and companionship amidst the ruins of the occupied city. In places like Elli's, itself a simple *Stricherkneipe* (rent-boy bar) with a colorful history, a wide range of people sought refuge from the drudgery of day-to-day life, "from intellectuals and train conductors to retirees, transvestites, leather types."[113] While there was some safety in community in places like Elli's, outside its doors, non-normative sexual practices underwent scrutiny of a different kind, landing practitioners, especially if they were young, in a host of institutions to help inculcate appropriate behavior. If modern sexual consciousness was the product both of liberatory and regulatory principles, then Berlin's incarceral spaces demonstrated that the East and West German states were still very much invested in controlling sexual desire. Just as the city was marked by sites of subculture, so too were there spaces set up to regulate the sexual comportment of youth.

5
Home

What is true of the family is also true of the great family of the nation!

Walter Ulbricht, *Five Year Plan, 1951–1955*[1]

In the interests of all residents, children are forbidden to play games.

House notice, West Berlin.[2]

In a federal youth services memorandum of April 1958, an unknown author outlined the current state of youth criminal policy in the German Democratic Republic. "Unlike in West Germany," they wrote, "in the GDR, delinquency is no longer the product of war and fascism as it was in the years after 1945." Implicitly connected to the evils of capitalism and not the aftermath of total war, juvenile delinquency was less of a problem in East Germany, apparently, due to the social character of the Workers' and Farmers' State. Contemporary cases of youth endangerment and criminality owed their existence not to the lingering stain of prewar social discipline, the author suggested, but to the inadequate application of socialist educational methods. Indeed, such programs were either unknown or "not uniformly applied by those responsible for instituting policy."[3] This example of double speak – the initial downplaying of youth crime followed by attempts to foist responsibility on the ill-conceived actions of rogue caseworkers and incomplete socialist acculturation – is illustrative of the mechanisms of governance at work in the insecure East German regime. What it fails to take into account, however, is that on both sides of the boundary, and in Cold War Berlin especially, the rise in postwar youth crime posed a host of difficult challenges for police, court, and youth welfare workers in the first decades after the war.[4]

While the previous chapters have explored geographies of leisure, memory, fear, experimentation, lust, emotion, and desire in the divided city, this chapter takes somewhat of a different tack. In surveying spaces within the city designed to prop up the faltering family unit, it focuses on efforts to stabilize the war-ravaged family home and the gender roles and sexual practices that gave it currency. In mapping out the network of incarceral spaces, those workhouses, jails, and remand homes set up to deal with the growing problem of youth crime, it analyzes how these institutions functioned as alternative geographies of home – places where adolescents were schooled in their future role as (re)productive citizens. Taking up the story of the rent boys and "loose girls" examined thus far in this book – the delinquent and endangered youth caught in homosexual liaisons with men at the train station, in underground bars, or in VD raids on city streets – it analyzes state, municipal, and, in the West, religious efforts to correct the problem of sexual unruliness in order to promote more appropriate contacts and encounters. Efforts to cement healthy social mores in these institutions, it was hoped, would chart a new life course for these wayward teens. This chapter suggests that parallel strategies were at work on both sides of the German–German boundary, which goes some way in explaining the tenor of moral panic affecting 1950s Germany, to say nothing of the widely held desire to stamp out anything that challenged the family construct as a cornerstone of rebuilding. These processes of moral reform, therefore, shed much-needed light on the tensions and spaces of modernity and reconstruction that remained unresolved in both postwar Germanys. Up until the building of the Berlin Wall, the vexing problem of errant sexual morals required direct intervention in the lives of adolescents to help prop up one of society's most basic of institutions. In these spaces of detention we see everyday evidence of the growing geopolitical divide between East and West.

Crime and Moral Refashioning

Research has shown that criminality, enforcement, and policing rates in the Federal Republic were higher than in the Weimar years.[5] West Germany was particularly intent on curbing male aggression and sexual violence, where young people were more than well represented. In East Germany, the situation was quite similar. The proliferation of petty criminality and crimes of morality, together with the economic pressures brought about by division that were more palpably felt in the GDR, forced authorities in East Berlin to consider new ways to tackle the ever-mounting problem of juvenile delinquency.[6] Coinciding with a flurry of legal and welfare reform measures that clarified anew the conditions under which young offenders could be forced into protective custody, both East and West Berlin governments resurrected the use of workhouses and special remand homes to deal with the incommodious problem of early sexual experimentation. Conceived as the final site of intervention once all other avenues for resocialization were exhausted, youth homes, numbering some 30 facilities by the 1950s, were designed to correct aberrant behavior and, crucially, to inculcate qualities of citizenship and personhood through a program of moral education and hard work.[7] Providing an education and limited instruction in household management, agricultural production, or industrial labor, caseworkers worked together with the police and youth courts in their respective halves of the city to devise practical solutions to what they believed was the growing passivity of the nation's young people. In these homes, abnormal and unwanted forms of sexual behavior and gender comportment fell under the microscope, since the task at hand was to inculcate healthful and productive qualities befitting the next generation of workers, students, fathers, and mothers. In the East, derailment (*Entgleisung*) was explicitly linked to failed socialist development, the antidote to which could only be an "active, positive, upbringing with...respect for the ten...commandments of the new socialist morality"[8] based on the model advanced by Walter Ulbricht in 1958 and put into practice in the day-to-day operation of the nation's workhouses and remand homes.[9] Across the border in West Berlin, meanwhile, group facilities based on the Anglo-American model likewise served as cauldrons of moral and gender acculturation where it was hoped that respect for home, hearth, and family would offset the "awful legacy of moral and material ruin" brought about by the war, and the possibly alienating impact of American-styled cultural consumption.[10]

As crucibles of regulation, negotiation, and often, but not solely, social control, these institutions were core agents in the Cold War struggle over nonconformism and moral reform.[11] The roots to this network of remand homes and workhouses extended back to well before Hitler; they owed their existence to a particular set of imperatives and practices for dealing with wayward youth that developed in the context of industrialization.[12] Although youth reformatory practices and justice legislation evolved over this long history from the nineteenth century through to National Socialism, many of the core assumptions about endangerment were re-applied willy-nilly after capitulation, especially the tremendous importance placed on buttressing family-based, heteronormative work and gender roles.[13] In particular, youth social policy in Cold War Berlin was oriented around a certain mode of thinking about the gender of deviance (*Verwahrlosung*). As places of acculturation and estrangement for those wards who failed to conform to society's dictates for normative behavior, these sites reflected and refracted a range of attitudes, expressions, and frameworks about how life was to be lived in the post-fascist city and, crucially, about how both postwar governments envisioned the scope and scale of intervention in the lives of their youngest citizens. An analysis of these spaces as building blocks of sexual citizenship brings back into view longstanding debates about the deleterious impact of city life, and the lengths to which East and West Berlin authorities would go to mediate its influence both in the aftermath of war and in the shadow of division. However, as this chapter will show, spaces of incarceration were not simply *reconstruction sites* for the recovery of past mores and values, but places where the future behavior of young citizens would be molded and shaped.

The Politics of Crime in Postwar Berlin

In the early postwar years, the causes of criminality were obvious. When looking for reasons to explain the problem in divided Germany, jurist Karl Bader was unequivocal: one need not look further than the contemporary adult generation, those who fought in the war and struggled to survive its aftermath. In many ways, his analysis was absolutely accurate. Of the men who did return from the front, many were broken physically and psychologically.[14] Poor living conditions and psychological war wounds go part of the distance in explaining the rise in criminal sexual convictions in the years after World Wars I and II, suggesting a relationship between mass violence and sexual intransigence in times of martial conflict and afterwards.[15] At the very least, the ongoing trauma of war posed unique challenges for men trying to reintegrate into the family fold upon return from the theaters of conflict and incarceration in prisoner-of-war camps in Soviet Russia. That this trauma played itself out in Weimar, East and West German statistics on youth crime cannot be coincidental. Although Bader was referencing the situation in West Germany, the social factors contributing to rising crime rates among adolescents were applicable to the East as well. "Of premier significance is the family," whether broken families, half families, or women standing alone.[16] The inability to reconstitute healthy family life was the "breeding ground for derailment," the single most determining factor for youth criminality.[17] Bader's description of the failings of family life was supported in statistics by sociologist Hilde Thurwald, who documented in great detail the plight of over 400 families struggling for an existence in capitulated Berlin.[18] Not only were entire city blocks leveled in the bombing, but useable housing stock was either requisitioned by the Allies, apportioned out, claimed via some madcap notion of squatter's rights, or shared by multiple family units. Literally and figuratively, defeat meant Berliners never really could go home again.[19]

For many Berlin youth, the street was their only refuge. Whether picked up at the train station, on the city street after dark, or in an underground bar, infected with syphilis from a zero-hour rape or through willing contact for food or fun, those youth sent through the system were unwilling participants in an ideological tug of war. While Nazi juvenile policy was formalized in the service of strengthening the national body with the objective of fighting a war of expansion, during the early years of postwar division, biopolitical maxims retreated from view, and the rehabilitation of offenders took on added meaning as each country competed for economic recovery. However, these places of confinement and moral reform retained their importance as spaces where the parameters of citizenship were constituted, frequently along pronounced gender lines. And yet, the objects of intervention, the young men and women relegated to these homes, were not just passive receptacles of the state's teaching. More often than not, they found unique and important ways of shaping their own experiences in these facilities, forging their own path through the system. Most importantly, the incarceration of young offenders – in this chapter, young men and women charged with morals offences – demonstrates, yet again, that definitions of deviance among male and female youth could bear striking similarities. Although Detlev Peukert, Kersten Kohtz, and Christina Benninghaus have argued that in imperial and Weimar Germany, male and female deviance was fundamentally different in scope and orientation, where boys were sent through the system for work-related infractions while young women almost always bore the brunt of moral panics surrounding their sexuality, the post-Hitler period ushered in significant changes. Adolescent male behavior was increasingly sexualized, confirming a shift already underway in late Weimar but unrecognized by most historians.[20] With the explicit cultivation of male aggressiveness and sexual prowess by the Nazis as part of its militarist, pronatalist agenda, sexuality – and heterosexuality in particular – increasingly formed a core component of young men's social as well as political identity, requiring appropriate guidance and streamlining to adequately take hold.[21]

Given the omnipresent fear of another armed confrontation on German soil, it is no surprise that adolescence would come under the microscope in both postwar Germanys with renewed vigor. Caught in the police dragnet for petty crime, vagrancy, prostitution, homosexuality, and general "hanging about' (*herumtreiben*), young offenders posed the ultimate challenge to state authorities intent on substantive ideological refashioning, while simultaneously gauging the challenge of the Cold War and rearming. Although division was formalized in the creation of two German states in 1949, West Germany left open the option of reunification while Soviet authorities continued to press for alternative solutions to the division of Berlin. Normalization of relations between the two countries was a series of fits and starts. The July 1955 Geneva Summit had carved out a new trade policy between the two Germanys and the Big Four Allied powers, but this also set a course for the war of consumption that would animate relations between East and West in the ensuing decades.[22] In the fall of that same year, West German Chancellor Konrad Adenauer would travel to Moscow and secure the release of the remaining 10,000 German prisoners of war held those last 10 years since capitulation in Soviet territory, all the while holding true to the policy of not officially recognizing the existence of the GDR. Within the push and pull of German–German relations, both countries took as aggressive a stance as possible to rearm their militaries and lay the foundation for the building of a citizen army, placing in the process renewed interest on questions of masculine comportment, since a new generation of youth would need to be convinced of duty of service without the overt militarism of the preceding Nazi regime.[23]

In iconic Berlin, symbol of the Cold War and site of a possible future war, relatively minor sexual offenses acquired additional meaning as challenges to the health and well-being of the national body politic. The involvement of youth in building socialism has formed a significant part of GDR historiography, one that has received much attention in recent years on both sides of the Atlantic.[24] Indeed, most historians agree that the quest to rehabilitate delinquent youth was anything but apolitical.[25] That the Cold War dividing line through the center of Berlin failed to curtail the porosity of city spaces, stop the movement of population, and limit the reach of consumer politics, advertising, and pop culture meant that each side of the city struggled with similar problems in reaching the youth with their respective messages of duty, respectability, and self-control. In the West, the way station for ever-increasing numbers of refugees fleeing Ulbricht's Germany, measures to impart important life skills were deemed crucial to the social, economic, and political well-being of core FRG institutions, chief of which was the family. In the East, caseworkers and reformers reevaluated prewar penal and welfare policy in their search for new ways to eradicate the remnants of capitalism so as to ease the transition to socialism. That all this took place in a physical landscape still haunted by chronic shortages, poor living conditions, broken families, and occupation gives a better understanding of the quest for moral boundary making as the key to social stability in the years leading up to the construction of the Berlin Wall.

Upon first glance, the divided city might not appear to provide the best vantage point from which to gauge the growing pains of reconstruction. Its special status certainly created extreme conditions that could not be replicated anywhere else in the two Germanys. Yet its very uniqueness as an icon of modernity and social engineering, the site where barbarism was planned and revenge unleashed, shaped the sense of urgency surrounding the rehabilitation of the city's disaffected and disenfranchised youth. Many of the policies crafted in the late 1940s were designed with the generation of *Flakhelfer* in mind, the term given to *Wehrmacht* and Hitler Youth anti-aircraft gunners who had manned the bunkers during the Battle of Berlin. This term was used to encapsulate those youths weaned on Nazi imperatives and institutions, and who experienced the *Untergang* (capitulation) cowered in cellars alongside their mothers or creeping through city streets in oversized helmets and ill-fitting greatcoats. By the mid-1950s, the youths under scrutiny by social services were too young to recall the deprivation of war's end, born instead into the rubble of the Reich's aftermath. This generation of rubble children represented a different set of challenges. As this cohort came of age they acquired the designation of *Halbstarke* or "toughs," a term that had been around since the nineteenth century but which quickly became the stuff of legend, sociological scrutiny, and pop culture in the 1950s. They were the rebellious youth involved in the infamous riots that rocked East and West Berlin, which, as Uta Poiger has documented, shocked both city administrations into action against delinquents.[26] These youths coveted the look of American film stars, dressed like James Dean and Marlon Brando, hung about street corners in Charlottenburg and Prenzlauer Berg, listened to jazz and rock 'n' roll, and fled the GDR in shocking numbers via the S-Bahn or by simply overstaying their work visas. At the same time that Allied, city, and state officials were busy enforcing political jurisdictions in the divided city, hammering out the terms of international law, trade, and migration while clamping down on border crossers, youth advocates, church charities, beat cops, and social workers likewise drew lines of demarcation between healthy and injurious behavior and intervened in an unparalleled degree in the lives of teenaged youths to control spaces of leisure, crime, and oppositionality with the hopes of guiding the emotional if not intellectual development of adolescents away from peril and back to respectability.

In this sense, Cold War Berlin is perhaps the perfect place to analyze the meanings associated with the search for home as both a metaphor into the role of the state in propping up the faltering family and the reliance on institutionalized care to further cement in society a foundation for a new way of life. Whether followed into the ruins for a quick transaction, surveyed at train stations for signs of solicitation, arrested in raids of underground bars or wrestling matches, or plucked off the street for fitting the profile of loose and endangered women, teenagers were subject to unyielding scrutiny at the hands of police, church, and welfare advocates. Without the intact nuclear family to domesticate errant desires, resocialization fell to a vast network of caseworkers and police who used makeshift bunker jails, workhouses, and remand homes to inculcate each state's vision of preferred gender roles, sexual moderation, and a healthy work ethic. In the process, these homes served as important geographies of socialization, regulation, and also encounter within and outside the city limits. As places where policies of the past rubbed up against the politics of the present, they were highly charged spaces of modernity and moral reform and, as we will see, vitally important reconstruction sites for social, sexual, and political normalization in the years leading up to the building of the Berlin Wall.

Criminality and Deviance

The postwar struggle over youth criminality and endangerment drew on three strands of nineteenth-century social policy forged during the consolidation of the German welfare state – penal reform, child welfare, and corrective education. From the 1850s onward, reformers, jurists, psychiatrists, and a host of self-proclaimed experts rallied the imperial governments to implement provisions guaranteeing the utility and function of public custodianship.[27] These efforts to refine the legalities of care and custodianship emerged on the scene around the same time as European nations looked to institutionalization broadly to tackle the problems associated with social unrest, rising crime, and urban poverty. In this way, alongside urban planning and modern police services, the growth of the caring professions and the zeal for incarceration, whether in mental facilities, workhouses, prisons, or remand homes, was a direct offshoot of modernization.[28] In Wilhelmine Germany, guardianship and welfare initiatives were continually debated in the formulation of the Civil Code (*Bürgerliches Gesetzbuch* or BGB), while adult correctional facilities, reformatories, and workhouses were licensed through the criminal statute, which as of 1923 included a separate code for young offenders (the *Reichsjugendgesetzbuch* or RJGG).[29] Youth reformatories entered on the scene around the same time, linking child welfare to penal reform by extending patriarchal authority from the confines of the family to the correctional institution. Reforms to the Imperial Penal Code (*Reichsstrafgesetzbuch* or RStGB) afforded the various German states the option of establishing criteria for reformatories in prevention of moral waywardness.[30] But the family was no longer out of the reach of the state entirely as a quasi-autonomous domain of unfettered patriarchal authority. In an admixture of custodial and criminal law, the state established Houses of Salvation (*Rettungshäuser*) for both criminal and socially endangered youth, laying claim in the process to public custodianship in a manner that previously had been reserved for household heads.[31] In fact, according to a prominent penal reformer of the day, correctional facilities were fully capable of inculcating paternal authority and discipline since wayward children could be instructed in the appropriate teachings of traditional society through a surrogate institutional setting.[32]

Although the product of conflicting visions of social reform, workhouses and reformatories embodied both valorization and fear of the family's role in socializing the young. Progressive reformers, coming from all sides of the political and confessional spectrum, called for the standardization of methods to treat social dislocation and help equalize the destructive aspects of modernity's relentless march. *Rettungshäuser*, workhouses, youth courts, jails, municipal youth bureaus (*Jugendämter*), and legal statutes for young offenders represented a collective strategy in socializing errant youths while integrating them into society as contributors to national, political, and economic life. But as moral failings, unruliness, and impoverishment became transformed into medically substantiated causes of endangerment by the 1920s, child welfare reformers gained unparalleled authority in defining the form and function of corrective intervention.[33] All this would be for naught, however, for by 1934 private charities and laypeople lost most of their real and imagined authority as the Nazi consolidation of power gave rise to initiatives like the National Socialist People's Welfare (*Nationalsozialistische Volkswohlfahrt* or NSV) in addition to new institutions designed to underscore the power of the state in structuring social identity.[34]

After World War II, the caring profession's preoccupation with youth initially formed part of a calibrated response to Nazi policies. Brought into public view by the misery of occupation and defeat, the soaring level of criminality reflected the war-ravaged conditions into which, quite literally, the younger generation had been born. Weaned on a virulent strain of Nazi population politics (*Bevölkerungspolitik*) which tied the Reich's reproductive health to the glory of the nation, many youths had come of age early in order to serve the nation as grist to the mill of battle, or as dutiful wives and mothers.[35] Alongside this *Flakhelfer* generation, now toddlers and small children were regarded as equally, if not more, endangered as anthropologists, psychologists, even sex therapists attempted to predict the long-term impact of war, privation, and social disarray.[36] Most shocking of all was the impact of the physical environment on biological rhythms as researchers documented what they saw as a connection between the trauma of war and the earlier onset of puberty among adolescents, suggesting a link between violence, space, and increased sexual permissiveness.[37] Placing blame for postwar lawlessness squarely on the shoulders of Hitler and the Nazis, local government, church officials, and social reformers debated ways in which to curb juvenile delinquency in order to begin the slow and arduous process of resocializing what they feared might be successive generations of morally decayed youth. Just as before the war, youth issues would reemerge as a crucial issue for jurists, child welfare advocates, police, and social workers as they sought ways to impart social policy in an occupied and divided Germany.

In the summer and fall of 1945, fears of ongoing societal decline did not only surface in the travelogues of expats and their rhetoric of civilization's ruin but was there for all to see in the very image of the broken cityscape, suggesting profoundly significant sociospatial moorings that few Germans failed to recognize. Indeed, capitulated Berlin showcased the endangerment of its youth in vivid color. Alongside the rawness of physical and material devastation and the macabre photos of children at play among the ruins, statistics gathered by the various city agencies testified to the enormity of the situation at hand. Whereas in 1938 there had been 286 young offenders registered aged from 14 to 18 years, a rate of 173 per 100,000 population, in 1946 this had risen by an unbelievable 850 percent, with over 1800 youths making their way through what little remained of the system. This figure of 1482 crimes per 100,000 population did not even include the so-called *Strafunmündige*, those

youths under the age of 14 who were deemed not criminally responsible for the over 2200 crimes registered in their names.[38] The question
of where to house the legions of unsupervised youth loomed large, and
once again the heterotopic potential of the city's militarized and incarceral spaces was swiftly brought to bear on the growing crisis. As we saw
in Chapter 1, no sooner had the flak guns stilled than bunker antechambers were converted into makeshift jails in addition to other essential
facilities like hospitals. Gestapo and criminal police holding cells were
hastily remodeled into makeshift dormitory spaces in what remained of
the police headquarters on Dircksenstrasse near Alexanderplatz. According to the *Sozialdemokrat* newspaper in February 1948, since it opened
its doors in June 1945 "over 10,000 male and female children and youth
had used the facility."[39] Even one of the city's most sinister Nazi execu-
tion sites was recalibrated to house the legions of young offenders picked
up on the streets of Berlin. Outbuildings on the Plötzensee prison compound were quickly converted to a youth jail, a short walk from the
place where over 3000 opponents of the regime – communists as well as
conservatives, potters, and politicians – were executed. Although it was
never expressly stated in the police and court registers, one can only
wonder whether the newly incarcerated knew of the macabre solemnity
of the site and the suffering that had only recently happened there.[40]

Despite word emanating from the city that all was not well in the former capital, the promise of making it back to Berlin held a tremendous
hold over the various transient populations tramping about the countryside and desperate for word from whatever family might have survived
deportation and the bombing.[41] It was here that criminologists and
sociobiologists, some of whom had made their careers serving the Nazis,
offered up the best of their knowledge to help refine policy and procedures on juvenile criminality. Despite disciplinary differences, most
agreed that the breakdown of the family was the single largest cause
of derailment. It was not just the collapse of the nuclear family that
brought such trouble, but the conditions under which remaining familial units struggled to survive. As a 45-page report from the Protestant
social welfare organization Innere Mission proclaimed in 1946, close
quarters and the fact that housing was in such short supply meant that
the rationing of space in Berlin and "the communal sharing of kitchen
and bath facilities among many families endangers the youth."[42] In his
1949 publication on the sociology of postwar crime, Karl Bader claimed
that austere living conditions were particularly deleterious for women
and girls, who lacked the strength and spirit of men and thus fell victim to jeopardy in far greater numbers. This gendering of susceptibility

was confirmed in Bader's thinking by the high VD transmission rate and the overwhelming frequency with which women and girls turned to prostitution. What manifested itself in male youths as robbery and petty theft, begging and vagabondage "evolves in girls as an early tendency towards promiscuity and ends in full-blown harlotry."[43] Despite the urgency of his intentions, hidden from view in Bader's account were the hundreds of rent boys and itinerant youths who likewise turned tricks in the shadow of the ruins, huddled about train station waiting rooms, and made their way in equally eyebrow-raising numbers into remand homes, jails, dormitories, and workhouses. Boyhood sexuality was certainly imperiled, yet interestingly, for jurists like Bader the sexual aspect of their behavior was often not cited as the dominant cause for concern.

Where Bader gleaned his analysis of Berlin from crime statistics and a long tradition of Lombrosian criminological literature that perpetuated this gendering of deviance, in a 1947 article in the newly minted liberal daily newspaper, *Der Tagesspiegel*, the soon-to-be world famous psychologist Alexander Mitscherlich claimed that delinquency was less a problem of gender or sexuality than of the mind, one that only psychoanalysis and compassionate therapy could truly hope to cure. Harking back to the human capacity for crime and violence explored at length in Freud's somber 1929 text *Civilization and Its Discontents*, Mitscherlich argued that postwar conditions, broadly defined, had contributed to the creation of an entire caste of *"homo lupus"* teens capable of tremendous asociality due the broad-based leveling of social values, the betrayal of generations, and the breakdown of the family. To counter the "physical and psychic effect of catastrophe which destroyed the family, and shook the foundation of parental authority," corrective institutions must shoulder this responsibility and provide "a stabile form of collective nurturing (*Erziehung*)." In one of many missives aimed at reestablishing a footing for a craft much maligned by the Nazis, Mitscherlich argued that spaces of detention must serve as ersatz families, creating a world in microcosm (*die Welt im Kleinen*) to shelter and nourish healthy, honest, compassionate relationships among wards. Although "military order and unconditional subservience might for the duration of inhabitancy appear to bring results," Mitscherlich underscored for his readership that much more might be achieved through compassion and patience. Indeed, the cost to society was great for failing to act, or for simply reapplying recent methods of confinement and custodianship. The continued alienation of youth threatened to endanger all of Germany at a time when it was most vulnerable. The only hope was to break from the extant welfare and penal tradition and begin completely anew. Failing to take these steps would only "rebury the hopes for our country's renewal alongside the happiness of our youth."[44]

Instead of blazing new trails as Mitscherlich suggested, welfare advocates, criminologists, and psychoanalysts initially put their faith in past practice to divine ways of dealing with the crush of statistics supporting the upsurge of youth criminality. So too did city and state authorities in divided Berlin. Overwhelmed by the situation at war's end, youth advocates in the Soviet Occupation Zone had no choice but to make a Faustian bargain and uphold several Nazi laws and ordinances maintaining curfews, restricting youth access to adult-oriented nightclubs, and limiting certain forms of employment deemed harmful to developing minds.[45] It was not just the East German dictatorship that deployed tactics honed under previous regimes, and amplified, often to deleterious ends, policies implemented by the Nazis. Well into the 1950s, jurists in the Federal Republic debated the usefulness of maintaining article 17 of the Juvenile Justice Act (*Jugendgerichtsbuch*), which stipulated the conditions under which a youth might be given an open-ended sentence (*unbestimmte Dauer*). Ideally not to exceed four years of incarceration in a youth facility or jail, this paragraph entered into the Nazi legal statute in 1943, serving that regime well in its effort to regulate the actions of its youngest citizens. Since these ideas had circulated before 1933 in juvenile justice and child welfare debates, this statute was not deemed representative of purely Nazi thinking and, like the anti-sodomy paragraph, it had some use for dealing with the postwar moral panic surrounding youth criminality. The postwar crime wave, the breakdown of the family, uncontrollable femininity, and challenges to the moral imperatives of Christian Democracy generally underscored the need for this level of intervention, provided the "educational" component of the sentence was made explicit in the courtroom.[46]

Enforcing Behavior in Heterotopic Spaces

Not only were policies from the Nazi regime applied over the boundaries of 1945 and perhaps more surprisingly over 1949, but often the homes themselves had earlier incarnations as Nazi, Weimar, and even Wilhelmine detention institutions. Some places, like Rummelsberg and Struveshof, had particularly nasty histories as centers of interrogation in the persecution of Berlin's known social outsiders, asocials, and homosexuals.[47] Within the walls of these structures, both of which were located in the Soviet Zone, the fledgling GDR sought to cement a foundation for its new social order, where young men and women would be educated through redemptive labor in the roles they would be expected to fulfill in the Worker's and Farmer's State.[48] In these institutions, criminality, especially crimes of a sexual nature, met with exacting punishment given the importance of moral righteousness in labeling the FRG as home to fear-mongering imperialists bent against the otherwise well-meaning attempts of Ulbricht and his coterie in the East to bring about peaceful reunification.[49] Securing a firmament for moral rebuilding in rhetoric and practice became the priority of all public officials, and police chief Paul Markgraf proclaimed as early as 1947 the readiness of police under his command in the eastern districts of the city to intervene in the interests of children, youth, and society.[50]

Applying youth policy on the mean streets of Cold War Berlin required the work of many different people, institutions, and ministries on both sides of the boundary. In fact, the incarceral map of the city not only blurred temporal and ideological distinctions in harking back to Nazi policy and institutions, it also transcended professional boundaries since it relied on a host of authorities from police to caseworker, physician to teacher. Remand homes and reformatories were governed by an onion-skin layering of directives, some welfare driven and educative, others purely punitive and penal in nature. As in the case of the Struveshof facility in Ludwigsfelde, just to the southwest of the city in the neighboring province of Brandenburg but connected by rail, these facilities might serve many purposes in housing wards of the state and orphans together with convicts and *Schwererziehbare* or difficult youth.[51] While the local youth service workers coordinated efforts in the city, certain military government laws also gave local authorities license to build and operate similar houses for more explicitly rehabilitative purposes. Designed primarily to combat the spread of venereal disease, police and health service workers drew on the constellation of reformatories as temporary housing for quarantined women in addition to the many "asocial persons without permanent living quarters or demonstrable work habits" at large and roaming throughout the city.[52] Youth under the age of 18 charged with a crime or suspected of general asociality, promiscuity, or of leading an itinerate lifestyle might be sent to homes operating under the auspices of the eastern sector's ministry of *Volksbildung* which, following Order No. 156 of the Soviet Military Authority, oversaw youth services in the eastern portion of Berlin as of 1947.[53] These *Jugendwerkhöfe* or youth workhouses were designed for the most difficult cases but included a degree of educational programming to "make [charges] into worthy citizens of the Workers' and

Farmers' State." If not via one of these routes then criminal youth might expect to be forwarded to a remand home after serving time in a youth facility so that further monitoring of their progress could be guaranteed. Despite the motivations for forwarding youth to one of these institutions, this complicated and sometimes overlapping network of facilities had one thing in common: above all else, caseworkers, jurists, and police, especially those in the emerging GDR, agreed that "the main ingredient for reforming wayward youth ... was work."[54]

But before reaching the ateliers and farms of remand homes and workhouses, youths first encountered reform policy in the neighborhood streets surrounding their communities. Among the most visible agents of youth reform were the special police detachments comprised largely of female officers tasked with policing sexual offenses and crimes involving children. Housed in precincts in each district, they worked in tandem with Allied Military Police (MP) conducting sweeps of local bars, movie houses, and cafés, and were often the first line of attack against promiscuous and endangered youth. Once a crime was committed and an offender identified, the women's police units documented the occurrence in their police ledger and, depending upon the nature of the crime, might enter the youth's profile into a general card index like those assembled for other sex offenses such as prostitution and homosexuality.[55] After the initial round of questions at the local police station, police forwarded the teens to a temporary outreach center (*Jugendhilfestelle*) in the basement of the Dircksenstrasse police headquarters, where, in consultation with the central youth bureau (*Hauptjugendamt*), they prepared the youth for a possible hearing in court. The *Jugendhilfestelle* near Alexanderplatz was in such high demand that it had to be renovated in 1948 since its facilities were no longer capable of dealing with the thousands of youths who had passed through its doors since the defeat of the Reich in May 1945. Despite the affirmed need for such a facility, the site was poorly equipped to deal with the increasing ranks of criminal youths from neighboring districts. The Dircksenstrasse facility, along with its overflow center on Greifswalder Strasse in Prenzlauer Berg, contained a mere 145 beds for temporary shelter, which, according to a 1948 newspaper report in *Sozialdemokrat*, hardly kept pace with the steady influx of detainees.[56]

Taking youths from the districts and then apportioning them to one of the many institutions in this diffuse patchwork of facilities served a logical purpose in these insecure first years of early state building since these spaces, and the bodies relegated there, helped reinforce boundaries of behavior and comportment through a relational process of identification. The more depraved or diseased the youth was, the greater the distinction from the social and national body – all the more important, then, to begin a thorough process of rehabilitation away from the home district and neighborhood so that youths might learn to cultivate more appropriate, healthful, and productive behavior. Indeed, the spaces that emerged out of the welfare and legal codes before and after 1945 played an indelible role in producing and sustaining dominant notions of gender and citizenship, both in the way youths were identified as needing intervention and in their treatment once incarcerated. Indeed, gender distinctions acquired spatial markers. Despite the network of facilities designed to educate youths about their plight and ostensibly to provide them with advice on how to access the system, young women and girls rounded up in raids typically bypassed these sites and were forcibly sent not to the *Jugendhilfestelle* but to VD clinics run by the Berlin Department of Health, where they could expect to be detained overnight before undergoing mandatory pelvic examinations for gonorrhea and syphilis. If diseased, they were committed by law for the duration of their illness while health officials forwarded their particulars to both the youth bureau and police, since the willful and wanton spread of disease constituted a misdemeanor according to both occupation health ordinances and the German Penal Code.[57] Meanwhile, boys and young men in the *Jugendhilfestelle* waited until police and social workers determined the appropriate course of action for them. Given the nature of the specific crime committed, a youth might be forwarded to one of the city's group homes to await a hearing in front of a juvenile court. In the meantime, the case came under the jurisdiction of the Youth Court Counseling Services (*Jugendgerichtshilfe*), whose task it was to research the background of the offender and document the charge's family history – even, if necessary, creating a psychological profile to help identify the cause and extent of moral endangerment. Social workers then submitted these reports to the particular judge presiding over the youth's case. A direct carry-over from the Weimar period, this service attempted to make the court more sensitive to the plight of wayward youth by drawing attention to milieu and family life as indicators of the need for corrective education instead of outright punishment. With careful intervention instead of incarceration, a young charge might learn the error of their ways and embrace reform.[58] Far from simply indicating a preexisting criminal predisposition, however, these profiles also reinforced widely held notions of asociality, tracing its origins and causes back to the broken and overburdened family. But in the early postwar era, such indicators as dirty living quarters and a working mother, which were frequently mentioned in these evaluations, were more often the rule than the exception. If an intact family was the measurement of a healthful maturation and social development, many Berliners in East and West alike certainly fell short of this mark.[59]

In a 1948 article in one of the Berlin dailies entitled "Mom threw me out! An afternoon at social services – helping hands, healing words," a reporter documented a day in the life at the municipal department of social services. The *mise en scène* follows the story of a typical parent during her visit to the offices of social services about her teenage son's predicament. Describing him as possessing a "mixture of stupidity and smarts," the mother outlined that Freddy had already spent time in the Fichtebunker youth detention center for breaking and entering, theft, and shirking work responsibilities. Returning to her home with the journalist, Freddy's mother added, "he stole anything that wasn't nailed down to buy cigarettes and chocolate," and brought shame and scandal upon the family by having "socialized with known homosexuals." As a result of his most recent crimes, Freddy was forwarded to the *Jugendhilfestelle* on Dirksenstrasse where he seemed to conduct himself well at the beginning of his stay. Eight days before Christmas, however, he ran away, only to be caught once more by police. This time, a youth court judge would decide Freddy's fate after a short psychiatric assessment. Whatever the outcome in the courts, the reporter suggested that the boy would be best served by a stay in the country, a phrase synonymous with a sentence in one of the city's workhouses and remand homes, often located in a leafy suburb or outside city limits entirely – a testament to the ongoing link between urbanity and illicit behavior.

The reporter's story draws attention to three distinct features of postwar criminality and rehabilitative care. In terms of a general profile, Freddy's crimes were quite typical of the period since his initial charges of petty theft and shirking were representative of the kinds of infractions committed by boys and male teens. In addition to this misbehavior, however, he is also described as sexually permissive, preferring to hang out with friends of dubious sexual orientation. Ultimately, when caught by police, the reporter's veiled reference to the practice of sending offenders to work facilities as a means by which to correct untoward behavior would have enjoyed widespread public agreement. If adult Germans perceived a threat from youth in a general sense, the specific acts of stealing, shirking, and sexual promiscuousness were the three main causes of alarm among youth service workers and police, and in the penal policies of the divided city, this behavior triggered immediate action.

Perils and Pitfalls

Despite the well-meaning intervention of youth service workers, material hardship, administrative chaos, and overlapping spheres of influence hampered efforts in effecting meaningful change in the lives of endangered youth. Until the currency reform of 1948, economic hardship was widespread and well documented in monthly statistical reports that charted increasing rates of malnutrition in addition to property and violent crimes.[60] General uncertainty about Soviet consolidation of power in the Soviet zone caused the flight and dislocation of a new wave of political refugees in to the American, British, and French sectors. By the end of 1949 alone, half a million youth aged 14 to 20 were registered in the newly established West Germany, many of whom lived in temporary camps and shelters after being initially interrogated at the Marienfelde refugee facility in West Berlin. After their exit interview (to ensure they were not members of the secret police), they joined the ranks of other displaced persons, some of whom had fled the former eastern territories in advance of the Russians at war's end.[61] Since West Berlin served as a kind of island in the storm, a Western toehold within the Eastern Bloc, it quickly became home to the many transient and disaffected youth whom eastern critics feared searched for escape, excitement, and leisure among the bright lights of the big city.

To be sure, Berlin's unique situation, as well as the challenging living conditions, ongoing privation, and the breakdown of the family unit caused alarm among police, social service workers, and health authorities on both sides of the boundary. But the steady stream of transient youths into the western districts from the surrounding eastern zone further taxed an already overburdened social system. Living on the margins of society had rendered refugees desperate and without means. As one healthcare worker noted in a Zehlendorf district health authority report in the far southwest quadrant of the city, delinquent refugees were the most difficult to handle since they were "without scruples...never ha[d] papers on them, and often use[d] false names."[62] Still, nothing worried the authorities more than the high levels of venereal disease transmission among this transient population. In order to protect against the moral endangerment of Berlin youth and curb the spread of disease, a vast network of public and private, short- and long-term care facilities marshaled their meager resources to intervene directly in curbing deviant behavior through elaborate educational and social welfare programs. In all too many cases, however, these facilities often contributed to the problems they were designed to prevent.

As in any institutional setting, difficulties arose in the youth facilities due to overcrowding, inadequate supervision, and, crucially, a lack of resources. In the *Jugendhilfestelle* on Dircksenstrasse near the S- and U-Bahn train station at Alexanderplatz, police forwarded teenaged boys caught hanging about without identification, since many runaways could be found there due to the austere conditions in the zone. Its central location and proximity to the railway line meant that it was chronically overpopulated. One of the facility's coordinators, Frau Hoffmann, described the setting as a dismal prison-like structure, with 47 beds available for 90 charges. The facility was poorly outfitted, dirty, and had no linen except that which was donated, and often boys were forced to sleep two to a bed, where they might be tempted to experiment and test out their erotic urges.[63] Unable to control what happened in this homosocial space, caseworkers as far away as Struveshof believed the situation in this single downtown institution was partially responsible for the rising number of young male hustlers making their way through the system and ultimately landing in their care far to the southwest of the city centre.[64] The boys in the Dircksenstrasse facility were not the only ones tempted by close quarters and an emboldened sense of camaraderie. In a 1951 report to the Ministry of Justice regarding the operation of workhouses throughout the GDR, the head of the East German Central Justice Administration reported that a facility as far away as Sachsen-Anhalt had a particularly vexing problem with its female wards, some of whom had been sent from trouble spots in Berlin. Drawing on the first-person account of one of the charges, Dr. Gentz described how the girl "found love among the women there." Confined to a room with 30 women, she found that the wards had fashioned a piece of wood into the shape of a phallus and had been caught pleasuring each other with the apparatus. When this was taken away, the girls collected carrots to serve in place of the wooden appendage. Dr. Gentz's mole ended her report to superiors with a plea to be placed in a suitable environment so that she might not revert to the error of her old ways, which had included prostitution in the streets of Berlin.[65] This plea, and the lesson this example was supposed to impart on justice ministry authorities in East Berlin, was to show the structural inadequacy of these workhouses and the moral depravity they ostensibly engendered, using the example of lesbianism to solidify the point. That they likewise underscored the continued link between nonconformist sexual practices and homosocial institutions like schools and jails was beyond their grasp.[66]

Unable to meet the immediate needs of its wards, the Dirckenstrasse facility began to operate more formally as a kind of clearinghouse where boys would receive short-term evaluation before being forwarded into youth jail or into workhouses. Despite the well-meaning intentions of youth services and the police, while in care many of these adolescents learned a variety of survival techniques – both good and bad – to better equip them for life on the streets. As criminologist Ernst Selig remarked in his 1951 textbook on crime, shirkers and asocials were thought to forge criminal networks and friendships with other delinquents while in group homes, sidestepping in the process all hope of reform.[67] For many, this was a simple survival mechanism, allowing them to earn money for food by navigating the underworld of the sex trade or finding out about sympathetic beat cops and social workers. Still, the fact that charges were housed together in a homosocial environment with more seasoned offenders meant many left more endangered than when they arrived. In one episode at Struveshof, two boys plotted a successful escape and managed to find a john, whom they ultimately robbed in order to secure their train fair back to Berlin.[68] This problem was so widespread that the Struveshof warden warned other youth service workers at a conference of the danger of exposing wards to more hardened male criminals, especially male prostitutes, since some had "over 150 infractions under their belt." His hope was that they might one day be housed in a special facility more suited to their needs where they could not "morally infect new arrivals."[69] In other words, the places of detention, although often located a distance away from the city's main thoroughfares, were themselves sexualized sites of erotic encounter that threatened efforts at rehabilitation. The answer to the problem lay both in reforming behavior and in constructing suitable spaces within which reformation might take place. Here, space and sexuality were mutually reinforcing, a symptom of the problem at hand and a sign of the extraordinary lengths to which charges went to buck the system.[70]

Sometimes wards fell even deeper into peril at the hands of staff, including caseworkers who abused the reach of their authority and the geographic isolation of many of these facilities, which were located on the periphery of the city or in its outlying districts. Even in the city center, increased visibility did not necessarily curb crimes of opportunity and access. In one notable instance, a caseworker with one of the juvenile court services was suspected of having sexual relations with two of the teenage clients while simultaneously romancing a secretary, prompting the director of the facility to alert the police and, more importantly (or so it seemed), to inform the man's fiancée of his wrongdoing.[71] In another, the director of operations at a youth home on Mittelstrasse reportedly raped young female charges allegedly procured by the director of the facility herself. In the Tannenhof correctional facility in the neighborhood of Lichtenrade, personal security was so lax that the girls frequently resorted to locking up their personal effects out of fear that the other wards and staff might steal them.[72] The list of abuse and neglect was long indeed, transcending sector boundaries and highlighting the dire material conditions affecting city services in the years leading up to 1949. In one girls' home just across the border in Brandenburg, where many city youth were sent for countryside rehabilitation, there were no stools or benches, wards routinely had little to eat, and educative programs were lacking, if planned at all[73]. This was no different in the central districts, where in Plötzensee inmates often went hungry, and were forced to eat whatever scraps were sent their way in tin cans cleaned with sand. And this was without the benefit of utensils. There was so little usable physical space in Struveshof that at one time wards reportedly had to sleep standing up. Most distressing of all, despite propaganda photos there was such a heavy turnaround in that facility that neither the janitorial staff nor the caseworkers were able to ensure basic cleanliness (Figures 5.1 and 5.2). As one report made

Figure 5.1 In the Struveshof youth reeducation home (today part of Ludwigsfelde), Berlin, where refugee children were housed, 1948.
Photo credit: Bildarchiv Preussischer Kulturbesitz/Art Resource, NY.

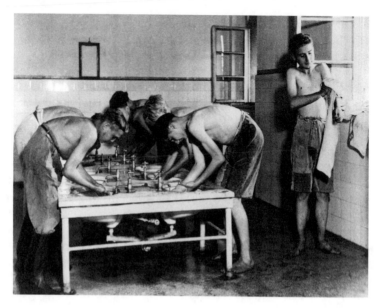

Figure 5.2 In the Struveshof youth reeducation home (today part of Ludwigsfelde), Berlin, where refugee children were housed, 1948.
Photo credit: Bildarchiv Preussischer Kulturbesitz/Art Resource, NY.

painfully clear, bed wetters – and there were many given the trauma the city youth had recently faced – slept in soiled bedding among the general population. The floors were lined with potato skins and beet-root, with books, cigarette butts, and maggots teaming about amidst the refuse. Without functioning lights in the outhouse, the boys literally "stepped into fecel matter and brought their dirty feet back under the covers of their comforters." As warden Goetze lamented in a report on the facility, "every single duvet had to be disinfected in Berlin. And we needed them that same evening for sleep."[74] If these institutions were intended to teach cleanliness of person and moral outlook as core features of rehabilitation, they failed miserably on both accounts.

The homes under East German authority in the eastern sector and in the province of Brandenburg remained committed to societal transformation even if these spaces were less than ideal for imparting the social mission. Interestingly, despite formal division in 1949 and a widening ideological gap resulting in diverging strands of social policy, East and West Berlin youth services continued to bear striking similarities in how they meted out welfare services and juvenile justice. With some exceptions, most notably the obvious emphasis on Christian values in the

West versus socialist humanism in the East, facilities in both halves of the city maintained a similar emphasis on (re)productive citizenship – ensuring young men and women understood their obligations to society as wives, mothers, fathers, and future workers. In other words, despite the changing cartography of the city, and some differences of emphasis, origin, and degree, youth policy and incarceration in Cold War Berlin reflected similar concerns about moral reform and gender normalization for girls, and increasingly for boys. That officials in East and West both looked to group homes as the answer to the ills that plagued their respective societies says much about the continued importance of spaces of incarceration in forging a core social and political grounding as the linchpin of society despite the lessons of institutionalization in their most radical form during the past regime.

Sites of Concern

What was palpably different about youth policy in divided Berlin was the kind of institution entrusted with carrying out initiatives. In the East, alongside police, juvenile delinquency was the preoccupation of the Ministry of *Volksbildung*, since it oversaw issues of societal transformation and socialist reorientation. In West Berlin, the Youth Services Bureau oversaw state-run facilities. But these institutions were supplemented by a network of church-run homes administered by the helping hands of the Protestant Innere Mission and Catholic Caritas service organizations. Despite the different mandates of the Ministry of *Volksbildung* and the Christian social services, these homes shared common perceptions of endangerment and even drew on similar touchstones for youth rehabilitation. Of course, the 1950s posed unique challenges as each city administration adapted to the changing political situation. Given the porosity of the internal boundary, in West Berlin youth policy the emphasis was more on policing dangerous city spaces, where challenges to the Christian Democratic Union's domestic ideology was believed to fester. The Innere Mission supplemented the police in identifying hotspots throughout the city, and resurrected the pre-Nazi train station mission services (*Bahnhofsmission*) to aid weary travelers in navigating the dangers of the city. The police, meanwhile, emboldened by the 1953 Law for the Protection of Youth, cracked down on other dangerous venues in the city, such as cinemas, jazz clubs, seasonal folk festivals, and penny carnivals (*Rummelplätze*) as well as pay-by-the-hour hotels, so as to remove impressionable youth from corrupting places where they might learn to enjoy the taste of tobacco and the company of occupation soldiers. Beyond these sites of concern, many of which were located on the boundary between East and West or were nestled into what remained of the city's ruins (as in the case of the traveling carnivals), division itself was a cause for alarm. In a 1951 memorandum on youth endangerment, Pastor Heyne of the Innere Mission dispatched a brief to the central administration in Bethel informing them that the western half of the city was in the midst of a particularly shocking rise in sexual crime, especially homosexuality, which he viewed as a symbol of the "insecurity of parents on sexual matters and a testament to the disharmony of marital relations such that children and youths internalize this sense of insecurity."[75] Formal division in 1949 had only exacerbated the problem for the West Berlin authorities, since they were now forced to deal with an even greater influx of refugees, removed from the care and protection of family and with little in the way of material support. Members of church social welfare organizations, together with youth bureau and *Jugendgerichtshilfe* social workers, understood this in particularly gendered ways. Whereas it remained a given that girls were prone to licentiousness and prostitution due to the absence of husbands or fathers and the loosening societal taboos that accompanied mass rape, the sexual endangerment of young boys was especially troubling since it severely undercut the possibility of normalization. Whereas girls and women might be set back on course through thoughtful intervention, custodianship, and with the careful guidance of male influence, the potential homosexualization of adolescents could not be undone, at least according to dominant sexological literature which underscored seduction as perpetuating the curse of outright homosexuality.[76] Not only were there new standards of masculinity unleashed by the war, according to Hans Giese, director of the Hamburg Institute for Sexual Science, but no amount of careful stewardship could counterbalance the deleterious impact of division in undermining the return to healthy heteronormative manliness. For Giese, these recent events had fundamentally altered the sanctity of the putatively private sphere. Since the state intervened with renewed vigor in protecting the family and marriage as a foundation of basic laws and principles of governance, sexual practices had acquired added political importance in the realm of everyday life.[77]

Suddenly, erotic experimentation, perceived licentiousness, and challenges to the family idyll were signs not just of endangered socialization but of imperiled political stabilization as well. This danger was felt especially in the border districts of the divided city, given the toothless enforcement of the boundary and the lack of affordable or adequate living space well into the 1950s. Not only had these liminal city spaces enabled the return of homosexual clubs in this difficult-to-police region, but the districts of Neukölln, parts of Tiergarten, and Wedding also happened to consist primarily of working-class neighborhoods that had experienced a disproportionate amount of the city's bombing damage. There were plans for large-scale housing reconstruction projects like those for the Ernst-Reuter-Siedlung along Wedding's Ackerstrasse or even for the showpiece Hansa Viertel, where architects like Le Corbusier and Walter Gropius took part in the International Design Exhibition (InterBau) of 1957, hoping to imbue West Berliners with the spirit of modernization and renewal, while serving as an ideological corollary to East Berlin's socialist boulevard, the Stalinallee. However, despite grand design, the plight of the city's most vulnerable was not easily cured by modular living space and modernist renewal.[78] Despite the pomp and circumstance of these much-needed building projects, lauded for the way in which they proposed to rehabilitate living quarters from the irrationality of pre-1933 design and provide postwar families with infrastructure and modern amenities instead of moldy apartments and cellar dwellings, the sad fact remained that "sexual assaults against children and youth [had] risen exponentially" in these areas. In the yearly report from the rather cumbersomely translated jurisdictional offices of the General German Union of Youth Courts and Court Advisory Services (Revitalized and Newly Constituted) to the director of Caritas in Freiburg, in these neighbourhoods "particularly noticeable is that, above all, the streams of impoverished youth from the East fall victim to homosexual circles."[79] In other words, those youths unhinged from home and hearth were vexing not simply because they formed part of the steady stream of migrants trickling through the porous boundary but because they promised to further compromise what little balance had been achieved on the western side of the city. If architectural competitions sought ways to concretize the "city of tomorrow" in bricks and mortar, linking living space and the nuclear family to the Cold War struggle, the homophobic panic surrounding border crossers proved what Hans Giese had suggested all along about the challenge to normative masculinity posed by wandering youths, expellees, and refugees from the East: that now more than ever before the public sphere was "an augmented projection of the private sphere." It was here that "sexuality takes on a particularly political role as a symbol of spiritual values that serve as the basis for healthy social behavior."[80]

With wide-reaching architectural plans unrealizable until the late 1960s, the western districts turned to special protection legislation to police places in the city where endangerment occurred, relying increasingly on Christian welfare organizations to help inculcate core social values. Across the border, despite the lack of material resources in the East, workhouses and remand homes were lauded by jurists and youth advocates there as progressive and humane sites of social betterment.[81] Although initially a stopgap measure, by the 1950s these facilities would be invested with the authority to help foster a sense of civic responsibility and an emerging socialist morality in addition to promoting healthful gender roles, especially at such a critical time in the personal and political development of the nation's youth. However, given the structural inability of East Berlin's administrative services to implement policy smoothly in the day-to-day management of delinquency, corrective education was not a panacea for rehabilitation.[82] At the very least, the remedial program promoted education in a trade for the young men and women in custody, enabling the fledgling East German state to promote a particular platform for social rehabilitation based less on revolutionary theory than on traditional notions of gender and the rudimentary necessities of economic stability.

After division in 1949, educators working for the Ministry of *Volksbildung* teamed up with the Ministry of Justice to find ways to correct behavior while simultaneously cultivating civic identification through the promotion of work and family values. This intervention was especially important since many youth "as a result of their asocial origins and development protest against all community standards." According to one advocate, this was particularly distressing since these youth were not simply rebelling against their parents' ways but were fostering generational angst and outright hostility toward the new organization of a socialist society.[83] In his capacity as head of the East German Central Justice Administration, Dr. Gentz responded to these fears by emphasizing that the purpose of rehabilitative justice was to "awaken social consciousness in the youth to such a degree that they undertake socially useful employment of their own free will." Indeed, only through "productive work" could a youth's educational and career path be secured. Of course, these concerns were not simply altruistic but also politically expedient, as Dr. Gentz himself outlined in describing the role both the Free German Youth (FDJ) and the Democratic Association of German Women (DFD) would play in these homes by aiding youth in making the best possible transition back into society.[84]

In other words, workhouses represented an important site of social and penal reform, while simultaneously being imbued with significant and overt political imperatives. Part of an overarching strategy of differentiating East German jurisprudence from that of the West, youth penal policy and welfare reform came into particularly sharp focus after 1949. At issue was precisely the role of the courts and welfare services in best serving the needs of contemporary youth. While some bureaucrats debated the merits of bypassing the courts entirely in favor of forwarding certain offenders directly to the state employment office (*Arbeitsamt*), youth workers in the GDR dealt with the day-to-day operation of a network of workhouses and youth facilities overburdened by the number of wayward teens still in the system.[85] Although frequently overextended, these facilities nevertheless played a significant role in the state's strategy to build healthy work and family relationships among a new generation of citizens and workers.[86]

Some workhouses were located in close proximity to the burgeoning number of the new people's-owned factories (*Volkseigenebetrieb* or VEB), making it easier for teenaged boys to participate in industrial production.[87] Indeed, most of the homes for boys involved a program of industrial labor, with the exception of one facility specifically designed to promote agriculture.[88] In learning a trade, they were given the skills needed to enable them to serve as providers and producers once they left the workhouse. Girls in protective custody for promiscuity and prostitution at the Heidekrug institution in Brandenburg/Havel, on the other hand, busied themselves with domestic chores such as cooking, washing, mending, and cleaning. In Werftpfuhl, "healthy behavior and lifestyle" was imparted to female charges through a program based on gardening, sewing, and nursing.[89] Of course, these skills were designed to facilitate the girls' behavioral reform so that they too could one day leave the facility with marketable skills while at the same time taking their proper place as morally upstanding wives and mothers.[90]

But reforming behavior required resources that these workhouses and reformatories simply did not have. As with the material hardships faced by the *Jugendhilfestelle* in town, these workhouse facilities frequently encountered similar problems. Although these institutions were designed to reform aberrant behavior and promote socialism, core organizational problems undermined the state's efforts at rehabilitation. In a real sense, these institutions contained the seeds of their own destruction in that the desired outcome, moral reform, was inhibited by the structure and operation of the social program itself. If domesticity and maternal instincts were the markers of young women's successful rehabilitation, then the success of these houses remained a source of frustration for wards and officials alike.

In Heidekrug, which could house up to 300 women, most of the guards and workers were SED party members. Although they had the authority of political affiliation, they worked without a proper uniform that would mark the separation of the staff from the inhabitants of the facility. Although chores included washing and cleaning, the charges went frequently without soap. Upon visiting Heidekrug, Käthe Kern of the DFD concurred with previous reports that the institution was in disrepair, lacking in soap, coal, and basic amenities. The situation was much worse at a reformatory for endangered girls in Thuringia, where guards reportedly begged for food from the inmates, since they received better food rations than the facility workers.[91] While material hardship threatened to end reform before it began, it was not the only issue hampering these facilities from carrying out their mandate. One report said that while the young women in Heidekrug spent their entire afternoon working in the fields, guards took the opportunity to take naps while on duty. If the organizational disarray hampered resocialization efforts, the "peculiar" relationship between a ward and a female guard suggests that for more reasons than one the family imperative was imperiled by the very system constructed to reinforce its viability.[92]

Although these workhouses and reformatories served as the primary tool to build healthful behavior by teaching youth the merits of productive labor, the zeal of reformers was stymied by the knowledge that it was impossible to gauge how deeply or genuinely the young men and women in custody internalized their reform messages. This bitter truth was not only debated privately among professionals and laypeople, but it also helped shape public perceptions about the success or failure of socialist reeducation. In a newspaper report for the *Neue Zeit* printed under the sensationalized title "Education with Top-Ten Hits. A Visit to a Reformatory for Endangered Girls," Dr. Fuchs-Kamp of the Institute for Psychiatry of Berlin visited a Brandenburg facility to evaluate the problem of institutionally rehabilitating "fallen" girls and women. None of the girls were any older than 18, and already, remarked Dr. Fuchs-Kamp, they had come in contact with the VD hospital, where they had presumably undergone quarantine after contracting gonorrhea or syphilis. Those forwarded to the Cottbus facility most likely were repeat offenders or suspected of being under-aged prostitutes who required a year in custody in order to "be placed on the right path through hard work." Given the depths to which these girls had apparently sunk, rehabilitating these girls "[was] no easy task."

On one night table, the doctor observed, there stood a number of pictures in a small gallery of beautiful men. One desk held three framed photos, all of them of different men, and the same was in evidence on another bedside table. As if to underscore the precise nature of the girls' depravity for the reading audience, Dr. Fuchs-Kamp asks one charge how she came to be institutionalized for long-term care in the workhouse. She responded, like so many other youth of her generation, that she just "wanted to have some fun." After all, she asked the doctor rhetorically, was she expected "to die an old virgin?" Seeking out another example to demonstrate the difficulties educators faced in reforming such debased girls, the doctor turned to another young girl who sat with her legs crossed during the interview and appeared very "ladylike" with her painted-on eyebrows, nail polish, and lipstick. When asked what motivated her to put such effort into her appearance while in custody, she answered, with a coquettish glance to the side, that "first of all, sometimes we get the odd visitor here" and, secondly, she hardly wanted "to become a wallflower."[93] These observations are significant as they provide insight into what qualities and behavior represented professional and popular visions of sexual delinquency at the time. Despite their lodging in an institution, these girls remained "on the make" and apparently beyond the reach of reform efforts. As members of the next generation, these young women served as the canvas upon which Germans, whether lay or professional, could express their own insecurities about the future and the consequences of their recent past. Although in a broad sense concern with girls' future reproductivity contrasted them with a concern for boys' productivity, they represented a conjoined problem for citizens and officials alike. Whether mingling with friends at the train station or staying out late at the cinema, the actions of youth assumed a threatening countenance that consumed considerable resources and defied both scientific management and moral rhetoric.

Spaces of Intervention

Despite these difficulties in applying policy uniformly, the rise in youth criminality in postwar Germany forced a renewed engagement among professionals with the question of the origins of criminal endangerment itself. Caseworkers and policy makers were baffled by the rise in crime. Were certain youths predisposed to criminal behavior by virtue of *Fehlentwicklung* or poor development? What role did the environment play in shaping delinquency? Was asociality a result of postwar hardship or, as the director of the Hephata-Treysa institution claimed in 1957 regarding the 80 percent of youth in his facility who fell under this category, due to a variety of neurological afflictions?[94] These contrasting claims continued to animate discussion in the years after the war and, with few changes, remained in circulation at least until the 1960s.

If there was one issue that most youth advocates on the ground could agree upon, despite the emerging ideological divide, it was that defeat in war had brought with it dramatic challenges to reforming wayward youth. "As a result of Hitler's war," stated a 1947 police memorandum on the fight against youth crime, "Germany emerged not simply as a rubble heap in a material sense" but it experienced "an unimaginable lowering of its moral and ethical worth."[95] Capitulation gave rise to "confused families and weakened family ties," and these poor household relationships now "played themselves out at an alarming rate on the situation of the youth."[96] The numerous cases of juvenile delinquency stemmed in large part from the rise of broken homes and so-called "half families" that confirmed for many Berliners that the world had been turned upside down with defeat.[97] By the time Hanns Eyferth wrote in 1950 that this generation of delinquents "might not be healed of their particular wounds," many people had begun to fear that the youth teetered dangerously toward out-and-out asociality.[98]

If initially the fear of youth delinquency transcended the boundaries that separated an emerging socialist state from its capitalist neighbor, in the language and imperatives of reform these common priorities changed as the 1950s unfolded.[99] Social policy on crime and juvenile delinquency suddenly became part of the Cold War battle, where the attitudes and behavior of the younger generation emerged as elemental in securing economic and political legitimacy in each of the two Germanys. Despite considerable fanfare, the founding of the Workers' and Farmers' State in October 1949 had not resulted in social and industrial stabilization, and the number of unregistered youth continued to alarm authorities as they frequently fell into criminal activity and prostitution.[100]

To combat the mounting threat of social and sexual dislocation, the *Jugendamt*, Department of Health, and Ministry of *Volksbildung* combined efforts to reform the function of the workhouses, reformatories, youth homes, and counseling services to realign priorities. Although never intended for hardened criminals or political prisoners, counseling services, workhouses, and reeducation facilities were sometimes used in ways other than planned. Overcrowding was still an issue, and the problems of the early postwar period continued to animate rehabilitative efforts. Added to the mix was the concerted effort to impart political education through carefully schooled educators. As law student Gerda

Grube remarked in a comprehensive GDR legal history, workhouses were successful when they operated with the principles of "work and self-discipline [as] the main forms of corrective education." A paragraph later, the same publication also mentions the "special importance in overcoming youth endangerment and criminality" that lay in the political work of "each and every youth and their educators."[101] In the best possible scenario, as in some of the privately run confessional group homes in and around Berlin, reformed youth were educated by example. Some even returned to the institution to hold marriage ceremonies and christenings, sharing their joy with the caseworkers who helped turn their lives around.[102]

As the 1950s unfolded, the problem of juvenile delinquency and youth crime became subsumed within social policy on the protection of youth generally. Tied to a wide-sweeping anti-smut and pornography campaign that targeted the corrupt West as the origin of all forms of immorality, measures to combat unhealthy sexual development linked unequivocally the physical and sexual health of the citizen to the overall productivity of the nation. Recidivism, sexual promiscuity, itinerate lifestyles, fears of American cultural exports like rock 'n' roll and jazz, and the flight of many young East Germans westward spurred the government to clamp down once and for all on all things counterproductive to the march of socialism.[103] Groups of youth hanging around Berlin's train stations were especially targeted since surveys and spot checks confirmed that many of them were uneducated and untrained, representing the loss of an important resource to the East German state. Ideally, every citizen's productive capacity had to be harnessed in support of population growth and industrial renewal.[104]

East Germany in practice adopted norms at times hardly distinguishable from "the bourgeois family" – but never acknowledged them as such. Like their counterparts in the West, officials targeted sexual comportment as a vital link in the transition from postwar chaos to postwar stability. In the end, however, the slow rebuilding of Berlin ultimately had to be waged on three fronts – on the streets, in the courts, and in care – where there were never any guarantees that aberrant behavior could be successfully modified to fit the new model of morality. Work, both domestic and industrial, held the promise of rehabilitating wayward youth by channeling their attention toward productive pursuits. The language of productivity also informed West Berlin juvenile penal policy on asocials and prostitutes, especially in cases where judges deliberated whether to send a repeat offender to youth jail or prison.[105] While workhouses were made possible in the postwar West German

Penal Code, in the East they formed part of a large-scale reorganization of the legal and social service system, which sought to implement more humanistic alternatives to imprisonment at the same time as the state divested local authorities of control over these matters. Only in these long-term institutions, which supplemented parallel measures for hardened criminals, could "routine work patterns and socially useful thinking and behavior" be taught.[106]

If the family served as the barometer of successful or failed socialization in the years leading up to and during World War II, then marriage and the family idyll continued to set the parameters of the debate for a uniform and successful postwar youth policy as well. As a kind of safe haven in troubled times, the family emerged in postwar German discourses of renewal and reconstruction as the locus of social and political stability. Challenges to the family, such as those manifested under the aegis of National Socialist population policies, engendered the utmost scrutiny and suspicion. As a corrective measure against a totalitarian relapse, the West German constitution enshrined the family as a necessary bulwark against possible future aggression – a liberal democratic private sphere that must be shielded from state intervention. More importantly still, the family emerged as the primary site of political power with prescribed roles for husband and wife forming the basis for what might be viewed as a kind of (re)productive citizenship.[107]

In the German Democratic Republic, too, the family ideal was likewise strong and similarly situated in party and constitutional discourses of appropriate civic comportment. But the image of the family propagated in the GDR was socialist-inspired and self-consciously devoid of the idolatry of the bourgeois *Sittenkodex*. Of course, popular and official discourses belied the fact that the family's bourgeois underpinnings remained partially intact despite claims to the contrary. Attempts to formulate a suitable proletarian moral code proliferated in the 1950s, and whether by force or by choice officials looked to the Soviet Union for inspiration. The late Soviet pedagogue Anton Makarenko's philosophical account of the place of law and morality in a socialist society provided a canonical account of the role class-consciousness and scientific humanism could play in forming a new kind of social relationality within an otherwise traditional family structure.[108] As late as the 1958 Fifth Party Congress of the reigning Socialist Unity Party (SED), GDR president Walter Ulbricht initiated a preemptive strike against what he feared was the continued influence of all things bourgeois in the fledgling socialist state. As part of a 10-point policy for the continued Sovietization of morality, Ulbricht outlined the steps his citizens should take to secure the path toward socialist renewal. With echoes of Moses' instructions, these socialist strictures sought equal resonance as citizens were instructed to "live a clean and respectable life and respect the family."[109]

Intent on limiting alternative forms of sexual expression, in a sense both the East and West German states were perhaps more similar than distinct in the 1950s. Despite their opposing ideological orientation and productive images of civic comportment, socialist and Christian democratic visions of the family bear striking resemblance to one another. Nowhere is this more demonstrable than in their concern for the younger generation and its compromised moral upbringing. But each state's safeguarding measures were not simply aimed at resocializing youth and eradicating criminality. Against the backdrop of increasing Cold War polarization, this generation of young up-and-coming citizens would not simply demonstrate to the world the scope and scale of German democratic renewal. As future contributors to the moral, civic, and political reconstruction of the East German state, the youth of the 1950s were essential elements in its ideological refashioning. Because family rhetoric united the personal and political spheres, linking generations of Germans together with shared experiences, fears, and expectations, it likewise functioned as an important site of legitimization for Ulbricht's regime. Since the family represented one of its foundational elements, any tangible threat to its ultimate stability had to be corrected by institutionalized disciplinary structures under the careful management of professionals and party officials.

Workhouses and reformatories operated as both welfare and legal measures involving the most difficult cases of asociality, juvenile delinquency, and promiscuity. They also reflected the pressures and needs of an embattled and divided city that still struggled well into the 1950s with the problem of moral reconstruction. While they were envisioned by postwar authorities as emblematic of education instead of incarceration, the line between welfare and penal policy was frequently blurred as they often contained wards who either were just released from jail, or, given the nature of their debasement, seemed likely candidates for future imprisonment. The way in which the state determined who could be forwarded to workhouses demonstrates the elasticity of the terms "endangerment" and "delinquency" in the years following the war. Gone was the language of biological determinism. But the criteria for determining what constituted aberrant behavior and who required the protection of the state remained relatively the same as those that saw other undesirables sent to workhouses during the Nazi period.[110]

Although the forced sterilization of criminals and asocials exemplified the perils associated with a biological understanding of deviance during

National Socialism, the postwar period was still influenced by medical-ization. Social policy on crime and endangerment applied in practice in the public and private curative institutes and workhouses indicates the ongoing preoccupation with identifying and overcoming unhealthy sexual practices before they could be transmitted to a new generation of outcasts. But important distinctions must be drawn. In the court counseling service and in the facilities themselves, psychiatrists, social workers, and psychologists interviewed family members to ascertain the extent of debasement within a particular family unit. In other words, the family environment and not genetics was recognized as playing a substantial role in contributing to delinquency. This distinction is sig-nificant, but it speaks less to the resolve of social workers and medical authorities in the postwar period than to the determination to move away from eugenic-inspired conceptions of deviance. More to the point, it highlights the continued insecurity on both sides of the boundary for leaving sexual acculturation to the intimate space of the biological family.

These local institutions complemented the state's efforts to secure the active participation of the nation's youth in reconstruction. In East Germany, in moving reformatories and youth services to the mantle of the Ministry of People's Education (*Volksbildung*) from their former place as part of the Ministry of Social Services (*Sozialwesen*), the ideological imperative becomes clear: remedying deviant behavior was intimately bound up with building socialism through (re)productive labor. In the West, similar concerns animated policies for promoting democratic fatherhood through corrective education. In this way, reforming way-ward youth was also about state building, since rehabilitative education protected and promoted the family while simultaneously harnessing the participation of the youth in strengthening the state in an era of remilitarization.

Despite efforts to blame first the war and then the West for the ideo-logical endangerment of the younger generation, child welfare workers, police, and members of the East German government itself quickly recognized the need to look internally for solutions. Petty criminality, delinquency, prostitution, and clique building plagued the divided city, acquiring the attention of GDR policy makers because officials feared that asocial young adults shirked work and family responsibilities and appeared especially susceptible to the influence of American-styled cultural capitalism.[111] The ongoing existence of youth criminality in the East underscored the state's particular inability to meet the chal-lenges of social and economic revitalization. The danger posed by the morally derailed (*Entgleist*) younger generation was indeed great, for without rehabilitation it was unclear who would shoulder the burdens of increased industrial productivity to help rebuild the war-torn and emerging GDR. As the situation worsened in the 1950s, the state employed a variety of methods to promote socialization. But aside from organized sport and leisure, Free German Youth retreats, and Young Pioneer parades, another form of intervention was found that borrowed from advancements made before the war in treating juvenile delinquents.[112] Targeting certain young offenders for rehabilitation through workhouses, remand homes, and reformatories, the East German state, its welfare services, police, and youth policy advocates, equated antisocial with anti-socialist behavior and sought retributive justice through hard work and austere living conditions. From here it was but a small step to the inhumane institutionalization of delinquents in the notoriously brutal Torgau facility.[113]

By this time, concern over Nazi-era policy and procedures fell by the wayside as the consolidation of East Germany took place in the shadow of American-backed consumer capitalism in the neighboring Federal Republic. Mirroring this change in priorities, the notion of *Rechtsgut* also changed, signifying a shift away from reconstruction issues toward the larger battle with the capitalist West. No longer preoccupied with the fascist past, and having met the challenge of postwar reconstruction at least in theory, GDR social policy found a new foil in Adenauer's Christian democracy. These stages in the development of East German social policy – engaging the specter of National Socialism, forging a platform for rebuilding, and legitimizing the current regime – guided the treatment of young offenders in the court system, in custody, and in care.

But this was not solely an East German policy and city facilities formed an essential part of East and West German attempts to define and delimit appropriate civic identity according to the dictates of familial roles, productive labor, and moral reform. As a result, hundreds of East and West Berlin youths were funneled through facilities and institutions designed to leave a distinct impression of their desired contribution to society. Just as health policy intimately linked the self-legitimization of East and West Germany with population politics, social policy on the problem of youth criminality reflected similar preoccupations and concerns.[114] Bringing the city's wayward teens into an awareness of healthful and, more importantly, heterosexual social mores meant instilling in them the knowledge of and respect for Ulbricht and Adenauer's family-based industrial political economy. To educate young offenders about their contribution to the health and prosperity of the nation, the Ministry of *Volksbildung* employed a variety of methods in the management of postwar delinquency, and Berlin's Protestant, Catholic and state-run institutions hoped to make good on the promises of protective legislation and anti-smut campaigns in eradicating the specter of early sexual experimentation in the West. In workhouses and remand homes in and around the divided city that promoted the retributive value of domestic, industrial, and agricultural labor, delinquent youth received careful instruction on how to fulfill their social obligations to state and society. Cloaking social policy in the language of morality and borrowing managerial strategies of containment and prevention from before the war, East and West Germany sought the support of average citizens equally invested in eradicating moral dissipation and confusion.

The Cold War city was a defining feature of social policy's mirror play. Ten years after war's end, the problem of youth waywardness was anything but solved. If anything, worsening living and working conditions in the neighboring Soviet zone meant that a stream of refugees tasked the already overburdened social system. In fact, a special commission was needed to redirect attention toward the issue of youth crime in the divided city of Berlin. The Committee for the Eradication of Youth Crime, under the supervision once again of the Ministry of *Volksbildung*, consisted of members of the East German criminal police, the prosecutor's office, the Ministry of Work and Apprenticeship, the Free German Youth, and the Association of German Democratic Women, in addition to the Free German Trade Union. An especially perplexing problem that attracted attention was *Republikflucht*, or defection, since an alarming number of teens found their way into the statistics. Whereas the early postwar period gave rise to widespread endangerment due to the degree of privation brought about by defeat, by the 1950s youth crime and waywardness was emblematic of a different sort of oppositionality. The fear for East German authorities was that these youth were not simply asocial, or even antisocial, but that they were in fact anti-state. Influenced by the "smut and dirt" of American cultural imperialism, turning their backs on family and factory, and lured by agents of the *Adenauerstaat* to a life in the West, GDR youth formed a sizeable impediment to the consolidation of state power and control over the private sphere. While the "extent and origins of endangerment" were not to be found in the character of the GDR at all, according to the party line, derailment could only be measured in the "difficulty in reforming waywardness, in the rise in crime, and also in the number of traitorous acts" committed against the state.[115] Socialist morality was not taking hold, and despite the most coercive attempts to reform aberrant behavior and repackage gender roles in support of the industrial economy, this goal remained elusive.

What were the governments protecting in sending their youth to places of detention? In fashioning a healthy work ethic, reinforcing the family, and promoting traditional gender roles, youth policy in divided Germany continued to gender delinquency in seeking ways to harness the supposedly natural capacities of young men and women under the guise of rehabilitation. Far from an organic feature of societal organization, the ideal family required the intrusion of the state in shaping behavior and tailoring morality to meet the imperatives of socialist comportment and democratic citizenship. Although attempts to impose state discipline and control over aberrant behavior resulted in incarceration for many, promiscuity and petty criminality marked the transition from young offender to young adult, as many East and West Berlin youths continued to live lives outside of the strictures and structures of appropriate identification.

While common assumptions informed social policy in both Germanys after 1949, in resurrecting reformatories for the purposes of behavioral and ideological reorientation, East Germany sought to sever its connection to the pre-1933 welfare tradition and heritage it shared with the West. Rehabilitation strategies established in remand homes and workhouses represented a conscious effort to refashion key social reform measures from the Weimar period in order to achieve a revolutionary transformation of society in what Konrad Jarausch has somewhat controversially claimed resulted in the creation of a welfare dictatorship.[116] Despite a full-frontal attack on the *Adenauerstaat* among criminologists and legal reformers, in applying penal and welfare strategies to combat youth waywardness the GDR emphasized a similarly traditional vision of delinquency, vice, and moral endangerment, which had much more in common with the Christian West than first imagined. As Günter Grau has argued elsewhere, attempts to promote a radical reorganization of society did not necessarily undercut the appeal of bourgeois morality, especially in the area of sexual comportment.[117]

In Cold War Berlin, juvenile delinquency and promiscuity, still understood in Lombrosian terms, represented a lapse not just in the social but in the moral development of future citizens, and could only be corrected by state involvement in propping up an alternative notion of "home" in the city's spaces of incarceration. In identifying which transgressions merited state intervention, penal and welfare institutions both reflected and refracted gendered notions of delinquency and deviance, as caseworkers across the divided city designed programs to meet the needs of their charges to best integrate them into healthful and productive work and family life. These programs, stressing household, agricultural, and industrial labor, although pragmatic in providing a trade and livelihood, nevertheless structured rehabilitation around the promotion of specifically gendered identities. Against the backdrop of the mass exodus of able-bodied citizens, a rise in the number of divorces, and continued concerns over the falling birth rate, youth policy sought to buttress the faltering family in crafting a particular vision of the roles these young citizens were to fulfill in their competing regimes. Although youth authorities emphasized civic responsibility, productive labor, and healthful gender roles in their institutions designed to safeguard the family, the inability to implement policy smoothly in the day-to-day process served as a challenge to the very utility of a family-based morality at the same time as it hinted that causes for failure could not be externalized indefinitely.

Examining the plight of the faceless adolescents who huddled in the air raid shelters, walked the streets, directed errant glances at waiting hopefuls on train station platforms, or accompanied a certain someone for a drink and a bite at a neighborhood bar, we see that the tactics employed to reeducate the fallen in the duties of citizenship took on distinct spatial components in Cold War Berlin. In the encounters that transpired in this vast network of institutions of confinement, the war, collapse, and ideological as well as physical division played a mediating role in how effective policies could be in inculcating a sense of "home" among wayward teens. At times, material shortage and the duplicitous desires of wardens proved more of a challenge than the promiscuousness of unruly charges, yet both East and West Berlin youth welfare authorities felt the need to intervene in the intimate sphere of their young wards. Concern was great, for as long as postwar youths refused to share the burden of reconstruction, the city, whether East or West Berlin, could not lay claim to a much-coveted world-class status. Although moral reform initiatives in these homes suggest the omnipresent stranglehold of the state in shaping the hearts and minds of its citizens, just as the ruins represent destruction and the possibility of a new beginning, perhaps it is best to view these spaces as in equal part repressive and productive. While certainly a sign of state paternalism and moral regulation, they also testify to the sustained efforts of a generation of nonconformist youth to challenge tradition and chart their own path through the rubble of broken families, hopes, and lives.

Conclusion: Borders and Boundaries

> Berlin tasted of the future, and that's why we gladly took the crap and the coldness.
>
> Carl Zuckmayer, "Als Wär's ein Stück von mir," 1966

For Rolf Schneider, it was a day like any other. He met an out-of-town relative at the Franziskaner restaurant under the arches of the Friedrichstrasse train station, and mused about the frequency of the vibrations that rocked the "furniture, glasses and the palms of our hands as a nervous tic" every two minutes, as each train rolled in. After a forgettable meal "unlovingly prepared but extremely cheap," they left the restaurant only to be bombarded by the illuminated political messages passing as text across the station arch, which, he notes sardonically, were "ignored by everyone." Going first to Ostbahnhof to ensure his relative caught his train, he then hopped on board a west-traveling S-Bahn, and was reminded when back at Friedrichstrasse by the dulcet tones of woman's voice over the loudspeaker that this was the last station stop "in the democratic sector of Berlin." Upon disembarking at Zoo Station, that curious "island of Eastern-bloc 'real socialism' at the heart of capitalism," his eyes were pulled toward the blue-uniformed train station police and the drunk staggering through the hall. Would he make it to the exit? He followed along, and turned towards the Kurfürstendamm, where he noticed across from the scaffolding surrounding the Memorial Church the outdoor tables of the Café Kranzler, where a "flock of elderly ladies, hats perched on top of blue-rinsed curls," did not seem to mind the noisy construction. They continued to "spear their forks into big, brightly-coloured slices of cake." He ambled down the Ku-damm to Schöller's bookshop, where he contemplated buying the last volume of Proust's *Remembrance of Things Past*, were it not so expensive given the day's currency rates. Little did he realize at the time that soon, he would "never be able to buy the book." Then it's a quick stop at the chemist's, where he bought his weekly allotment of Swiss dried milk powder for his six-month-old daughter, who had developed an unfortunate allergy to the milk available in the GDR. At a nearby cinema, posters advertised the anti-Nazi film *Aren't We Wonderful* (*Wir Wunderkinder*), which won the 1960 Golden Globe for best foreign film. "I must get around to seeing this film at last, definitely next week." But, as he notes mournfully, he would never get the chance. Finally, before boarding his train home, he stopped to buy bananas and carrots for his daughter, treating himself to a tin of Golden Mixture pipe tobacco. Happily, there were no checks again at Friedrichstrasse, which struck him neither as strange nor odd. In the time it took to travel back to the southeastern district of Erkner, he looked out the window and saw the passing of "old buildings, new buildings, ruins, stretches of grass, ugly scenes and idyllic scenes, the usual picture that I have known for a long time." Over the seven years he had spent in the city since moving from his hometown of Wernigerode, he managed to make peace with the schizophrenic nature of life in divided Berlin, even professing a kind of love for "the contradictions, the insanity, the imperfections, surprises, brutalities and dowdiness of the city." He continued his trek home. "The next day, 13 August 1961, the GDR start[ed] building the Berlin wall."[1]

In a coffee-table book published by the same publishing house he once led as a member of the East German cultural elite, Schneider's reminiscences of life in the shadow of the Wall provide a textual accompaniment to the photographs of an otherwise unknown photojournalist, who died shortly after its construction.[2] Walter Schulze's portrayal of divided Berlin is less well known than that of contemporaries like Henry Ries, Friedrich Seidenstücker, and Chargesheimer, whose images have gone on to acquire iconic status in what some have seen as a triumphalist take on "the early post-war years as a success story . . . free from all traces of damage."[3] Schultz's photos and Schneider's commentary portray an image of Berlin en passant. They harness the gaze of the viewer/reader and take it into the streets, squares, and backyards of the reconstructing city. With great sensitivity and pathos, both men portray the day-to-day lives of average citizens alongside the city's open wounds. Of course, the largest of all blights on the cityscape would be built in the middle of August 1961, on what Schneider tells us was just another sunny day.

This book has taken up this question of normality under extreme conditions by examining the iconic place of the city in the ebb and flow of twentieth-century history. In exploring the way physical spaces of contact and encounter connoted a host of sentiments and meanings about that city's moral reconstruction in the aftermath of World War II, it has attempted to present a case for the unique ways in which people made sense of division and occupation, building for themselves a sense of normalcy in abnormal times. Daily life in Cold War Berlin was not only marked by worsening political conditions, but the city lived under the specter of Nazi brutality and the lingering presence of what had come before, the struggle to cement a foundation for democracy in the 1920s and the chauvinism of Prussian rule.

Between 1945 and 1961, the ruins represented total destruction and tragedy. But they also heralded a period of unrelenting dynamism and change. In interesting ways, people sought to influence the course of their lives given the challenges they faced in the destroyed environment. Despite crippling devastation, mass rape, trauma, and deprivation, Berlin's broken state nevertheless served as an important conduit of memory. Its shattered landscape may not have resulted in an all-important coming-to-terms with the crimes of the Nazi state and the antecedents of authoritarianism, biopolitics, and race thinking, but it did conjure up a host of select memories about the cultural experimentation, illicit sexualities, and nonconformism of the 1920s. While both Berliners and foreign visitors to the city recalled with pleasure the excesses of Weimar, curiously they did not subject the National Socialist reaction to this period to rigorous analysis. In emphasizing the one without the other, the full scope of reconstruction paradoxes went overlooked. Faced with public licentiousness, disease transmission, difficulties reintegrating former soldiers, and the general breakdown of the family, it became easy to gravitate to pre-1945 policies and procedures despite serious attempts to distance both East and West German regimes from National Socialist racial teaching.

Betwixt and between the wreckage of Hitler's Germania, there lurked evidence of a not-too-distant past, one that once found itself at the apex of metropolitan modernity, revolutionary fervor, and cultural experimentation. Although the century's first experience with total war spared the city the misery of carpet bombing, food riots, general strikes and the violence of the fall and winter of 1918–19 left its mark on the beleaguered city, leading Walter Benjamin and Georg Simmel to note the existential quandaries raised by ruins between the quest to reminisce and the desire to rebuild.[4] One generation later, even if hardy Berliners generally preferred rationalism over nostalgia, as John Mander remarked in his 1959 study of the divided city, somehow they "made an exception of 'the Twenties' – the period that begins for our purposes about 1910 and ends very abruptly on the night of the 30th of January 1933." With memories still fresh of the violence few sanctioned, some would participate in, and many more simply ignored or condoned, by and large Berliners still "cherish(ed) the memories of that extraordinary decade."[5] This book argues that the memories of the period before Hitler were not just present in postwar Berlin, but would play a great role in shaping contemporary encounters in the destroyed capital. This held true for those traipsing through the rubble in search of family and shelter as much as for the postwar *flâneurs* that flocked to the city as members of the occupation and literary establishment to catch a glimpse of Berlin's historic fall from glory. Capitulation may have marked an end to the fighting, but as this book has shown, there was much in the way of continuity over the benchmark of 1945.

Although formal division in 1949 cut the city into two parts, formalizing a separation that was already palpable in local governmental affairs since the Berlin Blockade months earlier, the city was fractured in many more ways than simply politically. Like many metropolitan centers, modern urban planning initiatives in the nineteenth century had had little effect in fully eradicating its patchwork, premodern qualities, meaning that historic Berlin was marked by temporal divisions as well as political, economic, and societal ones. At the same time that hastily constructed tenement quarters well-nigh guaranteed the spread of class struggle and contagion in one quadrant of the city, across town grand boulevards were adorned with electrified streetlights and cafés quickly followed to ensure the adequate flow of human traffic as well as capital. As Christopher Isherwood noted throughout his travels in the 1920s, Berlin was always a "city with two centers," stratified according to class and status, something his compatriot and fellow novelist Michael Sadleir referred to as the difference between "official Berlin" and the more "noisy, bustling, and raffish" quarters where crime and vice flourished. "From the Zeughaus to Alexander-Platz [*sic*] is just over a kilometer," Sadleir noted, "yet the two belong to different worlds." Even the sight of rubble was not unique to the post-1945 period, for successive industrial spurts meant some area of the city was under perpetual construction for most of the twentieth century.[6] From the exposed bowels of the overland pipeline the young Vladimir Nabokov refers to in his short story "A Guide to Berlin," to the cracks and fissures in the pavement in Peter Schneider's *The Wall Jumper* decades later, this porous, evolving, and unfinished Berlin reinforced the notion that the city's past could never fully be paved over, processed, or forgotten.[7] This was especially the case in divided Berlin in the 1950s. As one woman was overheard to say on the Day of Penitence in the closing years of that decade, this was "a city whose wounds, after ten years, are not healed," in whose ruins "the bodies of men, women, and children still lie, without headstone or flowers upon their graves."[8] Like an archeological dig, Berlin's sites of reconstruction and encounter unearthed a rich texture of past lives, experiences, and practices all struggling to cope with the calamitous events of mid-century.

As I have tried to show, there were many places in divided Berlin that could count as reconstruction sites, places where rebuilding initiatives rubbed up against spontaneous use and the responses this engendered by both the East and West German regimes, similarly intent on safeguarding the family as the cornerstone of their moral and industrial refashioning. At any given time, in any culture, virtually all places of human encounter are sexualized and gendered, if we start from a point of departure that recognizes heterosexuality as an unstable construct requiring reinforcement to render it natural, transparent, and omnipresent through rituals of regulation, consumption, and the day-to-day ordering of space. In Cold War Berlin, however, this process of ensuring compliance through the regulation of difference was explicitly connected to the insecurities of both German regimes in failing to mediate the deleterious impact of unstable gender and sexual identities. That this also rested on a particular engagement (and sometimes non-engagement) with the Nazi and Weimar past forces further consideration of the reasons why these blind spots continued to exist. What is obvious is the way in which bourgeois norms of respectability and intimacy resurfaced on both sides of the boundary, couched in different rhetoric but essentially articulating the same moral panic over attempts to restore a homogenous and stable national identity as a bulwark against the excesses of the past and the dangers lurking across the border. It was not just heterosexuality that was imperiled by emasculated men, effeminate boys, and emboldened women who shirked their collective responsibilities to the postwar family, but the strength of the nation itself, suggesting a link between national identity, citizenship, and the perceived naturalness of marriage-based heterosexuality.

As both nations sought economic stability and remilitarization through the 1950s, even greater influence was placed on policing deviance, especially so for the generations of youth who had grown up in the shadow of war. By looking at the way in which many of these anxieties emerged out of the broken landscape – such that efforts to eradicate vice required the reconstruction not just of healthy lives but of the places where they gained succor – I have argued that the fears surrounding metropolitan identity are reflective of unresolved tensions amidst the push and pull of modernity generally, which held the possibility of extraordinary intervention in the sphere of personal autonomy. But as we see in Cold War Berlin, regulation was never absolute, but neither was emancipation. In the years before the so-called sexual revolution, gay bars remained captive to the whims of the criminal police, and progressive voices sacrificed their own subaltern on the altar of respectability. Still, people exploited existing mechanisms of control to find new and unique ways of organizing an opposition, any opposition, to the displacement of social anxieties onto sexual relations. Sometimes they were more successful than others. In the years leading up to the building of the Berlin Wall, there were more places to hide, considering the piecemeal forms of governance at work in the divided city.

The inexorable staying power of metropolitan modernity, for better and sometimes for worse, reminds us that Berlin's place in the historical imaginary was never fully bounded by borders or fixed in time. Indeed, Berlin's is a history of multiplicity, messiness, and overlap, what historical geographer Doreen Massey has termed "a momentary collection of trajectories and relations" forged in the context of a particular historical moment.[9] Geographers have made significant contributions recently in reinterpreting the history of the New Berlin as a period of rebuilding, which has centered on complex and sometimes contradictory processes of reflection, remembering, recasting, and retelling select elements of the city's storied past.[10] As Allan Cochrane reminds us, there really is no unitary or authentic Berlin. Like its borders and boundaries, changing and unstable, its "histories past and present are always in the process of being made, always provisional, never finalized."[11] But, as this book has shown, this holds true not just for contemporary Berlin; it was especially evident in this first phase of the Cold War when authorities on either side of the Iron Curtain embarked on a platform of deliberate self-fashioning. Of course, the city's historic development has always been somewhat peripatetic. Since the beginning of its recorded history, this cluster of settlements on the Havel and Spree rivers had proved an unlikely location for economic growth and cultural capital.[12] Unlike London, Paris, or even Vienna, steeped in courtly tradition and financial power, Berlin's emergence in the late nineteenth century as a major urban center was anything but self-evident, uncontested, singularly embraced, or guaranteed. The tug of war between its latent cosmopolitanism and a trenchant resistance to change percolated over the century divide, where throughout the course of subsequent decades, it would house elements of the radical left and right, emerging as the apogee of the avant-garde and home to a brewing crisis of civilization and ideology. Replete with political pageantry, it would serve as the nerve center of no fewer than five different German governments. Variously described as an island of freedom in a sea of communist red, and an experiment in peace if not prosperity in the westernmost reaches of the Eastern bloc, it was the much-feared front city in a highly anticipated World War III. In his famous speech at the Brandenburg Gate in 1963, in reference to the building of the Berlin Wall, John F. Kennedy could not be more correct: for much of the second half of the twentieth century, all roads no longer led to Rome, but to Berlin.

Notes

Introduction

1. Richard Brett-Smith, *Berlin '45: The Grey City* (London: Macmillan, 1966), 54.
2. Anke Pinkert, *Film and Memory in East Germany* (Bloomington: Indiana University Press, 2008); Robert R. Shandley, *Rubble Films: German Cinema in the Shadow of the Third Reich* (Philadelphia, PA: Temple University Press, 2001); Eric Rentschler, "The Place of Rubble in the *Trümmerfilm*," in Julia Hell and Andreas Schönle (eds.), *Ruins of Modernity* (Durham, NC: Duke University Press, 2010), 418–39; Wilfried Wilms and William Rasch, *German Postwar Films: Life and Love in the Ruins* (Basingstoke: Palgrave Macmillan, 2008).
3. *Histories of the Aftermath: The Cultural Legacies of the Second World War in Europe*, ed. Frank Biess and Robert Moeller (New York: Berghahn Books, 2010).
4. Dagmar Herzog, *Sex After Fascism: Memory and Morality in Twentieth-Century Germany* (Princeton, NJ: Princeton University Press, 2005), 1.
5. On this point, see the essays in Hell and Schönle (eds.), *Ruins of Modernity*, especially Andreas Huyssen, "Authentic Ruins: Products of Modernity" and Todd Samuel Presner, "Hegel's Philosophy of World History via Sebald's Imaginary of Ruins: A Contrapuntal Critique of the "New Space' of Modernity," pp. 17–28 and 193–211.
6. Dorothy Rowe, *Representing Berlin: Sexuality and the City in Imperial and Weimar Germany* (Aldershot: Ashgate Publishing Ltd, 2003); Eric D. Weitz, *Weimar Germany: Promise and Tragedy* (Princeton, NJ: Princeton University Press, 2007).
7. Paul Rutherford draws on Bruno Latour's *We Have Never Been Modern* (Cambridge, MA: Harvard University Press, 1993) in *A World Made Sexy: Freud to Madonna* (Toronto: University of Toronto Press, 2007), 9.
8. Deborah Ascher Barnstone, *The Transparent State: Architecture and Politics in Postwar Germany* (New York: Routledge, 2005); Paul Betts, *The Authority of Everyday Objects: A Cultural History of West German Industrial Design* (Berkeley: University of California Press, 2007); Greg Castillo, *Cold War on the Home Front: The Soft Power of Midcentury Design* (Minneapolis: University of Minnesota Press, 2010); György Péteri, "Nylon Curtain – Transnational and Transsystemic Tendencies in the Cultural Life of State-Socialist Russia and East-Central Europe," *Slavonica* 10.2 (2004): 113–23.
9. Atina Grossmann, *Jews, Germans, and Allies: Close Encounters in Occupied Germany* (Princeton, NJ: Princeton University Press, 2007); Robert G. Moeller, *Protecting Motherhood: Women and the Family in the Politics of Postwar West Germany* (Berkeley: University of California Press, 1993); Heide Fehrenbach, *Race After Hitler: Black Occupation Children in Postwar Germany and America* (Princeton, NJ: Princeton University Press, 2005); Wolfgang Schivelbusch, *In a Cold Crater* (Berkeley: University of California Press, 1998); Paul Steege,

Black Market, Cold War: Everyday Life in Berlin, 1946–1949 (Cambridge, MA: Cambridge University Press, 2007).

10. Walter Benjamin, *Berlin Childhood Around 1900* (Cambridge, MA: Belknap Press, 2006); Andreas Killen, *Berlin Electropolis: Shock, Nerves, and German Modernity* (Berkeley: University of California Press, 2006); Rudy Koshar, *From Monuments to Traces: Artifacts of German Memory, 1870–1990*, (Berkeley: University of California Press, 2000); Jennifer A. Jordan, *Structures of Memory: Understanding Urban Change in Berlin and Beyond* (Stanford, CA: Stanford University Press, 2006); Mel Gordon, *Voluptuous Panic: The Erotic World of Weimar Berlin* (Port Townsend, WA: Feral House, 2000); Alexandra Richie, *Faust's Metropolis: A History of Berlin* (New York: Carroll & Graf, 1998); Curt Moreck, *Führer durch das "lasterhafte" Berlin*, (Nicolaische Verlagsbuchhandlung, 2001); Karen E. Till, *The New Berlin: Memory, Politics, Place* (Minneapolis: University of Minnesota Press, 2005); Brian Ladd, *The Ghosts of Berlin: Confronting German History in the Urban Landscape* (Chicago, IL: University of Chicago Press, 1998).
11. Matt Houlbrook, "Towards a Historical Geography of Sexuality," *Journal of Urban History* 4.2 (2001): 497–504; Frank Mort, *Capital Affairs: London and the Making of Permissive Society* (New Haven, CT: Yale University Press, 2010).
12. Robert Beachy, "The German Invention of Homosexuality," *Journal of Modern History* 82.4 (December 2010): 801–38; Geoffrey Giles, "The Institutionalization of Homosexual Panic in the Third Reich," in Robert Gellately and Nathan Stolzfus (eds.), *Social Outsiders in Nazi Germany* (Princeton University Press, NJ: Princeton, 2001), 223–55; Annette F. Timm, *The Politics of Fertility in 20th Century Berlin* (Cambridge, MA: Cambridge University Press, 2010).
13. Greg Eghigian has done much to introduce Foucault's notion of governmentality to East German history. See especially "Homo Munitus: The East German Observed," in *Socialist Modern: East German Everyday Culture and Politics*, ed. Paul Betts and Katherine Pence (Ann Arbor; University of Michigan Press, 2008) and "The Psychologization of the Socialist Self: East German Forensic Psychology and Its Deviants, 1945–1975," *German History* 22 (2004): 181–205.
14. Mark Fenemore, *Sex, Thugs, and Rock n' Roll: Teenage Rebels in Cold-War East Germany* (Oxford and New York: Berghahn, 2007); Thomas Lindenberger, " 'Asoziale Lebensweise.' Herrschaftslegitimation, Sozialdisziplinierung und die Konstruktion eines "negativen Milieus' in der SED-Diktatur," *Geschichte und Gesellschaft* 31 (April–June, 2005), 227–54; Uta G. Poiger, *Jazz, Rock, and Rebels: Cold War Politics and American Culture in a Divided Germany* (Berkeley: University of California Press, 2000).
15. Much work has been written on the supposed naturalness of the heterosexual couple as the basic building block of social citizenship, in the United States and elsewhere. See Margot Canaday, *The Straight State: Sexuality and Citizenship in Twentieth-Century America* (Princeton NJ: Princeton University Press, 2009); David T. Evans, *Sexual Citizenship: The Material Construction of Sexualities* (London: Routledge, 1993); Jennifer V. Evans, "The Moral State: Men, Mining, and Masculinity in the Early GDR," *German History* 23.3 (2005): 355–70.
16. On the liminal status of Cold War Berlin, see Steege, *Black Market, Cold War*.

17. Benjamin, *Berlin Childhood Around 1900;* Susan Buck-Morss, *The Dialectics of Seeing: Walter Benjamin and the Arcades Project* (Cambridge, MA: MIT Press, 1991); David Patrick Frisby and Mike Featherstone, *Simmel on Culture: Selected Writings* (London: Sage Publications Ltd, 1998).
18. W. Byford-Jones, *Berlin Twilight* (London: Hutchinson, 1947), 46.
19. Gottfried Benn and Alfred Döblin are cited in Schivelbusch, *In a Cold Crater,* 12, 5; Isaac Deutscher, *Reportagen Aus Nachkriegsdeutschland* (Hamburg: Junius, 1980), 114; Manuel Gasser, *Erinnerungen und Berichte* (Zurich: Verlag der Arche, 1981), 113; Stephen Spender, *European Witness* (New York: Reynal & Hitchcock, 1946), 235.
20. Grossmann, *Jews, Germans, and Allies;* Elizabeth D. Heineman, "The Hour of the Women: Memories of Germany's 'Crisis Years' and West German National Identity," *American Historical Review* 101.2 (1996): 354–95; Norman Naimark, *The Russians in Germany: A History of the Soviet Zone of Occupation, 1945–1949* (Cambridge, MA: Belknap Press, 1997).
21. Svenja Golterman, *Die Gesellschaft der Uberlebenden: Deutsche Kriegsheimkehrer und ihrer Gewalterfahrungen im Zweiten Weltkrieg* (Munich: Deutsche Verlags-Anstalt, 2009).
22. Benjamin, *Berlin Childhood Around 1900.*; Walter Benjamin, *Gesammelte Schriften,* (Frankfurt am Main: Suhrkamp, 1972); Walter Benjamin, *Selected Writings* (Cambridge, Mass: Belknap Press, 1996); Buck-Morss, *The Dialectics of Seeing*; Moreck, *Führer durch das "lasterhafte" Berlin*; *Grosstadt-Dokumente*; Hans Ostwald, *Kultur- und Sittengeschichte Berlins* (Berlin: Grunewald, H. Kelmm, 1924); Georg Simmel, *Die Grossstadt: Vorträge und Aufsätze Zur Städteausstellung* (Dresden: von Zahn & Jaensch, 1903).
23. Georg Simmel, "Soziologie des Raumes," translated as "Sociology of Space" by Mark Ritter in *Simmel on Culture: Selected Writings*, ed. David Frisby and Mike Featherstone (London: Sage Publications Ltd, 1998).
24. Rowe, *Representing Berlin,* 72.
25. Moreck, *Führer durch das "lasterhafte" Berlin.*
26. Edward Dickinson, *The Politics of German Child Welfare from the Empire to the Federal Republic* (Cambridge, MA: Harvard University Press, 1996); Peter Fritzsche, *Reading Berlin 1900* (Cambridge, MA: Harvard University Presss, 1996); Corey Ross, *Media and the Making of Modern Germany: Mass Communications, Society, and Politics from the Empire to the Third Reich* (New York: Oxford University Press, 2008); Gary Stark, *Banned in Berlin: Literary Censorship in Imperial Germany, 1871–1918* (New York: Berghahn Press, 2009).
27. Frank Mort and Lynda Nead, *Sexual Geographies* (London: Lawrence and Wishart, 1999), 6.
28. Phil Hubbard, *Sex and the City: Geographies of Prostitution in the Urban West* (Aldershot: Ashgate, 1999); Judith Walkowitz, *City of Dreadful Delight: Narratives of Sexual Danger in Late-Victorian London* (Chicago: University of Chicago Press, 1992).
29. Steven Maynard. "Through a Hole in the Lavatory Wall: Homosexual Subcultures, Police Surveillance, and the Dialectics of Discovery, Toronto, 1890–1930," *Journal of the History of Sexuality* 5.2 (October 1994): 207–42.
30. Hubbard, *Sex and the City*, 103.
31. David Harvey, *Spaces of Capital: Towards a Critical Geography* (New York: Routledge, 2001); Henri Lefebvre, *The Production of Space* (Oxford, UK and

Cambridge, MA: Blackwell, 1991); Henri Lefebvre, *Everyday Life in the Modern World* (New Brunswick, NJ: Transaction Books, 1984); Allen J. Scott and Edward Soja, *The City: Los Angeles and Urban Theory at the End of the Twentieth Century* (Berkeley: University of California Press, 1996).

32. Fritzsche, *Reading Berlin 1900*.

1 The Cellar and the Bunker

1. Theo Findahl, *Untergang. Berlin 1939–1945*, trans. Thyra Dohrenburg (Hamburg: Hammerich & Lesser, 1946), 169.

2. Regina Stürckow argues that the Kurfürstendamm remained quite international during the early war years, with American films on offer, swing clubs (for a time), and international newspapers on sale in the kiosks and newsstands near Joachimstaler Strasse. See Regina Stürickow, *Der Kurfürstendamm: Gesichter einer Straße* (Berlin: Arani-Verlag GmbH, 1995), 130.

3. Although Berlin was bombed as early as 1940, the most damage was inflicted between November 1943 and May 1945. Reinhard Hellwig, ed., *Dokumente deutscher Kriegsschäden: Evakuierte, Kriegssachgeschädigte, Währungsgeschädige: Die geschichteliche und rechltiche Entwicklung*, Vol. IV/2: *Berlin – Kriegs- und Nachkriegsschicksal der Reichshauptstadt* (Bonn: Bundesminister für Vertriebene, Flüchtlinge und Kreigsgeschädigte, 1967), 3–5.

4. Volkmar Fichtner estimates 49,000 in *Die anthropogen bedingte Umwandlung des Reliefs durch Trümmeraufschüttungen in Berlin (West) seit 1945*, Vol. 21. (Berlin: Selbstverlag des geographischen Instituts der Freien Uni Berlin, 1977), 3. The figure of 56,000 is the number quoted in Hellwig, *Berlin – Kriegs- und Nachkriegsschicksal der Reichshauptstadt (=Dokumente deutscher Kriegsschäden, Bd. IV/2)*, Bonn, 1967, 77f.; see also Georg Homsten, *Die Berlin Chronik, Daten, Personen, Dokumente* (Düsseldorf: Droste Verlag, 1984), 384–5.

5. Nicholas Stargardt, *Witnesses of War: Children's Lives Under the Nazis* (London: Vintage Press, 2007).

6. Fichtner, *Die anthropogen bedingte Umwandlung*, 5; Frank Howley, *Berlin Command* (New York: G. P. Putnam and Sons, 1950), 8.

7. Howley, *Berlin Command*, 8; Reinhard Rürup, ed., *Berlin 1945: Eine Dokumentation* (Berlin: Stiftung Topographie des Terrors und Verlag Willmuth Ahrenhövel, 2005), 13–14.

8. For a fascinating discussion of Berlin's modernization through the lens of urban planning, see Nadine Roth's award-winning dissertation, "The Architecture of Identity: Re-imagining Berlin as Imperial Capital and Modern Metropolis, 1890–1936," PhD dissertation, University of Toronto, 2003.

9. W. Byford-Jones, *Berlin Twilight* (London: Hutchinson, 1947), 19.

10. For varying accounts and statistics, see Wolfgang Bohleber, *Mit Marshallplan und Bundeshilfe: Wohungsbaupolitik in Berlin 1945–1963* (Berlin: Duncker und Humblot, 1990), 15, together with "Verlust an Wohnungen durch den Krieg," in *Berlin in Zahlen*, 173, and Rürup, *Berlin 1945*, 59–60.

11. Gerhard Keiderling, *"Gruppe Ulbricht" in Berlin April bis Juni 1945. Von den Vorbereitungen im Sommer 1944 bis zur Wiedergründung der KPD im Juni 1945. Eine Dokumentation* (Berlin: Berliner Wissenschafts-Verlag, 1993), 307.

12. Atina Grossmann, *Jews, Germans, and Allies: Close Encounters in Occupied Germany* (Princeton, NJ: Princeton University Press, 2007), 16–17.
13. Georg Simmel, "The Metropolis and Modern Life," in *George Simmel on Individuality and Social Forms*, ed. Donald N. Levine (Chicago: University of Chicago Press, 1971), 325.
14. Aside from an earlier historiography of the history of sexuality that drew almost exclusively from a Foucauldian framework, attempts to think critically about the relationship between moral regulation, sexual identity, and urban experience have largely come out of human geography and historical sociology. Two examples include: Philip Hubbard, *Sex and the City: Geographies of Prostitution in the Urban West* (Aldershot: Ashgate, 1999); and Frank Mort and Lynda Nead, eds., *Sexual Geographies*, New Formations No. 37. (London: Lawrence and Wishart, 1999).
15. Stephen Spender, *European Witness* (New York: Reynal & Hitchcock, 1946), 229.
16. Wilhelm Hausenstein, *Europäische Hauptstädte* (Erlenbach-Zürich, 1932), 372–3.
17. W. H. Auden's impressions may be found in Alan Balfour's, *Berlin: The Politics of Order, 1737–1989* (New York: Rizzoli, 1990), 156. Peter Gay provides an interesting overview of contemporary impressions of the city during the Weimar Republic, from those enamored with the city to its detractors and critics. See his *Weimar Culture* (New York: Harper and Row, 1968), 129, 132. For the Nazi period, see Josef Goebbels, *Kampf um Berlin: Der Anfang* (Munich: Franz Eher nachf., 1937), 46.
18. Balfour, *Berlin: The Politics of Order*, 249.
19. Researchers have located the origins of around 779 bunkers in Berlin, although the plans for another 335 could not be verified with current evidence. See Dietmar Arnold, Reiner Janick, Ingmar Arnold, Gudrun Neumann, Klaus Topel (eds.), *Sirenen und gepackhte Koffer: Bunkeralltag in Berlin* (Berlin: Ch. Links Verlag, 2003), 13. The authors point to an article in *Abend* from July 18, 1947 which estimates the number of bunkers in Berlin to be roughly 1000. For contemporary use of the extant 22 bunkers in Berlin, see "Berlin's Bunkers in Party Alarm," *Deutsche Welle* (Dec. 3, 2001): www.dw-world.de/dw/article/0,2144,339896,00.html (accessed Apr. 7, 2011).
20. The Reichsluftschutzverbund or RLB was founded in 1933 and by the time war broke out, it boasted a hearty membership of over 13 million, with its own magazine, *Die Sirene*. See Arnold et al., *Sirenen und gepackhte Koffer*, 24–5.
21. Karl Friedrich Borée, *Frühling 45: Chronik einer Berliner Familie* (Darmstadt: Schneekluth, 1954), 47.
22. William Shirer quoted in Richard Brett-Smith, *Berlin '45: The Grey City* (London: Macmillan, 1966), 81–2.
23. Brett-Smith, *Berlin '45*, 84.
24. Helmut Altner, *Berlin Dance of Death* (Staplehurst: Spellmount, 2002), 126.
25. Hildegard Knef, *Der geschenkte Gaul: Bericht aus einem Leben* (Munich: Molden, 19870), 34.
26. Inga Pollack, "Zwischen Krieg und Frieden in Berlin," Tiergarten Mai '45. Zeitzeugenberichte. Mitte Museum und Archiv.
27. Pollack, "Zwischen Krieg und Frieden in Berlin."

28. Herr Homa, Zeitzeugenbefragung "Tiergarten Mai '45." Mitte Museum und Archiv.
29. Ursula von Kardoff, *Berliner Aufzeichnungen 1942–1945*, 134.
30. Hans-Dieter Schäfer, *Berlin im Zweiten Weltkrieg: Der Untergang des Reichshauptstadts in Augenzeugenberichte* (Munich: Piper, 1985), 300.
31. Dorothea von Schwanenflügel Lawson, *Laughter Wasn't Rationed: Remembering the War Years in Germany* (Alexandria, VA: Tricor Press, 1999), 371.
32. Borée, *Frühling 45*, 6.
33. Arnold et al., *Sirenen und gepackte Koffer*, 76, 79.
34. David Seamon, *The Geography of the Lifeworld* (London: Croom Helm, 1979).
35. Arnold et al., *Sirenen und gepackte Koffer*, 86.
36. Johanna Barthel, *Berlin nach dem Krieg – wie ich es erlebt habe* (Berlin: Berliner Forum, 1977), 32.
37. Hildegard Müller, in *1945 – Nun hat der Krieg ein Ende: Erinnerungen aus Hohenschönhausen*, ed. Thomas Friedrich and Monika Hansch (Berlin: Heimatmuseum Hohenschönhausen, 1995), 106.
38. Anneliese Hewig's memories were published by Claus Bernet, "Aus 'Berlins schweren Tagen': Ein Tagebuch vom 22. April bis zum 7. Mai 1945," *Der Bär von Berlin* (2007), 187.
39. Pollack, "Zwischen Krieg und Frieden in Berlin."
40. Ursula von Kardorff, *Berliner Aufzeichnungen aus den Jahren 1942 bis 1945* (Munich: Deutsche Taschenbuch Verlag, 1962), 95.
41. From the exhibit "Born in Flakturm Humboldthain" in the Heimatmuseum Wedding, held in 1995/96 and described in Arnold et al., *Sirenen und gepackte Koffer*, 87.
42. Jacob Kronika, *Der Untergang Berlins* (Flensburg and Hamburg: Wolff, 1946), 11.
43. Jeanne Mammen to Erich Kuby in Erich Kuby, *Mein Krieg: Aufzeichnungen aus 2129 Tagen* (Munich: Nymphenbruger, 1975), 309.
44. Horst Lange in Schäfer, *Berlin im Zweiten Weltkrieg*, 288.
45. Altner, *Berlin Dance of Death*, 159.
46. Erich Schneyder and Louis P. Lochner, "The Fall of Berlin," *The Wisconsin Magazine of History* 50.4. Unpublished documents on Nazi Germany from the Mass Communications History Center (Summer, 1967): 420.
47. Mark R. McGee, *Berlin. A Visual and Historical Documentation from 1925 to the Present* (Woodstock and New York: The Overlook Press, 2002), 158.
48. Kardorff, *Berliner Aufzeichnungen 1942–1945*, 134, 138.
49. Schneyder and Lochner, "The Fall of Berlin," 419.
50. In a Bremen bunker, one inhabitant noted that the bunker wardens had once been party members and members of the SA (*Sturmabteilung*). In the final days of the conflict, however, they increasingly found wardens in civil attire, presumably because most of the able-bodied had been redirected to other, more pressing, details. See Michael Foedrowitz, *Bunkerwelten: Luftschutanlagen in Norddeutschland* (Berlin: Christof Links Verlag, 1998), 106.
51. See "Bericht über den 'Sondereinsatz Berlin' für die Zeit vom 30.3.–7.4.1945," in Schäfer, *Berlin im Zweiten Weltkrieg*, 311.
52. Altner, *Berlin Dance of Death*, 113.
53. Anonymous, *A Woman in Berlin: Eight Weeks in the Conquered City, A Diary*, trans. Philip Boehm (New York: Picador, 2000), 9–10. In his diary of the end

of the war, Helmut Altner recalls how the SS went around to the cellars in a desperate search for any remaining recruits. Indignant, he claims: "no corner or apartment, no cellar or shed is safe from the patrols that drive anyone capable of bearing arms out into the streets." Altner, *Berlin Dance of Death*, 86.

54. Anonymous, *A Woman in Berlin*, 43. Interestingly, another diarist, Ruth Andreas-Friedrich, describes a more or less intact gender ordering among the remaining adherents of the Uncle Emil resistance group, suggesting an interesting link between gender, masculinity, and the culture of resistance. See Ruth Andreas-Friedrich, *Battleground Berlin: Diaries, 1938–49* (New York: Holt, 1947).
55. Knef, *Der geschenkte Gaul*, 34.
56. Marta Mierendorf in Claudia Schoppmann and Angela Martin (eds.), *Ich fürchte die Menschen mehr als die Bomben: Aus den Tagebüchern von drei Berliner Frauen 1938–1946* (Berlin: Metropol Verlag, 1996), 105.
57. Kurt Wafner in *1945 – Nun hat der Krieg ein Ende*, ed. Thomas Friedrich and Monika Hansch (Berlin: Heimatmuseum Hohenschönhausen, 1995), 33.
58. Anneliese Hewig's memories in Bernet, "Aus 'Berlins schweren Tagen,' " 189.
59. Müller, *1945 – Nun hat der Krieg ein Ende*, 10.
60. Franz Gröpler, in *1945 – Nun hat der Krieg ein Ende*, ed. Thomas Friedrich and Monika Hansch (Berlin: Heimatmuseum Hohenschönhausen, 1995), 10.
61. Altner, *Berlin Dance of Death*, 132.
62. Matthias Menzel, *Die Stadt Ohne Tod* (Berlin: Carl Habel Verlagsbuchhandlung, 1946), 177.
63. See Walli Schrade's reminiscence in LAB Rep. 240 Kleinschriftgut Zietgeschichtliche Sammlung. Erlebnisberichte aus der Berliner Bevölkerung über die Zeit des Zweiten Weltkrieges und danach. Acc. 2651, No. 419.
64. Submission #335 from Ursula Trappiel in LAB B Rep. 240. Erlebnisberichte aus der Berliner Bevölkerung über die Zeit des Zweiten Weltkrieges und danach. Acc. 2651, No. 4.
65. Submission #272 from Berta Wilinga in LAB B Rep. 240. Erlebnisberichte aus der Berliner Bevölkerung über die Zeit des Zweiten Weltkrieges und danach. Acc. 2651, N0. 2.
66. Ryan Cornilius, *Der letzte Kampf* (Munich: Droemer/Knaur 1966), 337. One diarist describes how the Russians sorted the bunker cells, placing men and women in different rooms. See the excerpt from Katharina Heinroth, *Mit Faltern begann's. Mein Leben mit Tieren in Breslau* (Munich: Kindler, 1979), 139–43 included in Schäfer, *Berlin im Zweiten Weltkriege*, 331.
67. Marta Mierendorf in Schoppman, *Ich fürchte die Menschen*, 137.
68. Anonymous, *A Woman in Berlin*, 77.
69. Karin Friedrich in Barthel, *Berlin nach dem Krieg*, 218.
70. Submission #324 from Agnes Trost in LAB B Rep. 240. Erlebnisberichte aus der Berliner Bevölkerung über die Zeit des Zweiten Weltkrieges und danach. Acc. 2651, No. 4.
71. Kurt Wafner in *1945 – Nun hat der Krieg ein Ende. Erinnerungen aus Hohenschönhausen*, ed. Thomas Friedrich and Monika Hansch (Berlin: Heimatmuseum Hohenschönhausen, 1995), 34, 43.
72. Grossmann, *Jews, Germans, and Allies*; Elizabeth D. Heineman, "The Hour of the Women: Memories of Germany's 'Crisis Years' and West German National Identity," *American Historical Review* 101.2 (1996): 354–95.

73. Menzel, *Die Stadt Ohne Tod*, 177.
74. Borée, *Frühling 45*, 15.
75. "Berlins Hochbunker – ein Jahr nach dem Kriege," *Der Kurier* (Mar. 13, 1946).
76. Brett-Smith, *Berlin '45*, 119.
77. "'Matterhorn' am Humboldthain," *Neue Humboldthain* (Nov. 17, 1950).
78. "Die Ende der Berliner Bunker," *Der Kurier* (Nov. 5, 1946).
79. Winfried Richard, "Noch schöner, noch grüner – Humboldthanin und Pankegrünzug im Wedding seit 1945," *Humboldthain und Pankegrünzug.* Undated publication in Mitte Museum und Archiv, Humboldt-Bunker Chronologie.
80. Pamela Swett, *Neighbours and Enemies: The Culture of Radicalism in Berlin, 1929–33* (Cambridge, MA: Cambridge University Press, 2007).
81. On consumerism and its role in both economies, see Paul Betts, *The Authority of Everyday Objects: A Cultural History of West European Industrial Design* (Berkeley: University of California Press, 2007); Paul Betts and Katherine Pence, *Socialist Modern: East German Everyday Culture* (Ann Arbor: University of Michigan Press, 2008); David Crew, ed., *Consuming Germany in the Cold War* (New York: Berg Press, 2004); Eli Rubin, *Synthetic Socialism: Plastics and Dictatorship in the German Democratic Republic* (Chapel Hill: University of North Carolina Press, 2008); Jonathan R. Zatlin, *The Currency of Socialism: Money and Political Culture in East Germany* (Cambridge, MA: Cambridge University Press, 2008).
82. LAB C Rep. 303/9 Polizeipräsident in Berlin, 1945–8, No. 259. Raid report, Bunker Schlesischer Bahnhof, dated 2.11.1946.
83. Benita Blessing, *The Antifascist Classroom: Denazification in Soviet-occupied Germany, 1945–49* (New York: Palgrave, 2006).
84. LAB C Rep. 303/9 Polizeipräsident in Berlin 1945–8, No. 259. Raid report from the Bahnhof Friedrichstrasse (precise date unspecified), some time in 1948.
85. Silvia Koerner, "Nach dem Kriege in Berlin." LeMO. Lebendiges Museum Online. Deutsche Historisches Museum, interview February 10, 2000.
86. Silvia Koerner, "Kinderalltag nach dem Krieg." LeMO. Lebendiges Museum Online. Deutsche Historisches Museum, interview March 9, 2000.
87. Atina Grossmann, "A Question of Silence: The Rape of German Women by Occupation Soldiers,' *October* 72 (Spring 1995): 43–63.
88. Curt Riess, *The Berlin Story* (New York: The Dial Press, 1952), 110.
89. Riess, *The Berlin Story*, 110, 111.
90. Walter Benjamin's writings, particularly his *Passagenwerk*, and *Berlin Childhood* advance arguments concerning the place of the city, specifically the street and commercial zones of the metropolis in the construction of modern identities. See Walter Benjamin, *The Arcades Project* (London and New York: Bellknap Press, 1999) and *A Berlin Childhood Around 1900* (London and New York: Bellknap Press, 2006).
91. Michel de Certeau, *The Practice of Everyday Life*, as cited in Tim Edensor, *Industrial Ruins: Space, Aesthetics, and Materiality* (New York: Berg, 2005), 82.
92. LAB C Rep. 341 Stadtbezirksgericht Mitte, No. 5635, Amts Berlin-Mitte Abt. 99 (Schöffengericht) 22.11.1949 case against 16-year-old Klaus S. accused of supporting himself as a rent boy at Bahnhof Zoo when approached by a man for sex while carrying his luggage. See also See Jennifer V. Evans, *"Bahnhof*

Boys: Policing Male Prostitution in Post-Nazi Berlin," *Journal of the History of Sexuality* 12.4 (October 2003): 605–36.

93. For a discussion of surveillance techniques see my article *"Bahnhof* Boys." On the postwar employment of judicial authorities, see Andreas Pretzel, *NS-Opfer unter Vorbehalt: Homosexuelle Männer in Berlin nach 1945* (Berlin: LIT Verlag, 2002).

94. LAB C Rep. 303/9 Polizeipräsident in Berlin, 1945–8, No. 248 Tätigkeitsbuch MII/1 – aussendienst – 8.5.1948–23.4.1949. Laufende No. 206 Verdacht der widernatürliche Unzucht, 19.5.1948.

95. LAB B Rep. 069 Jugendstrafanstalt Plötzensee, case against Gerhard P, 1.11.1950.

96. "Mutti hat mich rausgeschmissen – Ein vormittag auf dem Sozialamt – Helfende Hande, heilendes Wort," *Der Telegraf* no. 14, January 17, 1948.

97. "Die Besprisornies von Berlin. Jugendliche, die gestoheln haben – sind sie alle kriminell?' *Der Tagesspiegel* August 7, 1947.

98. Doreen Massey as referenced in Allan Cochrane, "Making Up Meanings in a Capital City: Power, Memory, and Monuments in Berlin," *European Urban and Regional Studies* 13.1 (2006): 22.

99. Byford-Jones, *Berlin Twilight*, 19.

2   The Street

1. Monika Maron, "Place of Birth: Berlin," in *Berlin Tales*, trans. Lyn Marven (Oxford: Oxford University Press, 2009), 67. Originally published in Monika Maron, *Geburtsort Berlin* (Frankfurt am Main: S. Fischer Verlag, 2003).

2. On the function of nostalgia in the former Eastern Bloc, see Svetlana Boym, *The Future of Nostalgia* (New York: Basic Books, 2002).

3. Nigel Thrift, *Non-representational Theory: Space, Time, Affect* (New York: Routledge, 2008), 87.

4. See Dorothy Rowe's first chapter "The Rise of Berlin in Imperial Germany" for an excellent overview of this material in *Representing Berlin: Sexuality and the City in Imperial and Weimar Germany*. Aldershot: Ashgate, 2003).See also Andreas Killen, *Berlin Electropolis: Shock, Nerves, and German Modernity* (Berkeley: University of California Press, 2006).

5. Patrice Petro, "After Shock/Between Boredom and History," in *Fugitive Images*, ed. Patrice Petro (Bloomington: Indiana University Press, 1995), 265.

6. Klaus Theweleit, *Male Fantasies* (Minneapolis: University of Minnesota Press, 1987).

7. Josef Goebbels, *Kampf um Berlin I. Der Anfang (1926–1927)* (Munich, 1937), 27.

8. Otto Friedrich, *Before the Deluge: A Portrait of Berlin in the 1920s* (New York: Harper and Row, 1972), 8.

9. Walter Benjamin, "The Work of Art in the Age of Technological Reproduction," in *Illuminations*, ed. and intro. Hannah Arendt. (New York: Harcourt, Brace, and World 1968), 253–64.

10. Evgenii Bershtein, "The Withering Away of Private Life: Walter Benjamin in Moscow," in *Everyday Life in Soviet Russia: Taking the Revolution Inside*, ed. Christina Kiaer and Eric Naiman (Bloomington: Indiana University Press, 2006), 220.
11. Walter Benjamin, *Moscow Diary* (Cambridge, MA: Harvard University Press, 1986), 73.
12. Friedrich, *Before the Deluge*, 5.
13. Humphrey Jennings in *The Humphrey Jennings Film Reader*, ed. Kevin Jackson. (Manchester: Carcanet, 1993),103.
14. Monica Black, *Death in Berlin From Weimar to Divided Germany* (Cambridge, MA: Cambridge University Press, 2010).
15. Walter Benjamin, "Theses on the Philosophy of History," in *Illuminations*, trans. Harry Zohn (New York: Schocken, 1969); Georg Simmel, "The Metropolis and Modern Life," in *George Simmel on Individuality and Social Forms*, ed. Donald N. Levine (Chicago: University of Chicago Press, 1971); Raymond Williams has identified that structures of feeling can help us understand the social structures binding together certain identities and social formations. Since feelings are linked to milieu, space, and time, they are historical reflections of the elements at work in self-fashioning, positioning people in the choices they undertake. See Raymond Williams, "Structures of Feeling," *Marxism and Literature* (Oxford: Oxford University Press, 1977), 128–35. See also Stephen Muecke, "The Archaeology of Feeling," *The UTS Review* 5.1 (1999): 1–5.
16. Joachim Schlör, *Nights in the Big City. Paris – Berlin – London, 1840–1930* (London: Reaktion Books, 1998), 241.
17. David Frisby, "Deciphering the Hieroglyphics of Weimar Berlin: Siegfried Kracauer," in *Berlin: Culture and Metropolis*, ed. Heidrun Suhr and Charles W. Haxthausen (Minneapolis: University of Minnesota Press, 1991), 152; Franz Hessel, *Spazieren in Berlin* (Munich: Rogner & Bernhard, 1968), 43; Mel Gordon, *Voluptuous Panic: The Erotic World of Weimar Berlin* (Port Townsend, WA: Feral House, 2000).
18. Curt Moreck, *Führer durch das "lasterhafte" Berlin* (Leipzig, 1931) (reprint Berlin 1987), 12.
19. Joseph Roth, "Berliner Vergnügungsindustrie (1930)," in *Großstadt-Feuilletons*, Vol. IV of *Werke*, ed. Hermann Kesten (Cologne and Amsterdam, 1976), 864, as cited in Schlör, *Nights in the Big City*, 279.
20. Klaud Herding and Hans-Ernst Mittig, *Kunst und Alltag im NS-System: Albert Speers Berliner Straßenlaternen* (Giess, 1975).
21. See the reports of the *Sondereinsatz Berlin* in Bundesarchiv-Militärararchiv Freiburg RW 4/ vorl. 266. Excerpted in *Militärgeschichtliche Mitteilungen* I (1967), 95–119 and also in Hans Dieter Schäfer, *Berlin im Zweiten Weltkreig. Der Untergang der Reichshauptstadt in Augenzeugenberichten.* (Munich: Piper, 1985).
22. Schlör, *Nights in the Big City*, 279; Marko Paysan, "Zauber der Nacht," in Bernd Poster, ed., *Swing Heil: Jazz im Nationalsozialismus* (Berlin, 1989), 76.
23. Martha Dodd, *My Years in Germany* (London: Victor Gollancz, 1939), 23.
24. Christopher Isherwood, *Goodbye to Berlin* (London: Hogarth Press, 1939), 460.

25. Dodd, *My Years in Germany*, 125–6.
26. Thomas Wolfe, "I Have a Thing to Tell You," *New Republic* 90, 1164 (March 24, 1937).
27. Howard Kingsbury Smith, *Last Train From Berlin: An Eyewitness Account of Germany at War* (New York: Knopf, 1942), 162.
28. Karen Blixen, *Breife aus einem Land im Krieg*, as cited in Oliver Lubrich, "Kontrastaufnahmen. Berlin in den Berichten ausländischer Reisender, 1933–1945," in *Weltfabrik Berlin: Eine Metropole als Sujet der Literatur*, ed. Matthias Harder and Almut Hille (Würzburg: Königshausen & Neumann, 2006), 156.
29. Matthias Menzel, *Die Stadt ohne Tod. Berliner Tagebuch 1943/45* (Berlin, 1946), 93.
30. Theo Findahl, *Untergang: Berlin 1939–1945* (Oslo: Aschehoug & Co, 1945), 102, excerpted in Hans Dieter Schäfer, *Berlin im Zweiten Weltkrieg. Der Untergang der Reichshauptstadt in Augenzeugenberichten* (Munich: Piper, 1985), 227.
31. Eric D. Weitz, *Weimar Germany: Promise and Tragedy* (Princeton, NJ: Princeton University Press, 2007), 312.
32. Uta G. Poiger, "Fantasies of Universality? *Neue Frauen*, Race and Nation in Weimar and Nazi Germany," in Modern Girl Around the World Research Project, ed. Alys Eve Weinbaum, Lynn M. Thomas, Priti Ramamurthy, Uta G. Poiger, & Madeleine Yue Dong, *The Modern Girl Around the World* (Durham: Duke University Press, 2008); "Beauty, Business and German International Relations," *WerkstattGeschichte* 16.45 (2007): 53–71.
33. Poiger, "Fantasies of Universality?" 317–46. On the fashion industry, see Irene Guenther, *Nazi Chic? Fashioning Women in the Third Reich* (New York: Berg, 2004).
34. Findahl, *Untergang*, 105, excerpted in Schäfer, *Berlin im Zweiten Weltkrieg*, 231.
35. This sentiment is evoked in Weitz, *Weimar Germany*, 313.
36. Wolfgang Schivelbusch, *In a Cold Crater: Cultural and Intellectual Life in Berlin, 1945–1948* (Berkeley: University of California Press, 1998).
37. Anthony Beevor in *Revealed: Hitler's Secret Bunkers*, documentary directed by George Pagliaro, 2008. For more on the battle of Berlin, see Beevor's book *Berlin: The Downfall 1945* (New York: Penguin Books, 2002).
38. Helmut Altner, *Berlin Dance of Death* (Staplehurst: Spellmount, 2002), 114.
39. Altner, *Berlin Dance of Death*, 124.
40. Altner, *Berlin Dance of Death*, 124.
41. Monica Black, *Death in Berlin*.
42. Monica A. Black, "Reburying and Rebuilding: Reflecting on Proper Burial in Berlin after 'Zero Hour,'" in *Between Mass Death and Individual Loss: The Place of the Dead in Twentieth-Century Germany*, ed. Alon Confino, Paul Betts, and Dirk Schumann (New York: Berghahn Books, 2008), 69.
43. Black, "Reburying and Rebuilding," 69.
44. Albert Speer in Alan Balfour, *Berlin: The Politics of Order 1737–1989* (New York: Rizzoli International Publications, 1990), 55.
45. Speer in Balfour, *Berlin: The Politics of Order*, 134.
46. Walli Sohrade's recollection is in LAB B Rep. 240 Kleinschriftgut. Zeitgeschichtliche Sammlung. Erlebnisberichte.

47. LAB DO 1 7.0 Deutsche Verwaltung des Innern (DVdI), No. 18 Sekretariat, Entwicklung des Deutschen Volkspolizei 1946–52. Abschrift von Befehl des Militärkommandanten der Stadt Berlin 25.5.45.

48. For the British perspective on the refugee crisis, see especially Matthew James Frank, *Expelling the Germans: British Opinion and Post-1945 Population Transfer in Context* (Oxford: Oxford University Press, 2008).

49. Richard Brett-Smith, *Berlin '45: The Grey City* (London: Macmillan, 1966), 118.

50. Curt Riess, *The Berlin Story* (New York: the Dial Press, 1952), 16.

51. John J. Maginnis, *Military Government Journal: Normandy to Berlin* (Amherst: University of Massachusetts Press, 1971), 269, 344–5.

52. Maginnis, *Military Government Journal*, 259.

53. Isaac Deutscher, "Berlin – September 1945," *The Economist* (September 29, 1945), reprinted in *Reportagen aus Nachkriegsdeutschland*, trans. Tamara Deutscher (Berlin: Junius, 1980), 114.

54. Werner Durth and Niels Gutschow, *Träume in Trummern: Planungen zum Wiederaufbau zerstörter Städte im Westen Deutschlands, 1940–1950* (Braunschweig: Vieweg, 1988).

55. Jens Lachmund, "Exploring the City of Rubble: Botanical Fieldwork in Bombed Cities in Germany after World War II," *Osiris* 18 (2003): 239.

56. Elke Sohn, *Zum Begriff der Natur in Stadtkonzepten anhand der Beiträge von Hans Bernhard Reichow, Walter Schwagenscheidt und Hans Scharoun zum Wiederaufbau nach 1945* (Münster: LIT Verlag, 2008), 85.

57. Hildemar Scholz, *Die Ruderalvegetation Berlins* (Berlin: Freie Universität, 1956).

58. Cornel Schmidt, "'Neues Leben aus Ruinen': Trümmerflora," *Orion* 5.3 (1950): 113. For an environmental history of European city centers, see *.Resources of the City: Contributions to an Environmental History of Modern Europe*, ed. Dieter Schott, Bill Luckin and Geneviève Massard-Guilbaud, Historical Urban Studies (Aldershot: Ashgate, 2005).

59. Jens Lachmund, "Die kartographische Organisation biologischen Wissens. Eine Fallstudie zur Geschichte stadtökologischer Kartierungen von Berlin (West)," in *Ganz normale Bilder: Zur visuellen Produktion von Selbstverständlichkeit*, ed. David Gugerli and Barbara Orland (Zürich: Chronos, 2002), 85.

60. Paul Steege, *Black Market, Cold War: Everyday Life in Berlin, 1946–1949* (Cambridge, MA: Cambridge University Press, 2007), 250.

61. Henri Lefebvre, *The Production of Space* (London: Blackwell, 1991).

62. For more on the history of privacy in the German Democratic Republic see Paul Betts, *Within Walls: Private Life in the German Democratic Republic* (Oxford: Oxford University Press, 2010) and "Manners, Morality and Civilization: Reflections on Post-1945 German Etiquette Books: Reflections on Post-1945 German Etiquette Book," in *Histories of the Aftermath: The Legacies of World War II in Comparative European Perspective*, ed. Frank Biess and Robert Moeller (New York: Berghahn, 2009).

63. Wolfgang Bohleber, *Mit Marshallplan Und Bundeshilfe. Wohnungsbaupolitik in Berlin 1945 Bis 1968* (Berlin: Duncker & Humblot, 1990); Robert G. Wertheimer, "The Miracle of German Housing in the Postwar Period," *Land Economics* 34.4 (1958): 338–45; Axel Schildt and Sywottek,

" 'Reconstruction' and 'Modernization:' West German Social History during the 1950s," in *West Germany under Construction: Politics, Society, and Culture in the Federal Republic of Germany*, ed. Robert G. Moeller (Ann Arbor: University of Michigan Press, 1997), 413–44.

64. Dorothea von Schwanenflügel Lawson, *Laughter Wasn't Rationed. Remembering the War Years in Germany* (Alexandria, VA: Tricor Press, 1999), 434.
65. Erna Saenger's story is in LAB B Rep. 240, Acc. 2651, No. 1 Erlebnisberichte aus der Berliner Bevolkerung uber die Zeit des 2. Weltkrieges und danach.
66. Daniela Berghahn, *Hollywood Behind the Wall: The Cinema of East Germany* (Manchester: Manchester University Press, 2005); Joshua Feinstein, *The Triumph of the Ordinary: Depictions of Daily Life in the East German Cinema 1949–1989* (Chapel Hill: University of North Carolina Press, 2002); Jennifer M. Kapczynsky, *The German Patient: Crisis and Recovery in Postwar Culture* (Ann Arbor: University of Michigan Press, 2008); Anke Pinkert, *Film and Memory in East Germany* (Bloomington: Indiana University Press, 2008).
67. Annette F. Timm, "The Legacy of Bevölkerungspolitik: Venereal Disease Control and Marriage Counselling in Post-WWII Berlin," *Canadian Journal of History/ annals canadiennes d'histoire XXXIII* (August 1998): 173–214.
68. John Borneman traces this phenomenon into the dwindling years of the Cold War. See John Borneman, *Belonging in the Two Berlins: Kin, State, Nation* (Cambridge, MA: Cambridge University Press, 1992).
69. Silvia Koerner, "Kinderalltag Ende der vierziger Jahre," LeMO. Lebendiges Museum Online. Deutsche Historisches Museum, interview 09.03.2000.
70. Wilfred Byford-Jones, *Berlin Twilight* (New York: Hutchinson, 1947), 54; Jennifer V. Evans, "*Bahnhof* Boys: Policing Male Prostitution in Post-Nazi Berlin," *Journal of the History of Sexuality* 12.4 (October 2003): 605–36.
71. Helmut Schelsky, *Die Skeptische Generation: Eine Soziologie des deutschen Jugend* (Düsseldorf: Eugen Diederichs, 1957). See also Sibylle Meyer and Eva Schultze, *Kurzfristige und langfristige Auswirkungen des II. Weltkriegs auf vollständige und unvollständige Familien. Ein Beitrag zum Wandel der Familie in Deutschland* (Berlin: Institut für Soziologie der Technischen Universität Berlin, 1989).
72. Gordon, *Voluptuous Panic*.
73. Judy Barden, "Candy Bar Romance – Women of Germany," in *This Is Germany. A Report on Post War Germany by 21 Newspaper Correspondents*, ed. Arthur Settel (New York: William Sloane Associates, 1950), 170.
74. Eric Rentschler, "The Place of Rubble in the *Trümmerfilm*," in Julia Hell and Andreas Schönle, *Ruins of Modernity* (Durham: Duke University Press, 2010), 418–39.
75. Georg Holmsten, *Berliner Miniaturen: Großstadtmelodie* (Berlin: Deutsche Buchvertriebs- und Verlags-Gesellschaft, 1946), 13.
76. Holmsten, *Berliner Miniaturen*, 13, 15.
77. Norman Palmer, "Prostitution Alarms Germans," *Stars and Stripes* 1.239 (December 5, 1945): 1.
78. Heinz Friese in LAB B Rep. 240 Kleinschriftgut. Zeitgeschichtliche Sammlung. Erlebnisberichte.
79. LAB C Rep. 118 Magistrat der Gesundheits- und Sozialwesen, No. 304 Protokoll einer Besprechung zur Koordinierung der Massnahmen zur

Bekämpfung der Prostitution 11. September 1950; see also Uta Falck, *VEB Bordell: Geschichte der Prostitution in der DDR* (Berlin: Ch Links Verlag, 1998).

80. LAB C Rep. 118 Magistrat der Gesundheits- und Sozialwesen. No. 668 Maßnahmen zur Bekämpfung der Geschlechtskrankheiten besonders bei Jugendlichen 1954–5. Letter from Dr. Gross to Frau Johanna Kuzia, 2.12.1954.

81. Dorothy Rowe, *Representing Berlin*, 147.

82. Cited in Siegfried Heimann, "Das Uberleben organisieren: Berliner Jugend und Jugendbanden in der vierziger Jahren," in Berliner Geschichtswerkstatt, ed., *Vom Lagerfeuer zur Musikbox: Jugendkuulturen 1900–1960* (Berlin: Elefanten, 1985), 125–6; Hilde Thurnwald, *Gegenwarts problem Berliner Familien: Eine soziologische Untersuchung von 498 Berliner Familien* (Berlin: Weidmannsche Verlagsbuchhandlung, 1948).

83. In the GDR, see D. Müller-Hegemann, *Moderne Nervosität* (Berlin: Volk & Gesundheit, 1959); W. Bretschneider, *Sexuell aufklären rechtzeitig und richtig* (Leipzig, Jena: Urania, 1956). In the FRG, see Hans Heinrich Muchow, *Sexualreife und Sozialstruktur der Jugend* (Reinbeck bei Hamburg, 1959), 27–70; Kurt Saller, *Zivilisation und Sexualität* (Stuttgart: Ferdinand Enke Verlag, 1956).

84. LAB B Rep. 210 Bezirksamt Zehlendorf. Acc. 840, No. 91/4 Tätigkeitsberichte des Gesundheitsamts vom 1. Januar bis 31. Dezember 1949.

85. LAB C Rep. 118 Magistrat der Gesundheits- und Socialwesen, No. 304 Protokoll einer Besprechung zur Koordinierung der Massnahmen zur Bekämpfung der Prostitution 11. September 1950.

86. *Berliner Zeitung* 14 (June 3, 1945), 3; "Berlins Strassen werden beleuchtet," *Nacht-Express, Der Berliner Abend-Zeitung* (December 14, 1945), 1.

87. LAB B Rep. 210 Bezirksamt Zehlendorf. Acc. 840, No. 91/1 Bericht über die Tätigkeit des Gesundheitsamts Zehlendorf für die Zeit vom 1. Juli bis 30. September 1946. See also Annette F. Timm's book on the role of these health units and marriage counseling centers in Berlin, *The Politics of Fertility in 20th Century Berlin* (Cambridge MA: Cambridge University Press, 2010).

88. LAB B Rep. 210 Acc. 840, No. 91/2 Tätigkeitsberichte des Geundheitsamts vom 1. Dezember 1946–31. Dezember 1947.

89. *Nacht-Express, Der Berliner Abend-Zeitung* (December 13, 1945), 6. See Timm, *The Politics of Fertility in 20th Century Berlin.*

90. Jennifer V. Evans, "Constructing Borders: Image and Identity in Die Frau von Heute, 1946–1948," in *Conquering Women: Women and War in the German Cultural Imagination*, ed. Hilary Sy-Quia and Susanne Baackmann (Berkeley: University of California Press, 2000), 30–61; Donna Harsch, *Revenge of the Domestic: Women, the Family, and Communism in the German Democratic Republic* (Princeton, NJ: Princeton University Press, 2007), 38; Norman Naimark, *The Russians in Germany: A History of the Soviet Zone of Occupation, 1945–1949* (Cambridge, MA, 1997), 129, 135.

91. BArch, DY 31/1640 Sitzungen des Zentralen Frauenausschusses; Protokolle und Berichte. Bericht aus der Frauensitzung vom 15.11.1945.

92. LAB C Rep. 303/9 Polizeipräsident in Berlin, 1945–48 No. 241. Wochen und Monatsberichte der Abteilung Kriminalpolizei 1945–48. See the report from 24.6.1948 Präsidialabteilung, Dezernet I by Hagendorff as well as the response from Markgraf dated 25.6.1948, which he forwarded to the Alliierte

Stadtkommandantur, Public Safety Committee, vorsitzfuhrender Stabschef in Berlin-Dahlem.

93. Silvia Koerner, "Nach dem Kriege in Berlin," LeMO. Lebendiges Museum Online. Deutsche Historisches Museum, interview 10.02.2000.

94. LAB C Rep. 303/9 Polizeipräsident in Berlin, 1945–48 No. 83. Dezernet II. Reports of the Prasidialabteilung, Polizeipräsident in Berlin. Tätigkeitsbericht der Abteilungen und Dienststellen in Wochen- und Monatsberichten Juli bis September 1945. Monatsbericht 1. Juli bis 31. Juli 1945 Abteilung K. For a discussion of the use of marriage counseling centers in disease control see Timm, "The legacy of 'Bevolkerungspolitik,'" 173–214.

95. LAB C Rep. 303/9 Polizeipräsident in Berlin, 1945–48. No. 85 Dezernet II, Tätigkeitsbericht der Abteilungen und Dienststellen in Wochen- und Monatsberichten. Here, in order, Wochenbericht 29.12.–4.1.1946, Wochenbericht 5.1.–11.1.1946, and Wochenbericht 12.1.–18.1.1946.

96. Maria Tatar, *Lustmord: Sexual Murder in Weimar Germany* (Princeton, NJ: Princeton University Press, 1997).

97. On the gendered and sexualized narratives of big city life before 1933, see Rowe, *Representing Berlin*.

98. "Remapping Berlin. A Modern Woman's Guidebook to the City," in Despina Stratigakos, *A Women's Berlin: Building the Modern City* (Minneapolis: University of Minnesota Press, 2008), 1–16.

99. LAB C Rep. 118, Magistrat der Gesundheits- und Sozialwesen No. 121 Anklageschriften und Genadengesuche Jugendliche, 1946–48.

100. On the issue of the sexual behavior of American forces in Germany, see Perry Biddiscombe, "Dangerous Liaisons: The Anti-Fraternization Movement in the U.S. Occupation Zones of Germany and Austria, 1945–1948," *Journal of Social History* 34.3 (2001): 611–47; Heide Fehrenbach, *Race after Hitler: Black Occupation Children in Postwar Germany and America* (Princeton, NJ: Princeton University Press, 2007); Petra Goedde, "From Villains to Victims: Fraternization and the Feminization of Germany 1945–47," *Diplomatic History* 23.1 (Winter 1999): 1–20; Maria Höhn, *GIs and Fräuleins: The German–American Encounter in 1950s West Germany* (Chapel Hill: University of North Carolina Press, 2001); Johannes Kleinschmidt, *Do Not Fraternize: die schwierige Anfänge deutsch-amerikanische Freundschaft 1944–49* (Trier: WVT Wissenschaftlicher Verlag, 1997); and John Willoughby, "Sexual Behavior of American GIs During the Early Years of the Occupation of Germany," *Journal of Military History* 62 (January 1998): 155–74.

101. NARA, College Park. RG 389 Provost Marshall General. Criminal Investigation Branch. 1946 and 1947 Statistical Reports, Boxes 1711/12. Data concerning the precise number of courts martial conducted in Berlin between 1945 and 1948 and the relative frequency of cases involving women is admittedly difficult to assemble. However, it is possible to sketch a general outline of criminality with the use of figures compiled from monthly CID reports for the Office of the Provost Marshal General. In 1947, the CID oversaw 1278 arrests of military personnel in the American zone of occupation in Germany. Of that number, 412 arrests involved assault, accounting for 32 percent of the total and forming the most frequent reason for incarceration, followed by rape/sodomy, which stood at 220 arrests

or 17 percent. Records for the previous year are incomplete, but for a six-month period ending December 1946 over 1100 military arrests were made. Despite the dramatically higher incarceration rate, the relative number of arrests involving assault and rape/sodomy remain in keeping with 1947 figures, accounting for 211 and 104 arrests, respectively.

102. In 1946 the CID included an aggregate snapshot of all arrests (military and civilian) by detachment with their monthly reports. On average, CID recorded 42.4 arrests in Berlin between June and December 1946. Utilizing the monthly reports in the same period, we learn that 55 percent (1103) of all arrests in the American zone involved military personnel while 45 percent (893) were civilian. Based on this differential, at least 23 arrests per month involved military personnel in Berlin. However, by 1947 this ratio undergoes a dramatic reversal, with civilians accounting for 66 percent (2718) of all arrests over the year, with military personnel accounting for 32 percent (1268).

103. LAB C Rep. 303/9 Ministerium des Innern, Der Polizeipräsident in Berlin. No. 249 Weibliche Kriminalpolizei 1945–48, 6–12.

104. During times of conflict, public safety and the guarding of military supplies and installations fell under the jurisdiction of the G-5 division of the Supreme Headquarters, Allied Expeditionary Forces (SHAEF) before being passed on to the postwar administrative agency of the US Forces, European Theater (USFET). Once the occupation of Germany was sorted out administratively, the portfolio on public safety was transferred to the Office of the Military Government of the United States (OMGUS) on October 1, 1945. From then on, the administration of military government activities in the zone, including initially control of German courts and German police, became the task of OMGUS and by October 1946 it acquired authority over public safety in general. Oliver J. Frederiksen, *The American Military Occupation of Germany, 1945–1953* (Historical Division Headquarters, United States Army, Europe, 1953), 58.

105. Frederiksen, *The American Military Occupation of Germany*, 61.

106. LAB, B Rep. 303/9 Polizeipräsidium Berlin, No. 84 Dezernet II, reports of the Prasidialabteilung, Polizeipräsident in Berlin. Tätigkeitsbericht der Abteilungen und Dienststellen in Wochen- und Monatsberichten Okt. Bis Dez. 1945. Wochenbericht 29.9.45. "Sittlichkeitsdelikt an 4 jähriges Kind."

107. LAB, B Rep. 303/9 Polizeipräsidium Berlin, Wochenbericht 23.2–1.3.46 dated March 2, 1946.

108. NARA, College Park. RG 260 OMGBS Staff Judge Advocate, Special Court-Martial Files, case dated October 14, 1946. Statement of Ursula V. to Criminal Investigation Division, undated.

109. NARA, College Park RG 260 OMGBS Staff Judge Advocate, Special Court-Martial Files, case dated October 14, 1946. Statement of SIS. Investigator Herbert B. taken on July 30, 1946 by Agent Milton M. of the 759th Military Police Battalion, Special Investigation Section Friedenau, Berlin.

110. NARA, College Park RG 260 OMGBS Staff Judge Advocate, Special Court-Martial Files, case dated October 14, 1946. Record of Trial by Special Court-Martial, Patton Barracks, Berlin Germany October 14, 1946.

111. LAB B Rep. 210 Bezirksamt Zehlendorf, Amerikanische Militär, Tätigkeitberichte (Fluchtlinge), 1945–50, Acc. 840, No. 88.

112. "Gross-Berlin gestern und heute – Berlin diskutiert," *Der Abend* August 4, 1947.

113. LAB C Rep. 303/9 Sittlichkeitsdelikte 1945–49, Polizeipräsident in Berlin, Kriminalpolizei MII. Abschrift, Polizeiinspektion Neukölln P.I.Nkl. Tgb. No. 2477/47 from August 21, 1947 to the Polizeisektor-Assistant im amerikanischen Sektor.

114. Clip from *Tägliche Rundschau* entitled "Und abends nur in Herrenbegeleitung? Drei Stimmen zum Thema: Durfen Frauen allein in Tanzlokale?" (31.12.1946), found in SAPMO DY 30/IV 2/17/28 Zentral Komittee der SED, Abteilung Frauen-Zeitungsauschnitte über Gleiche Lohn und Paragraph 218.

115. LAB C Rep. 303/9 Polizeipräsident in Berlin, 1945–48. No. 11 Präsidialabteilung, Polizeiverordnung zum Schutz der Jugend. Letter regarding "Polizeiliche Behandlung gefährdeter und hilfsbedurftiger Kinder, Jugendlicher und Minderjahriger," June 7, 1946.

116. Ellen Schlüchter, *Pladoyer für den Erziehungsgedanken* (Berlin: de Gruyter, 1994), 21.

117. Alfons Kenkmann, *Wilde Jugend: Lebenswelt großstädtischer Jugendlicher zwischen Weltwirtschaftskrise, Nationalsozialismus und Währungsreform* (Berlin: Klartext, 2002).

118. LAB C Rep. 303/9 Polizeipräsident in Berlin, 1945–48. No. 11 Präsidialabteilung, Polizeiverordnung zum Schutz der Jugend. Memo from Markgraf "Polizeiverordnung zum Schutze der Jugend," vom 10.6.1943 RGBl. I. S. 349.

119. See volume 23 by W. Hammer entitled *Zehn Lebensläufe Berliner Kontrollmädchen* in the 50-volume *Großstadt Dokumente* (*Big City Documents*) published between 1905 and 1908 under the editorial eye of Hans Ostwald. This guide is discussed in Rowe, *Representing Berlin*, 98–108. For the history of prostitution and Berlin's demimonde, see Lynn Abrams, "Concubinage, Cohabitation and Law: Class and Gender Relations in Nineteenth-Century Germany," *Gender and History* 5.1 (Spring 1993): 81–100; Richard J. Evans, *Tales from the German Underworld* (New Haven, CT: Yale University Press, 1998). See also Julia Roos, *Weimar through the Lens of Gender: Prostitution Reform, Woman's Emancipation and German Democracy 1919–33* (Ann Arbor: University of Michigan Press, 2010), as well as her articles "Backlash against Prostitutes" Rights: Origins and Dynamics of Nazi Prostitution Policies," *Journal of the History of Sexuality* 11.1/2 (January/April 2002): 67–94. Reprinted in Dagmar Herzog, ed., *Sexuality and German Fascism* (Oxford and New York: Berghahn Books, 2005); "Prostitutes, Civil Society, and the State in Weimar Germany," in *Paradoxes of Civil Society: New Perspectives on Modern German and British History*, ed. Frank Trentmann (New York and Oxford: Berghahn Books, 2000), 263–80.

120. John Borneman, *Belonging in the Two Berlins: Kin, State, Nation*, 161. Thomas Lindenberger, "Rowdies im Systemkonflikt. Geheime und öffentliche Bilder der Jugenddelinquenz im Staatssozialismus," *Jahrbuch für Jugendforschung* (2005): 51–70. See also Uta G. Poiger, *Jazz, Rock, and Rebels: Cold War Politics and American Culture in a Divided Germany* (Berkeley: University of California Press, 2000), 210.

121. Claudia Puttkammer and Sacha Szabo, *Gruß aus dem Luna-Park: Eine Archäologie des Vergnügens. Freizeit- und Vergnügungsparks Anfang des zwanzigsten Jahrhunderts* (Berlin: wvb Wissenschaftlicher Verlag, 2007).
122. LAB B Rep. 010 No. 2293 Letter from Abteilung IV Polizeipräsident in Berlin, 28.4.1954 regarding licensing of Beuermann's event.
123. "Lärm," *Der Tag* (12. Juni 1955). LAB B Rep. 069 Jugendstrafanstalt Plötzensee, No. 1032 case against Erhard S. geb. 24.6.1940.
124. Jennifer V. Evans, "Decriminalization, Seduction, and 'Unnatural Desire' in the German Democratic Republic," *Feminist Studies* 36.3 (Fall 2010): 553–77; and Günter Grau, "Im Auftrag der Partei: Versuch einer Reform der strafrechtlichen Bestimmungen zur Homosexualität in der DDR," *Zeitschrift für Sexualforschung* 9. Jg (1996): 109–30.
125. LAB B Rep. 013 No. 502. Memo to Ella Kay from Hauptjugendamt, Berlin-Reinickendorf dated July 21, 1955, entitled "Artikel in *Der Abend* vom 2.7.1955: Arbeitshaus für Strichjungen."
126. Archiv Diakonisches Werk. Central-Ausschuß für die Innere Mission der deutschen evangelischen Kirche, Geschäftsstelle Bethel (CAW). No. 585A Jugendprostitution. Entschliessund des Fachausschusses Jugendschutz zur Frage der Prostitution (Hamm/Westf., 7/8 Januar 1952).
127. Archiv Diakonisches Werk. (CAW). CA 551 Jugendgerichtshilfe. Jaharesbericht 1951 der Jugenderichtshilfe, Hauptjugendamt, Berlin-Schöneberg. February 19, 1952.
128. Poiger, *Jazz, Rock, and Rebels.*
129. Jörn Donner, *Report from Berlin* (Bloomington: Indiana University Press, 1961), 274.
130. Horst Claus, "Rebels With a Cause: The Development of the '*Berlin-Filme*' by Gerhard Klein and Wolfgang Kohlhaase," in *DEFA: East German Cinema, 1946–1992*, ed. Seán Allan and John Sandford (New York: Berghahn Books, 1999), 93–116; Feinstein, *The Triumph of the Ordinary*, esp. chapter 2.
131. Elizabeth Heineman, "The Economic Miracle in the Bedroom: Big Business and Sexual Consumer Culture in Reconstruction West Germany," *Journal of Modern History* 78.4 (2006): 846–77; Dagmar Herzog, *Sex After Fascism: Memory and Morality in 20th Century Germany* (Princeton NJ: Princeton University Press, 2005).
132. Donner, *Report from Berlin*, 39.
133. KuBa's poem is cited in Pinkert, *Film and Memory in East Germany*, 109.
134. Anke Pinkert makes the point that emotional and psychological breakdowns were typically cast as feminine, as emblems of weakness of constitution, mirroring some of the gender dynamics at work in GDR society at large. See Pinkert, *Film and Memory in East Germany*, 118–20. On the 1953 uprising in Berlin and in the countryside, see Andrew Port, *Conflict and Stability in the German Democratic Republic* (Cambridge, MA: Cambridge University Press, 2006).
135. Poiger, *Jass, Rock, and Rebels.*
136. Elmar Kraushaar, "Unzucht vor Gericht: Die 'Frankfurter Prozesse' und die Kontinuität des § 175 in den fünfziger Jahren," in *Hundert Jahre schwul: Eine Revue*, ed. Elmar Kraushaar (Berlin: Rowohlt, 1997), 60–9.
137. Donner, *Report from Berlin.*

138. William H. Conlan, *Berlin: Beset and Bedevilled (Tinderbox of the World)* (New York: Fountainhead Publishers, 1963), 29.
139. Conlan, *Berlin: Beset and Bedevilled*, 29.
140. Donner, *Report from Berlin*, 40.
141. Klaus D. Wiek, *Kurfürstendammund Champs-Elysees: Geographischer Vergleich zweier Weltstrassen – Gebiete* (Berlin: Dietrich Reimer Verlag, 1967), 43. See also Anna Teut, "Eher kurios denn wirklich überzeugend," *Die Welt* January 18, 1962; on the competition for the ruin see also Ulrich Conrads, "Die neue Kaiser-Wilhelm-Gedächtniskirche in Berlin," *Bauwelt* 4.53 (1962): 95–8.
142. Settel, *This Is Germany*, 25.
143. Franz Kain, *Romeo und Julia an der Bernauer Strasse* (Berlin: Aufbau Verlag, 1955), 21.
144. Rolf Schneider, "Als der Krieg zu Ende war," in *Heimkehr ins Leben: Berlin 1945–60* (Berlin: Aufbau Verlag, 2005), 131.
145. In fact, historians have begun to take issue with the notion that Walter Ulbricht was but a minor player in these deliberations. See Hope M. Harrison, *Driving the Soviets up the Wall: Soviet–East German Relations, 1953–1961* (Princeton, NJ and Oxford: Princeton University Press, 2003).
146. Patrick Major, "The Berlin Wall Crisis: The View from Below," *History in Focus* vol. 10 *The Cold War* (Spring 2006): www.history.ac.uk/ihr/Focus/cold/articles/major.html (accessed Apr. 8, 2011).
147. Lynn Millar und Will McBride, *Berlin und Die Berliner von Amerikanern Gesehen* (West Berlin: Rembrandt-Verlag, 1958), 6, 8.
148. Edith Rimkus and Horst Beseler, *Verliebt in Berlin: Ein Tagebuch in Bildern und Worten* (Berlin: Verlag Neues Leben, 1958), 18–19.
149. Rimkus and Beseler, *Verliebt in Berlin*, 163.
150. Rimkus and Beseler, *Verliebt in Berlin*, 187.
151. Ulrich Domröse, *Arno Fischer. Situation Berlin. Fotografien, Photographs, 1953–1960* (Berlin: Nicolaische Verlagsbuchhandlung GmbH, 2001), 24–8.
152. Hans Scholz and Chargesheimer, *Berlin: Bilder aus einer Grossen Stadt* (Cologne: Kiepenheuer & Witsch, 1959), inner sleeve.
153. Renate Gruber and L. Fritz Gruber, *The Imaginary Photo Museum* (New York: Harmony Books, 1982), 19.
154. Helmut Peitsch, "Das erzählte Berlin der 50er Jahre," in Dragica Horvat, *Eine Kulturemetropole wird geteilt: Literarisches Leben in Berlin (West) 1945 bis 1961.* (Berlin, 1987), 67–86; and Helmut Peitsch, "Von Ruinen und Erinnerung. Berlin-Topoi der Nachkriegsliteratur," in Matthias Harder and Almut Hille, *Weltfabrik Berlin: Eine Metropole als Sujet der Literatur* (Würzburg: Königshausen & Neumann, 2006), 181–204.
155. Domröse, *Arno Fischer*, 24.
156. Scholz and Chargesheimer, xxviii.
157. Steege, *Black Market, Cold War.*
158. Franklin M. Davis, *Come as a Conqueror: The United States Army's Occupation of Germany, 1945–1949* (New York: Macmillan, 1967).
159. Frank Biess, " 'Everybody Has a Chance.' Civil Defense, Nuclear *Angst*, and the History of Emotions in Postwar Germany," *German History* 27.2 (2009): 215–43 and "Feelings in the Aftermath: Toward a History of Postwar

Emotions," in *Histories of the Aftermath: The Legacies of the Second World War in European Perspective*, ed. Frank Biess and Robert Moeller (New York: Berghahn Books, 2011).

3   The Train Station

1. Uwe Johnson, "Postscript on the S-Bahn," in *Berlin Tales*, trans. Lyn Marven. (Oxford: Oxford University Press), 63–6.
2. "U-Bahnhof Mehringdamm," in *Bomben, Trümmer, Lucky Strikes: Die Stunde Null in bisher unbekannten Manuskripten*, ed. Peter Kruse (Berlin: Wolf Jobst Siedler, 2004), 235–6.
3. Wolfgang Schivelbusch, *The Railway Journey: The Industrialization of Time and Space in the 19th Century* (Berkeley: University of California Press, 1986) and Todd Presner, *Mobile Modernity: Germans, Jews, Trains* (New York: Columbia University Press, 2007). See also Peter Bailey, "Adventures in Space. Victorian Railway Erotics or Taking Alienation For a Ride," *Journal of Victorian Culture* 9.1 (April 2004): 1–21; Ralph Herrington, "Railway Journey and Crises of Modernity," *Pathologies of Travel* (Amsterdam: Rodophi, 2000), 229–60; Simone Gigliotti, *A Holocaust in Transit: Trains, Captivity, Witness* (New York: Berghahn Books, 2010) and " 'Cattle Car Complexes': A Correspondence with Historical Captivity and Post-Holocaust Witnesses," *Holocaust and Genocide Studies* 20.2 (2006): 256–77.
4. Presner, *Mobile Modernity*, 3.
5. On train stations and transit, see Clara Magdalene Oberle, "City in Transit: Ruins, Railways, and the Search for Order in Berlin, 1945–1948," PhD dissertation, Princeton University, 2006.
6. Michel Foucault, "Of Other Spaces," *Diacritics* 16.1 (Spring 1987): 24.
7. Marian Aguiar, "Making Modernity: Inside the Technological Space of the Railway," *Cultural Critique* 68 (Winter 2008): 66.
8. Bailey, "Adventures in Space," 1–21.
9. "The Adventure" (1910) in *Simmel on Culture: Selected Writings*, ed. David Frisby and Mike Featherstone (London and Thousand Oaks, CA: Sage Publications, 1997), 221–32.
10. Gayle Letherby and Gillian Reynolds, *Train Tracks: Work, Play, and Politics on the Railways* (New York: Berg, 2005), 8.
11. Pamela E. Swett, "Political Networks, Rail Networks: Public Transportation and Neighbourhood Radicalism in Weimar Berlin," in *The City and the Railway in Europe*, ed. Ralf Roth and Marie Noelle Polino (Aldershot: Ashgate, 2003), 222–3.
12. Brian Ladd, *The Ghosts of Berlin: Confronting German History in the Urban Landscape* (Chicago: University of Chicago Press, 1997), 140.
13. Albert Speer as cited in Jeffrey Richards and John M. MacKenzie, *The Railway Station: A Social History* (Oxford: Oxford University Press, 1986), 116.
14. Richards and MacKenzie, *The Railway Station*, 116.
15. Barbara Lovenheim, *Survival in the Shadows: Seven Jews Hidden in Hitler's Berlin* (Detroit, MI: Wayne State University Press, 2002), 151.
16. Ursula von Kardorff, *Berliner Aufzeichnungen Aus den Jahren 1942-45* (Munich: Deutscher Taschenbuch Verlag, 1962), 193.

17. Birthe Kundrus, "Forbidden Company: Romantic Relationships between Germans and Foreigners, 1939 to 1945," *Journal of the History of Sexuality* 11.1/2 (January–April 2002): 201–22.
18. Jeanne Mammen in Hans-Dieter Schäfer, *Berlin im Zweiten Weltkrieg: Der Untergang der Reichshauptstadt in Augenzeugenberichten* (Munich: Piper Verlag, 1985), 239.
19. von Kardorff, *Berliner Aufzeichnungen*, 220–1.
20. Helmut Altner, *Berlin Dance of Death* (Staplehurst: Spellmount, 2002), 152.
21. Hans Dieter Schäfer, *Berlin im Zweiten Weltkrieg: Der Untergang der Reichshauptstadt in Augenzeugenberichten* (Munich: Piper Verlag, 1985), 248.
22. Heinz Knobloch, *Angehaltener Bahnhof: Fantasiestücke, Spaziergänge in Berlin.* East Berlin: Das Arsenal, 1984),60.
23. Knobloch, *Angehaltener Bahnhof*, 60.
24. Cited in Anke Pinkert, *Film and Memory in East Germany* (Bloomington: Indiana University Press, 2008), 100.
25. Willi Besener and Heinrich Manier, "Im Unterleib von Berlin," in *Bomben, Trümmer, Lucky Strikes: Die Stunde Null in bisher unbekannten Manuskripten*, ed. Peter Kruse (Berlin: Wolf Jobst Siedler, 2004), 117.
26. Anke Pinkert, "Silent Mothers: Air Wars as Intimate Memory – *Rotation*," in *Film and Memory in East Germany* (Bloomington: Indiana University Press, 2008), 90–107.
27. Kracauer's fascination is cited in Peter Mugay, *Die Friedrichstrasse* (Berlin: Ch. Links Verlag, 1991), 86.
28. Dr. Annaliese Holzhausen-Rohr, "Ruhe vor der Sturm" Tiergarten Mai '45 Zeitzeugenberichte. Mitte Museum und Archiv am Festungsgraben; Ewan Butler, *City Divided 1955* (New York: Praeger, 1955), 96.
29. Wolfgang Schivelbusch, *The Culture of Defeat: On National Trauma, Mourning, and Recovery* (New York: Metropolitan Books, 2003), 277.
30. Jörn Donner, *Report from Berlin* (Bloomington: Indiana University Press, 1961), 57.
31. Army Times, *Berlin: The City That Would Not Die* (New York: Dodd, Mead and Company, 1968), 22.
32. John J. Maginnis, *Military Government Journal: Normandy to Berlin* (Amherst: University of Massachusetts Press, 1971), 258.
33. *Berlin: The City That Would Not Die*, 37.
34. Landrum Bolling, "Zone of Silence," in Arthur Settel, *This Is Germany: A Report on Post War Germany by 21 Newspaper Correspondents* (New York: William Sloane Associates, 1950), 375.
35. Richard Brett-Smith, *Berlin '45: The Grey City* (New York: St. Martin's Press, 1967), 119.
36. This condition continued into the 1950s given the fact that many people continued to live in cramped and awkward living spaces, with bunkers serving as inhabitable space until apartments could be built. See *Neue Berliner Illustrierte* 1954/2-2 Januarheft – X. Jahrgang, pp. 3–4.
37. Margret Boveri, *Tage des Uberlebens. Berlin 1945.* (Munich: SeriePiper, 1985), 125.
38. Claudia Schoppmann and Angela Martin, eds., *Ich fürchte die Menschen mehr als die Bomben: Aus den Tagebüchern von drei Berliner Frauen 1938–1946.* (Berlin: Metropol Verlag, 1996),139.

39. Brett-Smith, *Berlin '45*, 88.
40. Denis Martin, "March of Millions," in Arthur Settel, *This Is Germany* (New York: Sloane, 1950), 216–17.
41. Kristen Semmens, *Seeing Hitler's Germany: Tourism in the Third Reich* (Basingstoke: Palgrave Macmillan, 2005).
42. Peter Neumann, "Berlins vergessene Bahnhöfe," *Berliner Zeitung* March 4, 2004.
43. Walter Benjamin, *Berlin Childhood Around 1900*. (Cambridge, MA: Belknap Press, 2006), 35.
44. Knobloch, *Angehaltener Bahnhof*, 8–9; Presner, *Mobile Modernity*, 58.
45. Wilfred Byford-Jones, *Berlin Twilight* (New York: Hutchison Press, 1947), 49.
46. Dagmar Barnouw, *Germany 1945: Views of War and Violence* (Bloomington: Indiana University Press, 1996), 156–61.
47. Henry Ries, *Berlin Photographien, 1946–1949* (Berlin: Nicolaische Verlagsbuchhandlung Beuermann, 1998), 83.
48. Barnouw, *Germany 1945*, 158.
49. Erika Brüning as cited in Walter Schulze and Rolf Schneider, *Heimkehr ins Leben. Berlin 1945–1960* (Berlin: Aufbau-Verlag, 2005), 100.
50. See Zygmunt Bauman, *Modernity and the Holocaust* (Ithaca, NY: Cornell University Press, 2001). Here too see Presner, *Mobile Modernity*.
51. For a unique and compelling analysis of trains, transit, and the Holocaust see Gigliotti, *A Holocaust in Transit*.
52. Byford-Jones, *Berlin Twilight*, 52.
53. Byford-Jones, *Berlin Twilight*, 52.
54. Massimo Perinelli, *Fluchtlinien des Neorealismus: Der organlose Körper der italienischen Nachkriegszeit 1943–1949* (Bielefeld: Transcript, 2009).
55. Friedrich Luft, *Blick über den Zaun: Tagesblätter* (Berlin: Transit Buchverlag, 1999), 7.
56. Archiv des Diakonischen Werkes der EKD, CAW 573. Report entitled "Lebenprobleme [sic] der Gegenwart. Das Seelenleben des Jugendlichen," p. 10 by P.D. Dr. med. Et phil. M. Tramer. Undated.
57. Ralph Herrington, "The Railway Journey and the Neuroses of Modernity," in *Railway Journey and the Crises of Modernity*, ed. Richard Wrigley and George Revill (Amsterdam: Rodopi, 2000), 229.
58. Herrington, "The Railway Journey and the Neuroses of Modernity," 233.
59. Bettine Hitzer, *Im Netz der Liebe: Die Protestantische Kirche und ihre Zuwanderer in der Metropole Berlin, 1849–1917* (Cologne: Böhlau Verlag, 2006); Astrid Kirchhof, "Gefährdete Frauen und 'Warnende' Männer. Fürsorge am Bahnhof im Berlin der Kaiserzeit," *Informationen zur Modernen Stadtgeschichte* (2004) 1: 38–52; Warren Rosenblum, *Beyond the Prison Gates: Punishment & Welfare in Germany, 1850–1933* (University of North Carolina Press, 2008).
60. Burghard Ciesla, "'Uber alle Sektorengrenzen hinweg…' Die Deutsche Reichsbahn und die Berlinkrisen (1945–1958)," in *Stebern für Berlin? Die Berliner Krisen 1948: 1958*, ed. Burghard Ciesla, Michael Lemki, and Thomas Lindenberger (Berlin: Metropol Verlag, 2000), 133–52; Rudolf Heym, *Das Buch der Deutschen Reichsbahn* (Munich: Gera Mond Verlag, 2003); Erich Preuß, *Der Reichsbahn-Report* (Stuttgart: transpress Verlag, 2001). In an

example of the absurdity of Cold War governance, the underground network was run by the West. See Patrick Major, *Behind the Berlin Wall* (Oxford:
Oxford University Press, 2009), 28.

61. Butler, *City Divided*, 96.
62. Karl Bader, *Soziologie der Deutschen Nachkriegskriminalität* (Tübingen: JCB
Mohr, 1949); Hilde Thurnwald, *Gegenwartsprobleme Berliner Familien: Eine
soziologische Untersuchung an 498 Familien* (Berlin: Weidmann, 1948).
63. Atina Grossmann makes this point eloquently in her article on the rape of
German women by Soviet soldiers. See "A Question of Silence: The Rape of
German Women by Occupation Soldiers," *October* 72 (Spring 1995): 43–65.
64. See Peter von Rönn's recent article for a larger discussion of youth
corruptibility in the Nazi era. Peter von Rönn, "Politische und psychiatrische Homosexualitäts-Konstruktionen im NS-Staat," *Zeitschrift für
Sexualforschung* 11 (1998): 220–60. Special thanks to Dagmar Herzog for
this reference.
65. Many people who have examined the problem of incarceration have
confined their attention to either the Nazi or the postwar period.
Some important contributions in the German literature include: *Polizei:
Vom Zwangsverhältnis zur Zweckehe?* ed. Jens Dobler (Berlin: Verlag rosa
Winkel, 1996); *Eldorado: Homosexuelle Frauen und Männer in Berlin 1850–
1950: Geschichte, Alltag und Kultur*, ed. Jens Dobler for Verein der
Freunde eines schwulen Museums Berlin e.V (Berlin: Edition Hentrich,
1992); Rainer Hoffschildt, *Die Verfolgung der Homosexuellen in der NS-Zeit:
Zahlen und Schicksale aus Norddeutschland* (Berlin: Verlag rosa Winkel,
1999); Burkhard Jellonnek, *Homosexuelle unter dem Hakenkreuz. Die
Verfolgung der Homosexuellen im Dritten Reich* (Paderborn: Schöningh, 1990);
Rönn, "Politische und psychiatrische Homosexualitäts- Konstruktionen
im NS-Staat"; Claudia Schoppmann, *Nationalsozialistische Sexualpolitik
und weibliche Homosexualität* (Pfaffenweiler, 1991); Claudia Schoppmann,
Verbotene Verhältnisse (Berlin: Querverlag, 1999); "...wegen Vergehen nach
§ 175 verhaftet". *Die Verfolgung der Düsseldorfer Homosexuellen während
des Nationalsozialismus*, ed. Frank Sparing (Mahn- und Gedenkstätte
Düsseldorf: Grupello, 1997); Hans-Georg Stürmke, *Homosexuelle in
Deutschland: Eine politische Geschichte* (Munich, 1989). Recent examples
from the postwar period include: Burckhardt Riechers, "Freundschaft und
Anständigkeit: Leitbilder im Selbstverständnis männlicher Homosexueller
in der frühen Bundesrepublik," *Invertito – Jahrbuch für die Geschichte
der Homosexualitäten* (1999): 12–46; Kristof Balser, Mario Kramp, Jürgen
Müller, and Joanna Gotzmann, *Himmel und Hölle: Das Leben der Kölner
Homosexuellen, 1945–69* (Cologne: Emons, 1994); and the essays in *"Wegen
der zu erwartenden hohen Strafe...,"* *Homosexuellenverfolgung in Berlin 1933–
1945*, ed. Andreas Pretzel and Gabriele Roßbach (Berlin: Sponsored by the
Kulturring in Berlin e. V, 2000).
66. In recent years, many important studies have emerged that document
transgressive sexuality in the urban milieu. Some key examples of the city's
role in fostering discourses of belonging and the emergence of subcultural
identification include George Chauncey's *Gay New York: Gender, Urban Culture, and the Making of the Gay Male World* (New York: Basic Books, 1994);
Goodbye to Berlin? 100 Jahre Schwulenbewegung (Berlin: Verlag rosa Winkel,

1996); Dan Healey, *Homosexual Desire in Revolutionary Russia: The Regulation of Sexual and Gender Dissent* (Chicago, IL: University of Chicago Press, 2001); Steven Maynard, "Through a Hole in the Lavatory Wall: Homosexual Subcultures, Police Surveillance, and the Dialectics of Discovery, Toronto, 1890–1930," *Journal of the History of Sexuality* 5 (1994): 207–42; Frank Mort, "Mapping Sexual London: The Wolfenden Committee on Homosexual Offences and Prostitution, 1954–57," *New Formations* 37 (Spring 1999): 92–113; and Mark Stein, *City of Sisterly and Brotherly Loves: Gay and Lesbian Philadelphia, 1945–72* (Chicago, IL: University of Chicago Press, 2000).

67. On Berlin's vibrant history, see Dobler, *Polizei: Vom Zwangsverhältnis zur Zweckehe?*; Dobler, *Eldorado*.

68. For an example from the Weimar period, see John Henry Mackay's famous account of a callboy's life in the 1920s in *Der Puppenjunge*, reprint (Berlin: Verlag rosa Winkel, 1999). In English as *The Hustler* (Boston: Alyson, 1985).

69. See the police logbook entries for descriptions of the train stations most frequented by male prostitutes in LAB C Rep. 303/9 Polizeipräsident in Berlin, No. 248 Tätigkeitsbuch MII/I – Aussendienst – 8.5.1948–23.4.1949, 60.

70. Henning Bech, *When Men Meet: Homosexuality and Modernity* (Chicago, IL: University of Chicago Press, 1997).

71. This link between bestiality and homosexuality has been researched in the Swedish context by Jens Rydström. See his article " 'Sodomitical Sins are Threefold': Typologies of Bestiality, Masturbation, and Homosexuality in Sweden, 1880–1950," *Journal of the History of Sexuality* 9 (2000): 240–76. For early histories of the regulation of illicit sex and German masculinity, see Martin Dinges, ed., *Hausväter, Priester, Kastraten: zur Konstruktion von Männlichkeit in Spätmittelalter und Früher Neuzeit* (Göttingen: Vandenhoeck & Ruprecht, 1998); Ulrike Gleixner, *"Das Mensch" und "Der Kerl." Die Konstruktion von Geschlecht in Unzuchtsverfahren der frühen Neuzeit (1700–1760)* (New York: Campus Verlag, 1994); and Isabel V. Hull, *Sexuality, State, and Civil Society in Germany, 1700–1815* (Ithaca, NY: Cornell University Press, 1996).

72. Edward Ross Dickinson, "Policing Sex in Germany, 1882–1982. A Preliminary Statistical Analysis," *Journal of the History of Sexuality* 6.2 (2007): 268.

73. Jens Dobler, *Zwischen Duldungspolitik und Verbrechensbekämpfung. Homosexuellenverfolgung durch die Berliner Polizei von 1848 bis 1933* (Berlin: Verlag für Polizeiwissenschaft, 2008); Martin Lücke, *Männlichkeit in Unordnung: Homosexualität und männliche Prostitution in Kaiserreich und Weimarer Republik* (Frankfurt am Main: Campus Verlag, 2008).

74. Florence Tamagne and Gert Hekma both argue that the 1930s witnessed a Europe-wide increase in intolerance vis-à-vis homosexuals. See Florence Tamagne, *Histoire de l'homosexualité en Europe* (Paris, 2000) and Gert Hekma, "Same-sex Relations among Men in Europe, 1700–1990," in *Sexual Cultures in Europe*, Vol. 2: *Themes in Sexuality*, ed. Franz Eder, Lesley Hall, and Gert Hekma (Manchester: University of Manchester Press, 1999), 79–103.

75. There is a broad range of opinions about the exact nature and origins of Nazi animosity toward homosexuality and homosexuals. In his landmark study of nationalism and respectability, George Mosse contended that homosexuals represented the evils of modernity, posing a distinct challenge

to a militarized but chaste vision of male bonding. Harry Oosterhuis has suggested that initially Hitler tolerated homosociality as one aspect of the new militarized masculinity that Mosse referred to in the years after the Great War. In order to sustain power and legitimacy, homosociality had to be purged from this vision of the New Man. Robert Moeller advances a more pragmatic solution to this issue in arguing that although the "night of the long knives" was motivated by the need to eliminate a possible rival within the ranks, a more general disdain for Röhm's public sexual identity may have in fact aided the Nazis in winning broad-based support for the action against the SA (*Sturmabteilung*). Günter Grau moves away from militarized masculinity to emphasize instead that the new population policy helped marginalize homosexuals, who had removed their reproductive power from the regeneration of the German people. See George Mosse, *Nationalism and Sexuality* (New York: Howard Fertig, 1985); Harry Oosterhuis, "Male Bonding and Homosexuality in Nazi Germany," *Journal of Homosexuality* 22.1 (1991): 242–62; Harry Oosterhuis, "Medicine, Male Bonding, and Homosexuality in Nazi Germany," *Journal of Contemporary History* (Spring 1997): 187–205; Robert Moeller, "The Homosexual Man is a 'Man,' the Homosexual Woman Is a 'Woman': Sex, Society, and the Law in Postwar West Germany," in *West Germany under Construction*, ed. Robert G. Moeller (Ann Arbor: University of Michigan Press, 1995), 257; and Günter Grau, *Homosexualität in der NS-Zeit* (Frankfurt am Main: Fischer Verlag, 1993). See also Eleanor Hancock, " 'Only the Real, the True, the Masculine Held its Value': Ernst Röhm, Masculinity, and Male Homosexuality," *Journal of the History of Sexuality* 8 (1998): 616–41.

76. Interestingly, Heinrich Himmler's statements support the argument that the increased persecution of homosexuals after the Röhm putsch was part of National Socialist policy and not simply a knee-jerk reaction to the SA's pronounced homosexual contingent. In a speech to the SS leadership on February 18, 1937, he reminded the audience that "in the first six weeks of our work in this field in 1934 we sent more cases to trial than the entire Berlin police force over the past 25 years. Nobody can tell me that it was all on account of Röhm." See "The Question of Homosexuality," in Heinrich Himmler, *Geheimreden 1933–1945*, ed. B. F. Smith (Frankfurt, 1974), as cited in Hans-Georg Stümke and Rudi Finkler, *Rosa Winkel, rosa Listen* (Hamburg, 1981), 436.

77. Dickinson, "Policing Sex in Germany, 1882–1982."

78. Jürgen Baumann, *Paragraph 175: Über die Möglichkeit einfache, die nichtjugendgefährdende und nicht öffentliche Homosexualität unter Erwachsenen straffrei zu lassen* (Berlin: Luchterhand, 1968), 48–9. This change in legislation was immediately felt in terms of the number of men prosecuted under the new variant of the paragraph. Baumann gives figures which suggest that of the 41,116 Germans convicted of violating laws protecting morality (*Sittlichkeitsdelikte*) between 1931 and 1933, fully 2319 were prosecuted against Paragraph 175. In the two years before World War II, the numbers increase dramatically to 24,447 Paragraph 175 infractions out of a total of 65,155 *Sittlichkeitsdelikte*. See Baumann, 61 as quoted in Moeller, "The Homosexual Man is a 'Man,' " 259.

79. *Reichsgesetzblatt* (RGBl), 1935, part I, 839–41.

80. On the issue of prison sentences, see Rainer Hoffschildt, "Zuchthäuser," in *Die Verfolgung der Homosexuellen in der NS-Zeit: Zahlen und Schicksale aus Norddeutschland* (Berlin: Verlag rosa Winkel, 1999), 143–76. Efforts are underway to catalogue the exact number of men who perished in the camps, as well as those who fell victim to Nazi jurisprudence. Rainer Hoffschildt is currently constructing a database of names, while Andreas Pretzel is assembling a book of the dead that seeks to enumerate the number of men who may be traced through the Berlin police and court records as having died due to Nazi persecution. This is an especially difficult task, given the fact that many men had repeat offences; where access is granted, case files are often incomplete.

81. See also Soviet General Besarin's Order of the Military Commanders of the City of Berlin from May 25, 1945, which stipulated that "in the interest of reestablishing normal life for the citizens of Berlin, in the interest of fighting against criminal offences and disturbances of the peace... the self government of the city of Berlin has received authorization from the command of the Red Army to organize a civic police force, court, and an office of the public prosecutor. These organs have already been formed on the 20th of May and have started about their normal work." *Befehl des Militärkommandanten der Stadt Berlin*, 25.5.1945. BArch DO 1 5.0 Ministerium des Inneren, Hauptabteilung Kriminalpolizei. No. 18, 99.

82. *Amstblatt der Militärregierung Deutschland*, 1945, No. 1, 11. For a discussion of the Allied position vis-à-vis Nazi jurisprudence see *Die Rechtsprechung der DDR, Anspruch und Wirklichkeit*, ed. Uwe-Jens Heuer (Baden Baden: Nomos Verlagsgesellschaft, 1995).

83. Perhaps these attitudes in the East help explain why from 1946 until 1949 only 129 judgments were passed down on Paragraph 175. Günter Grau has made this point in two articles, both dealing with the fractious debate over the possible decriminalization of homosexuality in the GDR. See Günter Grau, "Return of the Past: The Policy of the SED and the Laws Against Homosexuality in Eastern Germany between 1946 and 1968," *Journal of Homosexuality* 37 (1999): 1–21 and "Im Auftrag der Partei: Versuch einer Reform der strafrechtlichen Bestimmungen zur Homosexualität in der DDR 1952," *Zeitschrift für Sexualforschung* 9 (1996): 109–29, which includes a transcript of the deliberations of the legal reform committee from the Bundesarchiv-Lichterfelde.

84. See Brandstetter, *StPO mit Nebengesetzen* (Berlin, 1951), 273. See also Mario Kramp and Martin Sölle, "§175 – Restauration und Reform in der Bundesrepublik," in *"Himmel und Hölle": Das Leben der Kölner Homosexuellen 1945–69*, ed. Kristof Balser, Mario Kramp, Jürgen Müller, and Joanna Gotzmann (Cologne, 2000), 125.

85. Kammergericht Berlin, "Urteil v. 21.2.1950," *Neue Justiz* 4 (1950): 129.

86. Again, see Grau, "Return of the Past," and "Im Auftrag der Partei."

87. On the regulation of homosexuality in West and East Germany, see Robert G. Moeller, "Private Acts, Public Anxieties, and the Fight to Decriminalize Male Homosexuality in the Federal Republic of Germany," *Feminist Studies* 36.3 (Fall 2010): 528–52 and Jennifer V. Evans, "Decriminalization, Seduction, and 'Unnatural Desire' in the German Democratic Republic," *Feminist Studies* 36.3 (Fall 2010): 553–77.

88. Klaus Ulrich Klemens, *Die kriminelle Belastung der männlichen Prostituierten: Zugleich ein Beitrag zur Rückfallsprognose* (Berlin: Duncker & Humblot, 1967), 15.

89. This notion surfaced in the case against Karl-Heinz A. in Amtsgericht Tiergarten. 274 Ds 100/55, June 1, 1955.

90. LAB, B Rep. 013. No. 502, letter from Der Senator für Jugend und Sport, Hauptpfelgeamt, Berlin-Reinickendorf, 21 July 1955 to Frau Kay regarding a newspaper article in *Der Abend* from 2.7.55 entitled: 'Arbeitshaus für Strichjungen.'

91. LAB, C Rep. 303/9 Polizeipräsident in Berlin, No. 248 Tätigkeitsbuch MII/I – Aussendienst – 8.5.1948–23.4.1949, 10.

92. LAB C Rep. 341 Stadtbezirksgericht Mitte, No. 4743, case against Hans. L. 18 Ju Js 585.50 – 99 Ds 100.50.

93. Landesarchiv Berlin (hereafter referred to as LAB) B Rep. 013 Senatverwaltung für Jugend und Familie, Acc. 1052, No. 39. Case number (507) Jug Kms 65/51 and 2 Ju Kms 8/51. For an interesting pre-1918 history of the courthouse and some of its famous cases, see Benjamin Hett, *Death in the Tiergarten: Murder and Criminal Justice in the Kaiserzeit* (Cambridge, MA: Harvard University Press, 2004).

94. In a different case file account of transgressions against Paragraph 175 of the German Penal Code, Ursula Meinhard shows that the Berlin district court continued to recognize previous convictions under the Nazi criminal code as late as 1961. See Ursula Meinhard, " 'Auch nach heutiger Rechtsauffassung keine Bedenken.' Der lange Weg durch die Instanzen. 1943–1961," in *"Wegen der zu erwartenden hohen Strafe…": Homosexuellenverfolgung in Berlin, 1933–1945*, ed. Andreas Pretzel and Gabriele Roßbach (Berlin: Sponsored by the Kulturring in Berlin e. V, 2000), 287–89. For an account of the post-1945 experiences of men convicted in Nazi-era Berlin, see *NS-Opfer unter Vorbehalt: Homosexuelle Männer in Berlin nach 1945*, ed. Andreas Pretzel (Münster: Lit-Verlag 2002). I thank Andreas Pretzel for sharing his interesting research with me at an earlier stage.

95. On female prostitution, see Abraham Flexner, *Prostitution in Europe* (1914; New York: Century, 1920); Richard J. Evans, "Prostitution, State, and Society in Imperial Germany," *Past & Present* 70 (1976): 106–29; Regina Schulte, *Sperrbezirke: Tugendhaftigkeit und Prostitution in der bürgerlichen Welt* (Frankfurt: Syndikat, 1984); Julia Roos, "Backlash against Prostitutes' Rights: Origins and Dynamics of Nazi Prostitution Policies," in *Sexuality and German Fascism*, ed. Dagmar Herzog (New York: Berghahn, 2005).

96. Richard Bessel, *Germany 1945: From War to Peace* (New York: HarperCollins, 2009), 225.

97. Female prostitution was located among the subsections of Paragraph 361 of the Penal Code generally associated with forms of asociality including chronic drunkenness, lascivious behavior, peregrination, drug abuse, and begging, whereas paragraphs 173 to 184b dealt with more severe forms of immorality, specifically crimes against public decency. These *Sittlichkeitsdelikte* include molestation, incest, rape, homosexuality, male prostitution, seduction, *lustmord*, and procurement. In a sense, the difference between these two sections was a question of behavior versus action, but generally criminals accused of committing the more serious infractions

were believed to possess many of the asocial traits housed under the asociality paragraph. In this way, criminals charged with "crimes against the family and marriage" (the heading under which *Sittlichkeitsdelikte* were listed in the Criminal Code) were recognized as coming from among the ranks of the asocial; but rarely were those criminals accused of *Sittlichkeitsdelikte* charged simultaneously with infractions under Paragraph 361. The difference in the legal statutes governing moral infractions of a sexual nature speaks to that which was recognized as protected through the state's intervention: integrity of personhood and the family idyll as in the case of *Sittlichkeitsdelikte*, and an esoteric sense of community mores as in Paragraph 361.

98. See Jeffrey Weeks, *The World We Have Won: The Remaking of Erotic and Intimate Life* (New York: Routledge Press, 2007).

99. Elizabeth D. Heineman, "The Hour of The Woman: Memories of Germany's 'Crisis Years' and West German National Identity,' *American Historical Review* 101 (April 1996): 354–96, in addition to her recent monograph, *What Difference Does a Husband Make? Women and Marital Status in Nazi and Postwar Germany* (Berkeley: University of California Press, 1999); see also Maria Höhn, "Frau im Haus, Girl im Spiegel: Discourse on Women in the Interregnum Period of 1945–1949 and the Question of German Identity," *Central European History* 26 (Winter 1993): 57–91; Petra Goedde, "From Villains to Victims: Fraternization and the Feminization of Germany, 1945–47," *Diplomatic History* 23 (Winter 1999): 17; John Willoughby, "The Sexual Behavior of American GIs During the Early Years of the Occupation of Germany," *Journal of Military History* 62 (January 1998): 156; Annemarie Tröger, "Between Rape and Prostitution: Survival Strategies and Possibilities of Liberation of Berlin Women in 1945–1948," in *Women in Culture and Politics: A Century of Change*, ed. Judith Friedlander, Alice Kessler-Harris, and Carol Smith-Rosenberg (Bloomington: Indiana University Press, 1986).

100. Frank Biess, "Survivors of Totalitarianism: Returning POWs and the Reconstruction of Masculine Citizenship in West Germany, 1945–55," in Hanna Schissler, *The Miracle Years: A Cultural History of West Germany, 1949–68* (Princeton, NJ: Princeton University Press, 2001), 57–82; Robert Moeller, "The Last Soldiers of the 'Great War' and Tales of Family Reunions in the Federal Republic of Germany," *Signs: Journal of Women in Culture and Society* 24.1 (1998): 129–45.

101. Despite empirical evidence to the contrary, in 1959 Inspector Schramm of the Landeskriminalamt Berlin stated that in the immediate postwar period there were no callboys on the streets of Berlin. Only with the stabilization of the social and political situation, he argues, did hustlers reemerge onto the scene. See Ernst Schramm, "Das Strichjungenunwesen," in *Sittlichkeitsdelikte: Arbeitstagung im Bundeskriminalamt Wiesbaden vom 20. – 25.4.1959 über die Bekämpfung der Sittlichkeitsdelikte*, ed. Bundeskriminalamt (Wiesbaden: Bundeskriminalamt, 1959), 90. For examples from a different context, in this case early 1950s Cologne, see Michael Schön, "Einsatz für die Sittlichkeit: Kölner Polizei und Homosexuelle," in *"Himmel und Hölle": Das Leben der Kölner Homosexuellen 1945–69*, ed. Kristof Balser, Mario Kramp, Jürgen Müller, and Joanna Gotzmann (Cologne, 1999), 155–68.

102. LAB B Rep. 051 Amtsgericht Tiergarten #10685.

103. For examples of the treatment of young offenders, in this case young men charged with male prostitution, see the court case files from the Amtsgericht Tiergarten in 1947, which include examples of information gathered both by the Department of Youth Services and the *Jugendgerichtshilfe* before the division of municipal services in 1948. LAB B Rep. 051 Amtsgericht Tiergarten.
104. LAB C Rep. 303/9 Polizeipräsident in Berlin 1945–48, No. 259. Again, this language suggests the fact that many officials dealing with male prostitution viewed the boys as in fact heterosexual, forced into the trade by circumstance not desire. Indeed, most (but not all) boys explicitly denied homosexual orientation (literally in German *Veranlagung*) although this admission must be viewed with some skepticism. Police statements suggest that callboys (and johns for that matter) framed their "disposition" in ways to minimize the harshness of the pending sentence. For male prostitutes, an admission of desire could eliminate the possibility of mitigating circumstances, which had a very tangible effect on the length and type of sentence.
105. On November 28, 1945, four 15- and 16 year-old-girls were rounded up by Steglitz police while returning from a Christmas shopping trip at 3 o'clock in the afternoon. Since they had no ID on them (which was suspicious enough for police to think they were possible prostitutes), the girls were taken to the local precinct and strip-searched. Afterwards, they were sent to the hospital for the pelvic examination, where they had to undress in view of the American MPs (military policemen) who took part in the raid. LAB C Rep. 303/9 Ministerium des Innern, Der Polizeipräsident in Berlin. No. 249 Weibliche Kriminalpolizei 1945–48, 6–12.
106. LAB C Rep. 303/9 Polizeipräsident in Berlin 1945–48, No. 243 Abteilung V. Meldungen und Berichte 1945–48. See also the "Survey of Juvenile Delinquency in Berlin" from the Office of the Military Government of the US Sector (OMGUS), Berlin Sector dated August–October 1946. This report outlines the material hardships endured by Berliners in the year following the war. The survey pays particular attention to the problem of fraternization among German "girls" and American soldiers and calls for the use of spot checks and raids (*Razzia*). In Zehlendorf, one of the districts in southwestern Berlin under American control, "the young girls are kept in locked rooms through the night and many remain there throughout the next morning for their turn for examination." US National Archives and Records Administration (NARA), College Park, Maryland. RG 260 OMGUS Berlin Sector, Public Welfare Branch, box 192.
107. Raid report, Bunker Schlesischer Bahnhof dated 2.11.46. LAB C Rep. 303/9 Polizeipräsident in Berlin 1945–48, No. 259, 310.
108. In fact, both youth services and the Protestant Church believed the "streams of impoverished eastern youth" regularly fell "victim to homosexual circles" in postwar Berlin. Consult the Berlin-Schöneberg Year End Report from 1951 submitted to the Prostestant mission from West Berlin Youth Services, Archiv Diakonisches Werk (ADW) Central-Ausschuß für die Innere Mission der deutschen evangelischen Kirche, Geschäftsstelle Bethel. CA 551.

109. Some, like 14-year-old Fred V. from the East Berlin district of Köpenick, heard about the city's hot spots from boys he had met in the Struveshof facility in provincial Brandenburg. Interestingly, he had originally been picked up in 1949 for suspicious behavior around Bahnhof Zoo in the West. See LAB C Rep. 341 Stadtbezirksgericht Mitte, No. 4433, case number 98 Ds 34/50, June 23, 1950.

110. Robert P. Stephens, *Germans On Drugs: The Complications of Modernization in Hamburg* (Ann Arbor: University of Michigan Press, 2006).

111. Stefan Zweig, *The World of Yesterday* (Lincoln: University of Nebraska Press, 1964), 313.

112. Andreas Butter, Hans-Joachim Kirsche, and Erich Preuß, *Berlin Ostkreuz – Die Drehscheibe des S-Bahn-Verkehrs* (Munich: Geramond Verlag, 2000).

113. Barry Read, *New York Hustlers: Masculinity and Sex in Modern America* (Manchester: University of Manchester Press, 2010).

114. C Rep. 303/9 Polizeipräsident in Berlin, No. 248 Tätigkeitsbuch MII/I – Aussendienst –, 8.5.1948–23.4.1949.

115. Clayton J. Whisnant, "Styles of Masculinity in the West German Gay Scene," *Central European History* 39 (2006): 359–93.

116. LAB, B Rep. 051 Amtsgericht Tiergarten, Acc. 1687 #100685. Statement of Jugendamt to Bezirksjugendgericht Belin-Schöneberg by social worker overseeing the case.

117. See Evans, "Decriminalization, Seduction, and 'Unnatural Desire' in the German Democratic Republic," 553–77.

118. LAB, B Rep. 051 Amtsgericht Tiergarten, Acc. 1687 #100685. Report from KIM II/I dated 30.6.1947.

119. LAB, B Rep. 051 Amtsgericht Tiergarten, Acc. 1687 #11282.

120. LAB, C Rep. 303/9 Polizeipräsident in Berlin, No. 248 Tätigkeitsbuch MII/I – Aussendienst –, 8.5.1948–23.4.1949, 26.

121. LAB, B Rep. 051 Amtsgericht Tiergarten, Acc. 1687 #100685. Report from KIM II/I dated 30.6.1947.

122. According to the police file, Werner was never charged but instead had to face an internal hearing to determine whether disciplinary charges would be made for conduct unbecoming an officer. See the police statements taken from both suspects in LAB C Rep. 341 Stadtbezirksgericht Mitte, No. 4433, case 98 Ds 34/50, June 23, 1950.

123. Fred was sent to no less than three different institutions before serving out his sentence in August 1952. See the letter from Child Protective Services dated January 1, 1952 in LAB C Rep. 341 Stadtbezirksgericht Mitte, No. 4433, case 98 Ds 34/50, June 23, 1950.

124. LAB, C Rep. 303/9 Polizeipräsident in Berlin, No. 248 Tätigkeitsbuch MII/I – Aussendienst –, 8.51948–23.41949, 60. In this case, it is important to stress that procedures dictated that Werner would likely receive notice in the mail as to a fine for having contravened the law. Should he wish to contest the terms of the charge, he had the opportunity to appear in court in a formal hearing. Transgressions of this sort frequently substituted a fine for time in jail, and, according to Tiergarten district court records, if they were able many johns opted to pay their fine.

125. Moeller, "Private Acts, Public Anxieties," 528–52.

126. See *Herbert Tobias: Blicke und Begehren, 1928–1982* (Berlin: Berlinische Gallerie, 2008).
127. Laserstein was a stridently outspoken critic of the Adenauer regime. He published widely in homosexual journals advocating the decriminalization of Paragraph 175, defended homosexuals in court cases, and empowered gay men accused under the article with his guidebook to defense strategies entitled *Angeklagte Steh Auf!*, published in the early 1950s. His flagrant disregard for the Adenauer state caused him to be placed under surveillance by the Department of Constitutional Protection *(Verfassungschutz)*, which investigated threats to the integrity of West German democracy. He committed suicide in 1955, tarnished in a blackmail campaign and vilified in the conservative press. See *Der unaufhaltsame Selbstmord des Botho Laserstein: Ein deutscher Lebenslauf*, ed. Herbert Hoven (Frankfurt am Main: Luchterhand-Literaturverlag, 1991).
128. For a filmic version of the seduction motif, see Veit Harlan's remake of the 1919 film of a similar name, for which Magnus Hirschfeld originally contributed the screenplay. The 1957 version, *Anders als Du und Ich (§175)*, filmed under consultation with Hans Giese, sparked a national discussion of the quest to decriminalize Paragraph 175 in West Germany. The film was inherently controversial, due to both the subject matter and the director's professional history as a filmmaker during the Nazi period; he was responsible for one of the worst anti-Semitic feature films, *Jüd Suß*. A spirited account of the film and the controversy that engulfed it may be found in Heide Fehrenbach, *Cinema in Democratizing Germany: National Identity after Hitler* (Chapel Hill: University of North Carolina Press, 1995), 174–7.
129. Botho Laserstein, *Strichjunge Karl: Ein kriminalistischer Tatsachenbericht* (Hamburg: Janssen Verlag, 1994), 37.
130. Laserstein, *Strichjunge Karl*, 54. Of course, the fear of solicitation and blackmail was intense during the Nazi period. In Hamburg, for example, members of the Hitler Youth served as decoys, pretending, as Stefan Micheler argues, "to offer sexual services in order to entrap men." See Stefan Micheler, "Homophobic Propaganda and the Denunciation of Same-Sex-Desiring Men under National Socialism," in *Journal of the History of Sexuality* 11 (2002): 125.
131. For a full-length study of blackmail, with an emphasis on the English and French contexts, see Angus McLaren, *Sexual Blackmail: A Modern History* (Cambridge, MA: Harvard University Press, 2002).
132. Lücke, *Männlichkeit in Unordnung*.
133. Court records from this period are difficult to work with, offering but a foggy window into the past. I wish to extend warm thanks to Herren Marx and Nanzka of the Amtsgericht Tiergarten, Berlin for arranging access to valuable case files not yet archived at the Landesarchiv Berlin.
   For a discussion of the role of courtroom dramas and the place of the law in crafting acceptable and aberrant identities during the Nazi period, see Patricia Szobar, "Telling Sexual Stories in the Nazi Courts of Law: Race Defilement in Germany, 1933 to 1945," *Journal of the History of Sexuality* 11 (2002): 131–63. For a self-conscious study of the possibilities provided by court cases and their place in narrating gay history, see

Steven Maynard, " 'Horrible Temptations': Sex, Men, and Working-Class Youth in Urban Ontario, 1890–1935," *Canadian Historical Review* 6 (1997): 99–124.

134. Jurist Botho Laserstein published a guidebook that served to acquaint the reader with the reconstructed legal process. His informal guide was rumored to be used by homosexuals wishing to adopt the best possible defense against charges incurred under Paragraph 175. See Laserstein, *Angeklagte Steh Auf*.

135. Despite the fact that these explanations fell on deaf ears, during the Nazi period police statements continued to reflect the accused's attempt to craft a narrative appeal to mitigating circumstances, which in the Weimar period would have been entered as evidence in court and considered in sentencing. For examples from Berlin, see the articles included in *"Wegen der zu erwartenden hohen Strafe..."* ed. Pretzel and Roßbach.

136. Amtsgericht Tiergarten, Case against Horst K. 277 Cs 399/56, December 22, 1956.

137. Horst's monthly income was tabulated in 1956 at about 400–500 DM, and, while the fine is onerous, as a comparison, a transport worker with the Berlin Transit Authority (BVG) charged in another case in 1956 earned 280 DM per month and was forced to pay the same fine. Amtsgericht Tiergarten, K. 277 Cs 399/56, 22.12.56. In some cases, the findings of the district court could be appealed by the state prosecutor if the sentence seemed too light. See the example of the case against Peter Z. from 15.5.56 276 Cs 111/57 Amtsgericht Tiergarten and (534) 66 ns 56.57 (196.57) *Landgericht Berlin kleine Strafkammer* dated 7.3.58.

138. Internist Dr. Kilian published the results of his research on the reintegration of returning soldiers into family life in a special edition of the *Beiträge zur Sexualforschung*. He found that between 10 and 20 percent of the soldiers had homosexual encounters while in captivity. See H. Kilian, "Das Wiedereinleben des Heimkehrers in Familie, Ehe und Beruf," *Beiträge zur Sexualforschung* 11 (1957): 32–4. For a similar mention of homosexual "derailment" among POWs, see Otto Tschadek, "Die Aufgabe des Staates gegenüber dem Heimkehrer," *Beiträge zur Sexualforschung* 11 (1957): 76–9. More recently, Frank Biess has uncovered this connection in his research on the reintegration of POWs into East and West German society. See Biess, "Survivors of Totalitarianism," 57–82.

139. The only circumstance in which lenience was rarely granted was in cases where the defendant had prior convictions during the Nazi period. Despite efforts to democratize the court system by removing National Socialist laws, case files suggest that previous convictions incurred during the Nazis' 12-year rule were viewed as damaging to one's defense (*Strafschärfend*) since they demonstrated a pattern of behavior. Even when years had transpired between convictions, those contesting the summary judgment found themselves in the position of accounting for transgressions that occurred under Nazi law. On this issue, see Meinhard, " 'Auch nach heutiger Rechtsauffassung keine Bedenken,' " 287–9.

140. This was a common charge against returning soldiers, that psychological trauma had a profoundly gendered impact on their marital and social lives. See Svenja Golterman, *Die Gesellschaft der Überlebenden: Deutsche*

Kriegsheimkehrer und ihrer Gewalterfahrungen im Zweiten Weltkrieg (Munich: Deutsche Verlags-Anstalt, 2009).

141. See the statements entered by the municipal social services department of the West Berlin district of Berlin-Tempelhof at the juvenile court proceeding against 18-year-old Peter S. LAB B Rep. 051 Amtsgericht Tiergarten Acc. 1687 No. 10685.

142. Again, see Gerhard Jörns,*Der Jugendwerkhof im Jugendhilfesystem der DDR* (Göttingen: Cuvillier Verlag, 1995).

143. Michelle Mouton, *From Nurturing the Nation to Purifying the Volk: Weimar and Nazi Family Policy 1918–45* (Cambridge, MA: Cambridge University Press, 2007), 255.

144. See the decision by the Merseberg court from 12.8.1947 on the continued use of the Nazi-era Young Offender's Act in Neue Justiz Jg. 2 No. 7/8 (July/August 1948). Many contemporaries believed that a heavy hand was needed in dealing with the rise in crimes committed by the young in the wake of the war.

145. On Fred V., see LAB C Rep. 341 Stadtbezirksgericht Mitte, No. 4433. On Alfred B. see LAB A Rep. 358-02 Generalstaatsanwaltschaft beim Landgericht Berlin 1933–45, No. 104046 from 1941.

146. See LAB C Rep. 341 Stadtbezirksgericht Mitte, No. 4779 in which the youth is examined on several occasions, once to determine if he had the maturity and mental capacity to stand trial, and twice after he made multiple suicide attempts while serving his sentence.

147. Detective Superintendant Schramm of the Landeskriminalamt Berlin outlined the case of the callboy known only as Esche, who had been charged with the murder of one of his johns in 1957. Esche surfaced in the police records examined for this project around the same period as the murder, when he was naming the many johns he had been with and cooperating with the police by taking them to their apartments. See Schramm, "Das Strichjungenunwesen," 90.

148. See again von Rönn, "Politische und psychiatrische Homosexualitäts-Konstruktionen im NS-Staat," for a larger discussion of youth corruptibility in the Nazi era.

4   Bars, Cafés, Clubs

1. Fritz Mierau, *Russen in Berlin, 1918–1923: Eine kulturelle Begegnung* (Berlin: Quadriga, 1988).

2. Viktor Schlowski, "Zoo oder Briefe nicht über die Liebe," in Fritz Mierau, *Russen in Berlin* (Berlin: Quadriga, 1988), 302.

3. Christian Bouchholtz, "*Kurfürstendamm*" (Berlin: Axel Juncker Verlag, 1921), 9.

4. Sabine Hake, *Topographies of Class: Modern Architecture and Mass Society in Weimar Berlin* (Ann Arbor: University of Michigan Press, 2008), 138.

5. Ursula von Kardorff, *Berliner Aufzeichnungen 1942 bis 1945* (Munich: C. H. Beck, 1994), 354.

6. Lieutenant-Colonel W. Byford-Jones, *Berlin Twilight* (London: Hutchinson, 1947), 19.

7. John Mander, *Berlin: The Eagle and the Bear* (Westport, Connecticut: Greenwood Press, 1959), 154.

8. On urban spectatorship, see Frank Mort, "Mapping Sexual London: The Wolfenden Committee on Homosexual Offences and Prostitution 1954–57," in the special edition of *New Formations* ("Sexual Geographies"), 37 (Spring 1999): 92–112.

9. Michel de Certeau, *The Practice of Everyday Life* (Minneapolis: University of Minnesota Press, 1998).

10. Laurence Knopp, "Sexuality and Urban Space: A Framework for Analysis," in *Mapping Desire: Geographies of Sexualities*, ed. David Bell and Gill Valentine (New York and London: Routledge Press, 1995), 149.

11. Georg Simmel, "The Metropolis and Modern Life," in *George Simmel on Individuality and Social Forms*, ed. Donald N. Levine (Chicago: University of Chicago Press, 1971), 325.

12. Reinhard Rürup, ed., *Berlin 1945: Eine Dokumentation* (Berlin: Stiftung Topographie des Terrors und Verlag Willmuth Ahrenhövel, 2005), 13–14.

13. Egon Weingartner, "Die Notzucht. Eine kriminologische Untersuchung unter besonderer Berucksichtigung des Erscheinungsbildes der Notzuchtskriminalität in der heutigen Nachkriegszeit," PhD dissertation, University of Freiburg, 1951.

14. Peter Fritzsche, *Reading Berlin 1900* (Cambridge, MA: Harvard University Press, 1996).

15. "New Berlins and New Germanies: History, Myth, and the German Capital in the 1920s and 1990s," in *Representing the German Nation: History and Identity in Twentieth-Century Germany*, ed. Mary Fulbrook and Martin Swales (Manchester and New York: Manchester University Press, 2000), 65. See also Fritzsche, *Reading Berlin 1900*; Joseph Roth, *Reports from Berlin, 1920–1933* (New York: W. W. Norton, 2004); Nadine Roth, "Metamorphoses. Urban Space and Modern Identity. Berlin 1870–1933," PhD dissertation, University of Toronto, 2003; Eric D. Weitz, *Weimar Germany: Promise and Tragedy* (Princeton NJ: Princeton University Press, 2007).

16. Siegfried Kracauer, *Strassen in Berlin und anderswo* (Frankfurt am Main: Suhrkamp, 1964), 53.

17. Richard Brett-Smith, *Berlin '45: The Grey City* (New York: St. Martin's Press, 1967), 71.

18. As geographer Karen Till has noted in the contemporary city, physical spaces only acquire meaning via the artifacts, traces, and ghosts of another era. Karen E. Till, *The New Berlin: Memory, Politics, Place* (Minneapolis: University of Minnesota Press, 2005), 9. See also Brian Ladd, *Ghosts of Berlin: Confronting German History in the Urban Landscape* (Chicago: University of Chicago Press, 1998).

19. Alan Cochrane, drawing on geographer Doreen Massey's influential work on cities, makes this point for contemporary Berlin in "Making Up Meanings in a Capital City: Power, Memory and Monuments in Berlin," *European Urban and Regional Studies* 13.5 (2006): 22.

20. Howard Kingsbury Smith, *Last Train From Berlin: An Eye-Witness Account of Germany at War* (New York: Alfred A. Knopf, 1942), 160–2.

21. Theo Findahl, *Undergang. Berlin 1939–1945*, as cited in Hans Dieter Schäfer, *Berlin im Zweiten Weltkrieg: Der Untergand der Reichshauptstadt in AUgenzeugenberichten* (Munich: Piper Verlag, 1985), 227–8.

22. See the 23 extant anonymous reports of the *Wehrmacht's* Berlin special detachment division responsible for monitoring public opinion in public transit, department stores, food queues, and bars and restaurants. Bundesarchiv-Militärarchiv Freiburg im Breisgau (BArch-MA) RW 4/266 Aktion "Mundpropaganda" (Flüsterpropaganda): Einsatz von Soldaten aller Dienstgrade in der Heimat, um das Vertrauen in der Heimat zu festigen, Gerüchten entgegenzutreten sowie bestimmte Parolen und Mitteilungen zu verbreiten. *Berichte über den "Sondereinsatz Berlin" Oktober 1944–April 1945.* Portions of these reports have been published in Volker Berghahn in *Militärgeschichtliche Mitteilungen* 1 (1967): 95–119 and cited in Schäfer, *Berlin im Zweiten Weltkrieg.*

23. Byford-Jones, *Berlin Twilight*, 48.

24. Stephen Spender, *European Witness* (London: H. Hamilton Ltd., 1946), 235.

25. Henry Ries, *Ich War Ein Berliner: Erinnerungen eines New Yorker Fotojournalisten* (Berlin: Parthas-Verlag, 2001), 78.

26. Atina Grossmann, *Jews, Germans, and Allies: Close Encounters in Occupied Germany* (Princeton, NJ: Princeton University Press, 2007), 17. See also Wolfgang Schivelbusch, *In a Cold Crater: Cultural and Intellectual Life in Berlin 1945–48* (Berkeley: University of California Press, 1998).

27. Sigmund Freud, *Delusion and Dream, and Other Essays*, ed. Philip Reiff (Boston, MA: Beacon Press, 1956), 175–6.

28. Wolfgang Langhoff, quoted in Meike Mayer, *Neubeginn: Wiederaufbau des zerstörten Berlins 1945–1960.* (Berlin: Nicolaische Verlagsbuchhandlung Beuermann GmbH, 1995), 12.

29. See David Bell and Gill Valentine (eds), *Mapping Desire: Geographies of Sexualities* (London: Routledge, 1995); N. Duncan, *Bodyspace: Destabilizing Geographies of Gender and Sexuality* (London: Routledge, 1994); Phil Hubbard, "Sexuality, Immorality and the City: Red-light Districts and the Marginalization of Female Street Prostitutes," *Gender, Place and Culture* 5 (September 1998): 55–72; Phil Hubbard, "Desire/Disgust: Mapping the Moral Contours of Heterosexuality," *Progress in Human Geography* 24.2 (2000): 191–217.

30. Ersnt Troeltsch's reminiscences from post-World War I Berlin are cited in Schivelbusch, *In a Cold Crater*, 21. Marta Mierendorff's diary from the end of the war is published in *Ich fürchte die Menschen mehr als die Bomben: Aus den Tagebüchern von drei Berliner Frauen 1938–1946*, ed. Claudia Schoppmann and Angela Martin (Berlin: Metropol Verlag, 1996), 130. On the post-World War I dance craze, see Wolfgang Schivelbusch, *The Culture of Defeat: On National Trauma, Mourning, and Recovery*, trans. Jefferson Chase (New York: Metropolitan Books, 2003), 267.

31. LAB B Rep. 240 Kleinschriftgut Zeitgeschichtliche Sammlung, Erlebnisberichte. Remembrance of Berta Wilinga.

32. LAB B Rep. 210. Bezirksamt Zehlendorf. Amerikanische Militär, Tätigkeitsberichte (Flüchtilinge), 1945–50. Letter from the Office of Military Government Berlin Sector, Dr. Eugene E. Schwarz, Deputy, Public Health Office, from July 9, 1947 to the Burgermeister of Berlin Zehlendorf regarding prostitution in the sector.

33. Atina Grossmann, "A Question of Silence: The Rape of German Women by Occupation Soldiers" *October* 72 (Spring 1995): 43–63; Jennifer V. Evans,

"Protection from the Protectors: US Court-Martial Cases and the Lawlessness of Occupation in Postwar Berlin," in *GIs and Germans: The Military Presence, 1945–2000*, ed. Detlev Junker and Phillip Gassert (Cambridge University Press, in press).

34. Curt Riess, *The Berlin Story* (New York: The Dial Press, 1952), 67.

35. Frank Biess, *Homecomings: Returning POWs and the Legacies of Defeat in Postwar Germany* (Princeton, NJ: Princeton University Press, 2006); Robert G. Moeller, *War Stories: The Search for a Usable Past in the Federal Republic of Germany* (Berkeley: University of California Press, 2001).

36. Riess, *The Berlin Story*, 67.

37. Patrice Petro has argued that Weimar Berlin was constituted through male desire for and fear of the modern woman. See Patrice Petro, "Modernity and Mass Culture in Weimar: Contours of a Discourse on Sexuality in Early Theories of Perception and Representation," *New German Critique* 40, Special Issue on Weimar Film Theory (Winter, 1987): 115–46.

38. Riess, *The Berlin Story*, 50. On the mystery of the New Woman, see Weitz, *Weimar Germany: Promise and Tragedy*, 329.

39. Von Kardorff, *Berliner Aufzeichnungen 1942 bis 1945*, 354.

40. Brett-Smith, *Berlin '45: The Grey City*, 103.

41. Ewan Butler, *City Divided, Berlin 1955* (New York: Frederick A. Praeger, 1955), 80.

42. Drew Middleton, *Where Has Last July Gone? Memoirs* (New York: Quadrangle, 1973), 148.

43. Elisabeth Langgässer, *Briefe*, ed. Elisabeth Hoffmann (Düsseldorf: Claasen, 1990), vol. 1, 537–8.

44. Curt Moreck, "Wir zeigen Ihnen Berlin," in *Führer durch das "lasterhafte" Berlin*. (Leipzig: Verlag moderner Stadtführer, 1930), as cited in *The Weimar Republic Sourcebook*, ed. Anton Kaes, Martin Jay, and Edward Dimendberg (Berkeley: University of California Press, 1995), 564.

45. Brett-Smith, *Berlin '45: The Grey City*, 103.

46. Manuel Gasser, *Erinnerungen und Berichte* (Zürich: Verlag der Arsch, 1981), 129.

47. Carl Zuckmayer, *A Part of Myself* (New York: New York: Carroll and Graf Publishers, 1984), 234.

48. Brett-Smith, *Berlin '45: The Grey City*, 106.

49. Butler, *City Divided, Berlin 1955*, 72.

50. Paul Steege, *Black Market, Cold War: Everyday Life in Berlin 1946-49* (Cambridge: Cambridge University Press, 2007).

51. Hnry Ries, *Ich War Ein Berliner*, 77.

52. Gasser, *Erinnerungen und Berichte*, 113.

53. Butler, *City Divided, Berlin 1955*, 75.

54. Jörn Donner, *Report From Berlin* (Bloomington: Indiana University Press, 1961), 82.

55. Von Kardorff, *Berliner Aufzeichnungen 1942 bis 1945*, 354.

56. Georg Homsten, *Berliner Miniaturen. Großstadtmelodie* (1946), 18, as cited in Regina Stürickow, *Der Kurfürstendamm: Gesichter einer Strasse* (Berlin: Arani Verlag, 1995), 146.

57. Donner, *Report From Berlin*, 22.

58. Brett-Smith, *Berlin '45: The Grey City*, 106.

59. Siegfried Kracauer, "Strasse ohne Erinnerung," *Frankfurter Rundschau* 16 (December 1932).
60. William H. Conlan, *Berlin: Beset and Bedevilled (Tinderbox of the World)* (New York: Fountainhead Publishers, 1963), 29.
61. Donner, *Report from Berlin*, 23, 35.
62. Donner, *Report from Berlin*, 34.
63. Brett-Smith, *Berlin '45: The Grey City*, 104.
64. Donner, *Report from Berlin*, 25; Stürickow, *Der Kurfürstendamm*, 205.
65. Femina, Programmhelft vom 1.5.1939, as cited in Knud Wolffram, *Tanzdielen und Vergnügungspaläste: Berliner Nachtleben in den dreissiger und vierziger Jahren, von der Friedrichstrasse bis Berlin W. Vom Moka Efti bis zum Delphi* (Berlin: Edition Heintrich, 1992), 153.
66. Wolffram, *Tranzdielen und Vergnügungspaläste*, 158.
67. *Berliner Herald* January 18, 1931, 3,
68. John J. Maginnis, *Military Government Journal: Normandy to Berlin* (Amherst: University of Massachusetts Press, 1971), 267.
69. Brett-Smith, *Berlin '45: The Grey City*, 105.
70. Brett-Smith, *Berlin '45: The Grey City*, 106.
71. *Berlin Kommt Wieder: Die Nachkriegsjahre 1945/46 Ausstellungskatalogue des Landesarchivs* 16, (Mai 2005), 5.
72. Peter Jelavich, *Berlin Cabaret* (Cambridge, MA: Harvard University Press, 1996), 239–40.
73. *Der Tagesspeigel* November 24, 1945.
74. Ina Merkel, "Leitbilder und Lebenswesen von Frauen," in *Sozialgeschichte der DDR*, ed. Hartmut Kaelble, Jürgen Kocka, and Hartmut Zwahr (Stuttgart: Klett-Cotta, 1994), 359–82.
75. Jennifer V. Evans, "Constructing Borders: Image and Identity in Die Frau von Heute, 1945–49," in *Conquering Women: Women and War in the German Cultural Imagination*, ed Hillary Collier Sy-Quia and Susanne Baackmann (Berkeley: University of California, 2000), 44.
76. Judy Barden, "Candy Bar Romance – Women of Germany," in Arthur Settel, *This Is Germany* (New York: Sloane, 1950), 170.
77. Uta G. Poiger, *Jazz, Rock and Rebels: Cold War Politics and American Culture in a Divided Germany* (Berkeley: University of California Press, 2000), 57.
78. Peter Gay, *Weimar Culture: The Outsider as Insider* (New York: W. W. Norton, 2001); Jelavich, *Berlin Cabaret*.
79. *Die Badewanne, Ein Künstlerkabarett der frühen Nachkriegszeit* (Berlin: Edition Hentrich, 1991), 28, 165–7, 181; Rolf Ulrich, *Alles sollte ganz anders werden: 40 Jahre Kabarett "Die Stachelschweine"* (Frankfurt am Main, Ullstein, 1990).
80. "Mensch, Pepper" *Der Spiegel* 39 (September 25, 1963), 96.
81. "Berlin kommt wieder," *Die Zeit* 25 (June 23, 1955).
82. Donner, *Report from Berlin*, 28.
83. Donner, *Report from Berlin*, 29.
84. Donner, *Report from Berlin*, 30.
85. Donner, *Report from Berlin*, 230.
86. Donner, *Report from Berlin*, 31.
87. Donner, *Report from Berlin*, 230.
88. Butler, *City Divided*, 63.

89. Jens Dobler, *Von anderen Ufern: Geschichte der Berliner Lesben und Schwulen in Kreuzberg und Friedrichshain* (Berlin: Bruno Gmünder Verlag, 2003), 110.
90. Dobler, *Von anderen Ufern*, 112–13.
91. Akantha (aka Werner Becker), "Berlin tanzt!" *Der Kreis* 17.9 (1949).
92. Landesarchiv Berlin, B Rep. 20 Acc. 993, No. 6975.
93. Dobler, *Von anderen Ufern*, 252.
94. On the history of lesbianism in pre- and post-1933 Germany, see Claudia Schoppmann, *Zeit der Maskierung: Lebensgeschichten lesbischer Frauen im "Dritten Reich"* (Berlin: Orlanda Frauenverlag, 1993) and *Nationalsozialistische Sexualpolitik und weibliche Homosexualität* (Herbolzheim: Centaurus-Verlag GmBH, 1991). Marti Lybeck, "Gender, Sexuality and Belonging: Female Homosexuality in Germany, 1890–1933," PhD dissertation, University of Michigan, 2008.
95. Clair Sponsler, *Drama and Resistance: Bodies, Goods, and Theatricality in Late Medieval England* (Minneapolis: University of Minnesota, 1997), 27. See also Marjorie Garber's iconoclastic work, *Vested Interests: Cross-Dressing and Cultural Anxiety* (New York: Routledge, 1997).
96. Mel Gordon, *Voluptuous Panic: The Erotic World of Weimar Berlin* (Los Angeles: Feral House, 2000) and Magnus Hirschfeld, *Transvestites: The Erotic Drive to Cross-Dress* (New York, Prometheus, 2003). See also Rainer Herrn, *Schnittmuster des Geschlechts: Transvestitismus und Transsexualität in der frühen Sexualwissenschaft* (Gießen, Psychosozial-Verlag, 2005).
97. Garber, *Vested Interests*.
98. *Schwule Lieder*, vol. 2, track 18. Anno Mungen, "'Anders als die Anderen' or Queering the Song. Construction and Representation of Homosexuality in German Cabaret Song Recordings Before 1933," in *Queering the Popular Pitch*, ed. Sheila Whitely and Jennifer Rycenga (New York: Routledge, 2006), 74–5.
99. Curt Moreck, *Führer durch das lasterhafte Berlin* (Leipzig: Verlag moderner Stadtführer, 1931), 145–56.
100. Dobler, *Von anderen Ufern*, 187.
101. Anne Clark, "Twilight Moments," *Journal of the History of Sexuality* 14.1/2 (2005): 139–60.
102. Bastian Schlüter, Karl-Heinz Steinle, and Andreas Sternweiler, *Eberthardt Brucks: Ein Grafiker in Berlin*. Herausgegeben analsslich der Ausstellung zum 90. Geburtstag des Berliner Grafikers Eberhardt Brucks, 11 April 1917 bis 11 August 2008. (Berlin: Schwules Museum, 2008), 158.
103. Schlüter, Steinle, and Sternweiler, *Eberthardt Brucks*, 158.
104. For an example of how these communication networks functioned in the United States, see Martin Meeker, *Contacts Desired: Gay and Lesbian Communications and Community, 1940s–1970s* (Chicago: University of Chicago Press, 2005).
105. Dobler, *Von anderen Ufern*, 254.
106. See discussion of the court case in Dobler, *Von anderen Ufern*, 254.
107. Marco Pulver, ed., *"Das war janz doll!" Gottfried Stechers Memoiren: Eine schwule Biographie* (Berlin: Books on Demand Gmbh, 2001), 99–100.
108. Dobler, *Von anderen Ufern*, 232–4.
109. Dobler, *Von anderen Ufern*, 236.

110. Charlotte von Mahlsdorf, *I am My Own Wife: The Outlaw Life of Charlotte von Mahlsdorf, Berlin's Most Distinquished Transvestite* (San Francisco: Cleis Press, 1995), 110.
111. Von Mahlsdorf, *I am My Own Wife*, 110.
112. Richard W. McCormick, *Gender and Sexuality in Weimar Modernity: Film, Literature, and "New Objectivity"* (New York: Palgrave Macmillan, 2001), 6.
113. Rosa von Praunheim, *Sex und Karriere* (Munich: Rogner & Bernhard, 1976), 51.

5   Home

1. *Gesetz über den Fünfjahrplan zur Entwicklung der Volkswirtschaft der Deutschen Demokratischen Republik 1951–1955* (Berlin: Amt für Information der Regierung der DDR, 1952).
2. Cited in Emnie Sevgi Özdamar, "My Berlin," in *Berlin Tales*, trans. Lyn Marven, ed. Helen Constantine (Oxford: Oxford University Press, 2009), 99.
3. Bundesarchiv Berlin (BArch Berlin), DC 4 Amt für Jugendfragen, No. 1401 Bekämpfung der Jugendkriminalität, Konzeption für die Abteilung Leiter Beratung am 22.4.1958 zur Vorbereitung einer zentralen Konferenz über Jugendschutzarbeit.
4. BArch Berlin, DC 4 Amt für Jugendfragen, No. 1401 Bekämpfung der Jugendkriminalität, Thesen für die Bezirksbeauftragten zur Zentralen Arbeitsgemeinschaft für Jugendschutz zur Vorbereitung und Durchführung der Konferenzen über die Fragen des Jugendschutzes in den Bezirken, circa 1958.
5. For a statistical analysis of pre- and post-1945 criminality and recidivism, see Edward Ross Dickenson, "Policing Sex in Germany, 1882–1982: A Preliminary Statistical Analysis," *Journal of the History of Sexuality* 6.2 (2007), 236.
6. Thomas Lindenberger, " 'Asoziale Lebensweise.' Herrschaftslegitimation, Sozialdisziplinierung und die Konstruktion eines 'negativen Milieus' in der SED-Diktatur,"*Geschichte und Gesellschaft* 32 (2005): 227–54; and "Rowdies im Systemkonflikt. Geheime und öffentliche Bilder der Jugenddelinquenz im Staatssozialismus," *Jahrbuch für Jugendforschung* (Wiesbaden: Verlag für Sozialwissenschaften, 2005), 51–70.
7. Gerhard Jörns suggests there were 36 actual *Jugendwerkhöfe* in the GDR by 1956. For more information see his *Der Jugendwerkhof im Jugendhilfesystem der DDR* (Göttingen: Cuvillier Verlag, 1995), 66. Aside from these work-houses, between 1945 and 1951 in and around Berlin there also existed a variety of remand homes and reformatories. According to one study conducted by the *Innere Mission*, public, private, and church-based organizations in Berlin oversaw as many as 36 youth facilities in all four occupation sectors with 690 spots allocated to boys, and 1425 to girls under the age of 18. These facilities ranged from protective custody facilities where young offenders awaited trial, to foster homes and specialty housing for those who traveled to Berlin to complete apprenticeship training. Fifteen institutions were operated by the city government directly, while the Innere Mission ran 11 and the Catholic welfare organization

Caritas administered nine. Some of these facilities, like Struveshof, would be renamed *Jugendwerkhöfe* in the early 1950s. Archiv Diakonisches Werk, Gesamtverband der Berliner Inneren Mission (GVB), No. 14 Verschiedenes 1945–51 "Jugendliche in Gefahr. Jugendliche Verbrechen in Berlin."
8. BArch Berlin, DC 4 Amt für Jugendfragen, No. 1401 Bekämpfung der Jugendkriminalität, Thesen für die Bezirksbeauftragten zur Zentralen Arbeitsgemeinschaft für Jugendschutz zur Vorbereitung und Durchführung der Konferenzen über die Fragen des Jugendschutzes in den Bezirken, circa 1958.
9. *Der V. Parteitag der SED (10.–16.7. 1958): Eine Analyse* (Berlin: Presse- und Informationsstelle Berlin, Bundesministerium für gesamtdeutsche Fragen, 1958), also printed in *Neues Deutschland*, July 18, 1958.
10. LAB B Rep. 280, Aufruf der CDU, June 26, 1945. See Uta G. Poiger, *Jazz, Rock and Rebels: Cold War Politics and American Culture in Divided Germany* (Berkeley: University of California Press, 1999), especially chapter 3, "Lonely Crowds and Skeptical Generations: Depoliticizing and Repoliticizing Consumer Culture," 106–36.
11. Sara Ahmed, Claudia Castañeda, Anne-Marie Fortier and Mimi Sheller, eds., *Uprootings/Regroundings: Questions of Home and Migration* (Oxford: Berg, 2006); Alison Blunt and R. Dowling, *Home* (London: Routledge, 2006); Alison Blunt and A. Varley, "Geographies of Home: An Introduction," *Cultural Geographies* 11 (2004): 3–6; David Sibley, *Geographies of Exclusion* (London: Routledge, 1995).
12. Edward Ross Dickinson, *The Politics of German Child Welfare from the Empire to the Federal Republic* (Cambridge, MA: Cambridge University Press, 1996); Dietrich Oberwittler, "Von Strafe zur Erziehung? Zur Entwickllung der Jugendkriminalpolitik in England und Deutschland, ca. 1850–1920," PhD dissertation, Trier, 1998, and *Von der Strafe zur Erziehung: Jugendkriminalpolitik in England und Deutschland 1850–1920* (Frankfurt am Main, 2000); Young Sun-Hong, *Welfare, Modernity, and the Weimar State* (Princeton, NJ: Princeton University Press, 1998).
13. Edward Ross Dickinson, " 'Until the Stubborn Will is Broken.' Crisis and Reform in Prussian Reformatory Education, 1900–1934," *European History Quarterly* (2002): 161–206; Michelle Mouton, *From Nurturing the Nation to Purifying the Volk: Weimar and Nazi Family Policy 1918–45* (Cambridge, MA: Cambridge University Press, 2007).
14. Frank Biess, *Homecomings: Returning POWs and the Legacies of Defeat in Postwar Germany* (Princeton, NJ: Princeton University Press, 2006); Robert G. Moeller, *War Stories: The Search for a Usable Past in the Federal Republic of Germany* (Berkeley: University of California Press, 2001).
15. Dickinson, "Policing Sex in Germany, 1882–1982," 239.
16. Elizabeth Heineman, *What Difference Does a Husband Make? Marital Status in Nazi and Postwar Germany* (Berkeley: University of California Press, 2003).
17. Karl Bader, "Soziologie der Jugendkriminalität," in *Bekämpfung der Jugendkriminalität. Arbeitsgagung im Bundeskriminalamt Wiesbaden vom 1. November bis 6. November über die Kriminalität der Jugendlichen und Heranwachsenden* (Bundeskriminalamt Wiesbaden, 1955), 68.
18. Hilde Thurnwald, *Gegenwartsprobleme Berliner Familien: Eine soziologische Untersuchung an 498 Familien* (Berlin: Weidmann, 1948).

19. On the British case, see Joanna Bourke, " 'Going Home': The Personal Adjustment of British and American Servicemen after the War," in *Life After Death: Approaches to a Culture and Social History of Europe During the 1940s and 1950s*, ed. Richard Bessel and Dirk Schumann (New York: Cambridge University Press, 2003), 149–60.

20. Christina Benninghaus, "Verschlungene Pfade. Auf dem Weg zu einer Geschlechtergeschichte der Jugend," in *"Sag mir, wo die Mädchen sind..."* *Beiträge zur Geschlechtergeschichte der Jugend*, ed. Christina Benninghaus and Kerstin Kohtz (Cologne: Böhlau, 1999), 19; Kersten Kohtz, " 'Ich war ihm zu Willen, trotzdem strauebte ich mich.' Zur Sexuaität, verwahrloster' Mädchen in der Weimarer Republik," in *"Sag mir, wo die Mädchen sind..."*, 169–71; Martin Lücke, *Männlichkeit und Unordnung: Homosexualität und männliche Prostitution in Kaiserreich und Weimarer Republik* (Frankfurt am Main: Campus Verlag, 2008), 152; and Detlev Peukert, *Grenzen der Sozialdisziplinierung: Aufstieg und Krise der deutschen Jugendfürsorge, 1878–1932* (Cologne: Bund, 1986).

21. Annette F. Timm, "Sex with a Purpose: Prostitution, Venereal Disease and Militarized Masculinity in the Third Reich," *Journal of the History of Sexuality* 11.1/2 (2002): 223–55.

22. *Cold War Respite: The Geneva Summit of 1955*, ed. Gunter Bischof and Saki Dockrill (Baton Rouge: Louisiana State University Press, 2000).

23. Andrew Bickford, "The Militarization of Masculinity in the Former German Democratic Republic," in *Military Masculinities: Identity and State*, ed. Paul Higate (New York: Praeger Publishers, 2003), 157–74.

24. In addition to Gerhard Jörns's book *Der Jugendwerkhof im Jugendhilfesystem der DDR*, recent examples include: Gerrit Bratke, *Die Kriminologie in der DDR und ihre Anwendung im Bereich der Jugenddelinquenz: Eine zeitgeschichtlich-kriminologische Untersuchung* (Münster: LIT Verlag, 1999); Thomas Lindenberger, "Aufklären, zersetzen, liquidieren: Policing Juvenile Rowdytum in East Germany, 1956–1968," unpublished paper presented to the annual German Studies Association conference, October 4–7, 2001, Arlington, VA; Dorothy Wierling, "Die Jugend als innerer Feind. Konflikte in der Erziehungsdiktatur der sechziger Jahre," in *Sozialgeschichte der DDR*, ed. Hartmut Kaelble, Jürgen Kocka, and Hartmut Zwahr (Stuttgart: 1994), 404–25;, "Der Staat, die Jugend und der Westen. Texte zu Konflikten der 1960er Jahre," in *Akten. Eingaben. Schaufenster. Die DDR und ihre Texte. Erkundungen zu Herrschaft und Alltag*, ed. Alf Lüdtke and Peter Becker (Berlin: 1997), 223–40; and "The Hitler Youth Generation in the GDR: Insecurities, Ambitions and Dilemmas," in *Dictatorship as Experience: Towards a Socio-Cultural History of the GDR*, ed. Konrad Jarausch (New York: Berghahn Press, 1999), 307–24; Molly Wilkinson, "Building Bodies, Building Culture: Sports, Citizenship and National Identity in the German Democratic Republic, 1948–1990," PhD (in progress). On the treatment of young offenders in West Germany, see Frank Kebbedies, *Außer Kontrolle: Jugendkriminalität und Jugendkriminalpolitik in der NS-Zeit und der frühen Nachkriegszeit* (Essen: Klartext Verlag, 2000).

25. Of course, social policy was never truly devoid of politics. A *Tagesspiegel* article from September 25, 1946 documents a strategy adopted in the French zone. The article states that youth under 18 are not housed in prison, but

sent to custodial homes where they receive instruction from experienced anti-fascists under the direction of former French officers who served in the "Maquis" or French Resistance. "These youth," the article makes plain, "demonstrate a fine sense of justice."

26. Poiger, *Jazz, Rock, and Rebels*.
27. Edward Dickinson suggests that during the Weimar Republic, two major pieces of legislation helped standardize a comprehensive, locally centralized child welfare policy, including municipal welfare agencies, the participation of religious charities, in addition to correctional education services and youth courts. See Dickinson, *The Politics of German Child Welfare from the Empire to the Federal Republic*, 153. For information on youth policy and penal reform initiatives in the Wilhelmine and Weimar years, see Christine Dörner, *Erziehung Durch Strafe: die Geschichte der Jugendstrafe 1871–1945* (Weinheim: Juventa Verlag, 1996); Elizabeth Harvey, *Youth and the Welfare State in Weimar Germany* (Oxford: Clarendon Press, 1993); Derek S. Linton, *"Who Has the Youth Has the Future": The Campaign to Save Young Workers in Imperial Germany* (Cambridge: Cambridge University Press, 1991); Peukert, *Grenzen der Sozialdisziplinierung*: and most recently Warren Rosenblum, *Beyond the Prison Gates: Punishment and Welfare in Germany 1850–1933* (Chapel Hill: University of North Carolina Press, 2008).
28. David Harvey, *Paris, Capital of Modernity* (New York: Routledge, 2003).
29. Peukert, *Grenzen der Sozialdisziplinierung*. There were a variety of ways in which adults could be committed to a workhouse, most notably through §361,5 or §42d of the Penal Code in addition to corresponding welfare legislation. For more information see Wolfgang Ayass, *Das Arbeitshaus Breitenau. Bettler, Landstreicher, Prostituierte, Zuhälter und Fürsorgeempfänger in der Korrektions- und Landarmenanstalt Breitenau (1874–1949)* (Kassel: Gesamthochschule Kassel, Verein für hessische Geschichte und Landeskunde e.V, 1992); Andrea Rudolph, *Die Kooperation von Strafrecht und Sozialhilferecht bei der Disziplinierung von Armen mittels Arbeit. Vom Arbeitshaus bis zur gemeinnützigen Arbeit* (Frankfurt am Main: Peter Lang, 1995).
30. See Deputy Wachler's comments advocating reform in *Stenographische Berichte über die Verhandlungen des preussischen Hauses der Abgeordneten* (1878), as cited in Dickinson, *The Politics of German Child Welfare from the Empire to the Reich*, 20.
31. These developments resulted from the amendment to the RStGB and gained expression in laws both in Prussia and Baden that allowed for the placement of youth in foster families or reformatories if the child's behavior indicated suitable cause for concern. Dickinson states that a number of other states passed similar legislation in the 1890s. Dickinson, *The Politics of German Child Welfare from the Empire to the Reich*, 21.
32. Hugo Appelius, *Die Behandlung jugendlicher Verbrecher und verwahrloster Kinder* (Berlin: J. Guttentag, 1892), 25.
33. For an analysis of the influence of medicalization on child welfare and penal reform advocates see Gabriel Finder, "Education Not Punishment: Juvenile Justice in Germany 1890–1930," PhD dissertation, University of Chicago, 1997; Michael Voss, *Jugend ohne Rechte: Entwicklung des Jugendstrafrechts* (Frankfurt: Campus Verlag, 1986).

34. Mouton, *From Nurturing the Nation to Purifying the Volk*; Young Sun-Hong, *Welfare, Modernity, and the Weimar State*, 230.

35. For an extended discussion of health policy and *Bevölkerungspolitik*, see Annette Timm, "The Legacy of *Bevölkerungspolitik*: Venereal Disease Control and Marriage Counseling in Post-WWII Berlin," *Canadian Journal of History* XVIII (August 1998): 173–214.

36. Dagmar Herzog, "Desperately Seeking Normality. Sex and Marriage in the Wake of War," in *Life After Death: Approaches to a Culture and Social History of Europe During the 1940s and 1950s*, ed. Richard Bessel and Dirk Schumann (New York: Cambridge University Press, 2003), 161–92.

37. In the GDR, see D. Müller-Hegemann, *Moderne Nervosität* (Berlin: Volk & Gesundheit, 1959); W. Bretschneider, *Sexuell aufklären rechtzeitig und richtig* (Leipzig, Jena: Urania, 1956). In the FRG, see Hans Heinrich Muchow, *Sexualreife und Sozialstruktur der Jugend* (Reinbeck bei Hamburg, 1959), 27–70; Kurt Saller, *Zivilisation und Sexualität* (Stuttgart: Ferdinand Enke Verlag, 1956).

38. *Berliner Statistik* I (1947). Heft 1, p. 22.

39. "Jugendhilfsstelle wird ausgebaut," *Sozialdemokrat* February 6, 1948.

40. Brigitte Oleschinski, *Gedenkstätte Plötzensee* (Berlin: Gedenkstätte Deutscher Widerstand, 1995); Thomas Waltenbacher: *Zentrale Hinrichtungsstätten: Der Vollzug der Todesstrafe in Deutschland von 1937–1945. Scharfrichter im Dritten Reich.* (Berlin: Zwilling-Berlin, 2008).

41. See Richard Bessel, *Germany 1945: From War to Peace* (New York: HarperCollins, 2009); Atina Grossmann, "Defeated Germans and Surviving Jews: Gendered Encounters in everyday life in U.S. Occupied Germany, 1945–49," in *German History From the Margins*, ed. Neil Gregor, Nils Roemer, and Mark Roseman (Bloomington: Indiana University Press, 2006).

42. Archiv des Diakonischen Werkes der EKD, Gesamtverband der Berliner Inneren Mission (GVB), No. 14 Verschiedenes 1945–51. "Jugendliche in Gefahr. Jugendliche Verbrechen in Berlin."

43. Karl Bader, *Soziologie der Deutschen Nachkriegskriminalität* (Tübingen: J. C. B Mohr, 1949), 155, 149.

44. Alexander Mitscherlich, "Verwahrlosung der Jugend," *Tagesspiegel* November 27, 1947. On the place of psychoanalysis under the Nazis and in the early postwar period, see Daniel Pick, "In Pursuit of the Nazi Mind? The Development of Psychoanalysis in the Allied Struggle Against Germany," *Psychoanalysis and History* 11 (2009): 137–57 and Martin Dehli, "Shaping History: Alexander Mitscherlich and German Psychoanalysis after 1945," *Psychoanalysis and History* 11 (2009): 57–74.

45. For an overview of the postwar reorganizaiton of youth criminal policy see Jörg Wolff, Margreth Egelkamp, Tobias Mulot, and Michael Gassert, *Das Jugendstrafrecht zwischen Nationalsozialismus und Demokratie: Die Rückkehr der Normalität* (Baden Baden: Nomos, 1997). With the founding of the German Democratic Republic in October 1949, these laws were finally rewritten along with a host of other policy directives aimed at purging the remnants of Nazi social engineering while streamlining youth support for state socialism.

46. Matthias Etzel, *Die Aufhebung von nationalsozialistischenGesetzen durch den Alliierten Kontrolrat (1945–48).* (Tübingen: J. C. B. Mohr, 1992), 164; Eva

Schumann, ed., *Kontinuitäten und Zäsuren: Rechtswissenschaft und Justiz im "Dritten Reich" und in der Nachkriegszeit* (Göttingen: Wallstein Verlag, 2008). See also the discussion entitled "Die Jugendstrafe unbestimmter Dauer" from the Amstgericht Heinen, Bonn in *Monatschrift für Deutsches Recht* 8.5 (May 1954): 264–6.

47. Thomas Irmer, Kaspar Nürnberg, und Barbara Reischl, "Das Städtische Arbeits- und Bewahrungshaus Rummelsburg in Berlin-Lichtenberg, Zur Geschichte und Gegenwart eines vergessenen Ortes der Verfolgung von 'Asozialen' in der NS-Zeit," *Gedenkstättenrundbrief* 144.8 (2008): 22–3.

48. See especially the 1950 law on youth's role in building socialism in *Gesetz über die Teilnahme der Jugend am Aufbau der GDR*, February 1950. Archiv Diakonisches Werk, Allg. Slg. C61.4 Jugend in der GDR.

49. See the *Gesetz über den Fünfjahrplan zur Entwicklung der Volkswirtschaft der Deutschen Demokratischen Republik 1951*.

50. Landesarchiv Berlin (LAB), C Rep. 303/9 Polizeipräsident in Berlin, 1945–48, Nr. 11. Präsidialabteilung, Schutz der Jugend memo from Markgraf dated February 1, 1947 to all the necessary departments including the Hauptjugendamt.

51. Despite a well-developed network of short-term counseling and care facilities, by 1950 public and private youth homes housed over 2000 boys and girls, and youth courts forwarded an additional 2000 per month to these longer-term institutions. Due to shortage of space and financial backing, young offenders sometimes shared the same quarters as general wards of the state, compromising in the minds of educators the effectiveness of contemporary youth policy. Archiv Diakonisches Werk (ADW) Gesamtverband der Berliner Inneren Mission (GVB), No. 14 Verschiedenes 1945–51, "Jugendliche in Gefahr. Jugendliche Verbrechen in Berlin," a 45-page report on youth homes in Berlin-Brandenburg, undated but written around 1950.

52. BArch Berlin, DO 1 7.0 Deutsche Verwaltung des Innern (DVdI), No. 355 Die Entwicklung der Kriminalpolizei in der SBZ von 1945–49. Correspondence from December 24, 1947 concerning the work of the Kriminalpolizei in policing sexual crimes.

53. The ministry of *Volksbildung* oversaw children's aid and traditional child welfare services (such as adoption and care facilities) while also coordinating penal policy and directives as they affected children and teens. For information on the SMAD Order, see Deutsche Verwaltung für Volksbildung in der SBZ, ed., *Jugendämter: Aufbau und Aufgaben* (Berlin 1948), 31.

54. BArch Berlin, DC 4 Amt für Jugendfragen, No. 1657 die Arbeit zwischen Jugendklubhäuser und Heimen und soziale Betreuung Jugendlicher 1952–56, Bericht über die Lage in den Jugendwerkhofen und die Perspektiven im 2. Fünfjahrplan (undated).

55. For a detailed discussion of the process of policing homosexual youth, see Jennifer V. Evans, "*Bahnhof* Boys: Promiscuity and the Policing of Sexual Comportment in Post-Nazi Berlin," *Journal of the History of Sexuality* 12.4 (October 2003): 605–36.

56. BArch Berlin, DQ 2 Ministerium für Arbeit und Berufsausbildung, No. 3772 Zeitungsausschnitte zur Bekämpfung gefährdete Jugendlicher 1946–48. The newspaper snippet dated February 6, 1948, entitled "Jugendhilfestelle wird

ausgebau," found in the files of the Ministry for Employment and Apprenticeship, states that over 10,000 young boys and girls employed the services of the *Jugendhilfestelle*. This number included those youth removed from difficult family situations as well as criminals.

57. For more information on the laws governing disease transmission and suspected prostitution, see Uta Falck, *VEB Bordell: Prostitution in der DDR* (Berlin: Ch. Links Verlag, 1998); and Annette Timm, "Guarding the Health of Worker Families in the GDR: Socialist Health Care, *Bevölkerungspolitik*, and Marriage Counselling, 1945–72," in *Arbeiter in der SBZ-DDR*, ed. Peter Hübner and Klaus Tenfelde (Essen: Klartext, 1999), 463–95.

58. Of primary importance to police and social services was the need to convince Berlin's youth that their job was to help them navigate a path through the judicial and reformatory system. Understandably, many youths remained wary of any help police sought to provide. See BArch Berlin, DO 1 7.0 Deutsche Verwaltung des Innern (DvdI), No. 353 Broschüren zur Verordnung zum Schutz der Jugend 1948, Merkblatt zur Bekämpfung der Jugendkriminalität, Zonenkriminalamt Referat K6, Berlin July 28, 1947, no author.

59. For examples of the treatment of young offenders, in this case young men charged with male prostitution, see the court case files from the Amtsgericht Tiergarten in 1947, which include examples of information gathered both by the Jugendamt and the *Jugendgerichtshilfe* before the division of municipal services in 1948. LAB B Rep. 051 Amtsgericht Tiergarten.

60. In Berlin in the first few years after capitulation, property crimes had risen 885 percent from the 1937 figures. See Richard Bessel, "Grenzen des Polizeistaates. Polizei und Gesellschaft in der SBZ und frühen DDR, 1945–1953," in *Die Grenzen der Diktatur: Staat und Gesellschaft in der DDR*, ed. Richard Bessel and Ralph Jessen (Göttingen: Vandenhoeck and Ruprecht, 1996), 225. But violent crime also climbed in the postwar period. For statistics governing violent criminal infractions see LAB C Rep. 303/9 Polizeipräsident in Berlin 1945–48, No. 246 Statistiken der Kriminalpolizei 1945–48.

61. Hermann Glaser, *Kleine Kulturgeschichte der Bundesrepublik Deutschland* (Bonn: Carl Hanser 1991), 72–3.

62. LAB, B Rep. 210 Bezirksamt Zehlendorf, Acc. 840, No. 91/3 Tätigkeitsberichte des Gesundheitsamts vom 1. Januar bis 31. Dezember 1948. Report for the period of 1. January to 31 March, 1948 signed by a caseworker identified only as S.E.

63. Frau Hoffmann describes the Dircksenstrasse facility in the Diakonisches Werk report on youth services. See Archiv Diakonisches Werk, Gesamtverband der Berliner Inneren Mission (GVB), No. 14 Verschiedenes 1945–51, "Jugendliche in Gefahr. Jugendliche Verbrechen in Berlin." See also the article in *Sozialdemokrat* from February 6, 1948, "Jugendhilfsstelle wird ausgebaut," regarding the desperately needed renovations to the facility.

64. LAB C Rep. 120 Magistrat der Stadt Berlin, Hauptabteilung Volksbildung. No. 2710 Geschäftstätigkeit des Jugendwerkhöfes Struveshof 1948–60, Paedagogisches Referent, Konferenz mit Heimleitern und Erziehern in

Struveshof über weglaufen, Schwarzurlaub, Schwarzmarkt, Heimdiebstaehle, Arbeitsverweigerung, und Strafen am Mittwoch den 16.2.1949, 283.

65. BArch DP1 Ministerium der Justiz, Verwaltungsarchiv, No. 107 Die Einrichtung von Arbeitshäusern. Memorandum zur Frage des Arbeitshauses, Dr. Gentz 12.12.1951.

66. Martha Vicinus, "Distance and Desire: English Boarding-School Friendships," *Signs* 9.4 (1984): 600–22; and Regina Kunzel, *Criminal Intimacy: Prison and the Uneven History of Modern American Sexuality* (Chicago, IL: University of Chicago Press, 2008).

67. Ernst Seelig, *Lehrbuch der Kriminologie* (Dusseldorf: Fachverlag Dr. N. Stoytscheff, 1951), 48. Selig suggests that "shirking career criminals take to a life of crime while teens, often remarking later in life that they couldn't find work as young adults. In reformatories (homes for wayward youth or similar institutions) they aren't cured, but instead learn from more established career criminals and refine their skills... once on the outside they continue to seek out established criminals and form small bands of grifters." Interestingly, Selig suggests that no form of state intervention will prevent these youths from re-offending. However, he notes that in a few cases marriage brings about resocialization.

68. LAB C Rep. 303/9 Polizeipräsident in Berlin, No. 248 Tätigkeitsbuch MII/I – Aussendienst, May 8, 1948–April 23, 1949.

69. LAB C Rep. 120 Magistrat von Berlin hauptabteilung Volksbildung, No. 2710 Geschäftstätigkeit des Jugendwerkhofes Struveshof 1948–60. Paedagogisches Referent, Konferenz mit Heimleitern und Erziehern in Struveshof über weglaufen, Schwarzurlaub, Schwarzmarkt, Heimdiebstähle, Arbeitsverweigerung, und Strafen am Mittworch den 16.2.1949.

70. See Kunzel, *Criminal Intimacy.*

71. See the letter from the Director of the Jugendhilfestelle Herr Weimann to the head of the Kriminalpolizei from 28.9.48 in LAB C Rep. 303/9 Polizeipräsident in Berlin 1945–48, No. 259 Weibliche Kriminalpolizei 1945–49.

72. See the weekly reports in LAB C Rep. 303/9 Polizeipräsident in Berlin 1945–48.

73. Archiv Diakonisches Werk, BP 1859 Mitteilungen unserer Fürsorgerinnen über Heidekrug und Bezirksfürsorgeheime vom November 1947.

74. LAB C Rep. 120 Magistrat von Berlin Hauptabteilung Volksbildung. Arbeitsbericht des Landeerziehungsheims Struveshof für die Zeit vom 15.2–30.9.1948.

75. ADW, BP 1859. Letter from Pastor Heyne to the central administration of the Innere Mission, Bethel. February 23, 1951.

76. Robert G. Moeller, "Private Acts, Public Anxieties, and the Fight to Decriminalize Male Homosexuality in the Federal Republic of Germany," *Feminist Studies* 36.3 (Fall 2010): 528–52; and Dagmar Herzog, *Sex After Fascism: Memory and Morality in Twentieth-Century Germany* (Princeton, NJ: Princeton University Press, 2005), especially chapter 2, "The Fragility of Heterosexuality."

77. Hans Giese, "Die politische Rolle der Frage nach dem Wesen der menschlichen Sexualität," *Beiträge der Sexualforschung* 1.1 (1952): 25.

78. On the use of home building and modernist architecture as part of the Cold War battle for Berlin, see *Interbau Berlin 1957. Amtlicher*

Katalog der Internationalen Bauausstellung Berlin 1957 (Berlin: Internationale Bauausstellung Berlin GmbH, 1957); Gabi Dolff-Bonekämper and Franziska Schmidt, *Das Hansaviertel: Internationale Nachkriegsmoderne in Berlin* (Berlin: Verlag Bauwesen, 1999); Sandra Wagner-Conzelmann, *Die Interbau 1957 in Berlin: Stadt von heute – Stadt von morgen. Städtebau und Gesellschaftskritik der 50er Jahre.* Techn. Universität, Dissertation, Darmstadt, 2006. (Petersberg: Michael Imhof Verlag, 2007).

79. ADW, Central-Ausschuß für die Innere Mission der deutschen evangelischen Kirche, Geschäftsstelle Bethel (CAW), 551 Jugendgerichtshilfe. Jahresbericht 1951, 19.2.1951.
80. Giese, "Die politische Rolle," 25.
81. BArch Berlin, DP 1 Ministerium der Justiz, Hauptabteilung Strafvollzug II-42 Jugendstrafvollzug 1949–52. For information about the East and West German debates concerning the reform of the Young Offenders Act in general and education in lieu of incarceration, see especially *Unsere Jugend* 10 (1949): 30, *Unsere Jugend* (1950): 10, *Unsere Jugend* (1949): 21. A series of warm reflections from one caseworker were published in 1961, based on his experiences at one GDR facility. Hans Joachim Mahlberg, *Man Muss Nur den Schlüssel Finden. Erzählung aus einem Jugendwerkhof* (Rudolstadt: Greifenverlag zuu Rudolstadt, 1961).
82. Despite efforts to promote education instead of incarceration for teenaged youth, in special circumstances charges could be kept in custody beyond their eighteenth birthday if the situation warranted continued supervision. BArch Berlin, DC 4 Amt für Jugendfragen, No. 1657 die Arbeit zwischen Jugendklubhäuser und Heimen und soziale Betreuung Jugendlicher 1952–56, Bericht über die Lage in den Jugendwerkhofen und die Perspektiven im 2. Fünfjahrplan (undated).
83. BArch Berlin, DP 1 Ministerium der Justiz, Hauptabteilung Strafvollzug II-42 Jugendstrafvollzug 1949–52. Report from 30.09.50 Ministerium für Volksbildung des Landes Sachsen, Jugendhilfe, und Heimerziehung entitled "Unsere kommenden Aufgaben in Jugendwerkhofen."
84. BArch Berlin, DP 1 Ministerium der Justiz, Hauptabteilung Strafvollzug II-42 Jugendstrafvollzug 1949–52. Working plan for the amelioration of youth workhouses as drafted by Dr. Gentz and submitted to the Ministerium der Justiz upon receipt of the 30.09.50 report from Saxony.
85. The problems affecting East Berlin and the emerging GDR were not necessarily specific to the East. Overcrowding of youth facilities, including the mixing of simple offenders and more advanced criminals, raised the ire of many youth advocates in the West as well. See the article "Jugend protestieren," in *Juna* from September 12, 1950 regarding the deplorable conditions in the Plötzensee youth facility. In an article in *Telegraf* from June 15, 1948 entitled "Sommersonntag hinter Gefangnismauern: als Chorsänger im Jugendgefängnis Plötzensee – Gespräche mit Haftlingen – Kriminelle, Gefährdete, Gestrauchelte," the author reports how the young prisoners eat their rations out of empty cans that have been cleaned with sand since there were no available dishes.
86. In the Treuenbrietzen facility, boys lived in small groups with a single caseworker in deliberately designed family-like environments. See Horning, "Die Arbeit des Jugendwerkhofes Treuenbrietzen an straffällig gewordenen

und erziehungsgefährdeten Jugendlichen," in *Neue Justiz* 3.3 (1949): 38–9.

87. For an example from Saxony, see the article by an Amtsgericht judge in Aue, "Erfahrungen mit dem produktiven Arbeitsansatz Strafgefangener," *Neue Justiz* 2.4 (1950): 57–8.

88. At Struveshof in Ludwigsfelde, boys could learn a variety of trades in the facility's workshops including roofing, carpentry, and electrical work. Generally, youths did not enjoy agricultural work, since the hours were long and the work hard. They were rarely embraced by local farmers, who often saw them as difficult city youths with a poor attitude and a lack of respect. See C Rep. 120 Magistrat von Berlin, Abteilung Volksbildung, No. 2710 Geschäftstätigkeit des Jugendwerkhofes Struveshof, 1948–60.

89. LAB C Rep. 120 Magistrat von Berlin, Abteilung Volksbildung, No. 2976 Tätigkeit der Berliner Heime und Jugendwerkhöfe. Die gegenwartige Situation in den Berliner Jugendwerkhöfen – no date but from 1956, 194–201 (undated but ca. 1956).

90. The persistence of traditional gender roles despite the language of equality has been emphasized in a variety of studies. For an example, see Ina Merkel, "Leitbilder und Lebensweisen von Frauen in der DDR," in *Sozialgeschichte der DDR*, ed. Hartmut Kaelble, Jürgen Kocka, and Hartmut Zwahr (Stuttgart: Klett Cotta, 1994).

91. See "Die Errichtung eines Fursorge-Erziehungsheimes für gefährdete Mädchen ist im Schloss Friedrichswert Friedrichswerth," in *Abendpost* August 16, 1947.

92. Brandenburgisches Landeshauptarchiv – Abteilung Bornim, Rep. 212 Ministerium der Justiz Hauptabteilung Justiz, No. 1266 Haftlager Heidekrug für Frauen 1947–49. Report from Gerda Konrad and Helene Wosniak from June 23, 1950. Conditions were also deplorable in the Landesmädchenheim Schenkendorf near Königs Wusterhausen. See No. 1366 Unterbringung weiblicher Jugendlicher im Landesmadchenheim Schenkendorf bei Königs Wusterhausen, 1951. The relationship between the guard and inmate was considered to be "peculiar" since they were spotted walking arm in arm on a couple of occasions. When the guard was taken aside and made aware of her behavior, she commented that she would try to effect some distance between her and her charge, but that she did not want to tell the woman directly.

93. All of these examples are from "Erziehung mit Schlägermusik. Ein Besuch im Erziehungsheim für gefährdete Mädchen," in *Neue Zeit* May 28, 1948.

94. Dr. Schimmelpfeng, "Die Betreuung von Kindern, Jugendlichen und Heranwachsenden in Heimen und Anstalten," in *Bekämpfung der Jugendkrimianlität. Arbeitstagung im Bundeskriminalamt Wiesbaden vom 1. November bis 6. November über die Jugendlichen und Heranwachsenden* (Wiesbaden: Bundeskriminalamt, 1955), 231.

95. Merkblatt zur Bekämpfung der Jugendkriminalität, Zonenkriminalamt Referat K6, Berlin dated 28.5.47, author unknown. BArch Berlin, DO 1 7.0 Deutsche Verwaltung des Innern (DvdI), No. 353 Broschüren Materialien zur Verordnung zum Schutz der Jugend 1948.

96. Merkblatt zur Bekämpfung der Jugendkriminalität, Zonenkriminalamt Referat K6, Berlin dated 28.5.47. BArch Berlin, DO 1 7.0 Deutsche Verwaltung des Innern (DvdI), No. 353 Broschüren Materialien zur Verordnung zum Schutz der Jugend 1948.

97. For more information and statistics from the early postwar situation in Berlin see Thurnwald, *Gegenwartsprobleme Berliner Familien*.

98. Hans Eyferth, *Gefährdete Jugend. Erziehungshilfe bei Fehlentwicklung* (Hannover: Wissenschaftliche Verlagsanstalt K.G, 1950), 4.

99. On cross-fertilization and sharing of resources, Uta Poiger points to the paradoxes provided by postwar Berlin. In the sensational court proceedings against gang member Werner Gladow held in East Berlin in 1950, the prosecution actually called for the expert testimony and opinion of a West Berlin psychiatrist. Despite the entrenched battle lines between the two states, this court case demonstrates the continued sharing of resources until the early 1950s. See Poiger's lively discussion of the case in *Jazz, Rock and Rebels*, 48–51.

100. Even as late as 1955, East Berlin health authorities continued to lament the influx of itinerate youth that lounged about in unsavory circles and frequently fell into prostitution. See LAB C Rep. 118 Magistrat der Gesundheits- und Sozialwesen, No. 555 Beratung zur Bekämpfung der Prostitution, Dezember 1955. Meeting on 6.12.1955 in the Headquarters of Committee to Fight the Spread of Venereal Disease. Responses to a report tabled by a representative of the district of Mitte on the importance of working together with the police and social services to combat the spread of disease in the East. According to the Director of the East Berlin Department of Health, Dr. Gross, each police precinct records between 800 and 1000 unregistered and homeless people, many of them youths. See his letter from 2.12.1954 to the representative of the mayor of Berlin, Frau Johanna Kuzia in LAB C Rep. 118 Magistrat der Gesundheits- und Sozialwesen, No. 668 Maßnahmen zur Bekämpfung der Geschlechtskrankheiten besonders bei Jugendlichen 1954–55.

101. *Zur Geschichte der Rechtspflege der DDR 1945–1949* was purportedly written by a collective of authors under the direction of Hilde Benjamin (Berlin: Staatsverlag der DDR, 1976), 277.

102. See the individual cases listed in Archiv Diakonisches Werk (ADW) Gesamtverband der Berliner Inneren Mission (GVB), No. 14 Verschiedenes 1945–51, "Jugendliche in Gefahr. Jugendliche Verbrechen in Berlin," A 45-page report on youth homes in Berlin-Brandenburg, undated but written around 1950.

103. See Uta Poiger, "Rock 'n' roll, Kalter Krieg und deutsche Identität," in *Amerikanisierung und Sowjetisierung in Deutschland 1945–1970*, ed. Konrad H. Jarausch, Siegrist (Frankfurt: Campus Verlag, 1997), 275–89, in addition to her article "A New, 'Western' Hero? Reconstructing German Masculinity in the 1950s," *Signs: Journal of Women in Culture and Society* 24.1 (1998): 147–62.

104. See the letter from the head of the East Berlin department of health dated 3.5.1955. LAB C Rep. 118 Magistrat der Gesundheits- und Sozialwesen, No. 668 Maßnahmen zur Bekämpfung der Geschlechtskrankheiten besonders bei Jugendlichen 1954–55.

105. See the psychological assessment and case file of the underage Erhard S. charged with homosexual prostitution in 1958 in LAB B Rep. 069 Jugendstrafanstalt Plötzensee, Acc. 4202, No. 1032.
106. See the article "Jugend protestieren" in *Juna* from September 12, 1950.
107. This argument was made in reference to West Germany in Robert Moeller, *Protecting Motherhood: Women and the Family in the Politics of Postwar Germany* (Berkeley: University of California Press, 1993).
108. Makarenko was highly regarded among pedagogues and his writings were frequently cited in the documents. He represents the Soviet state's efforts to deal with the growing problem, after 1917, of homeless children and juvenile crime. For one of his key contributions to juvenile delinquency and Soviet childrearing, see A. S. Makarenko, *Problems of Soviet School Education* (Moscow: Progress Publishers, 1965). Makarenko was especially lauded for his work with the *besprizornyi* or delinquents of the early post-revolutionary era. Wendy Goldman suggests that in Soviet Russia, by 1924, the state viewed young criminals as a distinct subculture that was "stubbornly entrenched and inimical to the ideals of the state." In order to deal with the problem posed by young offenders, the state sought new ways to channel their energy toward respect for the family and key social institutions. See Wendy Z. Goldman, *Women, the State, and Revolution: Soviet Family Policy and Social Life, 1917–36* (Cambridge: Cambridge University Press, 1993), 89. For additional information on the problem of child welfare and juvenile delinquency in post-1917 Soviet Russia, see Alan M. Ball, *And Now My Soul Is Hardened: Abandoned Children in Soviet Russia, 1918–1930* (Berkeley: University of California Press, 1994); Laurie Bernstein, "Fostering the Next Generation of Socialists: *Patronirovanie* in the Fledgling Soviet State," *Journal of Family History* 26.1 (January 2001): 66–89; Margaret K. Stolee, "Homeless Children in the USSR, 1917–1957," *Soviet Studies* 40.1 (1988); and Jennie A. Stevens, "Children of the Revolution: Soviet Russia's Homeless Children (Besprizorniki) in the 1920s," *Russian History/Histoire Russe* 9, pts 2–3 (1982): 250–2.
109. *Der V. Parteitag der SED (10.–16.7. 1958): Eine Analyse* (Berlin: Presse- und Informationsstelle Berlin, Bundesministerium für gesamtdeutsche Fragen, 1958), also printed in *Neues Deutschland*, July 18, 1958.
110. Elizabeth Heineman includes a short description of the use of workhouses for the work-shy, prostitutes, and asocials during the war. See *What Difference Does a Husband Make?*, 30.
111. The best monograph-sized analysis of influence of American culture on postwar German youth is Poiger, *Jazz, Rock, and Rebels*.
112. Much work has been done on the Free German Youth movement in English and in Germany. An interesting new analysis examines the role of sport in East Germany's quest to mold and shape healthy and active socialist citizens. See Wilkinson, "Building Bodies, Building Culture: Sports and the Building of Socialism in the German Democratic Republic, 1945–1965."
113. The closed workhouse of Torgau was regarded as the most heinous juvenile facility in the GDR. For information on its history see Jörns, *Der Jugendwerkhof im Jugendhilfesystem der DDR*, 149–78 and especially Norbert Haase and Brigitte Oleschinski, eds., *Das Torgau-Tabu*.

Wehrmachtsstrafsystem, NkWD-Speziallager, DDR-Strafvollzug (Leipzig: Forum Verlag, 1993).

114. Annette Timm argues that the ongoing importance of population politics in Berlin health policy suggests that the family occupied a primary role in shaping socialist citizenship. See "Guarding the Health of Worker Families in the GDR: Socialist Health Care, *Bevölkerungspolitik*, and Marriage Counselling, 1945–72."

115. Barch Berlin, DC 4 Amt für Jugendfragen, No. 1401 Bekämpfung der Jugendkriminalität, Thesen für die Bezirksbeauftragten zur Zentralen Arbeitsgemeinschaft für Jugendschutz zur Vorbereitung und Durchführung der Konferenzen über die Fragen des Jugendschutzes in den Bezirken, ca. 1958.

116. See Konrad H. Jarausch, "Care and Coercion: The GDR as Welfare Dictatorship," in *Dictatorship as Experience: Towards a Socio-Cultural History of the GDR*, ed. Konrad Jarausch (New York: Berghahn Press, 1999), 59.

117. Günter Grau, "Return of the Past: The Policy of the SED and the Laws Against Homosexuality in Eastern Germany between 1946 and 1968," *Journal of Homosexuality* 37.4 (1999): 1–21.

Conclusion

1. Rolf Schneider, "Als der Krieg zu Ende War," in Walter Schulze and Rolf Schneider, *Heimkehr ins Leben. Berlin 1945–60* (Berlin: Aufbau Verlag, 2005), 154.
2. Schulze and Schneider, *Heimkehr ins Leben*.
3. Bodo Niemann, "Through the Eyes of a Passer-By. The Photographer Walter Schulze," in *Heimkehr ins Leben*, 10.
4. George Simmel, "The Ruin," in *Essays on Sociology, Philosophy, and Aesthetics*, ed. Kurt H. Wolff (New York: Harper and Row, 1959), 259. See also Svetlana Boym, *The Future of Nostalgia* (New York: Basic Books, 2001), 28–9.
5. John Mander, *Berlin: The Eagle and the Bear* (Westport, CT: Greenwood Press, 1959), 106.
6. Isherwood and Sadleir quoted in Richard Brett-Smith, *Berlin '45: The Grey City* (London: Macmillan, 1966), 142, 143, 144. For women's roles in building modern Berlin see Despina Stratigakos, *A Women's Berlin: Building the Modern City* (Minneapolis: University of Minnesota Press, 2008).
7. These examples from Nabokov and Schneider are cited in Boym, *The Future of Nostalgia*, 176.
8. Evan Butler, *City Divided: Berlin 1955* (New York: Praeger, 1955), 93.
9. Doreen Massey, "On Space and the City," in *City Worlds*, ed. Doreen Massey, John Allan, and Steve (New York: Routledge, 2000), 171.
10. Karen E. Till, *The New Berlin: Memory, Politics, Place* (Minneapolis: University of Minnesota Press, 2005); Brian Ladd, *The Ghosts of Berlin: Confronting German History in the Urban Landscape* (Chicago: University of Chicago Press, 1998); Andreas Huyssen, *Present Pasts: Urban Palimpsests and the Politics of Memory* (Stanford, CA: University of California Press, 2003); Jennifer

Jordan, *Structures of Memory: Understanding Urban Change in Berlin and Beyond* (Stanford: Stanford University Press, 2006).

11. Allan Cochrane, "Making Up Meanings in a Capital City. Power, Memory and Monuments in Berlin," *European Urban and regional Studies* 13.1 (2006): 22.

12. David Clay Large, *Berlin* (New York: Basic Books, 2001).

Bibliography

Archival Sources

Amtsgericht Tiergarten, Berlin-Moabit
Aktenboden Case Files 1950–5

Archiv Diakonisches Werk, Berlin (ADW)
Allgemeine Sammlung (Allg. Slg.)
Central-Ausschuß für die Innere Mission der deutschen evangelischen Kirche, Geschäftsstelle Bethel (CAW)
Central-Ausschuß für die Innere Mission der deutschen evangelischen Kirche, Geschäftsstelle Berlin (CA/O)
Gesamtverband der Berliner Inneren Mission (GVB)
Provinzial-Ausschuß für Innere Mission in der Provinz Brandenburg (BP)

Brandenburgisches Landeshauptarchiv, Bornim
Rep. 212 Ministerium der Justiz
Rep. 241 Staatsanwaltschaft Potsdam

Bundesarchiv, Berlin (BArch B)
DC 4 Amt für Jugendfragen
DO 1 5.0 Ministerium der Inneren, Hauptabteilung Kriminalpolizei
DO 1 7.0 Ministerium der Inneren, Verwaltung des Inneren
DO 1 11.0 Ministerium der Inneren, Hauptverwaltung Deutsche Volkspolizei (HVDVP)
DO 1 32.0 Verwaltung Strafvollzug
DP 1 Ministerium der Justiz, Hauptabteilung Stravollzung
DP 1 Ministerium der Justiz, Verwaltungsarchiv
DP 3 Generalstaatsanwaltschaft der DDR
DQ1 Ministerium für Gesundheitswesen
DQ 2 Ministerium für Arbeit und Berufsausbildung

Bundesarchiv, Filmarchiv, Berlin (BArch FAB)

Landesarchiv, Berlin (LAB)
B Rep. 004 Senatsverwaltung für Inneren
B Rep. 008 Senatsverwaltung für Arbeit und Sozialwesen
B Rep. 012 Senatsverwaltung für Gesundheit, Landesgesundheitamt
B Rep. 013 Senatsverwaltung für Jugend und Familie
B Rep. 015 Senatsverwaltung für Schule, Beruf, Bildung, und Sport
B Rep. 020 Der Polizeipräsident in Berlin
B Rep. 051 Amtsgericht Tiergarten
B Rep. 069 Jugendstrafanstalt Plötzensee

B Rep. 210 Bezirksamt Zehlendorf
B Rep. 213 Bezirksamt Tempelhof
B Rep. 214 Bezirksamt Neukölln
B Rep. 240 Kleinschriftgut Zeitgeschichtliche Sammlung
C Rep. 101 Magistrat, Oberbürgermeister Aktengruppen der Abteilungen Gesundheitswesen östlichen Stadtbezirken
C Rep. 118 Magistrat, Abteilung Gesundheitswesen und Sozialwesen
C Rep 120 Magistrat von Berlin Hauptabteilung Volksbildung
C Rep. 303/9 Polizeipräsident der Berlin
C Rep. 303/26 Präsidium der Deutschen Volkspolizei Berlin
C Rep. 341 Stadtbezirksgericht Mitte

Bundesarchiv, Stiftung Archiv der Parteien und Massenorganisationen, Berlin (SAPMO)
AG IV Kulturbund der DDR
DDR IV Ministerium für Kultur
DY 30/IV 1/I–VIII, IX, X Parteitage der SED
DY 30/IV 2/1 Zentralkommitee Sitzungen
DY 30/IV 2/9.05 Abteilung Volksbildung
DY 30/IV 2/9.06 Abteilung Kultur
DY 30/IV 2/13 Abteilung Staat und Recht
DY 30/IV 2/17 Abteilung Frauen
DY 31 Demokratische Frauenbund Deutschland

LeMO Lebendiges Online Museum, Deutsches Historisches Museum
Silvia Koerner, "Nach dem Kriege in Berlin," LeMO. Lebendiges Museum Online. Deutsche Historisches Museum, interview 10.02.2000.
Silvia Koerner, "Kinderalltag nach dem Krieg," LeMO. Lebendiges Museum Online. Deutsche Historisches Museum, interview 09.03.2000.
Silvia Koerner, "Kinderalltag Ende der vierziger Jahre," LeMO. Lebendiges Museum Online. Deutsche Historisches Museum, interview 09.03.2000.

Mitte Museum und Archiv am Festungsgraben
Herr Homa, Zeitzeugenbefragung "Tiergarten Mai '45"
Annaliese Holzhausen-Rohr, "Ruhe vor der Sturm," "Tiergarten Mai '45," Zeitzeugenberichte.
Inga Pollack, "Zwischen Krieg und Frieden in Berlin," "Tiergarten Mai '45," Zeitzeugenberichte.

National Archives and Records Administration, College Park, Maryland (NARA)
RG 260 Office of the United States Military Government, Berlin Sector (OMGUS)
RG 260 OMGUS General Records of the Education and Cultural Relations Division
RG 260 OMGUS Records of the Community Education Branch, Records of Women's Affairs Section
RG 260 OMGUS, Berlin Sector, Records of the Public Welfare Branch. General Records
RG 260 OMGUS Berlin Sector, Records of the Educational and Cultural Relations Branch, General Records 1945–50

RG 260 OMGUS Records of Berlin Sector MP Blotters, January 1949–October 1949
RG 260 OMGUS Berlin Sector, Public Safety Branch, MP Blotters 1948–49
RG 260 Office of the United States Military Government for Germany (OMGUS)
RG 389 Provost Marshall General. Criminal Investigation Branch
RG 466 Records of the High Commissioner for Germany (HICOG)

Stiftung Deutsche Kinemathek, Berlin (SDK)

Newspapers and Periodicals

Abendpost
Allgemeine Zeitung
Amstblatt der Militärregierung Deutschland
Aufbau [Berlin]
Beiträge zur Sexualforschung
Berlin in Zahlen
Berliner Herold
Berliner Zeitung
Britische Besatzungzone
Das Tagesspiegel
Der Abend
Der Berliner
Der Berliner Abend-Zeitung
Der Kreis
Der Kurier
Der Morgen
Der Spiegel
Der Tag
Der Telegraf
Deutsche Volkszeitung
Deutsche Welle
Die Frau von Heute
Die Neue Zeitung
Die Welt
Die Weltbühne
Die Zeit
Frankfurter Rundschau
Freitag
Für Dich
Juna
Monatschrift für Deutsches Recht
Nachtexpress
Neue Berliner Illustrierte
Neue Humboldthain
Neue Justiz
Neue Zeit
Neues Deutschland
New Republic
New York Times

Reichsgesetzblatt
Sonntag
Sozialdemokrat
Stars and Stripes
Start: Illustriertes Blatt der jungen Generation
Tägliche Rundschau
Telegraf
Telegraph
The Economist
Tribüne
Unsere Jugend
Vorwärts
Zeitschrift für Sexualforschung

Books and Articles

Abrams, Lynn. "Concubinage, Cohabitation and Law: Class and Gender Relations in Nineteenth-Century Germany." *Gender and History* 5.1 (Spring 1993): 81–100.

Adams, Mary Louise. *The Trouble with Normal: Postwar Youth and the Making of Heterosexuality*. Toronto: University of Toronto Press, 1997.

Aguiar, Marian. "Making Modernity: Inside the Technological Space of the Railway." *Cultural Critique* 68 (Winter 2008): 66–85.

Ahmed, Sara, Claudia Castañeda, Anne-Marie Fortier, and Mimi Sheller, eds. *Uprootings/Regroundings: Questions of Home and Migration*. Oxford: Berg, 2006.

Altner, Helmut. *Berlin Dance of Death*. Staplehurst: Spellmount, 2002.

Andreas-Friedrich, Ruth. *Battleground Berlin. Diaries, 1938–49*. New York: Holt, 1947.

Anonymous. *A Woman in Berlin: Eight Weeks in the Conquered City, A Diary*. Trans. Philip Boehm. New York: Picador, 2000.

Appelius, Hugo. *Die Behandlung jugendlicher Verbrecher und verwahrloster Kinder*. Berlin: J. Guttentag, 1892.

Army Times, ed. *Berlin: The City That Would Not Die*. New York: Dodd, Mead and Company, 1968.

Arnold, Dietmar, Reiner Janick, Ingmar Arnold, Gudrun Neumann, and Klaus Topel, eds. *Sirenen und gepackhte Koffer: Bunkeralltag in Berlin*. Berlin: Ch. Links Verlag, 2003.

Ayass, Wolfgang. *"Asoziale" im Nationalsozialismus*. J. G. Cotta'sche Buchhandlung Nachfolger GmbH, 1995.

Ayass, Wolfgang. *Das Arbeitshaus Breitenau. Bettler, Landstreicher, Prostituierte, Zuhälter und Fürsorgeemppfänger in der Korrektions- und Landarmenanstalt Breitenau (1874–1949)*. Kassel: Gesamthochschule Kassel, Verein für hessische Geschichte und Landeskunde e.V, 1992.

Bach, Jr, Julian. *America's Germany: An Account of the Occupation*. New York: Random House, 1946.

Bader, Karl. *Soziologie der Deutschen Nachkriegskriminalität*. Tübingen: J. C. B. Mohr, 1949.

Bader, Karl. "Soziologie der Jugendkriminalität." In *Bekämpfung der Jugendkriminalität. Arbeitsgagung im Bundeskriminalamt Wiesbaden vom 1. November bis 6. November über die Kriminalität der Jugendlichen und Heranwachsenden.* Bundeskriminalamt Wiesbaden, 1955, pp. 63–70.

Bailey, Peter. "Adventures in Space. Victorian Railway Erotics or Taking Alienation For a Ride." *Journal of Victorian Culture* 9.1 (April 2004): 1–21.

Balfour, Alan. *Berlin: The Politics of Order, 1737–1989.* New York: Rizzoli, 1990.

Balibar, Etienne. "Propositions on Citizenship." *Ethics* 98 (1988): 723–30.

Ball, Alan M. *And Now My Soul Is Hardened: Abandoned Children in Soviet Russia, 1918–1930.* Berkeley: University of California Press, 1994.

Balser, Kristof, Mario Kramp, Jürgen Müller, and Joanna Gotzmann, eds. *Himmel und Hölle: Das Leben der Kölner Homosexuellen, 1945–69.* Cologne: Emons, 1994.

Banting, Keith G. "Social Citizenship and the Multicultural Welfare State." In *Citizenship, Diversity, and Pluralism: Canadian and Comparative Perspectives,* ed. Alan C. Cairns et al. Montreal and Kingston: McGill-Queen's University Press, 1999, pp. 108–36.

Barden, Judy. "Candy-Bar Romance – Women in Germany." In *This Is Germany. A Report on Post War Germany by 21 Newspaper Correspondents.* Ed. Arthur Settel. New York: William Sloane Associates, 1950, pp. 161–76.

Barnouw, Dagmar. *Germany 1945: Views of War and Violence.* Bloomington: Indiana University Press, 1996.

Barnstone, Deborah Ascher. *The Transparent State: Architecture and Politics in Postwar Germany.* New York: Routledge, 2005.

Barthel, Johanna. *Berlin nach dem Krieg – wie ich es erlebt habe.* Berlin: Berliner Forum, 1977.

Bauman, Zygmunt. *Modernity and the Holocaust.* Ithaca, NY: Cornell University Press, 2001.

Baumann, Jürgen. *Paragraph 175: Über die Möglichkeit einfache, die nichtjugendgefährdende und nicht öffentliche Homosexualität unter Erwachsenen straffrei zu lassen.* Berlin: Luchterhand, 1968.

Beachy, Robert. "The German Invention of Homosexuality." *Journal of Modern History* 82.4 (December 2010): 801–38.

Bech, Henning. *When Men Meet: Homosexuality and Modernity.* Chicago, IL: University of Chicago Press, 1997.

Beck, Karl. "Die Sexuelle Handlung." PhD dissertation, Faculty of Law, Universität Tübingen, 1988.

Beevor, Anthony. *Berlin: The Downfall 1945.* New York: Penguin Books, 2002.

Bekämpfung der Jugendkriminalität. Arbeitstagung im Bundeskriminalamt Wiesbaden vom 1. November bis 6. November 1954 über die Kriminalität der Jugendlichen und Heranwachsenden. Bundeskriminalamt Wiesbaden, 1955.

Bell, David and Gill Valentine, eds. *Mapping Desire: Geographies of Sexualities.* London: Routledge, 1995.

Benjamin, Hilde. "Recht und Rechtsbewusstsein." *Schriftenreihe der deutschen Volkspolizei* 1.1 (1955).

Benjamin, Walter. *The Arcades Project.* London and New York: Belknap Press, 1999.

Benjamin, Walter. *Berlin Childhood Around 1900.* Cambridge, MA: Belknap Press, 2006.

Benjamin, Walter. *Gesammelte Schriften.* Frankfurt am Main: Suhrkamp, 1972.

Benjamin, Walter. *Illuminations.* Trans. Harry Zohn. New York: Schocken, 1969.

Benjamin, Walter. *Moscow Diary.* Cambridge, MA: Harvard University Press, 1986.

Benjamin, Walter. *Selected Writings.* Cambridge, MA: Belknap Press, 1996.

Benjamin, Walter. "The Work of Art in the Age of Technological Reproduction." *Illuminations*. Ed. and intro. Hannah Arendt. New York: Harcourt, Brace, and World 1968, pp. 253–64.

Benninghaus, Christina and Kerstin Kohtz, eds. *"Sag mir, wo die Mädchen sind..." Beiträge zur Geschlechtergeschichte der Jugend*. Cologne: Böhlau, 1999.

Berghahn, Daniela. *Hollywood Behind the Wall: The Cinema of East Germany*. Manchester: Manchester University Press, 2005.

Berlin Kommt Wieder. Die Nachkriegsjahre 1945/46 Ausstellungskatalogue des Landesarchivs 16. Berlin, 2005.

Berlin. Kriegs- und Nachkriegsschicksal der Reichshauptstadt (=Dokumente deutscher Kriegsschäden, Bd. IV/2), Bonn, 1967.

Bernet, Claus. "Aus 'Berlins schweren Tagen': Ein Tagebuch vom 22. April bis zum 7. Mai 1945." *Der Bär von Berlin* (56. Folge, 2007).

Bernsdorf, Wilhelm, ed. *Wörterbuch der Soziologie*. Stuttgart: Ferdinand Enke Verlag, 1955.

Bernstein, Laurie. "Fostering the Next Generation of Socialists: *Patronirovanie* in the Fledgling Soviet State." *Journal of Family History* 26 (2001): 66–89.

Bershtein, Evgenii. "The Withering Away of Private Life: Walter Benjamin in Moscow." In *Everyday Life in Early Soviet Russia: Taking the Revolution Inside*. Ed. Christina Kiaer and Eric Naiman. Bloomington: Indiana University Press, 2006, pp. 217–29.

Besener, Willi and Heinrich Manier. "Im Unterleib von Berlin." In *Bomben, Trümmer, Lucky Strikes: Die Stunde Null in bisher unbekannten Manuskripten*. Ed. Peter Kruse. Berlin: Wolf Jobst Siedler, 2004.

Bessel, Richard. *Germany 1945: From War to Peace*. New York: HarperCollins, 2009.

Bessel, Richard. "Grenzen des Polizeistaates. Polizei und Gesellschaft in der SBZ und frühen DDR, 1945–1953." In *Die Grenzen der Diktatur. Staat und Gesellschaft in der DDR*. Ed. Richard Bessel and Ralph Jessen. Göttingen: Vandenhoeck and Ruprecht, 1996.

Betts, Paul. *The Authority of Everyday Objects: A Cultural History of West European Industrial Design*. Berkeley: University of California Press, 2007.

Betts, Paul. "Manners, Morality and Civilization: Reflections on Post-1945 German Etiquette Books." In *Histories of the Aftermath: The Legacies of World War II in Comparative European Perspective*. Ed. Frank Biess and Robert Moeller. New York: Berghahn, 2009, pp. 196–214.

Betts, Paul. *Within Walls: Private Life in the German Democratic Republic*. Oxford: Oxford University Press, 2010.

Betts, Paul and Katherine Pence, eds. *Socialist Modern: East German Everyday Culture*. Ann Arbor: University of Michigan Press, 2008.

Bickford, Andrew. "The Militarization of Masculinity in the Former German Democratic Republic." In *Military Masculinities: Identity and State*. Ed. Paul Higate. New York: Praeger, 2003, pp. 157–74.

Biddiscombe, Perry. "Dangerous Liaisons: The Anti-Fraternization Movement in the U.S. Occupation Zones of Germany and Austria, 1945–1948." *Journal of Social History* 34.3 (2001): 611–47.

Biess, Frank. " 'Everybody Has a Chance.' Civil Defense, Nuclear *Angst*, and the History of Emotions in Postwar Germany." *German History* 27/2 (2009): 215–43.

Biess, Frank. "Feelings in the Aftermath: Toward a History of Postwar Emotions." In *Histories of the Aftermath: The Legacies of the Second World War in European Perspective.* Ed. Frank Biess and Robert Moeller. New York: Berghahn Books, 2010. pp. 30–48.

Biess, Frank. *Homecomings: Returning POWs and the Legacies of Defeat in Postwar Germany.* Princeton, NJ: Princeton University Press, 2006.

Biess, Frank. "Survivors of Totalitarianism: Returning POWs and the Reconstruction of Masculine Citizenship in West Germany, 1945–1955." In *The Miracle Years: A Cultural History of West Germany.* Ed. Hannah Schissler. Princeton, NJ: Princeton University Press, 2001, pp. 30–48.

Biess, Frank. " 'Pioneers of a New Germany': Returning POWs from the Soviet Union and the Making of East German Citizens, 1945–1950." *Central European History* 32 (1999): 143–80.

Biess, Frank and Robert G. Moeller. *Histories of the Aftermath: The Cultural Legacies of the Second World War in Europe.* New York: Berghahn Books, 2010.

Binnie, Jon. *The Globalization of Sexuality.* Thousand Oaks, CA: Sage Publications, 2004.

Birtheler, M. *Die sozialistische Persönlichkeit als Erziehungsziel. Vortrag in der 31. Sitzung der Enquete-Kommission Aufarbeitung von Geschichte und Folgen der SED-Diktatur in Deutschland.* Berlin: Deutscher Bundestag, 1995.

Bischof, Gunter and Saki Dockrill. *Cold War Respite: The Geneva Summit of 1955.* Baton Rouge: Louisiana State University Press, 2000.

Bishop Jr., Joseph W. *Justice Under Fire: A Study of Military Law.* New York: Charterhouse, 1972.

Bittighöfer, B. "Sozialistische Geschlechtsmoral und Erziehung des jungen Genderation zu sittlichen wertvollen Partnerschaft." *Paedagogik* 20 (1965).

Bittighöfer, Bernd. *Moral und Gesellschaft. Entwicklungsprobleme der sozialistischen Moral in der DDR.* Berlin: Dietz Verlag, 1968.

Black, Monica. *Death in Berlin from Weimar to Divided Germany.* Cambridge, MA: Cambridge University Press, 2010.

Black, Monica. "Reburying and Rebuilding. Reflecting on Proper Burial in Berlin after 'Zero Hour.' " In *Between Mass Death and Individual Loss: The Place of the Dead in Twentieth-Century Germany.* Ed. Alon Confino, Paul Betts, and Dirk Schumann. New York: Berghahn Books, 2008.

Blessing, Benita. *The Antifascist Classroom: Denazification in Soviet-occupied Germany, 1945–49.* New York: Palgrave Macmillan, 2006.

Blunt, Alison and R. Dowling. *Home.* London: Routledge, 2006.

Blunt, Alison and A. Varley. "Geographies of Home: An Introduction." *Cultural Geographies* 11 (2004): 3–6.

Bock, Gisela. *Zwangssterilisation im Nationalsozialismus: Studien zur Rassenpolitik und Frauenpolitik.* Opladen, 1986.

Boehling, Rebecca. "The Role of Culture in American Relations with Europe: The Case of the United States's Occupation of Germany." *Diplomatic History* 23.1 (1999): 57–69.

Bohleber, Wolfgang. *Mit Marshallplan und Bundeshilfe: Wohungsbaupolitik in Berlin 1945–1963.* Berlin: Duncker und Humblot, 1990.

Boissier, Doris. "Die Antifaschistischen Frauenausschüsse als Wegbereiter des DFD." *Archivmitteilungen* 38.3 (1988): 85–8.

Boré, Karl Friedrich. *Frühling 45: Chronik einer Berliner Familie.* Darmstadt: Schneekluth, 1954.

Borneman, John. *Belonging in the Two Berlins: Kin, State, Nation.* New York: Cambridge University Press, 1992.

Bouchholtz, Christian. *Kurfürstendamm.* Berlin: Axel Juncker Verlag, 1921.

Bourke, Joanna. "'Going Home': The Personal Adjustment of British and American Servicemen After the War." In *Life After Death: Approaches to a Culture and Social History of Europe During the 1940s and 1950s.* Ed. Richard Bessel and Dirk Schumann. New York: Cambridge University Press, 2003, pp. 149–60.

Boveri, Margret. *Tage des Uberlebens. Berlin 1945.* Munich: SeriePiper, 1985.

Boym, Svetlana. *The Future of Nostalgia.* New York: Basic Books, 2002.

Bratke, Gerrit. *Die Kriminologie in der DDR und ihre Anwendung im Bereich der Jugenddelinquenz: Eine zeitgeschichtlich-kriminologische Untersuchung.* Münster: LIT Verlag, 1999.

Bretschneider, W. *Sexuell aufklären rechtzeitig und richtig.* Leipzig, Jena: Urania, 1956.

Brett-Smith, Richard. *Berlin '45: The Grey City.* London: Macmillan, 1966.

Bridenthal, Renate and Claudia Koonz. "Beyond *Kinder, Küche, Kirche*: Weimar Women in Politics and Work." In *When Biology Became Destiny: Women in Weimar and Nazi Germany.* Ed. Renate Bridenthal, Atina Grossmann, and Marian Kaplan. New York: Monthly Review Press, 1984.

Browder, Dewey A. "The Two Faces of the American Soldier in Germany." In *Amerika in Rheinland-Pfalz. Beiträge zu einem halben Jahrhundert deutschamerikanischer Nachbarshaft.* Ed. Winfried Herget. Trier, 1996.

Brubaker, Rogers. *Citizenship and Nationhood in France and Germany.* Cambridge, MA: Harvard University Press, 1992.

Buchholz, Erich. "Beratung über Ursachen der Kriminalität und ihre Bekämpfung." *Staat und Recht* 1 (1974): 853–6.

Buchholz, Erich. "Criminal Liability and Measures of Criminal Responsibility." In *Law and Legislation in the German Democratic Republic.* Berlin: Lawyers Association of the GDR, 1986.

Buchholz, Erich. "Einige Bemerkungen zur erzieherischen Rolle der Strafe in der Deutschen Demokratischen Republik." *Staat und Recht* 6 (1957): 37–49.

Buck-Morss, Susan. *The Dialectics of Seeing: Walter Benjamin and the Arcades Project.* Cambridge, MA: MIT Press, 1991.

Burleigh, Michael and Wolfgang Wippermann, eds. *The Racial State: Germany 1933–1945.* Cambridge: Cambridge University Press, 1991.

Butler, Ewan. *City Divided 1955.* New York: Praeger, 1955.

Butter, Andreas, Hans-Joachim Kirsche, and Erich Preuß. *Berlin Ostkreuz – Die Drehscheibe des S-Bahn-Verkehrs.* Munich: Geramond Verlag, 2000.

Byford-Jones, W. *Berlin Twilight.* London: Hutchinson, 1947.

Canaday, Margot. *The Straight State: Sexuality and Citizenship in Twentieth-Century America.* Princeton NJ: Princeton University Press, 2009.

Carter, Erica. "Alice in Consumer Wonderland: West German Case Studies in Gender and Consumer Culture." In *Gender and Generation.* Ed. Angela McRobbie and Mica Nava. New York: Macmillan, 1984, pp. 185–214.

Carvel, Terrell and Veronique Mottier, eds. *Politics of Sexuality: Identity, Gender, Citizenship.* London: Routledge Press, 1998.

Castillo, Greg. *Cold War on the Home Front: The Soft Power of Midcentury Design.* Minneapolis: University of Minnesota Press, 2010.

Cesarani, David and Mary Fulbrook, eds. *Citizenship, Nationality, and Migration in Europe.* London: Routledge Press, 1996.

Chauncey, George. *Gay New York: Gender, Urban Culture, and the Making of the Gay Male World, 1890–1940.* New York: Basic Books, 1994.

Ciesla, Burghard. "'Über alle Sektorengrenzen hinweg...' Die Deutsche Reichsbahn und die Berlinkrisen (1945–1958)." In *Stebern für Berlin? Die Berliner Krisen 1948: 1958.* Ed. Burghard Ciesla, Michael Lemki, and Thomas Lindenberger. Berlin: Metropol Verlag, 2000, pp. 133–52.

Clark, Anne. "Twilight Moments." *Journal of the History of Sexuality* 14.1/2 (2005): 139–60.

Claus, Horst. "Rebels With a Cause: The Development of the *'Berlin-Filme'* by Gerhard Klein and Wolfgang Kohlhaase." In *DEFA: East German Cinema, 1946–1992.* Ed. Seán Allan and John Sandford. New York: Berghahn Books, 1999, pp. 93–116.

Cochrane, Allan. "Making Up Meanings in a Capital City: Power, Memory, and Monuments in Berlin." *European Urban and Regional Studies* 13.1 (2006): 5–24.

Conlan, William H. *Berlin: Beset and Bedevilled (Tinderbox of the World).* New York: Fountainhead Publishers, 1963.

Connell, R. W. *Gender and Power: Society, the Person and Sexual Politics.* London: Weidenfeld & Nicolson, 1987.

Conrads, Ulrich. "Die neue Kaiser-Wilhelm-Gedächtniskirche in Berlin." *Bauwelt* 4.53 (1962): 95–8.

Cooke, Miriam and Angela Woolacott, eds. *Gendering War Talk.* Princeton, NJ: Princeton University Press, 1993.

Cornilius, Ryan. *Der letzte Kampf.* Munich: Droemer/Knaur 1966.

Crew, David, ed. *Consuming Germany in the Cold War.* New York: Berg Press, 2004.

Davidson, Arnold I. "Closing up the Corpses: Diseases of Sexuality and the Emergence of the Psychiatric Style of Reasoning." In *Meaning and Method: Essays in Honor of Hilary Putnam.* Ed. George Boolos. Cambridge: Cambridge University Press, 1990, pp. 295–326.

Davis, Jr., Franklin M. *Came as a Conqueror: The United States Army's Occupation of Germany 1945–49.* New York: Macmillan, 1967.

Davis, Natalie Zemon. *Society and Culture in Early Modern France.* Stanford, CA: Stanford University Press, 1975.

De Certeau, Michel. *The Practice of Everyday Life.* Berkeley: University of California Press, 1988.

Dehli, Martin. "Shaping History: Alexander Mitscherlich and German Psychoanalysis after 1945." *Psychoanalysis and History* 11 (2009): 57–74.

Delano, Paige Dougherty. "Making Up For War: Sexuality and Citizenship in Wartime Culture." *Feminist Studies* 26.1 (2000): 33–68.

Delanty, Gerhard. "Models of Citizenship: Defining European Identity and Citizenship." *Citizenship Studies* 5.1 (1997): 285–303.

Department of the Army Pamphlet, Military Justice Trial Procedure. Washington, DC: Department of the Army Headquarters, 1964.

Der V. Parteitag der SED (10.–16.7. 1958): Eine Analyse. Berlin: Presse- und Informationsstelle Berlin, Bundesministerium für gesamtdeutsche Fragen, 1958.

Deutsche Verwaltung für Volksbildung in der SBZ. *Jugendämter. Aufbau und Aufgaben.* Leipzig, Berlin, 1948.

Deutscher, Isaac. *Reportagen Aus Nachkriegsdeutschland.* Trans. Tamara Deutscher. Hamburg: Junius, 1980.

Dickinson, Edward Ross. "Policing Sex in Germany, 1882–1982. A Preliminary Statistical Analysis." *Journal of the History of Sexuality* 6.2 (2007): 204–50.

Dickinson, Edward Ross. *The Politics of German Child Welfare from the Empire to the Federal Republic.* Cambridge, MA: Harvard University Press, 1996.

Dickinson, Edward Ross. " 'Until the Stubborn Will is Broken.' Crisis and Reform in Prussian Reformatory Education, 1900–1934." *European History Quarterly* (2002): 161–206.

Die Badewanne, Ein Künstlerkabarett der frühen Nachkriegszeit. Berlin: Edition Hentrich, 1991.

Dietz, Mary. "Context is All: Feminism and Theories of Citizenship." *Daedelus* 116.4 (1987): 1–24.

Dinges, Martin, ed. *Hausväter, Priester, Kastraten: zur Konstruktion von Männlichkeit in Spätmittelalter und Früher Neuzeit.* Göttingen: Vandenhoeck & Ruprecht, 1998.

Dobler, Jens, ed. *Eldorado. Homosexuelle Frauen und Männer in Berlin 1850–1950. Geschichte, Alltag und Kultur.* For Verein der Freunde eines schwulen Museums Berlin e.V. Berlin: Edition Hentrich, 1992.

Dobler, Jens. *Polizei. Vom Zwangsverhältnis zur Zweckehe?* Berlin: Verlag rosa Winkel 1996.

Dobler, Jens. *Von anderen Ufern: Geschichte der Berliner Lesben und Schwulen in Kreuzberg und Friedrichshain.* Berlin: Bruno Gmünder Verlag, 2003.

Dobler, Jens. *Zwischen Duldungspolitik und Verbrechensbekämpfung: Homosexuellenverfolgung durch die Berliner Polizei von 1848 bis 1933.* Berlin: Verlag für Polizeiwissenschaft, 2008.

Dodd, Martha. *My Years in Germany.* London: Victor Gollancz, 1939.

Dolff-Bonekämper, Gabi and Franziska Schmidt, eds. *Das Hansaviertel: Internationale Nachkriegsmoderne in Berlin.* Berlin: Verlag Bauwesen, 1999.

Domröse, Ulrich. *Arno Fischer. Situation Berlin. Fotografien, Photographs, 1953–1960.* Berlin: Nicolaische Verlagsbuchhandlung GmbH, 2001.

Donner, Jörn. *Report From Berlin.* Bloomington: Indiana University Press, 1961.

Dörner, Christine. *Erziehung Durch Strafe: die Geschichte der Jugendstrafe 1871–1945.* Weinheim: Juventa Verlag, 1996.

Dörr, Margarete. *Wer die Zeit nicht miterlebt hat – Frauenerfahrungen im Zweiten Weltkrieg und in den Jahren danach.* Frankfurt: Campus Verlag, 1998.

Dubitscher, Fred. *Asoziale Sippen; erb- und sozialbiologische Untersuchungen.* Leipzig: G. Thieme, 1942.

Duncan, N. *Bodyspace: Destabilizing Geographies of Gender and Sexuality.* London: Routledge, 1994.

Durth, Werner and Niels Gutschow. *Träume in Trümmern: Planungen zum Wiederaufbau zerstörter Städte im Westen Deutschlands, 1940–1950.* Braunschweig: Vieweg, 1988.

Dworek, Günter. " 'Für Freiheit und Recht': Justiz, Sexualwissenschaft und schwule Emanzipation 1871–1896." In *Die Geschichte des §175: Strafrecht gegen Homosexuelle.* Freunde eines schwulen Museum in Berlin e.V in Zusammenarbeit mit Emanzipation e.V. Frankfurt am Main, 1990, pp. 42–61.

Edensor, Tim. *Industrial Ruins: Space, Aesthetics, and Materiality.* New York: Berg, 2005.

Eghigian, Greg. "Homo Munitus: The East German Observed." In *Socialist Modern: East German Everyday Culture and Politics*. Ed. Paul Betts and Katherine Pence. Ann Arbor: University of Michigan Press, 2008, pp. 37–70.

Eghigian, Greg. "The Psychologization of the Socialist Self: East German Forensic Psychology and Its Deviants, 1945–1975." *German History* 22 (2004): 181–205.

Eley, Geoff. "Nazism, Politics, and Public Memory: Thoughts on the West German *Historikerstreit* 1986–1987." *Past and Present* 121 (1988): 171–208.

Elias, Norbert. *The Civilizing Process.* Oxford: Basil Blackwell, 1978.

Elkin, Henry. "Aggressive and Erotic Tendencies in Army Life." *American Journal of Sociology* 51 (1945/46): 408–13.

Etzel, Matthias. *Die Aufhebung von nationalsozialistischenGesetzen durch den Alliierten Kontrolrat (1945–48).* Tübingen: J. C. B. Mohr, 1992.

Engelstein, Laura. *The Keys to Happiness: Sex and the Search for Modernity in Fin de Siecle Russia.* Ithaca, NY: Cornell University Press, 1992.

Engin F. Isin and Patricia K. Wood, eds. *Citizenship and Identity.* London: Sage Publications, 1999.

Entscheidungen des Bundesvergassungsgerichts. Vol. 6. Tübingen, 1957.

Ermarth, Michael, ed. *America and the Shaping of German Society, 1945–55.* Providence, RI: Berg Press, 1993.

Ernst, Anna-Sabine. "The Politics of Culture and the Culture of Everyday Life in the DDR in the 1950s." In *Between Reform and Revolution, Studies in the History of German Socialism from 1940–1990.* Ed David Barclay and Eric Weitz. London: Oxford University Press, 1995, pp. 489–506.

Evans, David, T. *Sexual Citizenship: The Material Construction of Sexualities.* London: Routledge, 1993.

Evans, Jennifer V. *"Bahnhof* Boys: Policing Male Prostitution in Post-Nazi Berlin." *Journal of the History of Sexuality* 12.4 (October 2003): 605–36.

Evans, Jennifer V. "Constructing Borders: Image and Identity in Die Frau von Heute, 1946-1948." In *Conquering Women: Women and War in the German Cultural Imagination.* Ed. Hilary Sy-Quia and Susanne Baackmann. Berkeley: University of California Press, 2000, pp. 30–61.

Evans, Jennifer V. "Decriminalization, Seduction, and 'Unnatural Desire' in the German Democratic Republic." *Feminist Studies* 36.3 (Fall 2010): 553–77.

Evans, Jennifer V. "The Moral State: Men, Mining, and Masculinity in the Early GDR." *German History* 23.3 (2005): 355–70.

Evans, Richard J. "Prostitution, State, and Society in Imperial Germany." *Past & Present* 70 (1976): 106–29.

Evans, Richard J. *Tales from the German Underworld.* New Haven, CT: Yale University Press, 1998.

Exner, Franz. *Kriminologie.* Berlin, 1944.

Eyferth, Hanns. *Gefärdete Jugend. Erziehungshilfe bei Fehlentwicklung.* Hannover: Wissenschaftliche Verlagsanstalt K.G., 1950.

Falck, Uta. *VEB Bordell: Geschichte der Prostitution in der DDR* Berlin: Ch. Links Verlag, 1998.

Fehrenbach, Heide. *Cinema in Democratizing Germany: Reconstructing National Identity After Hitler.* Chapel Hill: University of North Carolina Press, 1995.

Fehrenbach, Heide. *Race After Hitler: Black Occupation Children in Postwar Germany and America.* Princeton, NJ: Princeton University Press, 2005.

Fehrenbach, Heide. "Rehabilitating the Fatherland: Race and German Remasculinization." *Signs* (1998): 107–28.

Feinstein, Joshua. *The Triumph of the Ordinary: Depictions of Daily Life in the East German Cinema. 1949–1989*. Chapel Hill: University of North Carolina Press, 2002.

Feix, Gerhard. "Uberwindung gestörter Beziehungen zur Arbeit in der Familie, Schule, und Freizeit." *Staat und Recht* 21 (1972): 229–42.

Fenemore, Mark. *Sex, Thugs, and Rock 'n' Roll: Teenage Rebels in Cold-War East Germany*. Oxford, New York: Berghahn, 2007.

Fichtner, Volkmar. *Die anthropogen bedingte Umwandlung des Reliefs durch Trümmeraufschüttungen in Berlin (West) seit 1945*, Vol. 21. Berlin: Selbstverlag des geographischen Instituts der Freien Uni Berlin, 1977.

Findahl, Theo. *Untergang. Berlin 1939–1945*. Trans. Thyra Dohrenburg. Hamburg: Hammerich & Lesser, 1946.

Finder, Gabriel. "Education Not Punishment: Juvenile Justice in Germany 1890–1930." PhD dissertation, University of Chicago, 1997.

Fisher, Jaimey and Barbara Mennel, eds. Spatial Turns: Space, Place, and Mobility in German Literary and Visual Culture. Amsterdam: Rodopi, 2010.

Fitzpatrick, Sheila. *Everyday Stalinism. Everyday Life in Extraordinary Times: Soviet Russia in the 1930s*. Oxford: Oxford University Press, 2000.

Flexner, Abraham. *Prostitution in Europe (1914)*. New York: Century, 1920.

Foedrowitz, Michael. *Bunkerwelten: Luftschutanlagen in Norddeutschland*. Berlin: Christof Links Verlag, 1998.

Foucault, Michel. *Discipline and Punish: The Birth of the Prison*. Trans. Alan Sheridan. New York: Vintage Press, 1995.

Foucault, Michel. "Of Other Spaces." *Diacritics* 16.1 (Spring 1987): 22–7.

Foucault, Michel. *The History of Sexuality*. Vol. I, *An Introduction*. Trans. Robert Hurley. New York: Vintage Books, 1980.

Foucault, Michel. *The Order of Things: An Archeology of the Human Sciences*. New York: Vintage Press, 1973.

Frank, Matthew James. *Expelling the Germans: British Opinion and Post-1945 Population Transfer in Context*. Oxford: Oxford University Press, 2008.

Frederiksen, Oliver J. *The American Military Occupation of Germany, 1945–1953*. Historical Division Headquarters, United States Army, Europe, 1953.

Freud, Sigmund. *Delusion and Dream, and Other Essays*, ed. Philip Reiff. Boston: Beacon Press, 1956.

Freud, Sophie. "The Social Construction of Normality" *Families in Society* 80.4 (1999): 333–9.

Freund, Michaela. "Frauen, Prostitution und die Kontrolle weiblicher Sexualitaet in Hamburg in der Nachkriegszeit." PhD dissertation, Universität Hamburg, 1999.

Frevert, Ute. *Women in German History: From Bourgeois Emancipation to Sexual Liberation*. New York: Berg/St. Martin's Press, 1989.

Friedrich, Otto. *Before the Deluge: A Portrait of Berlin in the 1920s*. New York: Harper and Row, 1972.

Friedrich, Thomas and Monika Hansch, eds. *1945 – Nun hat der Krieg ein Ende. Erinnerungen aus Hohenschönhausen*. Berlin: Heimatmuseum Hohenschönhausen, 1995.

Frisby, David. "Deciphering the Hieroglyphics of Weimar Berlin: Siegfried Kracauer." In *Berlin: Culture and Metropolis.* Ed. Heidrun Suhr and Charles W. Haxthausen. Minneapolis: University of Minnesota Press, 1991, pp. 152–65.

Frisby, David Patrick and Mike Featherstone. *Simmel on Culture: Selected Writings.* London: Sage Publications Ltd, 1998.

Fritzsche, Peter. *Reading Berlin 1900.* Cambridge, MA: Harvard University Press, 1996.

Garber, Marjorie. *Vested Interests: Cross-Dressing and Cultural Anxiety.* New York: Routledge, 1997.

Gasser, Manuel. *Erinnerungen und Berichte.* Zurich: Verlag der Arche, 1981.

Gay, Peter. *Weimar Culture.* New York: Harper and Row, 1968.

Geertz, Clifford. *The Interpretation of Cultures.* New York: Basic Books, 1973.

Gehltomholt, Eva and Sabine Hering. *Das verwahrloste Mädchen. Diagnotistik und Fürsorge Zwischen Kriegsende und Reform (1945–65)* Siegen: Verlag Barbara Bodrich, Opladen, 2006.

Gellner, Ernst. *Nations and Nationalism.* Oxford: Basil Blackwell, 1983.

Gerhard, Uta. "Zur Geschichte der Geschlechterverhältnisse in der DDR." In *Sozialgeschichte der DDR.* Ed. Hartmut Kaelble, Jürgen Kocka, and Hartmut Zwahr. Stuttgart: Klett Cotta, 1994, pp. 383–403.

Gesetz über den Fünfjahrplan zur Entwicklung der Volkswirtschaft der Deutschen Demokratischen Republik 1951–1955. Berlin: Amt für Information der Regierung der DDR, 1952.

Giese, Hans. "Die politische Rolle der Frage nach dem Wesen der menschlichen Sexualität." *Beiträge der Sexualforschung* 1.1 (1952): 20–6.

Gigliotti, Simone. *A Holocaust in Transit: Trains, Captivity, Witness.* New York: Berghahn Books, 2010.

Gigliotti, Simone " 'Cattle Car Complexes': A Correspondence with Historical Captivity and Post-Holocaust Witnesses." *Holocaust and Genocide Studies* 20.2 (2006): 256–77.

Giles, Geoffrey. "The Institutionalization of Homosexual Panic in the Third Reich." In *Social Outsiders in Nazi Germany.* Ed. Robert Gellately and Nathan Stolzfus. Princeton, NJ: Princeton University Press, 2001, 223–55.

Glaser, Hermann. *Kleine Kulturgeschichte der Bundesrepublik Deutschland.* Bonn: Carl Hanser 1991.

Gleixner, Ulrike. *"Das Mensch" und "Der Kerl." Die Konstruktion von Geschlecht in Unzuchtsverfahren der frühen Neuzeit (1700–1760).* New York: Campus Verlag, 1994.

Göbbels, Hans. *Die Asozialen. Über Wesen und Begriff der Asozialität.* Hamburg: H. H. Nölke Verlag, 1947.

Goebbels, Josef. *Kampf um Berlin I: Der Anfang (1926–1927).* Munich: Franz Eher nachf., 1937.

Goedde, Petra. *GIs and Germans: Gender, Culture, and Foreign Relations, 1945–1949.* New Haven, CT: Yale University Press, 2003.

Goedde, Petra. "From Villains to Victims: Fraternization and the Feminization of Germany, 1945–47." *Diplomatic History* 23.1 (1999): 1–20.

Goldman, Wendy Z. *Women, the State, and Revolution: Soviet Family Policy and Social Life, 1917–36.* Cambridge: Cambridge University Press, 1993.

Golterman, Svenja. *Die Gesellschaft der Uberlebenden: Deutsche Kriegsheimkehrer und ihrer Gewalterfahrungen im Zweiten Weltkrieg*. Munich: Deutsche Verlags-Anstalt, 2009.

Goodbye to Berlin? 100 Jahre Schwulenbewegung. Berlin: Verlag rosa Winkel, 1996.

Gordon, Mel. *Voluptuous Panic: The Erotic World of Weimar Berlin*. Port Townsend, WA: Feral House, 2000.

Grau, Günter. *Homosexualität in der NS-Zeit*. Frankfurt am Main: Fischer Verlag, 1993.

Grau, Günter. "Im Auftrag der Partei. Versuch einer Reform der strafrechtlichen Bestimmungen zur Homosexualität in der DDR 1952." *Zeitschrift für Sexualforschung* 9 (1996): 109–30.

Grau, Günter. "Return of the Past: The Policy of the SED and the Laws Against Homosexuality in Eastern Germany Between 1946 and 1968." *Journal of Homosexuality* 37 (1996): 1–21.

Grau, Günter. "Sozialistische Moral und Homosexualität. Die Politik der SED und das Homosexuellenstrafrecht 1945 bis 1989 – ein Rückblick." In *Die Linke und das Laste. Schwule Emanzipation und linke Vorurteile*. Hamburg, 1995, pp. 85–141.

Gross, Johann. *Spiegelgrund. Leben in NS-Erziehungsanstalten*. Vienna: Ueberreuter, 2000.

Grossmann, Atina. "A Question of Silence: The Rape of German Women by Occupation Soldiers." *October* 72 (1995): 43–65.

Grossmann, Atina. "Defeated Germans and Surviving Jews: Gendered Encounters in Everyday Life in U.S. Occupied Germany, 1945–49." In *German History From the Margins*. Ed. Neil Gregor, Nils Roemer, and Mark Roseman. Bloomington: Indiana University Press, 2006, pp. 204–25.

Grossmann, Atina. *Jews, Germans, and Allies: Close Encounters in Occupied Germany*. Princeton, NJ: Princeton University Press, 2007.

Grossmann, Atina. "Pronatalism, Nationbuilding, and Socialism: Population Policy in the SBZ/DDR, 1945 to 1960." In *Between Reform and Revolution, Studies in the History of German Socialism*. Ed. David Barclay and Eric Weitz. London: Oxford University Press, 1995, pp. 443–66.

Grossmann, Atina. *Reforming Sex: The German Movement for Birth Control and Abortion Reform, 1920–1950*. New York: Oxford University Press, 1995.

Grossmann, Atina. "Women and National Socialism." *Gender and History* 3 (1991): 350–8.

Gruber, Renate and L. Fritz Gruber. *The Imaginary Photo Museum*. New York: Harmony Books, 1982.

Guenther, Irene. *Nazi Chic? Fashioning Women in the Third Reich*. New York: Berg, 2004.

Gutjahr, W. "Elterliches Versagen und Jugendkriminalität." In *Jugendkriminalität und ihre Bekämpfung in der sozialistischen Gesellschaft*. Berlin: Staatsverlag der DDR, 1965, pp. 235–45.

Haase, Norbert and Brigitte Oleschinski, eds. *Das Torgau-Tabu. Wehrmachtsstrafsystem, NkWD-Speziallager, DDR-Strafvollzug*. Leipzig: Forum Verlag, 1993.

Hake, Sabine. *Topographies of Class: Modern Architecture and Mass Society in Weimar Berlin*. Ann Arbor: University of Michigan Press, 2008.

Hancock, Eleanor. " 'Only the Real, the True, the Masculine Held its Value': Ernst Röhm, Masculinity, and Male Homosexuality." *Journal of the History of Sexuality* 8 (1998): 616–41.

Harder, Matthias and Almut Hille. *Weltfabrik Berlin: Eine Metropole als Sujet der Literatur.* Würzburg: Königshausen & Neumann, 2006.

Harland, Harri. "Jugendkriminalität und ihre Bekämpfung." *Neue Justiz* (1956): 396–400.

Harland, Harri. "Die Kriminalität in den beiden deutschen Staaten im Jahre 1960." *Neue Justiz* (1961): 561–6.

Harrison, Hope M. *Driving the Soviets up the Wall: Soviet–East German Relations, 1953–1961.* Princeton, NJ, Oxford: Princeton University Press, 2003.

Harrtmann, Richard. "Zur Aufdeckung feindlicher ideologischer Einflüsse im Jugendstrafverfahren." *Forum der Kriminalistik* (1970): 450–2.

Harsch, Donna. *Revenge of the Domestic: Women, the Family, and Communism in the German Democratic Republic.* Princeton, NJ: Princeton University Press, 2007.

Harsch, Donna. "Society, the State, and Abortion in East Germany, 1950–72." *American Historical Review* (1997): 53–84.

Harvey, David. *Paris, Capital of Modernity.* New York: Routledge, 2003.

Harvey, David. *Spaces of Capital: Towards a Critical Geography.* New York: Routledge, 2001.

Harvey, Elizabeth. *Youth and the Welfare State in Weimar Germany.* Oxford: Clarendon Press, 1993.

Hausenstein, Wilhelm. *Europäische Hauptstädte.* Zürich: Erlenbach, 1932.

Healey, Dan. *Homosexual Desire in Revolutionary Russia: The Regulation of Sexual and Gender Dissent.* Chicago, IL: University of Chicago Press, 2001.

Heimann, Siegfried. "Das Überleben organisieren: Berliner Jugend und Jugendbanden in der vierziger Jahren." In *Vom Lagerfeuer zur Musikbox: Jugendkuulturen 1900–1960.* Ed. Berliner Geschichtswerkstatt. Berlin: Elefanten, 1985.

Heineman, Elizabeth. "The Economic Miracle in the Bedroom: Big Business and Sexual Consumer Culture in Reconstruction West Germany." *Journal of Modern History* 78.4 (2006): 846–77.

Heineman, Elizabeth. "The Hour of the Woman: Memories of Germany's 'Crisis Years' and West German National Identity." *American Historical Review* 101.2 (April 1996): 354–96.

Heineman, Elizabeth. *What Difference Does a Husband Make? Women and Marital Status in Nazi and Postwar Germany.* Berkeley: University of California Press, 1999.

Hekma, Gert. "Same-sex Relations among Men in Europe, 1700–1990." In *Sexual Cultures in Europe.* Vol. 2. *Themes in Sexuality.* Ed. Franz Eder, Lesley Hall, and Gert Hekma. Manchester: University of Manchester Press, 1999, 79–103.

Hell, Julia and Andreas Schönle, eds. *Ruins of Modernity.* Durham, NC, London: Duke University Press, 2010.

Hellwig, Reinhard, ed., *Dokumente deutscher Kriegsschäden: Evakuierte, Kriegssachgeschädigte, Währungsgeschädige: Die geschichteliche und rechltiche Entwicklung.* Vol. IV/2, Berlin – Kriegs- und Nachkriegsschicksal der Reichshauptstadt. Bonn: Bundesminister für Vertriebene, Flüchtlinge und Kreigsgeschädigte, 1967.

Herbert Tobias. Blicke und Begehren, 1928–1982. Berlin: Berlinische Gallerie, 2008.

Herding, Klaud and Hans-Ernst Mittig. *Kunst und Alltag im NS-System. Albert Speers Berliner Straßenlaternen.* Giess, 1975.

Herrington, Ralph. "Railway Journey and Crises of Modernity." *Pathologies of Travel.* Amsterdam: Rodophi, 2000, pp. 229–60.

Herrn, Rainer. *Schnittmuster des Geschlechts: Transvestitismus und Transsexualität in der frühen Sexualwissenschaft.* Gießen, Psychosozial-Verlag, 2005.

Herzog, Dagmar. "Desperately Seeking Normality. Sex and Marriage in the Wake of War." In *Life After Death: Approaches to a Culture and Social History of Europe During the 1940s and 1950s.* Ed. Richard Bessel and Dirk Schumann. New York: Cambridge University Press, 2003, pp. 161–92.

Herzog, Dagmar. *Sex After Fascism. Memory and Morality in Twentieth-Century Germany* Princeton, NJ: Princeton University Press, 2005.

Hessel, Franz. *Spazieren in Berlin.* Munich: Rogner & Bernhard, 1968.

Hett, Benjamin. *Death in the Tiergarten. Murder and Criminal Justice in the Kaiserzeit.* Cambridge, MA: Harvard University Press, 2004.

Heuer, Uwe-Jens, ed. *Die Rechtsprechung der DDR, Anspruch und Wirklichkeit.* Baden Baden: Nomos Verlagsgesellschaft, 1995.

Heym, Rudolf. *Das Buch der Deutschen Reichsbahn.* Munich: Gera Mond Verlag, 2003.

Hirschfeld, Magnus. *Transvestites: The Erotic Drive to Cross-Dress.* New York: Prometheus, 2003.

Hitzer, Bettine. *Im Netz der Liebe: Die Protestantische Kirche und ihre Zuwanderer in der Metropole Berlin, 1849–1917.* Cologne: Böhlau Verlag, 2006.

Hoerning, Erika M. "Frauen als Kriegsbeute: Der Zwei-Fronten-Krieg. Beispiele aus Berlin." In *"Wir Kriegen jetzt andere Zeiten" – Auf der Suche nach der Erfahrung des Volkes in nachfaschistischen Ländern: Lebensgeschichte und Sozialkultur im Ruhrgebiet 1930 bis 1960,* vol. 3. Ed. Lutz Niethammer and Alexander von Plato. Berlin: Verlag J. H. W. Dietz Nachf., 1985.

Hoffschildt, Rainer. *Die Verfolgung der Homosexuellen in der NS-Zeit. Zahlen und Schicksale aus Norddeutschland.* Berlin: Verlag Rosa Winkel, 1999.

Höhn, Maria. "Frau im Haus, Girl im Spiegel: Discourse on Women in the Interregnum Period of 1945–1949 and the Question of German Identity." *Central European History* 26.1 (1993): 57–91.

Höhn, Maria. *GIs and Fräuleins: The German–American Encounter in 1950s West Germany.* Chapel Hill, NC: University of North Carolina Press, 2001.

Holmsten, Georg. *Berliner Miniaturen. Großstadtmelodie.* Berlin: Deutsche Buchvertriebs- und Verlags-Gesellschaft, 1946.

Holmsten, Georg. *Die Berlin Chronik, Daten, Personen, Dokumente.* Düsseldorf: Droste Verlag, 1984.

Hornung, K. "Die Arbeit des Jugendwerkhofes Treuenbrietzen an straffällig gewordenen und erziehungsgefährdeten Jugendlichen." *Neue Justiz* 3 (1949): 38–9.

Horvat, Dragica. *Eine Kulturemetropole wird geteilt. Literarisches Leben in Berlin (West) 1945 bis 1961.* Berlin, 1987.

Houlbrook, Matt. "Towards a Historical Geography of Sexuality." *Journal of Urban History* 4.2 (2001): 497–504.

Hoven, Herbert. *Der unaufhaltsame Selbstmord des Botho Laserstein: ein deutscher Lebenslauf* Frankfurt am Main: Luchterhand-Literaturverlag, 1991.

Howley, Frank. *Berlin Command.* New York: G. P. Putnam and Sons, 1950.

Hubbard, Phil. "Desire/Disgust: Mapping the Moral Contours of Heterosexuality." *Progress in Human Geography* 24.2 (2000), 191–217.

Hubbard, Phil. *Sex and the City: Geographies of Prostitution in the Urban West.* Aldershot: Ashgate, 1999.

Hubbard, Phil. "Sexuality, Immorality and the City: Red-light Districts and the Marginalization of Female Street Prostitutes." *Gender, Place and Culture* 5 (September 1998): 55–72.

Hull, Isabel V. *Sexuality, State, and Civil Society in Germany, 1700–1815.* Ithaca, NY: Cornell University Press, 1996.

Hütter, Jörg. "§175 RStGB im Zweiten Deutschen Reich 1890–1919." In *Die Geschichte des §175: Strafrecht gegen Homosexuelle.* Freunde eines schwulen Museum in Berlin e.V in Zusammenarbeit mit Emanzipation e.V. Frankfurt am Main, 1990.

Huyssen, Andreas. *Present Pasts: Urban Palimpsests and the Politics of Memory.* Stanford, CA: University of California Press, 2003.

Interbau Berlin 1957. Amtlicher Katalog der Internationalen Bauausstellung Berlin 1957. Berlin: Internationale Bauausstellung Berlin GmbH, 1957.

Irmer, Thomas, Kaspar Nürnberg, and Barbara Reischl. "Das Städtische Arbeits- und Bewahrungshaus Rummelsburg in Berlin-Lichtenberg, Zur Geschichte und Gegenwart eines vergessenen Ortes der Verfolgung von 'Asozialen' in der NS-Zeit." *Gedenkstättenrundbrief* 144.8 (2008): 22–31.

Isherwood, Christopher. *Goodbye to Berlin.* London: Hogarth Press, 1939.

Jackson, Kevin, ed. *The Humphrey Jennings Film Reader.* Manchester: Carcanet, 1993.

Jäger, Herbert. "Strafgesetzgebung und Rechtsgüterschutz bei Sittlichkeitsdelikten. Eine kriminalsoziologische Untersuchung." In *Beiträge zur Sexualforschung* (1957).

Jarausch, Konrad. "Care and Coercion: the GDR as Welfare Dictatorship." In *Dictatorship as Experience: Towards a Socio-Cultural History of the GDR.* Ed. Konrad Jarausch. New York: Berghahn Press, 1999, pp. 47–72.

Jarausch, Konrad and Hannes Siegrist, eds. *Amerikanisierung und Sowjetisierung in Deutschland 1945–1970.* Frankfurt am Main: Campus Verlag, 1997.

Jelavich, Peter. *Berlin Cabaret.* Cambridge, MA: Harvard University Press, 1996.

Jellonnek, Burkhard. *Homosexuelle unter dem Hakenkreuz: Die Verfolgung der Homosexuellen im Dritten Reich.* Paderborn: Schöningh 1990.

Jescheck, Hans-Heinrich. "Zur Frage der Kuppelei gegenuber Verlobten." *Monatschrift für Deutsches Recht* 8.11 (1954): 645–9.

Johnson, Uwe. "Postscript on the S-Bahn." *Berlin Tales.* Trans. Lyn Marven. Oxford: Oxford University Press: 63-66.

Jones, Kathleen B. "Introduction." *Hypatia: A Journal of Feminist Philosophy. Special Issue Citizenship in Feminism: Identity, Action, and Locale* 12.4 (1997): 1–5.

Jordan, Jennifer A. *Structures of Memory: Understanding Urban Change in Berlin and Beyond.* Stanford, CA: Stanford University Press, 2006.

Jörns, Gerhard. *Der Jugendwerkhof im Jugendhilfesystem der DDR.* Göttingen: Cuvillier Verlag, 1995.

Jürgens, Hans. *Asozialität als biologisches und sozialbiologisches Problem.* Stuttgart: Ferdinand Emke Verlag, 1961.

Kaes, Anton. *From Hitler to Heimat: The Return of History as Film.* Cambridge, MA: Harvard University Press, 1989.

Bibliography 295

Kaes, Anton. "German Cultural History and the Study of Film." *New German Critique* 65 (1995): 49–56.

Kaes, Anton, Martin Jay, and Edward Dimendberg, eds. *The Weimar Republic Sourcebook*. Berkeley: University of California Press, 1995.

Kain, Franz. *Romeo und Julia an der Bernauer Strasse*. Berlin: Aufbau Verlag, 1955.

Kapczynsky, Jennifer M. *The German Patient: Crisis and Recovery in Postwar Culture*. Ann Arbor: University of Michigan Press, 2008.

Katz, Jonathan Ned. *The Invention of Heterosexuality*. New York: Dutton Books, 1995.

Kebbedies, Frank. *Außer Kontrolle: Jugendkriminalität und Jugendkriminalpolitik in der NS-Zeit und der frühen Nachkriegszeit*. Essen: Klartext Verlag, 2000.

Keiderling, Gerhard. *"Gruppe Ulbricht" in Berlin April bis Juni 1945. Von den Vorbereitungen im Sommer 1944 bis zur Wiedergründung der KPD im Juni 1945. Eine Dokumentation*. Berlin: Berliner Wissenschafts-Verlag, 1993.

Kenkmann, Alfons. *Wilde Jugend: Lebenswelt großstädtischer Jugendlicher zwischen Weltwirtschaftskrise, Nationalsozialismus und Währungsreform*. Berlin: Klartext, 2002.

Kilian, H. "Das Wiedereinleben des Heimkehrers in Familie, Ehe und Beruf." *Beiträge zur Sexualforschung* 11 (1957): 32–4.

Killen, Andreas. *Berlin Electropolis: Shock, Nerves, and German Modernity*. Berkeley: University of California Press, 2006.

Kirchhof, Astrid. "Gefährdete Frauen und 'Warnende' Männer. Fürsorge am Bahnhof im Berlin der Kaiserzeit." *Informationen zur Modernen Stadtgeschichte* (2004): 38–52.

Kleinschmidt, Johannes. *Do Not Fraternize: die schwierige Anfänge deutsch-amerikanische Freundschaft 1944–49*. Trier: WVT Wissenschaftlicher Verlag, 1997.

Klemens, Klaus Ulrich. *Die kriminelle Belastung der männlichen Prostituierten. Zugleich ein Beitrag zur Rückfallsprognose*. Berlin: Duncker & Humblot, 1967.

Klessmann, Christoph. *Die doppelte Staatsgründung: Deutsche Geschichte*. 5th edition. Bonn: Bundeszentrale für politische Bildung, 1991.

Klessmann, Christoph. "Verpflectung und Abgrenzung: Aspekte der geteilten und zusammengehörigen deutschen Nachkriegsgeschichte." *Aus Politik und Zeitgeschichte* 29–30 (1993): 30–41.

Klimmer, Rudolf. "Die Homosexualität und ihre Bestrafung." *Neue Justiz* 4 (1950): 109–11.

Klimmer, Rudolf. *Die Homosexualität als biologisch-soziologische Zeitfrage*. Hamburg, 1958.

Knef, Hildegard. *Der geschenkte Gaul: Bericht aus einem Leben*. Munich: Molden, 1987.

Knobloch, Heinz. *Angehaltener Bahnhof. Fantasiestücke, Spaziergänge in Berlin*. Berlin: Das Arsenal, 1984.

Knopp, Laurence. "Sexuality and Urban Space: A Framework for Analysis." In *Mapping Desire: Geographies of Sexualities*. Ed. David Bell and Gill Valentine. New York and London: Routledge Press, 1995, pp. 149–61.

Koshar, Rudy. *From Monuments to Traces: Artifacts of German Memory, 1870–1990*. Berkeley: University of California Press, 2000.

Kracauer, Siegfried. *Straßen in Berlin und anderswo*. Frankfurt am Main: Suhrkamp, 1964.

Kramp, Mario and Martin Sölle, "§175 – Restauration und Reform in der Bundesrepublik." In *"Himmel und Hölle": Das Leben der Kölner Homosexuellen 1945–69*. Ed. Kristof Balser, Mario Kramp, Jürgen Müller, and Joanna Gotzmann. Cologne: Emons, 1994, pp. 146–9.

Kraushaar, Elmar. "Unzucht vor Gericht: Die 'Frankfurter Prozesse' und die Kontinuität des §175 in den fünfziger Jahren." In *Hundert Jahre schwul: Eine Revue*. Ed. Elmar Kraushaar. Berlin: Rowohlt, 1997, pp. 60–9.

Kröger, Peter. "Entwicklungsstudien der Bestrafung der widernaturlichen Unzucht und kritische Studie zur Berechtigung der §§175, 175a, 175b de lege fetenda." Doctor of Law dissertation, Freie Universität Berlin, 1957.

Kronika, Jacob. *Der Untergang Berlins*. Flensburg and Hamburg: Wolff, 1946.

Kuby, Erich. *Mein Krieg: Aufzeichnungen aus 2129 Tagen*. Munich: Nymphenbruger, 1975.

Kuhn, Annette. "Der Refamilialisierungsdiskurs nach '45." *Beiträge zur Geschichte der Arbeiterbewegung* 33.5 (1991): 593–606.

Kuhn, Annette. "Power and Powerlessness: Women after 1945, or the Continuity ofthe Ideology of Femininity." *German History* 7.1 (1989): 35–46.

Kundrus, Birthe. "Forbidden Company: Romantic Relationships between Germans and Foreigners, 1939 to 1945." *Journal of the History of Sexuality* 11.1/2 (January–April 2002): 201–22.

Kunzel, Regina. *Criminal Intimacy: Prison and the Uneven History of Modern American Sexuality*. Chicago, IL: University of Chicago Press, 2008.

Kymlicka, Will and Wayne Norman. "Return of the Citizen: A Survey of Recent Work on Citizenship Theory." *Ethics* 104 (January 1994): 352–81.

Lachmund, Jens. "Exploring the City of Rubble: Botanical Fieldwork in Bombed Cities in Germany after World War II." *Osiris* 18 (2003): 234–54.

Lachmund, Jens. "Kartennaturen. Zur Historischen Soziologie der Stadtökologie von Berlin (West)."In *Ganz normale Bilder. Zur visuellen Produktion von Selbstverständlichkeit*. Ed. David Gugerli and Barbara Orland. Zürich: Chronos, 2002, pp. 85–104.

Ladd, Brian. *The Ghosts of Berlin: Confronting German History in the Urban Landscape*. Chicago, IL: University of Chicago Press, 1998.

Langgässer, Elisabeth. *Briefe*. Ed. Elisabeth Hoffmann. Düsseldorf: Claasen, 1990.

Large, David Clay. *Berlin*. New York: Basic Books, 2001.

Laserstein, Both. *Strichjunge Karl: Ein kriminalistischer Tatsachenbericht*. Hamburg: Janssen Verlag, 1994.

Lawson,Dorothea von Schwanenflügel. *Laughter Wasn't Rationed: Remembering the War Years in Germany*. Alexandria, VA: Tricor Press, 1999.

Lefebvre, Henri. *Everyday Life in the Modern World*. New Brunswick, NJ: Transaction Books, 1984.

Lefebvre, Henri. *The Production of Space*. Cambridge, MA: Blackwell, 1991.

Letherby, Gayle and Gillian Reynolds. *Train Tracks: Work, Play, and Politics on the Railways*. New York: Berg, 2005.

Levine, Donald N., ed. *George Simmel on Individuality and Social Forms*. Chicago, IL: University of Chicago Press, 1971.

Liebman, Stuart and Annette Michelson. "After the Fall: Women in the House of the Hangman." *October* 72 (Spring 1995): 5–14.

Lindenberger, Thomas. "'Asoziale Lebensweise'. Herrschaftslegitimation, Sozialdisziplinierung und die Konstruktion eines 'negativen Milieus' in der SED-Diktatur." *Geschichte und Gesellschaft* 31 (April–June, 2005): 227–54.

Lindenberger, Thomas. "Aufklären, zersetzen, liquidieren: Policing Juvenile Rowdytum in East Germany, 1956–1968." Unpublished paper presented to the annual German Studies Association conference, October 4–7, 2001, Arlington, VA.

Lindenberger, Thomas. "Rowdies im Systemkonflikt. Geheime und öffentliche Bilder der Jugenddelinquenz im Staatssozialismus." *Jahrbuch für Jugendforschung* (2005): 51–70.

Linton, Derek S. *"Who Has the Youth Has the Future": The Campaign to Save Young Workers in Imperial Germany*. Cambridge: Cambridge University Press, 1991.

Lister, Ruth. *Citizenship: Feminist Perspectives*. London: Macmillan, 1997.

Lombroso, Caesar and Gugliemo Ferrero. *La Femme criminelle et la prostituée*. Paris, 1896.

Lovenheim, Barbara. *Survival in the Shadows: Seven Jews Hidden in Hitler's Berlin*. Detroit: Wayne State University Press, 2002.

Lubrich, Oliver. "Kontrastaufnahmen. Berlin in den Berichten ausländischer Reisender, 1933–1945." In *Weltfabrik Berlin: Eine Metropole als Sujet der Literatur*. Ed. Matthias Harder and Almut Hille. Würzburg: Königshausen & Neumann, 2006, pp. 145–64.

Lücke, Martin. *Männlichkeit in Unordnung: Homosexualität und männliche Prostitution in Kaiserreich und Weimarer Republik*. Frankfurt am Main: Campus Verlag, 2008.

Luft, Friedrich. *Blick über den Zaun. Tagesblätter*. Berlin: Transit Buchverlag, 1999.

Lurie, Jonathan. *Arming Military Justice: The Origins of the United States Court of Military Appeals*. Princeton, NJ: Princeton University Press, 1992.

Lurie, Jonathan. *Pursuing Military Justice: The History of the US Court of Appeals for the Armed Forces, 1951–80*. Princeton, NJ: Princeton University Press, 1998.

Lybeck, Marti. "Gender, Sexuality and Belonging: Female Homosexuality in Germany, 1890–1933." PhD dissertation, University of Michigan, 2008.

Mackay, John Henry. *Der Puppenjunge*. Reprint. Berlin: Verlag rosa Winkel, 1999.

Maginnis, John J. *Military Government Journal. Normandy to Berlin*. Amherst: University of Massachusetts Press, 1971.

Mahlberg, Hans Joachim. *Man Muss Nur den Schlüssel Finden: Erzählung aus einem Jugendwerkhof*. Rudolstadt: Greifenverlag zuu Rudolstadt, 1961.

Maier, Charles S. *The Unmasterable Past: History, the Holocaust, and German National Identity*. Cambridge, MA: Harvard University Press, 1988.

Major, Patrick. *Behind the Berlin Wall*. Oxford: Oxford University Press, 2009.

Major, Patrick. "The Berlin Wall Crisis: The View from Below." *History in Focus* 10 (Spring 2006). Online journal: www.history.ac.uk/ihr/Focus/cold/articles/major.html (accessed April 20, 2011).

Makarenko, A .S. *Problems of Soviet School Education*. Moscow: Progress Publishers, 1965.

Mander, John. *Berlin: The Eagle and the Bear*. Westport, CT: Greenwood Press, 1959.

Mannschatz, Eberhard. *Charakter und Aufgaben der Jugendhilfe in der Deutschen Demokratischen Republik. Referat auf der Zentralen Konferenz für Jugendhilfe in Weimar am 14. und 15. Januar 1954*. Berlin: Ministerium für Volksbildung der Deutschen Demokratischen Republik, Abteilung Jugendhilfe/Heimerziehung, 1952.

Marshall, Barbara L. *Engendering Modernity: Feminism, Social Theory, and Social Change*. Boston, MA: Northeastern University Press, 1994.

Marshall, T. H and T. Bottomore, eds. *Citizenship and Social Class*. London: Pluto Press,1992.

Maron, Monika. "Place of Birth: Berlin." *Berlin Tales*. Trans. Lyn Marven. Oxford: Oxford University Press, 2009. Originally published in Monika Maron, *Geburtsort Berlin* (Frankfurt am Main: S. Fischer Verlag, 2005).

Mason, Tim. "Man and Woman in Socialist Iconography." *History Workshop Journal* 6 (1992): 121–38.

Massey, Doreen. "On Space and the City." In *City Worlds*. Ed. Doreen Massey, John Allan, and Steve Pile. New York: Routledge, 2000, pp. 151–74.

Mayer, Meike. *Neubeginn. Wiederaufbau des zerstörten Berlins 1945–1960*. Berlin: Nicolaïsche Verlagsbuchhandlung Beuermann GmbH, 1995.

Maynard, Steven. "Through a Hole in the Lavatory Wall: Homosexual Subcultures, Police Surveillance, and the Dialectics of Discovery, Toronto, 1890–1930." *Journal of the History of Sexuality* 5.2 (October 1994): 207–42.

Maynard, Steven. " 'Horrible Temptations': Sex, Men, and Working-Class Youth in Urban Ontario, 1890–1935." *Canadian Historical Review* 6 (1997): 99–124.

Mayntz, Renate. *Die Moderne Familie*. Stuttgart: Ferdinand Enke Verlag, 1955.

McCormick, Richard W. *Gender and Sexuality in Weimar Modernity: Film, Literature, and "New Objectivity."* New York: Palgrave Macmillan, 2001.

McGee, Mark R. *Berlin: A Visual and Historical Documentation from 1925 to the Present*. Woodstock and New York: The Overlook Press, 2002.

McLaren,Angus. *Sexual Blackmail: A Modern History*. Cambridge, MA: Harvard University Press, 2002.

Meeker, Martin. *Contacts Desired: Gay and Lesbian Communications and Community, 1940s–1970s*. Chicago, IL: University of Chicago Press, 2005.

Meinhard, Ursula. " 'Auch nach heutiger Rechtsauffassung keine Bedenken.' Der lange Weg durch die Instanzen, 1943–1961." In *"Wegen der zu erwartenden hohen Strafe...": Homosexuellenverfolgung in Berlin, 1933–1945*. Ed. Andreas Pretzel and Gabriele Roßbach. Berlin: Sponsored by the Kulturring in Berlin e. V, 2000, pp. 287–9.

Menzel, Matthias. *Die Stadt Ohne Tod. Berliner Tagebuch 1943/45*. Berlin: Carl Habel Verlagsbuchhandlung, 1946.

Merkel, Ina. "Leitbilder und Lebensweisen von Frauen in der DDR." In *Sozialgeschichte der DDR*. Ed. Hartmut Kaelble, Jürgen Kocka, and Hartmut Zwahr. Stuttgart: Klett Cotta, 1994.

Merritt, Richard. *Democracy Imposed: US Occupation Policy and the German Public, 1945–49*. New Haven, CT: Yale University Press, 1995.

Meyer, Sibylle and Eva Schultze. *Kurzfristige und langfristige Auswirkungen des II. Weltkriegs auf vollständige und unvollständige Familien. Ein Beitrag zum Wandel der Familie in Deutschland*. Berlin: Institut für Soziologie der Technischen Universität Berlin, 1989.

Mezger, Edmund. *Persönlichkeit und strafrechtliche Zurechnung*. Munich: J. F. Bergmann, 1926.

Mezger, Edmund. *Strafrecht: Ein Lehrbuch*. Munich, Leipzig: Duncker & Humblot, 1931.

Micheler, Stefan. "Homophobic Propaganda and the Denunciation of Same-Sex-Desiring Men under National Socialism." *Journal of the History of Sexuality* 11 (2002): 95–130.

Middleton, Drew. *Where Has Last July Gone? Memoirs.* New York: Quadrangle, 1973.

Mierau, Fritz. *Russen in Berlin, 1918–1923. Eine kulturelle Begegnung.* Berlin: Quadriga, 1988.

Mieskes, H. *Der Jugendliche in der Situation der Straffälligkeit. Untersuchung zum Problem Erziehung oder Strafe.* Jena, 1956.

Millar, Lynn und Will McBride. *Berlin und Die Berliner von Amerikanern Gesehen.* West Berlin: Rembrandt-Verlag, 1958.

Moeller, Robert G. "Private Acts, Public Anxieties, and the Fight to Decriminalize Male Homosexuality in the Federal Republic of Germany." *Feminist Studies* 36.3 (Fall 2010): 528–52.

Moeller, Robert G. *Protecting Motherhood: Women and Family in the Politics of Postwar Germany.* Berkeley: University of California Press, 1993.

Moeller, Robert G. "Reconstructing the Family in Reconstruction Germany: Women and Social Policy in the Federal Republic, 1949–1955." In *West Germany under Construction.* Ed. Robert G. Moeller. Ann Arbor: University of Michigan Press, 1997.

Moeller, Robert G. "Remembering the War in a Nation of Victims: West German Pasts in the 1950s." In *The Miracle Years: A Cultural History of West Germany.* Ed. Hannah Schissler. Princeton, NJ: Princeton University Press, 2001.

Moeller, Robert G. "The Homosexual Man is a 'Man,' the Homosexual Woman is a 'Woman': Sex, Society, and the Law in Postwar West Germany." In *West Germany under Construction.* Ed. Robert G. Moeller. Ann Arbor: University of Michigan Press, 1997.

Moeller, Robert G. " 'The Last Soldiers of the 'Great War' and Tales of Family Reunions in the Federal Republic of Germany." *Signs: Journal of Women in Culture and Society* 24.1 (1998): 129–45.

Moeller, Robert G. *War Stories: The Search for a Usable Past in the Federal Republic of Germany.* Berkeley: University of California Press, 2001.

Moreck, Curt. *Führer durch das "lasterhafte" Berlin: Grosstadt-Dokumente.* Ed. Hans Ostwald. Berlin, Leipzig: J. Singer Verlag, 1905–8.

Morrison, Wayne. *Theoretical Criminology: From Modernity to Post-modernity.* London: Cavendish Publishing, 1995.

Mort, Frank. *Capital Affairs: The Making of a Permissive Society.* New Haven, CT: Yale University Press, 2010.

Mort, Frank. *Dangerous Sexualities: Medico-moral Politics in England since 1830.* London: Routledge and Kegan Paul, 1987.

Mort, Frank. "Mapping Sexual London: The Wolfenden Committee on Homosexual Offences and Prostitution, 1954–57." *New Formations* 37 (Spring 1999): 92–113.

Mort, .Frank and Lynda Nead, eds. *Sexual Geographies.* New Formations, vol. 37. London: Lawrence and Wishart, 1999.

Mosse, George. *Nationalism and Sexuality.* New York: Howard Fertig, 1985.

Mouffe, Chanta, ed. *Dimensions of Radical Democracy: Pluralism, Citizenship, Community.* London: Verso, 1992.

Mouton, Michelle. *From Nurturing the Nation to Purifying the Volk: Weimar and Nazi Family Policy 1918–45.* Cambridge, MA: Cambridge University Press, 2007.

Muchow, Hans Heinrich. *Sexualreife und Sozialstruktur der Jugend.* Reinbeck bei Hamburg, 1959.

Muecke, Stephen. "The Archaeology of Feeling." *The UTS Review* 5.1 (1999): 1–5.

Mugay, Peter. *Die Friedrichstrasse.* Berlin: Ch. Links Verlag, 1991.

Mühlberg, Dietrich. "Sexualität und ostdeutscher Alltag" *Mitteilungen aus der kulturwissenschaftlichen Forschung Differente Sexualitäten* 8.36 (1995): 8–40.

Müller-Hegemann, D. *Moderne Nervosität.* Berlin: Volk & Gesundheit, 1959.

Munson, Granville F. and Walter H. E. Jaeger, eds. *Military Law and Court-Martial Procedure: "Army Officers' Blue Book".* Washington, DC: National Law Book Company, 1941.

Naimark, Norman. *The Russians in Germany: A History of the Soviet Zone of Occupation, 1945–1949.* Cambridge, MA: Harvard University Press, 1997.

Neff, Anette. " 'Border Kreise': Fostering Democracy in the Face of Communism." Unpublished paper.

Niemann, Bodo. "Through the Eyes of a Passer-By. The Photographer Walter Schulze." *Heimkehr ins Leben. Berlin 1945–60.* Berlin: Aufbau Verlag, 2005, pp. 9–18.

Nuys-Henkelmann, Christian. " 'Wenn die rote Sonne abends im Meer versinkt…' Die Sexualmoral der fünfziger Jahre." In *Sexualmoral und Zeitgeist im 19. Und 20. Jahrhundert.* Ed. Anja Bagel-Bohlan and Michael Salewski. Opladen, 1990, pp. 107–95.

Oberle, Clara Magdalene. "City in Transit: Ruins, Railways, and the Search for Order in Berlin, 1945–1948." PhD dissertation, Princeton University, 2006.

Oberwittler, Dietrich. "Von Strafe zur Erziehung? Zur Entwickllung der Jugendkriminalpolitik in England und Deutschland, ca. 1850–1920." PhD dissertation, Trier, 1998.

Oberwittler, Dietrich. *Von der Strafe zur Erziehung: Jugendkriminalpolitik in England und Deutschland 1850–1920.* Frankfurt am Main, 2000.

O'Connor, John F. "Don't Know Much About History: The Constitution, Historical Practice, and the Death Penalty Jurisdiction of Courts-Martial." *University of Miami Law Review* 52 (1997): 177–240.

Oleschinski, Brigitte. *Gedenkstätte Plötzensee.* Berlin: Gedenkstätte Deutscher Widerstand, 1995.

Oosterhuis, Harry. "Male Bonding and Homosexuality in Nazi Germany." *Journal of Homosexuality* 22.1 (1991): 242–62.

Oosterhuis, Harry. "Medical Science and the Modernisation of Sexuality." In *Sexual Cultures in Europe: National Histories.* Ed. Franz Eder, Lesley Hall, Gert Hekma. Manchester: Manchester University Press, 1999.

Oosterhuis, Harry. "Medicine, Male Bonding, and Homosexuality in Nazi Germany." *Journal of Contemporary History* (Spring 1997): 187–205.

Ostwald, Hans. *Kultur- und Sittengeschichte Berlins.* Berlin: Grunewald, H. Kelmm, 1924.

Özdamar, Emnie Sevgi. "My Berlin." In *Berlin Tales.* Trans. Lyn Marven, ed. Helen Constantine. Oxford: Oxford University Press, 2009, pp. 97–106.

Pateman, Carol. *The Sexual Contract.* Stanford, CA: Stanford University Press, 1987.

Paysan, Marko. "Zauber der Nacht." In *Swing Heil: Jazz im Nationalsozialismus.* Ed. Bernd Poster. Berlin, 1989.

Perinelli, Massimo. *Fluchtlinien des Neorealismus: Der organlose Körper der italienischen Nachkriegszeit 1943–1949.* Bielefeld: Transcript, 2009.

Péteri, György. "Nylon Curtain – Transnational and Transsystemic Tendencies in the Cultural Life of State-Socialist Russia And East-Central Europe." *Slavonica* 10.2 (2004): 113–23.

Petro, Patrice. "After Shock/Between Boredom and History." *Fugitive Images*. Ed. Patrice Petro. Bloomington: Indiana University Press, 1995, pp. 265–84.

Petro, Patrice. "Modernity and Mass Culture in Weimar: Contours of a Discourse on Sexuality in Early Theories of Perception and Representation." *New German Critique* 40. Special Issue on Weimar Film Theory (Winter, 1987): 115–46.

Peukert, Detlev. *Grenzen der Sozialdisziplinierung: Aufstieg und Krise der deutschen Jugendfürsorge von 1878 bis 1932*. Cologne: Bund-Verlag, 1986.

Peukert, Detlev. *Inside Nazi Germany*. New Haven, CT: Yale University Press, 1987.

Phillips, A. *Engendering Democracy*. Cambridge: Polity Press, 1991.

Pick, Daniel. "In Pursuit of the Nazi Mind? The Development of Psychoanalysis in the Allied Struggle Against Germany." *Psychoanalysis and History* 11 (2009): 137–57.

Pike, David. "Cultural Politics in Soviet Occupied Germany 1945–46." *Journal of Contemporary History* 24 (1989).

Pike, David. *The Politics of Culture in Soviet-Occupied Germany, 1945–1949*. Stanford, CA: Stanford University Press, 1992.

Pinkert, Anke. *Film and Memory in East Germany*. Bloomington: Indiana University Press, 2008.

Ploetz, Alfred. *Die tüchtigkeit unserer Rasse und der Schutz der Schwachen. Ein Versuch über Rassenhygiene und ihr Verhältnis zu den humanen Ideen, besonders zum Sozialismus*. Berlin, 1895.

Poiger, Uta. "A New, 'Western' Hero? Reconstructing German Masculinity in the 1950s." *Signs: Journal of Women in Culture and Society* 24.1 (1998): 147–62.

Poiger, Uta. "Beauty, Business and German International Relations," *WerkstattGeschichte* 16.45 (2007): 53–71.

Poiger, Uta. "Fantasies of Universality? Neue Frauen, Race, and Nation in Weimer and Nazi Germany." *The Modern Girl Around the World: Consumption, Modernity, Globalization*. Ed. Alys Eve Weinbaum, Lynn M. Thomas, Priti Ramamurthy, Uta G. Poiger, and Madeleine Yue Dong. Durham, NC: Duke University Press, 2008, pp. 317–44.

Poiger, Uta. *Jazz, Rock, and Rebels: Cold War Politics and American Culture in a Divided Germany*. Berkeley: University of California Press, 2000.

Poiger, Uta. "Rock 'n' roll, Kalter Krieg und deutsche Identität." In *Amerikanisierung und Sowjetisierung in Deutschland 1945–1970*. Ed. Konrad H. Jarausch, Siegrist. Frankfurt: Campus Verlag, 1997, pp. 275–89.

Port, Andrew. *Conflict and Stability in the German Democratic Republic*. Cambridge, MA: Cambridge University Press, 2006.

Poutrus, Kirsten. "Die Frau ist der Feind: Vergewaltigungen in Berlin bei Kriegsende." *Freitag* 21 (1995): 13–15.

Presner, Todd. *Mobile Modernity: Germans, Jews, Trains*. New York: Columbia University Press, 2007.

Pretzel, Andreas. *NS-Opfer unter Vorbehalt: Homosexuelle Männer in Berlin nach 1945*. Berlin: LIT Verlag, 2002.

Pretzel, Andreas and Gabriele Roßbach, eds. *"Wegen der zu erwartenden hohen Strafe..."*. *Homosexuellenverfolgung in Berlin 1933–1945*. Berlin: Sponsored by the Kulturring in Berlin e. V, 2000.

Preuß, Erich. *Der Reichsbahn-Report*. Stuttgart: Transpress Verlag, 2001.

Pritchard, Gareth. *The Making of the GDR, 1945–53: From Anti-fascism to Stalinism*. Manchester: Manchester University Press, 2000.

Pulver, Marco, ed. *"Das war janz doll!" Gottfried Stechers Memoiren. Eine schwule Biographie*. Berlin: Books on Demand Gmbh, 2001.

Puttkammer, Claudia and Sacha Szabo. *Gruß aus dem Luna-Park. Eine Archäologie des Vergnügens. Freizeit- und Vergnügungsparks Anfang des zwanzigsten Jahrhunderts*. Berlin: wvb Wissenschaftlicher Verlag, 2007.

Read, Barry. *New York Hustlers: Masculinity and Sex in Modern America*. Manchester: University of Manchester Press, 2010.

Redhardt, Reinhard. "Zur gleichgeschlechtlichen mannlichen Prostitution." In *Beiträge zur Sexualforschung* (1954).

Rentschler, Eric. "The Place of Rubble in the *Trümmerfilm*." In *Ruins of Modernity*. Ed. Julia Hell and Andreas Schönle. Durham, NC: Duke University Press, 2010, pp. 418–39.

Richard, Winfried. "Noch schöner, noch grüner – Humboldthanin und Pankegrünzug im Wedding seit 1945." *Humboldthain und Pankegrünzug*. Undated publication in Mitte Museum und Archiv, Humboldt-Bunker Chronologie.

Richards, Jeffrey and John M. MacKenzie. *The Railway Station: A Social History*. Oxford: Oxford University Press, 1986.

Richardson, Diana. "Claiming Citizenship: Sexuality, Citizenship, and Lesbian/Feminist Theory." *Sexualities* 3.2 (2000).

Richie, Alexandra. *Faust's Metropolis: A History of Berlin*. New York: Carroll & Graf, 1998.

Riechers, Burckhardt. "Freundschaft und Anständigkeit: Leitbilder im Selbstverständnis männlicher Homosexueller in der frühen Bundesrepublik." *Invertito – Jahrbuch für die Geschichte der Homosexualitäten* (1999): 12–46

Ries, Henry. *Berlin Photographien, 1946–1949*. Berlin: Nicolaische Verlagsbuchhandlung Beuermann GmbH, 1998.

Ries, Henry. *Ich War Ein Berliner: Erinnerungen eines New Yorker Fotojournalisten*. Berlin: Parthas-Verlag, 2001.

Riess, Curt. *The Berlin Story*. New York: Dial Press, 1952.

Rimkus, Edith and Horst Beseler. *Verliebt in Berlin: Ein Tagebuch in Bildern und Worten*. Berlin: Verlag Neues Leben, 1958.

Rode, Christian. *Kriminologie in der DDR. Kriminalistätsursachenforschung zwischen Empirie und Ideologie*. Freiburg i. Br.: Max-Planck-Institut für ausländisches und internationales Strafrecht, 1996.

Roos, Julia. "Backlash against Prostitutes' Rights: Origins and Dynamics of Nazi Prostitution Policies." *Journal of the History of Sexuality* 11.1/2 (January/April 2002): 67–94.

Roos, Julia. "Prostitutes, Civil Society, and the State in Weimar Germany." In *Paradoxes of Civil Society: New Perspectives on Modern German and British History*. Ed. Frank Trentmann. New York, Oxford: Berghahn Books, 2000, pp. 263–80.

Roos, Julia. *Weimar through the Lens of Gender: Prostitution Reform, Woman's Emancipation and German Democracy 1919–33*. Ann Arbor: University of Michigan Press, 2010.

Rosario, Vernon, ed. *Science and Homosexualities*. New York: Routledge, 1997.

Rose, Sonya O. "Sex, Citizenship, and the Nation in World War II Britain." *American Historical Review* 103.4 (October 1998): 1147–76.

Rosenblum, Warren. *Beyond the Prison Gates: Punishment & Welfare in Germany, 1850–1933.* Chapel Hill: University of North Carolina Press, 2008.

Ross, Corey. *Media and the Making of Modern Germany: Mass Communications, Society, and Politics from the Empire to the Third Reich.* New York: Oxford University Press, 2008.

Roth, Joseph. *Reports from Berlin, 1920–1933.* New York: W. W. Norton and Company, 2004.

Roth, Michael S. with Claire Lyons and Charles Merewether. *Irresistible Decay: Ruins Reclaimed.* Los Angeles, CA: The Getty Research Institute for the History of Art and the Humanities, 1997.

Roth, Nadine. "Metamorphoses. Urban Space and Modern Identity. Berlin 1870–1933." PhD dissertation, University of Toronto, 2003.

Rowe, Dorothy. *Representing Berlin: Sexuality and the City in Imperial and Weimar Germany.* Aldershot: Ashgate, 2003.

Rubin, Eli. *Synthetic Socialism: Plastics and Dictatorship in the German Democratic Republic.* Chapel Hill: University of North Carolina Press, 2008.

Rudolph, Andrea. *Die Kooperation von Strafrecht und Sozialhilferecht bei der Disziplinierung von Armen mittels Arbeit. Vom Arbeitshaus bis zur gemeinnützigen Arbeit.* Frankfurt am Main: Peter Lang, 1995.

Rupieper, Hermann-Josef. "Bringing Democracy to the Frauleins: Frauen als Zielgruppe der amerikanischen Demokratisierungspolitik in Deutschland 1945–1952." *Geschichte und Gesellschaft* 17.1 (1991): 61–91.

Rürup, Reinhard, ed. *Berlin 1945: Eine Dokumentation.* Berlin: Stiftung Topographie des Terrors und Verlag Willmuth Ahrenhövel, 2005.

Rutherford, Paul. *A World Made Sexy: Freud to Madonna.* Toronto: University of Toronto Press, 2007.

Rydstrom, Jens. " 'Sodomitical Sins are Threefold': Typologies of Bestiality, Masturbation, and Homosexuality in Sweden, 1880–1950." *Journal of the History of Sexuality* 9 (2000): 240–76.

Sachße, Christoph. *Mütterlichkeit als Beruf: Sozialarbeit, Sozialreform, und Frauenbewegung 1871–1929.* Frankfurt am Main: Suhrkamp, 1986.

Saller, Kurt. *Zivilisation und Sexualität.* Stuttgart: Ferdinand Enke Verlag, 1956.

Sander, Helke and Barbara Johr, eds. *BeFreier und Befreite: Krieg, Vergewaltigungen, Kinder.* Munich: Antje Kunstmann Verlag, 1992.

Schäfer, Hans-Dieter. *Berlin im Zweiten Weltkrieg: Der Untergang des Reichhauptstadts in Augenzeugenberichte.* Munich: Piper, 1985.

Schelsky, Helmut. *Die skeptische Generation: Eine Soziologie der deutschen Jugend.* Cologne: Eugen Diederichs, 1957.

Schelsky, Helmut. "Die sozialen Formen der sexuellen Beziehungen." In *Die Sexualität des Menschen: Handbuch der medizinischen Forschung.* Ed. Hans Giese. Stuttgart, 1955.

Schelsky, Helmut. *Soziologie der Sexualität: Uber die Beziehungen zwischen Geschlecht, Moral und Gesellschaft.* Hamburg: Rowohlt Taschenbuch, 1955.

Schelsky, Helmut. *Wandlungen der deutschen Familie in der Gegenwart: Darstellung und Deutung einer empirisch-soziologischen Tatbestandsaufnahme.* Dortmund: Ardey, 1953.

Schikorra, Christa. "Kontinuitäten der Ausgrenzung: 'Asoziale' Häftlinge im Frauen-Konzentrationslager Ravensbrück." PhD dissertation, Humboldt Universität Berlin, 2000.

Schildt, Axel and Arnold Sywottek. " 'Reconstruction' and 'Modernization:' West German Social History during the 1950s." In *West Germany under Construction: Politics, Society, and Culture in the Federal Republic of Germany.* Ed. Robert G. Moeller. Ann Arbor: University of Michigan Press, 1997, pp. 413–44.

Schimmelpfeng, H. "Die Betreuung von Kindern, Jugendlichen und Heranwachsenden in Heimen und Anstalten." In *Bekämpfung der Jugendkrimianlität. Arbeitstagung im Bundeskriminalamt Wiesbaden vom 1. November bis 6. November über die Jugendlichen und Heranwachsenden.* Wiesbaden: Bundeskriminalamt, 1955.

Schissler, Hannah. *The Miracle Years.* Princeton, NJ: Princeton University Press, 2001.

Schivelbusch, Wolfgang. *In a Cold Crater: Cultural and Intellectual Life in Berlin, 1945–1948.* Berkeley: University of California Press, 1998.

Schivelbusch, Wolfgang. *The Culture of Defeat: On National Trauma, Mourning, and Recovery.* Trans. Jefferson Chase. New York: Metropolitan Books, 2003.

Schivelbusch, Wolfgang. *The Railway Journey: The Industrialization of Time and Space in the 19th Century.* Berkeley: University of California Press, 1986.

Schlör, Joachim. *Nights in the Big City. Paris – Berlin – London, 1840–1930.* London: Reaktion Books, 1998.

Schlüchter, Ellen. *Pladoyer für den Erziehungsgedanken.* Berlin: De Gruyter, 1994.

Schlüter, Bastian, Karl-Heinz Steinle, and Andreas Sternweiler. *Eberthardt Brucks: Ein Grafiker in Berlin.* Herausgegeben anlasslich der Ausstellung zum 90. Geburtstag des Berliner Grafikers Eberhardt Brucks, 11. April 1917 bis 11. August 2008. Berlin: Schwules Museum, 2008.

Schmidt, Cornel. " 'Neues Leben aus Ruinen': Trümmerflora." *Orion* 5.3 (1950): 113–16.

Schmidt-Harzbach, Ingrid. "Eine Woche im April. Berlin 1945. Vergewaltigung als Massenschicksal." *Feministische Studien* 5 (1984): 51–62.

Schneider, Rolf. "Als der Krieg zu Ende War." In *Heimkehr ins Leben. Berlin 1945–60.* Berlin: Aufbau Verlag, 2005, pp. 97–155.

Schneyder, Erich and Louis P. Lochner. "The Fall of Berlin." *The Wisconsin Magazine of History* 50.4 (Summer, 1967): unpaginated.

Scholz, Hans and Chargesheimer. *Berlin: Bilder aus einer Grossen Stadt.* Cologne: Kiepenheuer & Witsch, 1959.

Scholz, Hildemar. *Die Ruderalvegetation Berlins.* Berlin: Freie Universität, 1956.

Schön, Michael. "Einsatz für die Sittlichkeit: Kölner Polizei und Homosexuelle." In *"Himmel und Hölle": Das Leben der Kölner Homosexuellen 1945–69.* Ed. Kristof Balser, Mario Kramp, Jürgen Müller, and Joanna Gotzmann. Cologne, 1999, pp. 155–68.

Schoppmann, Claudia. *Nationalsozialistische Sexualpolitik und weibliche Homosexualität.* Pfaffenweiler, 1991.

Schoppmann, Claudia. *Verbotene Verhältnisse.* Berlin: Querverlag, 1999.

Schoppmann, Claudia. *Zeit der Maskierung: Lebensgeschichten lesbischer Frauen im "Dritten Reich".* Berlin: Orlanda Frauenverlag, 1993.

Schoppmann, Claudia and Angela Martin, eds. *Ich fürchte die Menschen mehr als die Bomben. Aus den Tagebüchern von drei Berliner Frauen 1938-1946.* Berlin: Metropol Verlag, 1996.

Schott, Dieter, Bill Luckin, and Geneviève Massard-Guilbaud, eds. *.Resources of the City: Contributions to an Environmental History of Modern Europe.* Historical Urban Studies. Aldershot: Ashgate, 2005.

Schott, Robin May. "Gender and 'Postmodern War.'" *Hypatia* 11.4 (1996).

Schramm, Ernst. "Das Strichjungenunwesen." In *Sittlichkeitsdelikte: Arbeitstagung im Bundeskriminalamt Wiesbaden vom 20. - 25.4.1959 über die Bekämpfung der Sittlichkeitsdelikte*, ed. Bundeskriminalamt. Wiesbaden: Bundeskriminalamt, 1959.

Schulte, Regina. *Sperrbezirke: Tugendhaftigkeit und Prostitution in der bürgerlichen Welt*. Frankfurt: Syndikat, 1984.

Schulze, Walter and Rolf Schneider. *Heimkehr ins Leben. Berlin 1945–1960*. Berlin: Aufbau-Verlag, 2005.

Schumann, Eva, ed. *Kontinuitäten und Zäsuren: Rechtswissenschaft und Justiz im "Dritten Reich" und in der Nachkriegszeit*. Göttingen: Wallstein Verlag, 2008.

Schwule Lieder, vol. 2, track 18. Anno Mungen, "Anders als die Anderen."

Scott, Allan J. and Edward Soja. *The City: Los Angeles and Urban Theory at the End of the Twentieth Century*. Berkeley: University of California Press, 1996.

Seamon, David. *The Geography of the Lifeworld*. London: Croom Helm, 1979.

Seelig, Ernst. *Lehrbuch der Kriminologie*. Dusseldorf: Fachverlag Dr. N. Stoytscheff, 1951.

Semmens, Kristin. *Seeing Hitler's Germany: Tourism in the Third Reich*. Basingstoke: Palgrave Macmillan, 2005.

Settel, Arthur, ed. *This Is Germany: A Report on Post War Germany by 21 Newspaper Correspondents*. New York: William Sloane Associates, 1950.

Shandley, Robert R. *Rubble Films: German Cinema in the Shadow of the Third Reich*. Philadelphia, PA: Temple University Press, 2001.

Shanor, Charles A. and Timothy P. Terrell, eds. *Military Law in a Nutshell*. St. Paul, MN: West Publishing, 1980.

Sheehan, James. "National History and National Identity in the New Germany." *German Studies Review* 15 (1992): 163–74.

Sibley, David. *Geographies of Exclusion*. London: Routledge, 1995.

Simmel, Georg. *Die Grossstadt. Vorträge und Aufsätze Zur Städteausstellung*. Dresden: von Zahn & Jaensch, 1903.

Simmel, Georg. "The Metropolis in Mental Life." In *The Sociology of Georg Simmel*, Trans. and ed. Kurt Wolff. New York: Free Press, 1964, pp. 409–17.

Simmel, Georg. "The Ruin." In *Essays on Sociology, Philosophy, and Aesthetics*. Ed. Kurt H. Wolff. New York: Harper and Row, 1959, pp. 259–66.

Sittlichkeitsdelikte. Bundeskriminalamt Wiesbaden, 1957, p. 90.

Smail, Deborah and Corey Ross. "New Berlins and New Germanies: History, Myth, and the German Capital in the 1920s and 1990s." In *Representing the German Nation: History and Identity in Twentieth-Century Germany*. Ed. Mary Fulbrook and Martin Swales. Manchester, New York: Manchester University Press, 2000, pp. 63–76.

Smith, Howard Kingsbury. *Last Train From Berlin: An Eyewitness Account of Germany at War*. New York: Knopf, 1942.

Sohn, Elke. *Zum Begriff der Natur in Stadtkonzepten anhand der Beiträge von Hans Bernhard Reichow, Walter Schwagenscheidt und Hans Scharoun zum Wiederaufbau nach 1945*. Münster: LIT Verlag, 2008.

Sparing, Frank, ed. "…wegen Vergehen nach § 175 verhaftet." *Die Verfolgung der Düsseldorfer Homosexuellen während des Nationalsozialismus. Mahn- und Gedenkstätte*. Düsseldorf: Grupello 1997.

Spender, Stephen. *European Witness*. New York: Reynal & Hitchcock, 1946.

Sponsler, Clair. *Drama and Resistance: Bodies, Goods, and Theatricality in Late Medieval England.* Minneapolis: University of Minnesota, 1997.

Stargardt, Nicholas. *Witnesses of War: Children's Lives Under the Nazis.* London: Vintage Press, 2007.

Stark, Gary. *Banned in Berlin: Literary Censorship in Imperial Germany, 1871–1918.* New York: Berghahn Press, 2009.

Steege, Paul. *Black Market, Cold War: Everyday Life in Berlin, 1946–1949.* Cambridge, MA: Cambridge University Press, 2007.

Stein, Mark. *City of Sisterly and Brotherly Loves: Gay and Lesbian Philadelphia, 1945–72.* Chicago, IL: University of Chicago Press, 2000.

Stephens, Robert P. *Germans On Drugs: The Complications of Modernization in Hamburg.* Ann Arbor: University of Michigan Press, 2006.

Stevens, Jennie A. "Children of the Revolution: Soviet Russia's Homeless Children (Besprizorniki) in the 1920s." *Russian History/Histoire Russe* 9 (1982): 250–2.

Stolee, Margaret K. "Homeless Children in the USSR, 1917–1957." *Soviet Studies* 40.1 (1988): 64–88.

Stoler, Ann Laura. *Race and the Education of Desire: Foucault's History of Sexuality and the Colonial Order of Things.* Durham, NC: Duke University Press, 1995.

StPO mit Nebengesetzen. Berlin 1951.

Strafgesetzbuch und andere Strafgesetze. Berlin, 1954.

Stratigakos, Despina. *A Women's Berlin: Building the Modern City.* Minneapolis: University of Minnesota Press, 2008.

Strumpf, Fritz. "Jeder Ofizier der Volkspolizei muss ein Erzieher sein." *Schriftenreihe der deutschen Volkspolizei* 2/2 (1956).

Stümke, Hans-Georg. *Homosexuelle in Deutschland: Eine politische Geschichte.* Munich, 1989.

Stümke, Hans-Georg and Rudi Finkler, eds. *Rosa Winkel, rosa Listen.* Hamburg, 1981.

Stürickow, Regina. *Der Kurfürstendamm: Gesichter einer Straße.* Berlin: Arani-Verlag GmbH, 1995.

Sun-Hong, Young. *Welfare, Modernity, and the Weimar State.* Princeton, NJ: Princeton University Press, 1998.

Swett, Pamela. *Neighbours and Enemies: The Culture of Radicalism in Berlin, 1929–33.* Cambridge, MA: Cambridge University Press, 2007.

Swett, Pamela. "Political Networks, Rail Networks: Public Transportation and Neighbourhood Radicalism in Weimar Berlin." In *The City and the Railway in Europe.* Ed. Ralf Roth and Marie Noelle Polino. Aldershot: Ashgate, 2003, pp. 222–3.

Szobar, Patricia. "Telling Sexual Stories in the Nazi Courts of Law: Race Defilement in Germany, 1933 to 1945." *Journal of the History of Sexuality* 11 (2002): 131–63.

Tamagne, Florence. *Histoire de l'homosexualité en Europe.* Paris, 2000.

Tatar, Maria. *Lustmord: Sexual Murder in Weimar Germany.* Princeton, NJ: Princeton University Press, 1997.

Theweleit, Klaus. *Male Fantasies.* Minneapolis: University of Minnesota Press, 1987.

Thrift, Nigel. *Non-representational Theory: Space, Time, Affect.* New York: Routledge, 2008.

Thurnwald, Hilde. *Gegenwartsprobleme Berliner Familien: Eine soziologische Untersuchung an 498 Familie.* Berlin: Weidmann, 1948.

Till, Karen E. *The New Berlin: Memory, Politics, Place*. Minneapolis: University of Minnesota Press, 2005.

Timm, Annette F. "Birth, Health, and the State: Medical Politics in Berlin, 1920–72." PhD dissertation, University of Chicago, 1999.

Timm, Annette F. "Guarding the Health of Worker Families in the GDR: Socialist Health Care, *Bevölkerungspolitik*, and Marriage Counselling, 1945–72." In *Arbeiter in der SBZ-DDR*. Ed. Peter Hübner and Klaus Tenfelde. Essen: Klartext, 1999.

Timm, Annette F. "The Legacy of *Bevölkerungspolitik*: Venereal Disease Control and Marriage Counseling in Post-WWII Berlin." *Canadian Journal of History* 18 (August 1998): 173–214.

Timm, Annette F. *The Politics of Fertility in 20th Century Berlin*. Cambridge, MA: Cambridge University Press, 2010.

Timm, Annette F. "Sex with a Purpose: Prostitution, Venereal Disease and Militarized Masculinity in the Third Reich." *Journal of the History of Sexuality* 11.1/2 (2002): 223–55.

Tröger, Annemarie. "Between Rape and Prostitution: Survival Strategies and Possibilities of Liberation of Berlin Women in 1945–1948." In *Women in Culture and Politics: A Century of Change*. Ed. Judith Friedlander, Alice Kessler-Harris, and Carol Smith-Rosenberg. Bloomington: Indiana University Press, 1986.

Tschadek, Otto. "Die Aufgabe des Staates gegenüber dem Heimkehrer." *Beiträge zur Sexualforschung* 11 (1957): 76–9.

Turner, B. S., ed. *Citizenship and Social Theory*. London: Sage Press, 1993.

Ulbricht, Walter. *Today's Youth – Tomorrow's Heads of Household*. Berlin: Dietz Verlag, 1963.

Ulrich, Rolf. *Alles sollte ganz anders werden: 40 Jahre Kabarett "Die Stachelschweine."* Frankfurt am Main: Ullstein, 1990.

Varga-Harris, Christine. "Green is the Colour of Hope?: The Crumbling Façade of Postwar *Byt* through the Public Eyes of *Vecherniaia Moskva*." *Canadian Journal of History* 34 (August 1999): 193–219.

van Gunsteren, Herman R. "Admission to Citizenship." *Ethics* 98 (1988).

Vicinus, Martha. "Distance and Desire: English Boarding-School Friendships." *Signs* 9.4 (1984): 600–22.

von Friedeburg, Herbert. *Die Umfrage der Intimsphäre*. Stuttgart: Ferdinand Enke, 1953.

von Hentig, Hans. "Die Kriminalität des Zusammenbruchs." *Schweizerische Zeitschrift für Strafrecht* 62 (1947): 337–41.

von Kardorff, Ursula. *Berliner Aufzeichnungen aus den Jahren 1942 bis 1945*. Munich: Deutscher Taschenbuch Verlag, 1962.

von Mahlsdorf, Charlotte. *I am My Own Wife: The Outlaw Life of Charlotte von Mahlsdorf, Berlin's Most Distinguished Transvestite*. San Francisco, CA: Cleis Press, 1995.

von Praunheim, Rosa. *Sex und Karriere*. Munich: Rogner & Bernhard, 1976.

von Rönn, Peter. "Politische und psychiatrische Homosexualitäts-Konstruktionen im NS-Staat." *Zeitschrift für Sexualforschung* 11 (1998): 220–60.

Voss, Michael. *Jugend ohne Rechte: Entwicklung des Jugendstrafrechts*. Frankfurt: Campus Verlag, 1986.

Wagner, Emmy. *Grundfragen einer artbeweußten Fürsorge*. Berlin, 1935.

Wagner, Patrick. *Volksgemeinschaft ohne Verbrecher: Konzeptionen und Praxis der Kriminalpolizei in der Zeit der Weimarer Republik und des Nationalsozialismus.* Hamburg, 1996.

Wagner-Conzelmann, Sandra. *Die Interbau 1957 in Berlin: Stadt von heute – Stadt von morgen. Städtebau und Gesellschaftskritik der 50er Jahre.* Dissertation, Techn. Universität, Darmstadt, 2006. (Petersberg: Michael Imhof Verlag, 2007).

Walby, S. "Is Citizenship Gendered?" *Sociology* 28.2 (1994): 379–95.

Walkowitz, .Judith. *City of Dreadful Delight: Narratives of Sexual Danger in Late-Victorian London.* Chicago, IL: University of Chicago Press, 1992.

Waltenbacher, Thomas. *Zentrale Hinrichtungsstätten. Der Vollzug der Todesstrafe in Deutschland von 1937–1945. Scharfrichter im Dritten Reich.* Berlin: Zwilling-Berlin, 2008.

Weber, Eugen. *Peasants into Frenchmen: The Modernization of Rural France 1870–1914.* Stanford, CA: Stanford University Press, 1979.

Weeks, Jeffrey. *Sexuality and Its Discontents: Meanings, Myths, and Modern Sexualities.* London: Routledge & Kegan Paul, 1985.

Weeks, Jeffrey. *Sex, Politics and Society: The Regulation of Sexuality since 1800.* London: Longman, 1989.

Weeks, Jeffrey. *The World We Have Won: The Remaking of Erotic and Intimate Life.* New York: Routledge, 2007.

Weingartner, Egon. "Die Notzucht. Eine kriminologische Untersuchung unter besonderer Berücksichtigung des Erscheinungsbildes der Notzuchtskriminalität in der heutigen Nachkriegszeit." PhD dissertation, Faculty of Law, University of Freiburg, 1951.

Weitz, Eric D. *Weimar Germany: Promise and Tragedy.* Princeton, NJ: Princeton University Press, 2007.

Werner, E. "Der Begriff der Prostitution in der neuesten Rechtsprechung." *Kriminalistik* 3.10 (1956): 84–6.

Wertheimer, Robert G. "The Miracle of German Housing in the Postwar Period." *Land Economics* 34.4 (1958): 338–45.

Wetzell, Richard. *Inventing the Criminal: A History of German Criminology 1880–1945* Chapel Hill: University of North Carolina Press, 2000.

Whisnant, Clayton J. "Styles of Masculinity in the West German Gay Scene." *Central European History* 39 (2006): 359–93.

Whitely, Sheila and Jennifer Rycenga, eds. *Queering the Popular Pitch.* New York: Routledge, 2006.

Whitney, Susan B. "Embracing the Status Quo: French Politics, Young Women, and the Popular Front." *Journal of Social History* 30 (1996): 29–53.

Wiek, Klaus D. *Kurfürstendamm und Champs-Elysees. Geographischer Vergleich zweier Weltstrassen – Gebiete.* Berlin: Dietrich Reimer Verlag, 1967.

Wierling, Dorothy. "Der Staat, die Jugend und der Westen. Texte zu Konflikten der 1960er Jahre." In *Akten. Eingaben. Schaufenster. Die DDR und ihre Texte. Erkundungen zu Herrschaft und Alltag.* Ed. Alf Lüdtke and Peter Becker. Berlin: 1997, pp. 223–40.

Wierling, Dorothy. "Die Jugend als innerer Feind. Konflikte in der Erziehungs-diktatur der sechziger Jahre." In *Sozialgeschichte der DDR.* Ed. Hartmut Kaelble, Jürgen Kocka, and Hartmut Zwahr. Stuttgart: 1994, pp. 404–25.

Wierling, Dorothy. "The Hitler Youth Generation in the GDR: Insecurities, Ambitions, and Dilemmas." In *Dictatorship as Experience: Towards a Socio-Cultural History of the GDR.* Ed. Konrad Jarausch. New York: Berghahn Books, 1999.

Wierling, Dorothy. "Mission to Happiness: The Cohort of 1949 and the Making of East and West Germans." In *The Miracle Years: A Cultural History of West Germany*. Ed. Hannah Schissler. Princeton, NJ: Princeton University Press, 2001.

Wiethold, F. "Kriminalbiologische Behandlung von Sittlichkeitsverbrechern." *Beitrage zur Sexualforschung* 2 (1952).

Wilkinson, Molly. "Building Bodies, Building Culture: Sports and the Building of Socialism in the German Democratic Republic, 1945–1965." PhD dissertation, University of Illinois, Urbana-Champaign, in progress.

Williams, Raymond. "Structures of Feeling." *Marxism and Literature*. Oxford: Oxford University Press, 1977, pp. 128–35.

Willoughby, John. "The Sexual Behavior of American GIs During the Early Years of the Occupation of Germany." *Journal of Military History* 62 (January 1998): 155–74.

Wilms, Wilfried and William Rasch. *German Postwar Films: Life and Love in the Ruins*. Basingstoke: Palgrave Macmillan, 2008.

Wolfe, Thomas. "I Have a Thing to Tell You." *New Republic* 90.1164 (March 24, 1937).

Wolff, Jörg, Margreth Egelkamp, Tobias Mulot, and Michael Gassert, eds. *Das Jugendstrafrecht zwischen Nationalsozialismus und Demokratie: die Rückkehr der Normalität*. Baden Baden: Nomos, 1997.

Wolffram, Knud. *Tanzdielen und Vergnügungspaläste. Berliner Nachtleben in den dreissiger und vierziger Jahren, von der Friedrichstrasse bis Berlin W. Vom Moka Efti bis zum Delphi*. Berlin: Edition Heintrich, 1992.

Wrigley, Richard and George Revill, eds. *Railway Journey and the Crises of Modernity*. Amsterdam: Rodopi, 2000.

Wrobel, Hans. *Verurteilt zur Demokratie: Justiz und Justizpolitik in Deutschland 1945–49*. Heidelberg, 1989.

Zatlin, Jonathan R. *The Currency of Socialism: Money and Political Culture in East Germany*. Cambridge, MA: Cambridge University Press, 2008.

Zerle, H. *Sozialistisch leben: Arbeitsmoral, Familienmoral, Erziehung*. Berlin: Volk und Wissen Volkseigener Verlag Berlin, 1964.

Zuckmayer, Carl. *A Part of Myself*. New York: Carroll and Graf Publishers, 1984.

Zur Geschichte der Rechtspflege der DDR 1945–1949. Berlin: Staatsverlag der DDR, 1976.

Zweig, Stefan. *The World of Yesterday*. Lincoln: University of Nebraska Press, 1964.

Index

Note: references to figures are in **bold**; references to notes are indicated by *n*.